INCOMPARABLE EMPIRES

Modernist Latitudes

MODERNIST LATITUDES

Jessica Berman and Paul Saint-Amour, Editors

Modernist Latitudes aims to capture the energy and ferment of modernist studies by continuing to open up the range of forms, locations, temporalities, and theoretical approaches encompassed by the field. The series celebrates the growing latitude ("scope for freedom of action or thought") that this broadening affords scholars of modernism, whether they are investigating little-known works or revisiting canonical ones. Modernist Latitudes will pay particular attention to the texts and contexts of those latitudes (Africa, Latin America, Australia, Asia, Southern Europe, and even the rural United States) that have long been misrecognized as ancillary to the canonical modernisms of the global North.

Barry McCrea, *In the Company of Strangers: Family and Narrative in Dickens, Conan Doyle, Joyce, and Proust*, 2011
Jessica Berman, *Modernist Commitments: Ethics, Politics, and Transnational Modernism*, 2011
Jennifer Scappettone, *Killing the Moonlight: Modernism in Venice*, 2014
Nico Israel, *Spirals: The Whirled Image in Twentieth-Century Literature and Art*, 2015
Carrie Noland, *Voices of Negritude in Modernist Print: Aesthetic Subjectivity, Diaspora, and the Lyric Regime*, 2015
Susan Stanford Friedman, *Planetary Modernisms: Provocations on Modernity Across Time*, 2015
Steven S. Lee, *The Ethnic Avant-Garde: Minority Cultures and World Revolutions*, 2015
Thomas S. Davis, *The Extinct Scene: Late Modernism and Everyday Life*, 2016
Carrie J. Preston, *Learning to Kneel: Noh, Modernism, and Journeys in Teaching*, 2016

Incomparable Empires

MODERNISM AND THE TRANSLATION OF SPANISH
AND AMERICAN LITERATURE

Gayle Rogers

COLUMBIA UNIVERSITY PRESS   NEW YORK

COLUMBIA UNIVERSITY PRESS
Publishers Since 1893
NEW YORK   CHICHESTER, WEST SUSSEX
cup.columbia.edu
Copyright © 2016 Columbia University Press
Paperback edition, 2019
All rights reserved

"Ur-cantos," drafts and typescripts, by Ezra Pound © 2015
Mary de Rachewiltz and the Estate of Omar S. Pound. Reprinted
by permission of New Directions Publishing Corp.

Library of Congress Cataloging-in-Publication Data
Names: Rogers, Gayle, 1978– author.
Title: Incomparable empires : modernism and the translation of Spanish and
  American literature / Gayle Rogers.
Description: New York : Columbia University Press, [2016] | Series: Modernist
  latitudes | Includes bibliographical references and index.
Identifiers: LCCN 2016010615 | ISBN 9780231178563 (cloth) |
  ISBN 9780231178570 (pbk.) |ISBN 9780231542982 (e-book)
Subjects: LCSH: Modernism (Literature)—Spain. | Modernism
  (Literature)—United States. | Spanish literature—Translations—History
  and criticism. | American literature—Translations—History and criticism. |
  Spanish literature—20th century—History and criticism. | American literature—
  20th century—History and criticism.
Classification: LCC PQ6073.M6 R636 2016 | DDC 860.9/112—dc23
LC record available at https://lccn.loc.gov/2016010615

Cover design: Jason Heuer

CONTENTS

ACKNOWLEDGMENTS   vii

Introduction: Modernism, Translation,
and the Fields of Literary History   1

I. American Modernism's Hispanists

1. "Splintered Staves": Pound, Comparative Literature,
   and the Translation of Spanish Literary History   37

2. Restaging the Disaster: Dos Passos, Empire,
   and Literature After the Spanish-American War   76

II. Spain's American Translations

3. Jiménez, Modernism/o, and the Languages
   of Comparative Modernist Studies   109

4. Unamuno, Nativism, and the Politics of the Vernacular;
   or, On the Authenticity of Translation   137

III. New Genealogies

5. Negro and *Negro*: Translating American Blackness in the Shadows of the Spanish Empire   167

6. "Spanish Is a Language Tu": Hemingway's Cubist Spanglish and Its Legacies   199

   Conclusion: Worlds Between Languages— The Spanglish *Quixote*   227

NOTES   237
INDEX   287

ACKNOWLEDGMENTS

I BEGAN THIS BOOK AS A JUNIOR FACULTY MEMBER AT THE University of Pittsburgh, and as I now thank various entities and colleagues across the university, I am overwhelmed by the amount of support—both institutional and personal—I have received in my time here. I am very grateful to the following: the Department of English; the Humanities Center, for a faculty fellowship and an endless series of engaging events; the Dietrich School of Arts and Sciences, for a Richard D. and Mary Jane Edwards Endowed Publication Fund Award, Faculty Research and Scholarship Program subventions, and a Summer Research Stipend; the University Center for International Studies, for a faculty fellowship; the Hewlett International Grant fund, the European Union Center of Excellence/European Studies Center, the Global Studies Center, and the Center for Latin American Studies, for funding my travel to archives and conferences; and the Provost's Year of the Humanities in the University initiative, for subvening conferences and colloquia that I helped organize. The staff of the English department and the Humanities Center deserve my ongoing thanks, as do the graduate and undergraduate students who shared crucially in the inquiries that motivated this book. A department of our size turns the act of singling out all of one's colleagues into a long list that appears impersonal. I'll therefore mention those who kindly read drafts and discussed this book at length with me and thank the rest as a whole: Don Bialostosky, Adam Lowenstein, Colin MacCabe, Neepa Majumdar, Ryan McDermott, Imani Owens, Shalini Puri, and Autumn Womack. Jonathan Arac has been both a reader and a collaborator of a decidedly singular nature.

Cowriting a book on modernism with Sean Latham while intermittently composing this one dramatically changed my approach to *Incomparable Empires*, and more important, his friendship provided continual energy for both projects. A number of generous and insightful friends read multiple parts of this book in manuscript, often through writing exchanges that enlivened and refreshed me at sorely needed moments: Magalí Armillas-Tiseyra, Rebecca Beasley, María del Pilar Blanco, Harris Feinsod, Leah Flack, Benjy Kahan, Catherine Keyser, and Carrie Preston. Rebecca Walkowitz showed me what I still needed to wrestle with; I appreciate her suggestions here and in our many ongoing conversations across several years now. Christine Froula returned to Pound and to me in illuminating, rejuvenating ways. John Dos Passos Coggin, Vanessa Fernández, Leslie Harkema, María Julia Rossi, and Kirsten Silva Gruesz helped me through both archives and translational questions alike. Jerome Branche, Neil Doshi, Josh Lund, and Dan Morgan were all rich and challenging interlocutors. Andrés Pérez-Simón, Alejandro Mejías-López, Melissa Dinverno, and Ignacio Infante staged a conversation in Cincinnati and beyond that gave this project momentum. The librarians at the Yale Collection of American Literature's Beinecke Rare Book and Manuscript Library provided me great assistance, too. I have benefited from the kindness of a number of colleagues in and from Spain, who have answered my naïve questions and helped me understand histories that I am still attempting to grasp fully: Domingo Ródenas de Moya, Javier Zamora Bonilla, Darío Villanueva, Juan Herrero Senés, María Jorquera, and José Luis Venegas. The Fundación Ortega y Gasset-Gregorio Marañón and the librarians at the Biblioteca Nacional de España remain great fonts of support and archival access.

Before I knew what this project was, conversations with Mark Wollaeger prompted me—as they have for almost two decades now—to frame and attempt to solve puzzles that mattered to me. At critical junctures, Jessica Berman and Paul Saint-Amour gave generous feedback that was, in reality, an extension of the support that they have both shown me for years now, and I'm beyond grateful to be included in their series. The anonymous readers of this manuscript were at once schematic and meticulous in their very useful and germane criticisms and suggestions. Philip Leventhal, Miriam Grossman, Robert Fellman, Kathryn Jorge, and the production team at Columbia were exceedingly responsive, professional, and kind to me. Ryan McGinnis, once again, has been an invaluable indexer and proofer. Audiences and colleges at a number of schools and conferences shaped this book indelibly: Pennsylvania State University, for which I thank Nicolás Medina-Fernández and Maria Truglio for the opportunity to speak; Northwestern University, for which I thank Harris Feinsod and Allen Young; Ithaca College, for which I thank Chris Holmes and Jennifer Spitzer; Princeton University, for which I thank Cliff Wulfman; Harvard University, for which I thank Paige Reynolds and John Paul Riquelme; the Modernist Studies Association, the Modern Language Association, the Society for Novel Studies, the American Comparative Literature Association, the Midwest Modern Language Association, La Generación de 1914 en su circunstancia europea y transatlántica symposium, and the colloquium series of the Humanities Center at the University of Pittsburgh. Writing projects commissioned by Eric Hayot and Rebecca Walkowitz, Josh Miller, Ania Spyra, and the *LA Review of Books*, and the conversations we had about them, helped me formulate some of the central ideas of this book, and further conversations with Greg Barnhisel, Christopher Bush, Joanne Diaz, and Jed Esty were always stimulating.

My friendships and regular reunions with Greg Downs, Erik Gellman, Guy Ortolano, David Smith, and Abram Van Engen somehow make writing books fun, if for no other reason than the fodder it provides us all. Jules Law has been an incomparable friend and guide. The vast majority of this book was written at Tazza d'Oro on Highland Avenue in Pittsburgh, which afforded me more tea and generosity than anyone should enjoy.

My family has been the constant source of life in and apart from my work. I am endlessly grateful to Alice and Britt Rogers, Laura Rogers, Meghan Frank and Britt Rogers, and my beautiful nieces Tatum, Cordie, and Frances. I am also fortunate to share a family life with Debbie and Eric Nieman, Tracy Nieman, Andy Drucker, and Patricia Horwitz-Lippman, and to have known the magnanimity of the late Jordan Lippman. The first glimmer of this book came long ago in Madrid at the Sorolla Museum, where Audrey had taken me. She has watched me grapple with its converging and diverging ideas ever since then and has only been supportive and loving all along. In the meantime, Ella and Aiden came into our lives. As they find their names here, may they know that this book is for them. Few of the daily, myriad, miraculous joys I have been so lucky to share with them have been greater than watching them begin learning to read— to create new worlds. But even words only hint faintly at the world we inhabit together and that I cherish beyond what I am capable of expressing. And so, as every day, I give my family all my love.

An earlier version of chapter 2 appeared as "Restaging the Disaster: Dos Passos and National Literatures After the Spanish-American War," *Journal of Modern Literature* 36, no. 2 (Winter 2013): 61–79. Reprinted with permission of Indiana University Press.

An earlier version of chapter 3 appeared as "Jiménez, Modernism/o, and the Languages of Comparative Modernist Studies," *Comparative Literature* 66, no. 1 (Winter 2014): 127–147. Copyright © 2014 University of Oregon. All rights reserved. Republished by permission of the present publisher, Duke University Press.

A section of chapter 6 appeared as "'Spanish Is a Language Tu': Hemingway's Cubist Spanglish," *NOVEL: A Forum on Fiction* 48, no. 2 (August 2015): 224–242. Copyright © 2015 NOVEL Inc. All rights reserved. Republished by permission of the present publisher, Duke University Press.

Unpublished materials are quoted courtesy of the Yale Collection of American Literature, Beinecke Rare Book and Manuscript Library; and the Fundación Ortega y Gasset-Marañón, Madrid. I thank both of these archives.

All translations mine unless otherwise noted. In most cases, I have preserved the errors in orthography and the variant spellings found in my subjects' publications and letters. These include missing diacritical marks, the distortions of English in Pound's or Hemingway's correspondence, and Jiménez's self-devised system of Spanish orthography ("jeneración" for "generación"; "esterior" for "exterior"). All other errors and faults in transcription or translation are mine.

INCOMPARABLE EMPIRES

INTRODUCTION

Modernism, Translation, and the Fields of Literary History

> *Spaniards know that there is no agreement, neither the landscape with the houses, neither the round with the cube, neither the great number with the small number, it was natural that a Spaniard [Picasso] should express this in the painting of the twentieth century, the century where nothing is in agreement, neither the round with the cube, neither the landscape with the houses, neither the large quantity with the small quantity. America and Spain have this thing in common, that is why Spain discovered America and America Spain, in fact it is for this reason that both of them have found their moment in the twentieth century.*
>
> —GERTRUDE STEIN, *Picasso* (1938)

A CROSSING OF TWO INFLUENTIAL MODERNISTS IN 1916: the American John Dos Passos sailed from New York City to Spain to begin his sustained project of translating, interpreting, promoting, and even imitating the works of Spanish writers such as Pío Baroja and Antonio Machado. After a return trip several years later, he published in tandem his study of Spanish culture, *Rosinante to the Road Again*, and his collection of largely Spanish-inspired poems, *A Pushcart at the Curb* (both 1922). The Spaniard Juan Ramón Jiménez sailed in the opposite direction to New York City in 1916. He composed during his journey and his stay a hybrid collection of poetry, prose, and translations—*Diario de un poeta recién casado* [*Diary of a Newlywed Poet*, 1917]—that he believed captured his simultaneous "rebirth" in both Anglophone American modernism and the new mode of Spanish lyricism that he was articulating.[1] These two figures also met in Madrid, and Dos Passos praised Jiménez in print. Through this crossing and the texts it yielded, we might plot additional points on the ever-growing map of interconnected global modernisms, but in fact, they should make us rethink the structure and teleologies of our comparative literary histories of the early twentieth century. Dos Passos and Jiménez were intervening in intense and protracted debates, amplified by the Spanish-American War of 1898, about the relationships among literature, history, and geopolitics. As they did so, they were attempting to reshape the burgeoning and newly powerful fields of Hispanism and American literary studies; to revise the exceptionalist narratives that governed those fields and popular notions of American and Spanish literature alike; to launch sweeping attacks on the reigning assumptions and modes of literary historiography built on versions of Herder, Hegel, Arnold, and even Social Darwinism; to recast the genealogies and maps of literary movements and translation across time; indeed, to theorize how their respective countries' cultural and linguistic exchanges were to be measured against waxing (U.S.) and waning (Spanish) empires on a shifting world stage. And as this book shows, they were hardly alone: they were joined in both their travel routes and their propositions by Ezra Pound, Miguel de Unamuno, Langston Hughes, Emilio Ballagas, Ernest Hemingway, Felipe Alfau, and many lesser-known critics in the overlapping Anglo- and Hispanophone literary spheres.

If it is not intuitively obvious that so much was at stake here, or why these topics mattered so much to modernist writers, it is because of our limited sense of translation and its contexts in this moment. In their practices, the authors treated here constantly blurred the conventional lines between translation and *poeisis*, between credentialing oneself as an authority and fashioning a signature authorial style, often in early moments in their careers. Pound and Unamuno were most explicit about the inseparability of composition, scholarship, criticism, and translation, but even in the case of Pound—the modernist writer whose translations have been studied most extensively—we have typically isolated better-known aesthetic achievements (especially in formal and linguistic innovation) as our historiographical landmarks. Translation names the commonality of cross-linguistic transfer that bound together the multifarious practices that this book examines, thereby conceptually organizing them into one highly integrated but internally variegated endeavor.[2] The multilingualism, foreign-language juxtapositions, and translingual fusions associated with modernist movements in several tongues often had significant roots in such undertakings; most modernists were translators of some type, after all. But more than an effort to break with inflexible Victorian standards or to give the kind of account of interlingual relationships made famous by Walter Benjamin, translation, for many modernists, composed an immense and complex domain of methods, techniques, and arguments. Through translation, they might reopen what the U.S. and Spanish empires, along with the fields of study that interpreted their cultures, had foreclosed. Far from minor preludes or footnotes to now-canonical works, translational labors were crucial parts of diverse agendas through which they channeled and spoke through voices of foreign pasts, inserted or removed themselves from national movements or "generations," and negotiated controversies of language politics. In short, translation aimed to make literature reorganize and transform, rather than simply reflect or express, political history.

In such work, modernists in the United States and in Spain were reformative Hispanists and Americanists, whether in experimental poems, professorships, Spanish Civil War ballad books, or textbooks and journals. The global movements that have come to be gathered by the sign "modernism" and its cognates were built substantively on engagements with two evolving fields—Hispanism and American studies—that were creating bodies of knowledge and were finding prevalent purchase in the early twentieth century.[3] In an exemplary instance, Pound, after giving up on a potential career as a professional scholar of Spanish literature, relentlessly disparaged the philologists who controlled the field by way of the combined poetics, criticism, and radical translations that he used to elaborate his aesthetic agendas in the 1910s. In 1915, he made the point forcefully that "the study of 'comparative literature' received that label about eighty years ago. It has existed for at least two thousand years. The best Latin Poets knew Greek. The troubadours knew several jargons."[4] Texts such as Pound's "Three Cantos" (1917) and Jiménez's *Diary* thus function at once as literary texts and as semischolarly, often polemical and unorthodox contributions to modern language studies—and to the overlapping discipline of comparative literature. (By the same token, many scholars, translators, and cultural diplomats addressed throughout this book were now-forgotten poets or novelists.) Some figures went so far as to transplant their own authorial identities: Hemingway, a self-styled expert on Spanish culture, fantasized that he was "considered a Spanish author who happened to be born in America" and quixotically rendered himself "Ernest de la Mancha Hemingway," and Unamuno claimed that he found his authentic voice in Spanish by translating Thomas Carlyle, then recreated Carl Sandburg's works in deeply personal poems.[5] Their own publications, as they circulated in translation both within and beyond their purviews, supplemented and revised such claims; Jiménez even devotes a prose poem in his *Diary* to discrediting the English translations of his poems by Britain's most renowned Hispanist, James Fitzmaurice-Kelly.

Incomparable Empires therefore understands translation as a constitutive, rather than a constituent, element of literary histories. And to study translation *within* literary formations, I argue, is simultaneously to study those formations—even on the level of their names—*through* translation.[6] By this I mean to affirm that modernism was a "great age of translations," in Pound's terms, but rather than assuming the intelligibility or coherence of periodizing terms such as "modernism" or of proposed national literary traditions or imperial identities, we must see them as the writers assembled here did: as precisely at stake across languages, as unsettled and fluctuating modern creations.[7] As a tool and a rubric, translation inhabited such a dualistic, mediating role, complete with both limits and failures. It frames specifically the historical relationship between literature and imperialism that motivates this book's inquiries. In a set of remarkable, broad-scale developments just after 1898, when the United States and Spain had spent boundless energy vilifying each other, numerous figures in both countries invested themselves in the idea that their recent adversary was home to a literary history that must be studied, disseminated, and even absorbed, all while a sense of competition and anxious comparison was still palpable. In this process, the renovated fields of American studies and Hispanism propagated mutually enriching exceptionalisms that bolstered one another at home and abroad.[8] Exceptionalism proved ideologically flexible enough to shift quickly, almost silently, from affirming nationalist ideals through denigration to affirming them through cooperation. Here, these fields were following the precedent set several decades prior in one originary site for comparative literary studies: after the Franco-Prussian War, French- and German-language scholars looked across the Rhine with a conjoined and not at all antithetical nationalism and cosmopolitanism.[9] In both the United States and Spain, the professional study of national literature created knowable units of literary history, usually as an extension of the state and the empire—sometimes explicitly, as in the work of the Royal Spanish Academy, and sometimes implicitly, when American studies gained institutional footholds alongside the growth of the U.S. empire and its increased global interventionism. In a period of swelling monolingual, racially exclusive nativism in both countries, these disciplines helped reduce multilingual, multiethnic, multimedia, and plurinational texts into stable, singular, ethnocentric, and exceptional literatures neatly attached to empires. They fashioned core identities around which the diverse, uncountable products and contacts of empire could be either assimilated or excluded. From studies of Anglo-Saxon literature to modern Spanish philology, major scholars and writers cemented the genealogies, chronologies, and patrimonies of national and imperial literary traditions. In the United States, they did so in a manner that Van Wyck Brooks found restrictive when he noted in 1918 that "our professors continue to pour out a stream of historical works repeating the same points of view to such an astonishing degree that they have placed a sort of Talmudic seal upon the American tradition," leaving writers without a "usable past."[10] So attenuated and uninspiring were such formulations in Spain that the Nicaraguan writer Rubén Darío would bluntly condescend, as he led *modernismo*'s "inverted conquest" of the former colonizer, that "Spain—amputated, aching, defeated—is in no state for letters."[11]

These well-known histories and narratives have been studied almost exclusively in national contexts, yet they were crafted through international symbiosis, with cooperation from multiple intermediaries and foreign partners. The term "Hispanism" in English bears out this point: it had long referred variously to Orientalist fantasies or an appreciation of Spanish culture, but roughly by the 1920s, it coherently signified a professional field of study devoted to Spain.[12] New centers of knowledge, such as the Hispanic Society in New York City (founded 1904) and the Centro de Estudios Históricos in Madrid (founded 1910), supported this work, and the writers examined here frequented them. Federico García Lorca, José Moreno Villa, Gertrude Stein, Vicente Blasco Ibáñez, William Carlos Williams, and many others also traversed, for a variety of reasons, the institutional and imaginative pathways opened up between the United States and Spain in this moment.[13] This work quickly spread to other arenas of culture as the study of Spain's language and literature saw a meteoric rise in popularity and translation in the United States in the 1910s. This unprecedented and arguably unequaled rise in attention to non-Anglophone foreign literatures composed a "collective fever" dubbed by one historian a "Spanish craze."[14] It reached from high-school classrooms—where Spanish enrollments increased by 700 percent during World War I—to museums, from formalist poetics to bestsellers, even to architectural trends, all with few degrees of separation. The newly founded Association of American Teachers of Spanish made Spanish instruction into a patriotic obligation, adopting as its slogan in 1918, "The war will be won by the substitution of Spanish for German."[15] All of this helped rapidly convert the United States into the preeminent—and most sympathetic, Hispanophilic—source of the study and translation of Spanish literature in the world. Simultaneously, principal voices in Spanish academic and literary cultures similarly helped bring U.S. literature, which previously commanded little respect in Spain, to domestic audiences, through magazines and newspapers, new college courses, and mass-market translations. Even while fears of U.S. cultural hegemony were peaking, Whitman became a household name, a jazz craze took hold, and Hughes became a translated voice of a fermenting political and social revolution. By 1932, the compelling works of contemporary leftist U.S. novelists demanded, as one Spanish critic stated in terms that resonate with Stein's above, that his compatriots "discover America for the second time," only from a markedly different vantage.[16]

Amid these processes, American literature was imagined as carrying the products of a rich civilization to new corners of the world on the wings of a growing overseas empire. Spanish literature, meanwhile, was asserted to have declined into near-obscurity just as its once-mighty empire—whose literature putatively peaked in its Golden Age of conquest—was reduced to a few tiny holdings. These compatible, self-fulfilling prophecies were promulgated, of course, in order to consolidate and justify an expansionist, English-only, and aggressively masculinist Anglo-Saxon nationalism in the United States. In Spain, they were employed after 1898 in an effort to harden a Castilian-language, nativist, Catholic identity around which the crumbling empire's subjects might rally to purify and regenerate an endangered tradition by shrinking the field of literary production but amplifying the intrinsic worth of a select few writers.[17] And indeed, if we follow this dual process and the coalescing exceptionalist narratives to midcentury, we see that such theses might seem to have been confirmed by the course of history. Buffered by everything from puppet governments to cultural diplomacy, from Hollywood films to recorded music, U.S. literature became a foremost global force. Meanwhile, Spanish literature completed its slow, centuries-long descent into international invisibility under an autarkic Francoist regime known mostly for having assassinated Spain's most promising modern author (Lorca); meanwhile, the celebrated Latin American Boom emerged from its former colonies.[18] Likewise, it appears that the victorious United States devoured and reinterpreted the culture of its vanquished imperial opponent, whose previous mantle of world power it still holds in the present, while Spain could only entrench a xenophobic, rearguard identity. Such retrospective readings have made 1898 seem like a chiastic marker—to return to my key term—of *translatio studii et imperii* conveniently situated at the cusp of a new century. In both countries, across many spheres of thought and cultural production, divine sanction and politicized fantasies seemed to have delineated what U.S. and Spanish literatures had been and could be in the twentieth century, creating a feedback loop between political history and literary formations.[19] This process annealed the longstanding, common assumption that great imperial and literary eras necessarily flourished together; thus, in Spain's case, imperial greatness was reconstrued as the concentration of an impalpable "spirit" accrued in the metropolis from past imperial expanse, now commensurate with a circumscribed set of national writers who did not seek global fame.

This assumption was the product of modern literary historiography's having arisen and become institutionalized alongside modern nation-states and the cresting European and British empires. A tradition of translation undergirded and established certain political histories as the source for tracking and periodizing literature. Translation functioned both as a crucial concept in the history of imperialism at large and as a versatile apparatus that facilitated narratives and connections while covering over contradictions. For the new classes of scholars of American studies, Hispanism, and comparative literature in the early twentieth century, and even for large publishing houses and small independent presses, translation generally aimed to stabilize and monumentalize the text, to enrich the dominant native language's resources while affirming the distance and difference of the source text, and to professionalize the accurate, invisible translator. In these same fields, comparisons elided other available nodes of comparison (such as minor-language or politically oppositional texts) and centered on a single narrative, while commentaries on foreign texts subjugated both politics and the critic's own relationship to the text. In all of these practices, imperialism, which was a ubiquitous topic of deliberation in both the United States and Spain at the time, explained literary formations rather than distorting them or even being shaped *by* them. These narrow alignments and hierarchies of geopolitics and literature, of implied pasts and presents, also abounded in public intellectualism and in exported texts, where translation chiefly furthered the post-1898 arrangements of U.S.-Spanish collaboration. Translation thus was carefully divided from other activities and bound up with selected projects that served the needs of empires in transition (whether expanding or contracting), and had little potential to question the alliances and processes that it was supporting.

While both drawing energy from and railing against predominant narratives and protocols, the writers analyzed in *Incomparable Empires* worked to destabilize and redesign these hardening conceptions of U.S. and Spanish literatures with premises and tactics that sometimes defy logic. To return to the crossing in 1916 with which I began, on the same day he left the United States, Dos Passos published his caustic article "Against American Literature," which called for the dismantling of a U.S. literary tradition forged in the exhilaration imbued by centuries of expansionism. He looked to Spain because he believed that its defeat in 1898 and its crumbling empire had created the conditions for a *flourishing* of new literature. In his translations, the young, emerging author sought to repoliticize and then mimic Spanish literature as he simultaneously staked a claim to public expertise against his fellow Hispanophilic socialists and anti-imperialists William Dean Howells and Waldo Frank. Jiménez, for his part, saw 1898 as having ushered in a distinct era in global letters by bringing all of the combatant countries and their dominant languages closer together, fostering an uneven but interconnected renaissance of Spanish, Spanish American, and U.S. letters. His own translational models would embody these connections, and he would then rearrange them across decades of lectures and criticism during his time as a professor in exile in the United States and Puerto Rico. Such uncommon, perhaps counterintuitive suggestions—that imperial and literary greatness are inversely proportional or that wars over colonial territories are a generative, rather than divisive, force—militated against the cultural and political work for which translational practices had been marshaled and confined.

Finding different heuristic and hermeneutic affordances in translation, the writers considered here also embraced derivation, unoriginality, distortion, or mistranslation, and they worked in ways that sometimes had more in common with medieval translation than with the prevailing norms of naturalness and fluidity indebted to Dryden and Arnold. They even manipulated "translation" as a term, from Pound's "traductions" to Ilan Stavans's "transladation," which I address in the conclusion. Translation, they asserted, could also unmake and redraw the artificial and dry portraits of a global cultural past—and could forecast new literary futures. They carved out critical and creative spaces that disconnected and reconfigured, compressed and radically realigned the given spatial politics and chronotopes of literary histories. In capitalizing on the newfound interest in U.S./Spanish connections, some writers drew damning, antiexceptionalist parallels between the imperial cultures of Golden Age Spain and the contemporary United States or between the Inquisition and American censorial codes. Others proposed literary maps that linked sixteenth-century Seville to the plantation U.S. South by way of twentieth-century Havana or put a Klansman's hood on Franco's head; others still rewrote, with concerted anachronisms, a buried history of interanimation and interpenetration between Anglo- and Hispanophone literatures and their associated empires since the 1500s. Translation created comparisons and narratives in which "American literature" and "Spanish literature" appeared *less* coherent, unconnected—reconstellated as *literatura yanqui* ("Yankee literature") or as prenational troubadour traditions in unfamiliar and recontextualized ambits. It had sociological and commercial capacities, too: in Spain, one might find poets like Whitman and Hughes and Hispanists like George Ticknor translated beside one another, perhaps for the first time, and grouped as exemplars of "North American literature"—a category barely intelligible to most North Americans. Rather than agreeing that New York City and Madrid ought to share in a cultural exchange that would increase the prestige and value of their respective native literatures, Dos Passos and Jiménez insisted that these two cities should *not* be connected as sites of exciting new literary production. They held—and many others in this book agreed—that both cities were mostly cultural wastelands, stale metropolitan capitals of homogenizing, decadent societies created by unremarkable empires; Berlin, Paris, and London, from which global literary repute issued, hardly fared better. They countered that the United States and Spain instead were generating together the new realist novel for a dawning international socialist revolution or were reviving a line of mysticism and antiorthodoxy that skipped over several centuries.

By reanimating such coordinates, I intend to modify the practices of comparison that connect international literatures in a manner that presumably enriches all; such an approach is a legacy of the period treated in this book, and we should see it skeptically.[20] Instead, I highlight methodologically the effects of the interlingual tensions and conflicts, rather than fluidity and translatability, between (in this case) English and Spanish. Thus, I do not use translation to expand or redescribe existing, already hegemonic fields such as modernist studies or American studies, nor do I fill in more spaces on the global maps they have produced. Rather, as Brent Hayes Edwards has shown in other contexts, translation—by opening a broad and incongruous register of allusion, parataxis, and argumentation—alternately bridged and created gaps, built up and disorganized fields.[21] Translation, like comparison, allows us to question their very vocabularies. Jiménez's speculations on the tension between "modernism" and "*modernismo*," which I investigate in chapter 3, are one example, and as I show in chapter 5, a loose collection of writers and critics in Spain and the Hispanophone Americas translated, for anthologies that aspired to professional authority, the works of Hughes, Claude McKay, and other New Negro writers with a distinct anxiety about this new *literatura negra* (black literature) and its name. The Spanish word *negro* had returned, thanks to the spread of the U.S. cultural empire, as an Anglophone term (Negro) in a global battle for political and civic rights, and conservative Spaniards and leftist Cubans together theorized controversially that the roots of black diasporic writing lay in baroque Spanish poetry. The concern in such cases was the epistemology and incommensurability, more than the debates over ontology, of terms like "black literature"/*literatura negra* that oscillated irreconcilably between English and Spanish at critical junctures. This irreconcilability feeds both the promise and the disquiet found in several writers' predictions that the twentieth century would be defined by the future union of a global English and a global Spanish.

This approach to translation emerges from the historical configurations of the empires and their relations in question here. Within modernist studies, the temporalities and spaces through which global modernisms are periodized, and through which modernism, imperialism, and colonialism are conjoined, have been revolutionized by postcolonial and transnational literary studies.[22] The recent emphasis on contact zones and territories, borderlands and border crossings, and subjectivities and migrations has productively complicated the familiar narratives of modernism too, and linguistic interactions and translational topics have played an important, though sometimes subdued, role in this work. But overlooked in questions of metropole/periphery relations, in versions of creolité or hybridity, or in subaltern approaches is the need for a comparative model that can apprehend the sense of "imperialism" as *competition* that Fredric Jameson recovers from the early twentieth century. "The word 'imperialism' designates, not the relationship of metropolis to colony," Jameson writes, "but rather the rivalry of the various imperial and metropolitan nation states among themselves."[23] Jameson himself has rarely pursued that sense, but it is vital here, as it was in the Great War and as it was for Lenin. For the centuries in which they were imperial competitors, Spain and the United States—both marginal players at the Berlin Conference that Jameson cites—had consolidated their national identities around the denigration of the other. The War of 1898 only accelerated this process, most famously in American yellow journalism and in Spanish popular media. The fact that the highly symbolic imperial crossing in 1898 was called a "splendid little war" in one country and a "Disaster" in the other makes the cultural cooperation that followed between the two countries all the more surprising and perhaps suspicious.[24] Spain was both dead and alive to Americans; the United States was both crass and inspiring to Spaniards.

To capture this—to compare these empires and their literatures without replicating the terms and assumptions that they propounded—we must explore "inter-imperiality" (to invoke Laura Doyle's useful, dialectical formulation) through translation, as opposed to looking primarily to form as an effect of historical conditions.[25] The disparate collectivity of writers that I gather here charted U.S. and Spanish literatures on an unsettled world stage by casting them simultaneously through interimperial dynamics and cross-linguistic traffic. As a malleable resource, translation thus was operating beyond the familiar paradigm in which it usually either shores up or resists imperial power, as critics including Edward Said, Mary Louise Pratt, Tejaswini Niranjana, Gauri Viswanathan, and Eric Cheyfitz have adumbrated it.[26] It was working instead to restructure or break open familiar imperial histories. Though the writers at hand shared in a networked array of practices and engagements, no single politics, aesthetics, sensibility, or genre unites them, and their work was too complex to be reduced simply to opposition to ascendant or ingrained narratives. The far left and the far right are both present, and Dos Passos's readings of modern Spanish literature, for instance, were in uncanny agreement with conservative Spanish nationalists. Pound and Unamuno both vacillated or contradicted themselves over time, and Hughes was implicated, as a translator, in a stunning mode of anti-African racism. Moving more or less chronologically but tacking back and forth across languages and contexts, I focus in the first four chapters on pronounced arcs in the careers of four major figures—precisely because the convoluted paths of their careers demonstrate the depth and breadth of their arguments. I pair two

American Hispanists, Pound and Dos Passos, with the former opening this book's approach to translation and the latter centering the arguments about post-1898 empire. Next, I pair two Americanists from Spain, Jiménez and Unamuno, whose works respectively theorize the problems of modernism in translation and of translation as a structure for demarcating literary history through contingent notions of innovation or authenticity. In the final two chapters, I further explore and test some of the synthetic genealogies these writers proposed and the methods by which they were devised. I take a wide-angle view of the making and the historicization of a literary-cultural formation (*literatura negra*) in chapter 5 and then, in chapter 6, concentrate on a single novel (*For Whom the Bell Tolls*, 1940), in which Hemingway stretches the bounds of translation to produce an estranged, invented tongue that registers the historical collisions of English and Spanish. (Hemingway's protagonist Robert Jordan, we might recall, was an American Spanish instructor steeped in knowledge of baroque Spanish literature.) In these final two chapters, academic fields and the immediate post-1898 world move to the background while the racial and political realities of the growing global force of American English in the late 1930s and early 1940s come to the foreground. From here, I trace new genealogies of late modernism and postmodernism through an optic of translation that clarifies the contributions of outlying or less obvious texts and writers. I conclude by pushing beyond the Spanish Civil War or World War II as a natural endpoint—just as World War I remains mostly a minor context for this book—and by looking to Felipe Alfau, Malcolm Lowry, and the contemporary author/translator Ilan Stavans. Here, I track the development of Spanglish not as a marker of bilingual immigrant subjectivity but as a literary dialect made possible by the entwined but fragmented histories of Spanish and Anglophone literatures. The alternative genealogies that I recover and offer urge us to reconsider the histories not only of our fields but also of our own critical habits.

* * *

It is not the case that the figures under scrutiny here somehow got things right—that they were more just comparatists or translators of foreign literatures and ought to be lauded, especially for something as banal as transgressing a national border or speaking against a statist or imperial vision. Undoubtedly, they were enmeshed in the contradictions of empire: they appreciated and drew on the global materials to which empire gave them access, and they glorified Spain's accretion of internal diversity, which was a direct result of the country's violent imperial past. They also praised eras of increased translation in ways that naturalized the very political histories that made those translations possible, and they developed sympathetic theories of the effects of territorial expansion and geopolitical power on literary production. Most of the authors I study are male, and several were invested in paradigms of masculinity or vitality that were coupled with regressive politics. They often operated in an almost exclusively male world of cultural historiography; most had little interest in opening up genealogies to women writers and only allowed black poets to enter as derivative. We find, then, that Dos Passos substantively blamed women for the poor state of writing in the United States, Jiménez sometimes took credit for translations that his wife Zenobia Camprubí first carried out, Hemingway's Maria is a helpless damsel in distress who could hardly be said to represent Spanish women, and Archer Milton Huntington's Hispanic Society of America was founded on a belief in the subjugated roles of women. Concomitant with such conceptions of gender was a typical condescension or excision of Spanish America, which I discuss in the middle part of the book, and a recurring portrayal of Spain as feminized and weak. Germany, by contrast, was demonized as a hyperindustrial war machine by Dos Passos, the headquarters of retrograde philology by Pound, and the producer of racist vitriol by Hughes, all in service of very different Hispanophilic literary ends. And what was deemed a benighted state program of *Kultur* in modern Germany was a useful counterexample to the theory that empire and culture thrive together.

It would take several more books to do justice to these topics—and some such books already exist[27]—but I mention them to signpost the arguments that this book aims to avoid. One possible version of this book would tell the entangled histories of Anglophone U.S. modernism and Spanish Silver Age letters roughly between 1898 and the Spanish Civil War (1936–39).[28] While fruitful, such a story would buy into the self-proclaimed narratives of native renaissance that I am attempting to historicize and disorient. The same holds for a version in which I would remap given works into a single field of cooperation—perhaps a transatlantic one—with various strands of connectivity cohering as a central plotline; but that kind of connectivity, as I indicated above, reproduces a familiar story.[29] Still another line of argument would hold that when Spain was newly defeated and converted into a historical monument, it became an exotic, semicolonial wellspring of inspiration across U.S. culture, and critics such as María DeGuzmán have demonstrated that some modernists participated in propagating such images.[30] In that version, however, a basic American identity is presupposed, and then Spain strengthens it by enabling the consolidation of Americanness. Instead, we need to rethink how the retroactively applied triumphalist tale of the American Century relies on a number of clichéd motifs of U.S. continuity and ascendancy, much in the same way that the deterministic story of Spanish decline recycles tropes of Iberian decadence from the Black Legend of the country's barbarism in its New World conquest. We must revisit skeptically the history of these mutually enriching exceptionalisms and the connections they created.

In this introduction, I aim to clarify the unintended, even occluded effects of American studies and Hispanism's post-1898 collaborations—to historicize the fields to which this book contributes. A somewhat granular replotting of 1898 and its ramifications across the following decades demonstrates why the infrastructure built by Hispanists and Americanists who crisscrossed the Atlantic became an unlikely resource for modernists in several countries. To see this, we need to unsettle the native formations and follow the foreign configurations of Spanish and U.S. literatures—to sketch the intellectual and methodological battles in which the writers gathered in this book were engaged, the experts and antagonists they found and attacked, and the successes and failures they encountered. I end with the means by which Hispanism and American studies, with their adaptable groundings in conceptions of essence, identity, democracy, or progress, actually concealed their links to one another through new Cold War and dictatorial mandates of professionalization and study. Thus we find that Hispanism and American studies seem to be discrete enterprises in the present whereas a century ago the two were often held in an array of uneven balances.[31]

Stein posits a related kind of mutual enrichment operating in the twentieth century and sees a certain amount of irony in the way that Americans like herself had "discovered" Spain by collecting Picasso's works. But her claim that both countries then "found their moment" together, and that they shared a propensity toward cubist forms, makes too hasty a logical leap.[32] She flattens the asymmetries of power, patronage, prestige, and more into a celebration (a paradoxical valuation of agreement upon aesthetic disagreement) that overlooks the great hostility and disproportionate exchanges between the two countries. Perhaps what the United States and Spain shared most saliently in this moment was a conviction of incomparability—a belief that their unique natures put them beyond comparison.³³ The reality is that sustaining such myths required constant, frequently anxious and self-subverting comparisons, and those comparisons laid the groundwork for other revisionary practices. Long before a field like American studies found itself overhauled in recent decades, the questions it deemed closed and the objects it aimed to amalgamate were forced open by a host of writers and critics working in a deep, sometimes strange tradition.

The United States as the New Spain

Comparison is embedded in exceptionalism, but not the kind of comparison that most contemporary critics find useful or worthwhile. Historically, Americans and Spaniards actually compared their empires to each other and to many others, for a variety of ends. Academic and popular authors from around the world compared them, too, with increased frequency beginning in the second half of the nineteenth century. (John Dos Passos's own father contributed to that trend; see chapter 2.) Yet, in following a selective range of comparative paths from among many posited in the past, few contemporary scholars of American literary studies have thought comparatively about the United States *as* an empire, one that emerged in competition with other empires and, in doing so, selectively appropriated and rejected their cultures.³⁴ A comparative approach to empires and their rivalries is common among world historians but rare among literary scholars in general, who tend to compare the national or linguistic tradition, period, genre, form, or movement, however modified.³⁵ A reluctance to compare the U.S. empire at all and to understand its literatures through interimperial dynamics pervades the fields to which I contribute in the chapters that follow—modernist studies, comparative literary studies, postcolonial and transnational literary criticism, Spanish literary historiography, and African American cultural studies—despite their otherwise abundant and rich intersections. Scholars of modernism, for instance, have looked primarily to European imperial histories and the literatures of postcolonies, neglecting the imperial United States; in their studies, they also have tended to focus on form rather than comparison. Within Spain, comparative studies remain almost wholly aesthetic in focus, removed from political contexts such as empire, and the United States is hardly mentioned.³⁶

The risk of such a singular approach to U.S. empire, even in postexceptionalist and transnational American studies, is high because it reinscribes exceptionalism and thereby perpetuates the myth of the United States as an exceptional empire.[37] It risks, in other words, continuing a pattern that Donald Pease has noted, in which American studies replicates the logic of U.S. imperial expansionism.[38] The fact that translation has been silently assumed and scarcely studied within the field, as Kirsten Silva Gruesz has shown, only magnifies this risk.[39] Here, the particular blindness to Spain within contemporary American studies is telling, and it has a discrete history that explains the large gap between the robust comparative studies of both early modern Anglo-/Hispanophone exchanges and contemporary Spanglish and bilingualism. The early English colonists in the United States even modeled their venture on the successes of Spanish conquest—so much so that John Smith warned against becoming "Spanolized English"—and Americans adopted practices and even racial terminologies of slavery from Spain (see chapter 5).[40] But shortly after the Revolutionary War, Spain began to function more consistently as a convenient Other around which U.S. identity formed, and this would continue during periods of territorial expansion. Americans impatiently awaited the collapse of the Spanish Empire and the opportunity to build their own empire to the west. Thomas Jefferson cautioned his compatriots not to rush to acquire lands held by Spain but instead to let "feeble" Spain retain them until the fledging United States was "sufficiently advanced" to take them "piece by piece"; meanwhile, he urged Americans to learn Spanish because of their necessary "future connections with Spain" and because "the antient history of a great part of America, too, is written in [Spanish]."[41] As Henry Adams wrote,

> Between the Americans and the Spaniards [around 1800] no permanent friendship could exist. Their systems were at war, even when their nations were at peace.... Spain represented despotism, bigotry, and corruption.... Spain had immense influence over the United States; but it was the influence of the whale over its captors,—the charm of a huge, helpless, and profitable victim.[42]

In a series of treaties, land purchases and seizures, and battles in the first half of the nineteenth century capped by the Mexican-American War (1846–48) and the Gadsden Purchase (1854), the United States claimed the territories north of the Rio Grande that once composed New Spain. The War of 1898 continued this process in which the United States' imperial advances were predicated on Spain's imperial losses.

Generations of eminent scholars, from Henry Wadsworth Longfellow to Henry Charles Lea to Irving Babbitt, read Spain's literature in modes that abutted that same process. The historian Richard L. Kagan has coined the term "Prescott's paradigm" (after William Hickling Prescott) to explain the ways in which the allegedly inevitable decline of Spain was a structuring narrative for studies of Spanish political and cultural history in the United States, where this narrative almost always fit into an exceptionalist agenda of naturalizing the coeval rise of the United States.[43] At the same time, Castilian, imperial Spain was circumscribed as an object of knowledge for a modern disciplinary formation; the varied modes of thinking about Spanish culture that had arisen across U.S. history were winnowed down just as the multiple states and languages within Iberia were. Ticknor's monumental *History of Spanish Literature* (1849) was, in the words of James Turner, "the solidest work of humanistic learning yet to appear in the United States," and it concluded—just after the Mexican-American War—that if Spaniards "have failed to learn this solemn lesson [of the danger of] blind submission to priestly authority, . . . inscribed everywhere, as by the hand of Heaven, on the crumbling walls of their ancient institutions, then is their honorable history, both in civilization and letters, closed forever."[44] A half-century later, the Spanish-born American and Harvard professor George Santayana admitted that he felt "almost a relief" at the demise of the Spanish Empire, whose "weakness" he saw as born of "Quixotic frailty."[45] In a patriotic poem, "Spain in America" (1901), he commemorated the U.S. victory in 1898 as proof that Spain had "taught the younger world" all that "she had to teach"—including "her faith and heart and speech"—but that Spain was now being rightfully eclipsed.[46] Spain became a cautionary example: a great empire that squandered its political power and cultural riches by refusing to tolerate secular democracy. Most Hispanists sympathized with Spain and saw its imperial decline as a tragedy—one that the United States could then rectify.

A similar logic was reinforced beyond academia, as is visible in the works of the diplomat and popular author John Hay.[47] Indeed, it was accelerated and amplified during the hysteria fomented in the United States over Spain's brutality during the Cuban War of Independence in the years leading up to 1898. In popular media and yellow journalism,

Spain was depicted, in recycled Black Legend imagery, as a conniving, murderous, cloaked coward; a fiery, hot-blooded, incompetent matador; a decrepit, dying woman; or a blood-covered simian with fangs. Cheap romance fictions told of brave Anglo-Saxon heroes who liberated the noble savages of Cuba from their oppression by a hot-tempered Latin master. By the early twentieth century, Americans were certain and proud that their country was *not* Spain, that it was a different kind of empire. The post-1898 exceptionalist narrative made white Americans heirs instead to a tradition of civilizing missions that dated back to Greece but that now required the uniformity and Anglo-Saxon expansionist spirit of the British Empire that the United States was also succeeding. In a revamped genealogy influenced by Arthur de Gobineau's thought, the decadent imperial systems of the racially mixed Latin countries (France, Italy, Portugal, and Spain) were contrasted with those of the progressive, pure Teutonic and Nordic peoples (Germany, England, and the United States) and with the reemergent "Asiatic" empires of Russia and Japan.

English-only white nativism peaked, that is, not only when African Americans were freed from slavery and when immigration surged in New York City but also when the U.S. empire reached further into non-Anglophone lands formerly held by Spain. Theodore Roosevelt, nationally famous for his role in the Spanish-American War, crafted a political identity around calls to make the United States a monolingual state defined by purported Anglo-Saxon principles and by a hypermasculinity that was opposed to the weak, feminized Latin type.[48] Such thought was not limited to the United States' imperial apologists: white supremacists in the South looked back to John C. Calhoun's understanding of the detrimental effects of racial mixing in the Spanish Empire and opposed the War of 1898 on the grounds that it would add nonwhite (Spanish, mestizo, Afro-Caribbean, indigenous, and more) voting subjects to the U.S. population. The abolitionist minister Theodore Parker charged that having adopted slavery practices from Spain had corrupted Anglo-Saxons and would degenerate them into Spaniards. The anti-imperialist William Graham Sumner, in his speech "The Conquest of the United States by Spain" (1899), asserted that the United States had "beaten Spain in a military conflict" but was "submitting to be conquered by her on the field of ideas and policies . . . which have brought Spain to where she is now," a subject of its own colonial "tyrann[y]."[49]

The profound shared fear of becoming Spain consolidated national identities, and it erased Spain from the New World. A dark, weird, crumbling Spain was relegated to the Old World and to the past, where it was no longer threatening. And, as has been well documented, the United States eagerly but anxiously accepted Spain's former commission as the primary power in the Americas and ambivalently acquired Spanish-speaking subjects.[50] As American studies rose in disciplinary stature in the first decades of the twentieth century, it maintained this logic and pushed Spain out of its view. More recently, Latino/a, Chicano/a, and various Hispanophone American studies have greatly diversified and challenged a field notorious for its near-exclusive focus on Anglophone texts produced in the territorial United States. And while figures such as Álvar Núñez Cabeza de Vaca are now seen to have an imprint on early U.S. literature, and while early modern scholars have long seen Spain and the United States as sharing in multiform cultural transactions, Spain still disappears from scholarly view when the United States claims its former lands. When American studies, particularly in the mid–twentieth century, fortified itself as a monolingual English enterprise, there was little room to recover a Spanish presence. Spain was transformed from sociopolitical entity into a language (Spanish) spoken by its former colonial subjects. The peninsula remained confined to itself; Spain had no territories and few subjects in the United States, after all.

American studies, in other words, in large part has treated "Spanish" as American Hispanists, nostalgic imperial apologists in Spain, and even the U.S. census did: as a confused, shifting signifier of some combination of ethnicity and language unclearly tied to the Iberian peninsula.[51] The prevailing approach to Spain in studies of U.S. culture follows from Stanley T. Williams's *The Spanish Background of American Literature* (1955). Williams, who was instrumental in founding American literary studies as an academic field and who sat on the inaugural board of *American Literature* (1929–), argued that Ticknor, Prescott, Henry Wadsworth Longfellow, Washington Irving, Bret Harte, Mark Twain, and William Dean Howells belonged to a century-long " 'Golden Day,' not merely of American literature itself but of some more or less united group eager to plunder for the young Republic the cultural riches of Spain."[52] Thus, for Williams, who tellingly casts Spaniards and Spanish speakers as virtually interchangeable, "the diverse channels by which Spanish culture has become part of our own" have made U.S. literature wealthier and more cosmopolitan, eclectic.[53] Here, "America" is solidified as an exceptional medley—a revised melting pot—and Spain becomes a residual source of prosperity for both American literary production and American studies. At the same time, as Williams's book indicates, by the turn of the twentieth century, the United States had—in a classic model of the effects of Orientalism—a groundswell of knowledge, professional expertise, public intellectualism, and newly translated materials regarding Spain. Irving spent years in Spain and became a respected international authority, Ticknor arranged to have the sole manuscript of the *Poema del Cid* brought to Boston in hopes of fostering its popularity, and bilingual textbooks and translation guides were being produced almost from the moment the United States acquired Puerto Rico. Williams, like a number of contemporary scholars of U.S. literature, looks only for how such a history informed a knowable, canonical American literature; to the figures in this book, and to many others, such exceptionalist presumptions are the problem. A space for revaluating Spain and repurposing its culture was already present in the United States, it turns out, and the post-1898 *hispanistas* in the United States and Spain would quickly enter it, spurring the debates in which modernist writers intervened in efforts to defamiliarize and denaturalize American cultural history. To understand the opportunities and mixed results of this moment, we must turn to Spain.

Tío Sam and the Anxious Embrace of an American Planet

In Spain, the War of 1898 prompted depictions and narratives of Yankee imperialism and belligerence across the spectrum of national media. An upstart country and culture to which Spaniards had paid little attention or had dismissed hastily as grotesque materialist offshoots of the British Empire suddenly shifted many national conversations. Uncle Sam was portrayed as a vulgar, ruthless henchman of rapacious industrialist oligarchs, and Americans often were pigs and deceptive heathens.[54] The racism of white Americans and the violence of the lynching epidemic were contrasted in the 1890s with the Spaniards' supposedly humane treatment of Afro-Cubans, and Americans were seen to be siding with the colonial natives *against* civilization. Powerful Spanish clerics and rightists denounced the United States as an abomination that combined all things ungodly. To the Spanish left, the United States was the mechanized imperialistic leviathan. These typologies were blended with a figuration of Robinson Crusoe, in whom Spaniards saw a ruthless Protestant (and thus heretical) devotion to material progress and economic power that had transferred from England to the United States. Crusoe was symbolically pitted, time and again, against Don Quixote, who signaled spiritual values and the Spanish conquest of the Americas by divine providence.[55] Latin empires, the Spanish argued in an adaptation of Giuseppe Sergi's valorization of the "Mediterranean race," gave the indigenous peoples both civilization and salvation; Teutonic empires were crude, avaricious, and dependent mostly on brute force. The implication was that even if the United States could dominate the markets of Spanish American states, it could never dominate their populations' souls—their impenetrable essences endowed to them by the immutable Catholic spirit and blood of their Spanish conquerors.

The war was popularly referred to as *El Desastre* (The Disaster). In Madrid, the newspaper *El Liberal* lamented after the cessions of the Treaty of Paris that "we have lost everything," for after Spain "returned to the West Indies, which we had discovered, and to the Far East, which we civilized," it was sent home like "evicted tenants" and "morose deportee[s]."[56] Another paper added in despair: "everything is broken in this unhappy country; there is no government, no electorate, no political parties. . . . All is fiction, all decadence, all ruin."[57] Other Spaniards saw the U.S. victory as punishment for Spain's mismanaging its colonies or as divine providence having chosen the Anglo-Saxons over Latin peoples. The war was contextualized as the endpoint of the long-festering *problema de España*, the unsolvable question of why Spain's once-robust empire had declined.[58] Spain received no support from Europe against the United States, confirming its fall from membership in the continental community. (The loss motivated, furthermore, another disaster for Spain: its botched attempt to invade and colonize Morocco that began just a decade later.) The year 1898 remains a turning point in modern Spanish history on a par with the Spanish Civil War and the post-Franco transition to democracy.

As in the United States, the responses to the war solidified the claims of racial exclusivity, nativism, and exceptionalism, here tied to Spain's unique destiny—whether that destiny was as a world power or as a minor European state, as an empire to be reinvigorated or to be eulogized. For all factions, the question of the nature of *hispanismo*—meaning all things essentially Spanish—weighed heavily on the racialized thought that had been building dramatically since 1892, the celebrated quadricentennial of Columbus's landfall. *Hispanistas* argued that there was an immaterial Spanish "spirit" that unified the Spanish people worldwide into one *raza*: *la raza española*. Anthropologists, ethnographers, and scientists scrutinized Spanish soldiers to see if they could understand the reasons why the Spanish *raza* had been defeated by an alliance of Africanized Cubans (as they saw them) and unintelligent Americans. The historian Julián Juderías's seminal and internationally influential history of the Black Legend (*la leyenda negra*, a term he coined in 1912) was at once an apologetic nationalist treatise and an investigation of the psychology and cultural productions of mostly Anglo-Saxon Protestants. Juderías concluded that Spaniards themselves were "principally to blame" for the Black Legend not because of their religious intolerance but because of their lack of introspective immersion in their own history: "we have had to learn about ourselves in books written by foreigners and inspired, as a general rule, by contempt for Spain."[59] Such nativism became further entrenched when, in light of Franco's enlisting "Moorish" troops to fight in the Spanish Civil War, both Loyalists and Nationalists recycled images over a thousand years old to depict one another as Africanized invaders of the true Spain.

The one-time anarchist writer Azorín turned sharply to the right after 1898 and, in 1913, gave what remains an influential and contentious name to a collection of authors and intellectuals whom he saw galvanized by the war: the Generation of '98.[60] The figures of this generation, including Azorín himself, Unamuno, Ángel Ganivet, Pío Baroja, Ramón del Valle-Inclán, Antonio and Manuel Machado, and others, were said to embody the persisting greatness of what was truly Spanish even after the Disaster. They were heralded as the greatest collective since Spain's Golden Age of Cervantes, Calderón, Lope de Vega, and Góngora; indeed, the period from 1898 to roughly 1939 came to be called the Silver Age.[61] Spanish literature was—and mostly remains—understood as having bloomed at the height of Spain's empire and then declined during the Counter-Reformation, Inquisition, and the New World independence movements: so much so that romanticism, at best, was faint in Spain, while realism and naturalism were largely belated, derivative movements.[62] For decades, the '98 writers' national introspection and plans to reinvent Spanish literature for a new century (known as *regeneracionismo*) proved, for conservative and nationalist voices, that the Disaster had magically purified Spanish culture—that it had concentrated that ineffable essence (*hispanismo*) that Spaniards had searched for and lost in imperial misadventures and had given birth to a rich new cultural movement locally. Spain's imperial size and literary greatness were recalibrated: "we must not pretend we have arsenals and shipyards where we have only buildings and installations that guard nothing and construct nothing," wrote the academic and politician Francisco Silvela, who urged that Spain instead reconstitute "all the organisms of the national life on modest but firm foundations that our means will allow us."[63] Accordingly, Spanish America was marginalized, and a new national Spanish literature was imagined by a professional and statist class of philologists to endow the country once again with mystique, privilege, and a realm of imagined *aesthetic* domination. The compensation for imperial loss was a crucible of spirit and a linguistic empire that Unamuno—an outlier in this book, except for how he undermines himself—would paradoxically defend. As part of this logic, Castilianism further asserted its domestic power, laying the groundwork for the suppression of provincial languages such as Catalan and Basque that would become law under Franco.

As many critics and translators used this moment to gauge the current state of Spanish letters by way of its international reception and influence—asking the same questions that Juderías did about international perceptions—Spain's apologists and cultural ambassadors promoted this fantastic abundance of new letters abroad.[64] A formation such as '98 might seem scarcely compatible with a new attention to U.S. literature, but in fact, these same critics attempted to reconcile post-1898 cultural relations with both the United States and Spanish America. This required sympathetic partners, and as it turned out, Spain's liberal establishment included federalist blocs that, for decades, had been sympathetic to U.S. intervention in Spain's former colonies. Recasting the common denunciative comparisons with the United States, the influential republican politician and writer Francisco Pi y Margall praised the United States as a true democracy with separation of church and state, a beacon of freedom and refuge from the tumult that engulfed many European states and their colonies. Some antimonarchists and anticolonialists even argued that the United States should replace Spain's own despotic rule in Cuba and the Philippines, for in the United States, "men of all nationalities and of all races live . . . together, free and in peace."[65]

A great shift in international literary and scholarly relations then took place. Liberal men of letters in Spain such as Rafael Altamira, Pascual de Gayangos, Amador de los Ríos, Juan C. Cebrián, the Duke of Rivas, Ramón Menéndez Pidal, and Juan Valera developed relationships with Anglophone Hispanists and created reciprocal circuits of study and exchange—and lectured, published, and sometimes took up academic positions in the United States—in order to tell a new story of a reconceived, postimperial Spain. This international project centered on the concept of *hispanismo*, which gradually came to signify also the work of spreading Spain's past and present cultural patrimony to new lands, and on the achievements of the Generation of '98 within a reconceived schema of Spain's literary past. *Hispanismo* required seeing the barbaric Anglo-Saxons of the United States as the most valuable and clear-sighted interpreters of the essence of Spain and acknowledging that the United States was a powerful new empire where Spanish literature could be translated and renovated. Altamira, for example, identified an emblematic collaborator in Charles Lummis, best known for his role as a promoter of travel and relocation in the U.S. southwest. In his history *The Spanish Pioneers* (1893), Lummis—paving the way for the post-1898 detente with Spain— first stressed his own "Puritan" and "Saxon" credentials in the preface, then praised the Spanish conquistadors and translated them as the palatable, classically American "pioneers."[66] Altamira wrote a lengthy, sympathetic prologue for the very popular translation of Lummis's book into Spanish in 1916 as *Los exploradores españoles del siglo XVI: vindicación de la acción colonizadora española en América* (literally: The Spanish explorers of the sixteenth century: a vindication of the Spanish colonial efforts in America). Soon, a condensed version of Altamira's widely translated *Historia de España y de la civilización española* (1900–1911) became the standard history textbook on Spain in the United States for decades.[67] This new reciprocity gave birth to a brief period of shared cultural prosperity for the United States and Spain in each other's countries and thus to a variety of literary products that the principal disciplines at work here—Hispanism and American studies—ultimately could neither compare nor comprehend.

Spain in America, Again

Hispanismo, as Frederick B. Pike has documented, crossed the Atlantic rapidly and effectively.[68] In its first decades, the Modern Language Association (founded in 1883) hardly mentioned Spanish in its publications or programs. But with the establishment of comparative literature departments around the turn of the century, Spanish literary studies, with the help of *hispanistas* and the ideological formations they proffered, found a belated foothold. By 1906, Miguel de Unamuno asserted that the United States had the greatest Hispanists in the world, and in 1909, the acclaimed British Hispanist Martin Hume conceded the same. The Spanish philologist and historian Miguel Romera-Navarro, a close friend of Pound's mentor Hugo Rennert, would spend the latter part of his career at the University of Pennsylvania and in 1917 would devote an entire book to *El hispanismo en Norte-América*. "Prescott's paradigm" had changed, and Spain was now to be elevated, if not emulated; at the same time, American Hispanists elevated their own institutional prestige and the international prestige of U.S. universities at large.

No figure better captures this transitional moment than Archer Milton Huntington, who saw Spain no longer as an imperial competitor but as something historically grand and forever new.[69] A scholar, translator, polymath, collector, and sponsor who came from a family of railroad magnates, Huntington founded the Hispanic Society of America, a museum and cultural center that both mummified and enlivened Spain. He brought the Valencian artist Joaquín Sorolla to his society in New York City for an exhibit in 1909 that drew nearly 160,000 visitors in the first month alone, the largest crowd for an art show to that date in U.S. history. Sorolla himself expanded his vision of Spain in articles for U.S. magazines and newspapers, where he suggested, "the Spain of Gil Blas? Ah, that has gone forever. . . . We are very modern in Spain today. . . . Spain, having lost her colonies, must now develop her great resources and compete in the markets of the world. . . . So we have great hopes for the new Spain."[70] For Sorolla, the "new Spain" was a rustic *Volk* of peasants whom he would paint in giant murals across the Sorolla Room at the Hispanic Society.

Huntington, who would bring dozens of Hispanists and Hispanophone writers to New York in the next two decades, then worked with the American Association of Teachers of Spanish (he was the inaugural honorary president) to sponsor the teaching of Spanish in New York City schools and at Columbia University. This occurred, perhaps surprisingly, in the same moment that bilingual schools were being closed across the country, when Spanish was being suppressed across the territories and new states of the southwest, when French was proscribed in Louisiana, and when the Trading with the Enemy Act (1918) made it illegal to disseminate many foreign-language texts without first having secured approval from the postmaster. The fiery and anti-German first leader of the AATS, Lawrence Wilkins, asserted in an opening salvo for the organization's journal *Hispania* (1917–) that "many are beginning to realize . . . that we Anglo-Saxons may possibly, after all, have overestimated our 'superiority' and underestimated the Iberian and Iberian-American nations, their past glories and their present capabilities—in art, in literature, in politics."[71] By studying Spanish, he argues, not only will one "develop as many brain loops as will the study of Sanscrit [*sic*] or Russian," but also, "much can be done to ward off the possibility of our hemisphere becoming some day the shambles that the Old World is now."[72] Another scholar proclaimed in *Hispania* that "Spanish was the first European language used on the North American continent. It was the language of the discoverer, the explorer, and the conqueror," and it was a tongue that conveyed the truth of Christianity.[73] Spanish literature was both foreign and native to the United States in this formulation, and it had merits for study that both included and exceeded the expression of a normative white U.S. identity. Middle- and high-school Spanish-language study, as mentioned above, skyrocketed in this moment. As Mary Louise Pratt writes of the language battles in the southwestern United States at this time, "Spanish as a native tongue was a threat; as a second, nonnative language, an asset" useful in conquering markets in Spanish America, among other things.[74] And accordingly, there was a powerful and mostly successful concomitant effort to limit "Spanish"—the literature, vocabulary, and accent taught to students—to Castilian Spain, excluding both Spain's provinces and Spanish America and implicitly reasserting the Monroe Doctrine on the level of foreign-language education.[75]

Huntington also advised Columbia University's president Nicholas Murray Butler, a strong Spanish sympathizer, to hire Federico de Onís, a student of Unamuno's and a prominent pan-Hispanist, to lead the Spanish department that Onís would quickly make the most influential in the country. At Columbia, Onís used money from the new Junta para la Ampliación de Estudios, a Spanish fund to promote the country's culture abroad, to create the Instituto de las Españas en los Estados Unidos (now the Hispanic Institute for Latin American and Iberian Cultures) in 1920. By 1922, nearly 57,000 college students were enrolled in Spanish courses in the United States, and publishing houses asked Onís, who taught Lorca during the poet's stay in the city, for names of Spanish writers to translate into English.[76] This celebration and elevation of Spain, which was documented enthusiastically by many Hispanists up to the 1940s, continued across society; the *New York Times* reported that even U.S. tourists to Spain increased from three thousand in 1923 to forty thousand in 1925, just when Spain's struggling economy aided the fantasy of the country as the cheap, exotic space that Hemingway would portray.[77] Gilded Age collectors and their heirs developed in this moment an acute taste for Spanish Golden Age masterpieces, and contemporary Spanish art traveled the country in several high-profile expositions.[78] "Spain sank low in our defeat of her, [and] she has replied with the lightnings of art," wrote one critic, in an inversion of the customary narrative of imperial and aesthetic greatness.[79] Giralda-style towers adorned a number of new buildings during the Spanish Colonial Revival style in architecture (1915–1931), Hispanophone media flourished in places like the bustling "Little Spain" neighborhood in Manhattan, while leading Spanish writers made regular trips to New York City.[80] Both translations of contemporary Spanish literature and anthologies of Spanish literary history reached new heights. Ten of Pío Baroja's novels were translated between 1917 and 1928, along with nine works by Ramón del Valle-Inclán between 1918 and 1935; Vicente Blasco Ibáñez's novel *Four Horsemen of the Apocalypse* (the best-selling book in the United States in 1919 and, soon after, a blockbuster film starring Rudolph Valentino) gained enormous popularity, and the author was awarded an honorary doctor of letters at George Washington University in 1920; Gregorio Martínez Sierra's plays found success in translation on Broadway; and translators and publishers such as Samuel Putnam and Thomas Walsh issued a spate of new Spanish texts for U.S. audiences.[81] This trend continued through the Spanish Civil War, which brought Spain anew into U.S. consciousness and which led exiled Spanish scholars to take up posts at U.S. universities—most famously, Américo Castro, who used his position at Princeton to promulgate a vision of a tolerant, multicultural Spanish modernity that held purchase for both the left and right in Spain.

These translations, trends, and phenomena—along with the many amnesiac "rediscoveries" of Spain in the early twentieth century—could hardly be said to have contributed univocally to the consolidation of a singular notion of American identity. Rather, they pointed and branched in multiple directions, from Blasco Ibáñez's radical politics to Putnam's creative translations. But as American studies narrowed and erased Spain and as the treatment of Hispanophone texts was relegated to Spanish language departments, texts that were widely visible in multiple cultures in their moment became difficult to see historically. In this way, Hispanism's success came at a price. But the many new doors opened for engaging with Spanish texts were now fully accessible beyond academic and disciplinary confinements. The history of English translations of the twelfth-century Spanish epic *Poema del Cid*, which figured importantly in Pound's early work (see chapter 1), bears out this process. The poem, which became the archnationalist text in Spain in the early 1900s, saw no translations into English until 1808; the first scholarly edition appeared in 1879 and was followed by another by Huntington himself in 1897–1903. By 1919, a new translation aimed at broader and popular audiences had appeared, and another followed in 1930. Between 1957 and 1966, three more translations were published (one by the Hispanist Lesley Byrd Simpson and two others by the poets W. S. Merwin and Paul Blackburn), and the feature film *El Cid*, starring Charlton Heston, was released in 1961. A text recovered and disseminated by modern Hispanism now became commercialized by Hollywood: the spaces for thinking beyond narratives of Spain's past glory or America's modern exceptionalism were plentiful.

Americanism in Spain: An Unfamiliar History of Familiarity

The coeval rise of the study of U.S. literature in Spain necessarily invokes the complexity of names and configurations by which "American literature" has been known abroad. Here, the foreign formations of American literature, as Brian T. Edwards, Sonia Torres, Wlad Godzich, Winfried Fluck, and others have shown, cast a different light on the nativist bearings and political assumptions that created that conceptual category domestically.[82] Various terms such as *literatura norteamericana* (North American literature, implicitly Anglophone), *literatura anglosajona* (literally, Anglo-Saxon literature, referring to English-language literature from the United Kingdom and United States), *literatura inglesa* (English literature, usually referring to England, but sometimes meaning Anglophone), and *literatura estadounidense* (United States literature, usually meaning Anglophone but sometimes including works in other languages such as Spanish) are still used to denote literatures from the present-day United States. (*Literatura americana* referred to writing from the Spanish colonies and former colonies in the Americas; the less formal *literatura yanqui* actually comes the closest to the exceptionalist portrait.) In Spain, U.S. literature took centuries to become respected and differentiated from the literature of England. Furthermore, the institutions in which U.S. literature was read did not have the structure of nation/language-based literary formations as ingrained as their peers in the United States did, and the power of the state and church over higher education made change difficult. For these and other reasons—and because of the relative youth of the United States—the life of U.S. studies in Spain is briefer and less documented (enrollment numbers, for instance, are not available). *Literatura norte-américana*, in fact, was popular well before it was an academic subject. The series Todas las literaturas, published by La España Editorial from the late 1800s to the early 1900s, produced a collection of profiles of U.S. writers in 1902 called *Literatura norte-americana*.[83] This volume only appeared, however, after some twenty other volumes covering the literatures of Rome, India, Norway, Russia, and many others had been published; English literature still towered over its North American offspring. *Literatura norte-americana* featured familiar names such as Mather, Emerson, Whitman, Poe, Bryant, Hawthorne, Melville, Stowe, Howells, Twain, and Harte. In other words, it was, by another name, an Anglophone U.S. canon whose compilation scholars have historicized in recent years, and many of the translations actually were made from preexisting French versions.

Spaniards across the political, academic, and popular spectrums were especially quick to comment on and critique U.S. histories of their country and its letters; the works of U.S. Hispanists, from Irving and Longfellow to Ticknor and Rennert, were entrées into the broader study of U.S. letters in many cases. The burgeoning intellectual and academic reciprocity was a starting point for fashioning a version of American literature that was compatible with *hispanismo* after 1898, when the U.S. tradition was understood through aesthetic forms and spiritual essence rather than as an expression of materialism and geopolitical conquest. By 1916, enough U.S. literature had been translated and discussed in Spain that a Columbia graduate student, John Delancey Ferguson, could publish a dissertation, *American Literature in Spain*, with a capacious bibliography. Ferguson saw that even though the "discreditable war of 1898" meant that "our manners and institutions no longer command ... the wholehearted admiration of the Spanish people," U.S. literature thrived in Spain.[84] Spaniards now looked to U.S. writers who embodied a spirit that was prior to and distinct from the belligerent culture of the present, and Whitman, he concludes, was read as representing the energies of progress that Anglo-Saxons endowed to the mixed races of the United States in order to guide them.[85] Julián Juderías himself praised Ferguson's work in a popular review and noted that it helped to discern why Spaniards welcomed a line of protest against material progress that runs through U.S. poetry.[86] In an important article in 1924, Enrique Díez-Canedo, a translator and scholar, called the United States "the country where poetry flourishes." He surveyed the scene through little magazines and declared that "American poetry [now] begins to feel the struggles of independence, not in isolated individuals, but as a body and as a separate literary state" that must be recognized.[87] U.S. literature appeared in discussions and translations across Spanish media with increasing frequency and enthusiasm in the 1920s. *El Sol*, the *Revista de Occidente*, and *La Gaceta Literaria* (the final of these featured a section called "Libros Yankis") became steady outlets; presses published an abundance of new translations of contemporary U.S. authors: Crane, Dos Passos, Dreiser, Eliot, Faulkner, Fitzgerald, Hemingway, James, Pound, and Steinbeck.[88] Where foreign critics had derided Spain in the early 1900s for its lack of interest in the outside world, translations from all over the world now were ubiquitous: Miguel Gallego Roca estimates that 80 percent of publications in Spain in 1925 were translations. One Spanish critic labeled this moment a dangerous "invasión literaria" and, with others, stereotyped local consumers of translations as boorish, uncultured nouveau-riche readers who enjoyed things like jazz and gramophone records—in other words, as Americans.[89]

At the same time, educational institutions were changing rapidly; the first secular university had opened in 1876, and the distinguished Residencia de Estudiantes opened in Madrid in 1910 as a direct model of the Oxbridge system. The latter offered extensive classes in English and, later, U.S. literature, and it hosted American students for summer courses and exchanges (*Hispania* contained many advertisements and curricula for these programs for U.S. students).[90] Figures such as Onís, the educational reformers María de Maeztu and José Castillejo, and the diplomat Juan Riaño y Gayangos set up more U.S./Spanish university exchanges (and Riaño personally aided Dos Passos). But the backlash against *yanqui* culture in Spain after 1898 meant a constant battle to elevate the prestige of U.S. literature. The two art forms often associated most closely with the United States—cinema and jazz—were deemed base, primitive, and obscene. Conservative and traditionalist Spaniards maintained an essentially tepid appreciation of U.S. letters as a belletristic tradition that ended, more or less, with Whitman. Perhaps surprisingly, the young, mostly anti-American Spanish left developed a dynamic, ambivalent sense of contemporary U.S. writing that influenced the large-scale rethinking of what "American literature" included and how it signaled as a political category. Nowhere is this clearer than in the socialist politician and writer Luis Araquistaín's widely circulated ethnography *El peligro yanqui* (The Yankee peril, 1921), which warned that "this great nation looks to us like a copy of Germany when it bathed itself in pride and messianism from 1870 to 1914."[91] Yet Spaniards must understand the United States, and, indeed, they can find hope in the literature of the U.S. left, whose writers Araquistaín catalogs and surveys capaciously, from Waldo Frank to Max Eastman. By 1932, books such as Julián Gómez Gorkin's *10 novelistas americanos* had appeared; Gorkin would also collaborate with U.S. publishers on translations of contemporary Spanish literature, especially socialist writing.[92] At the same time, the prominent critic of Anglophone literature Antonio Marichalar traced the poetic lines of what we now call U.S. modernism in a series of articles for Spanish journals, and he gave extensive genealogies of "novelistas norteamericanos" that ranged from Hawthorne to Wharton, Dos Passos, Frank, Hemingway, McKay, and Faulkner. The Second Republic's brand of internationalism meant new state sponsorship for different types of translations, consonant with the League of Nations' establishing its Index Translationum in 1932.

Franco's victory in 1939 foreclosed what comparative potential we might see in this moment, when many versions and visions of American literary genealogies coexisted. The Franco government's alignment with the U.S. state meant that Spain's state-sponsored academics revised the foundations for studying U.S. literature that had been laid by the Spanish left. Francoist scholars thus created a depoliticized canon and a historical narrative familiar to most Americans. This canon was promulgated by the Fulbright program and by programs with covert funding from the U.S. government—"Yankee imperialism in Spain," as the Spanish left called it—and American studies in Spain quickly found institutional security.[93] The government decreed programs in modern philology (English, French, German, and Italian were included) in Salamanca, Madrid, and then Barcelona between 1952 and 1955.[94] All offered courses on

English, "Anglo-Saxon," and North American literature, sometimes under classifications such as "Germanic linguistics" (which grouped German, Scandinavian, and English literature). At the same time, the Franco regime had exiled or prompted the exile of many cultural figures who would find homes in U.S. universities and would, in turn, promote U.S. literature in their native country. By 1956, Concha Zardoya's influential textbook *Historia de la literatura norteamericana* was published, and soon after, students were defending dissertations on Emerson and on Hemingway. New student exchanges with U.S. universities and new centers of study were established in the 1960s. English departments (again, under various names) were established in Valladolid, Seville, Santiago de Compostela, and, most important, Oviedo, which would eventually house the new organization AEDEAN (Asociación Española de Estudios Anglo-Norteamericanos) and its journal *Atlantis* in 1976—the year after Franco died.[95] In the post-Franco era, American studies flourished in Spain and continues to do so, and English remains as popular a choice of second language in Spain as Spanish does in the United States. The geopolitics behind this formation also remain mostly unremarked in Spanish criticism and scholarship, where U.S. literature's presence in the country is presented as a one-sided story of influence and diffusion. A conservative U.S. canon persists across the various configurations in which "American literature" is inscribed; the American-generated narrative of emergence is rarely questioned, and Spain is rendered distinct and unrelated to U.S. literature except as a residual source of material.

* * *

Underlying much of this work in both the United States and Spain were anxieties and assumptions highlighted in the chapters the follow. Beginning just before the turn of the twentieth century, the question of where U.S. and Spanish literatures stood in relation to the longstanding dominance of France and Britain and the more recent rise of Russia elicited much commentary among American and Spanish scholars and indeed drew in theorists from around the world. In an inquiry that the editors of the new journal *American Literature* would echo, John A. Macy asked in 1913 whether U.S. literature, in its hesitating emergence, was sufficient to the "opportunity" presented by the "multifarious immensity of the country" and where it should be situated on the global stage.⁹⁶ Spaniards such as Eduardo Gómez de Baquero measured and oftentimes lamented their country's influence abroad; Baroja and others disparaged Spanish letters as fallow and infertile.⁹⁷ The British writer Arnold Bennett, the Italian Hispanist Arturo Farinelli, and the Cuban revolutionary José Martí joined these conversations too, asking whether the international successes of Henry James or Benito Pérez Galdós were singular or whether they allowed new measurements of national prestige that might align with or diverge from geopolitics. Most who took part in these debates, and indeed most scholars and educators at the time, from Ticknor to Marcelino Menéndez y Pelayo to Brander Matthews, believed that an empire's literary fortunes and its geopolitical standing naturally rose and fell together. This inhered in the sense of "literature" itself; as Nancy Glazener explains, "as is the case with many other beliefs embedded in European imperialism, literature was understood as a human accomplishment and value at which Europe excelled and to which other parts of the world ought to aspire, universal in scope but taking distinctive national forms."⁹⁸ Matthew Arnold, when asking which literatures of the past will be worthy of study in the present, elaborated an influential sense of "adequacy" that captures this assumption:

> a significant, a highly-developed, a culminating epoch, on the one hand,— a comprehensive, a commensurate, an adequate literature, on the other,— these will naturally be the objects of deepest interest to our modern age. Such an epoch and such a literature are, in fact, *modern*, in the same sense in which our own age and literature are modern; they are founded upon a rich past and upon an instructive fulness of experience.⁹⁹

Great political and literary epochs rise together, Arnold argues; concentrations of talent and creativity, expanded resources and systems of patronage and/or commerce, endowed prestige and historical magnitude, and much more contribute to making this union seem universal, whether in the early modern Ottoman empire or the Qing dynasty in the eighteenth century. Such assumptions and such self-defining modes of thinking about creative or weak periods of literary production became increasingly common in the racialized and historicist readings of imperial "types" in the second half of the nineteenth century. They undergirded both the coupled consolidation of U.S. and Spanish literary studies in academies and the broader consolidation of national identities as they were putatively expressed through literary artifacts. But if we imagine comparison and translation as operating in multiple directions—as variously enriching and disaggregating those resources deemed "local" in any context—we can see that the fictions of incomparability quietly obscure a host of arguments about why (as Arnold asked) we study literatures that we do not presume to own.

I
American Modernism's Hispanists

CHAPTER I

"Splintered Staves"

Pound, Comparative Literature, and the Translation of Spanish Literary History

Why write what I can translate out of Renaissance Latin or crib from the sainted dead?
—EZRA POUND, letter to William Carlos Williams (1908)

This much is apparent: Spanish literature declined with Spanish world power; people came to Madrid to look at the "Fénix de los ingenios," Lope de Vega y Carpio, but since his time no man has gone to Spain to pay intellectual homage.... Was Madrid ever a metropolis; was Spain ever a centre of thought, ever, that is, after the fall of the Moorish dominion and the devastation of Cordova?
—EZRA POUND, "Some Notes on Francisco de Quevedo Villegas" (1921)

BEFORE HE WAS AN AVANT-GARDE POET, A FOUNDER OF movements, a modernist kingmaker, an international provocateur, or a political ideologue, Ezra Pound was a grad school dropout. Around 1906, the young scholar at the University of Pennsylvania abandoned his thesis on the *gracioso*, or buffoon figure, in the plays of Spain's renowned baroque poet and playwright Félix Lope de Vega. The common reading of Pound's career assumes that the poet's experiences in graduate seminars on medieval Spanish literature, in archives in Madrid while on a research fellowship, and among the ruins of the legendary Spanish hero El Cid's castle in Burgos matter only insofar as they provided pieces of material that he later recycled in the *Cantos*. Such a reading yields limited fruit: even by the time Pound published *A Draft of XVI. Cantos* in 1925, Spain and its literature had all but receded from his purview; Browning, Italy, Greek mythology, and countless other figures and sites instead had come to the foreground. Thus, in *The Pound Era* (1971), Hugh Kenner glides over and reduces Pound's Spanish allusions—and he mistakes them at that: he refers briefly to "Le Cid" of Canto III, thereby conflating the subject of a twelfth-century Spanish epic (El Cid) with the title of the French playwright Pierre Corneille's 1637 adaptation of the poem (*Le Cid*).[1]

To recover Pound's sustained grappling with Spain's cultural and political history is to do much more than flesh out a footnote for the *Cantos*. Pound might have quit the academy, but he continued practicing the skills he learned there—indeed, he renovated them into his own semiacademic "New Method of Scholarship" that he called "Luminous Detail," elaborated first in 1911.[2] Pound's Spanish engagements were a foundation for what was an ongoing major intellectual project in which he wove the texts that he discovered in his training into his interconnected poetry, translations, criticism, scholarship, and cultural politics. By focusing intensely on Pound's works in this period without assuming the *Cantos* as the only meaningful *telos*, we can see the formation of a headstrong, multipronged plan with several goals. Pound first wanted to dismantle the practices of Germanic philology, then to revise the shape of comparative literary studies (and American universities as a whole) for a new century. He would do so by overturning the reigning norms of translation and by bringing disorienting foreign texts to broader publics. Such labor, he believed, would allow him to theorize the conditions and possibilities of an "American Risorgimento" and, ultimately, to outline the structure of a new transtemporal, global literary history.[3]

That is to say, in the 1910s Pound articulated imagism, vorticism, and several aesthetic theories that would provide influential concepts for the history of Anglophone modernism all while he was slowly and sometimes bitterly letting go of his dream of becoming a professional scholar of Spanish and Romance-language literatures. His key Spanish text in this work was the *Poema del Cid* (ca. 1140–1207), the oldest surviving Castilian epic poem and the one that many Hispanists and cultural commentators in several countries had established, at the turn of the twentieth century, as the seminal text in Spanish literary history.[4] In fact, Pound once intended to translate the *Poema del Cid* in full, but he instead translated and retranslated sections of it at least four different times between 1906 and 1925.[5] In these translations and in his commentaries on the text in his groundbreaking study *The Spirit of Romance* (1910), he read the *Poema*'s protagonist El Cid, who was popularly understood as a national hero and a legendary figure in the Reconquista, as an emblematic bandit: a betrayed exile, a mercenary, and a multiply translated icon whose exploits were recounted in an imperfect, anonymously authored, incomplete text. Along the way, the inconsistent and ambivalently iconoclastic Pound rebuked the international Hispanist establishment by reading El

Cid as inassimilable to the national literary history that Pound's mentors had fashioned. The Cid instead belongs, Pound insisted, to the dispersed and forgotten patrimony of a Romance-language network of troubadours who had been excised, rather than nationalized, by scholars of late medieval Romance tongues. He would aim not only to explicate and reanimate this network but also to expand it through connections both to the classical world and to his own poetry.

Pound's unorthodox and contentious participation in the newly dominant Hispanist and comparatist scholarship that had stabilized the national legend of the Cid continued in several sites. First, he offered, in a series of articles for the English *New Age* in 1911–1913, his theories of translation's role in literary historiography and of the depressing state of translation practices in the new American empire. He then proposed that Spain's literary past can be both monumentalized and brought to life anew through reformative poetics, as evinced by the first drafts of the epic that consumed his adulthood: the "Ur-Cantos." This chapter therefore treats the "Ur-Cantos" as more than a poetic beginning; they are a poeticized document of translation, comparison, and commentary, the culmination of a decade of work and thought that began with medieval Romance studies and carried through to Pound's attempts to channel Spain's past.[6] Indeed, these critical practices were so fundamental to Pound's ambitions that he worried, in an early draft, that his poem was "too full of footnotes."[7] As he constantly repositions himself as storyteller, narrator, and translator, Pound uses the polyvalent figure of "splintered staves" in the "Ur-Cantos" to bind together his own fragmentation of poetic form and his discomposition of Spanish literary history.

Pound's translational and poetic configurations of Spain's literary history prompted him, furthermore, to consider comparatively the topics of cultural coherence and change—which appear more famously later in his thoughts on kulchur and paideuma—with an emerging sense that, as he put it in 1915, "when words cease to cling close to things, kingdoms fall, empires wane and diminish."[8] As he looks to the moments of Spain's imperial origins and to its decline, he sees Spanish literature's zenith in a polyglot moment when Romance demotics still interpenetrated one another. Spain's "vitality," he argues, *preceded* its high imperial period, which first augmented that vitality by increasing the country's translational exchanges, then corrupted it and killed it off. He thereby contends, in an acerbic article on Spanish literature that he published in the Spanish magazine *Hermes* in 1921, that Spain fell from literary greatness when it stopped translating, when the new codes of the Counter-Reformation and Inquisition closed the country's cultural borders. Thus, for important reasons I explore below, Pound turned on and dismissed his former object of study: by the time of the *Cantos*, Lope de Vega provides little more than a series of corpses through which Pound critiques the baroque and its use of ornament. Spanish literary history is strewn across a fragmented collage of global history in the *Cantos*, far from the narratives of Spain's national self-sufficiency that Pound had encountered in his graduate studies. And so, before he looked to currencies, banking systems, or Jewish lending practices as causes of decay, Pound, who was in many ways more pensive and interdisciplinary at this point in his career, understands Spain as an imperial ruin to be compared to the United States of his moment. He dramatizes Spain's decline and asserts, through metaphors of health, vitality, and "disease" in his poetry and criticism, a reading of both Spain's and the United States' imperial destinies—of the Inquisition and the early twentieth-century field of literary publishing—as bleak and unexceptional.

Pound, the Hispanist

As Pound later recalled, he entered college "at 15 with intention of studying comparative values in literature (poetry) and began doing so unbeknown to the faculty. . . . I began an examination of comparative European literature in or about 1901; with the definite intention of finding out what had been written, and how."[9] In his undergraduate years at Hamilton College, where he settled after his precocious time at the University of Pennsylvania, Pound pursued a program of comparative literary study in which he enthusiastically put himself "at risk of being perceived as arrogantly cross-grained," as A. David Moody writes.[10] He studied Spanish alongside several other Romance languages with the scholar of Provençal William P. Shepard, whose imprint remains visible in *The Spirit of Romance*. Pound joked about his work in "Dago lit," using the derogatory term for Spaniards and Italians at the time.[11] He also read modern German, French, and Spanish (including Benito Pérez Galdós's *Doña Perfecta*, to which he would return several times in his critical essays) alongside troubadour poetry, Dante, Anglo-Saxon poetry, the Bible, and Chaucer. Coupling this work with his translational poetics from the start, Pound also published his first translation, a bilingual "alba" or dawn poem, in Hamilton's literary magazine. When he arrived at the University of Pennsylvania for his graduate studies in 1905, the budding scholar immersed himself in late medieval and early modern Romance literatures—especially Spanish—by taking six of his seven courses with Hugo Rennert. Rennert, the world's leading authority on Lope de Vega, had just published the definitive biography of the playwright in 1904; he would become a member of both Archer Milton Huntington's Hispanic Society in the United States and the Royal Order of Isabella the Catholic in Spain. Under Rennert's tutelage and influence but with strongly internationalist sensibilities, Pound took his first steps toward becoming a scholar of Spanish letters by starting his thesis on Lope de Vega.

Rennert helped secure Pound a Harrison Foundation Fellowship to continue his archival work in Madrid. In May 1906, Pound arrived in Spain with letters that allowed him access to manuscripts in the Biblioteca Nacional de España. (A librarian in Madrid asked him why he was studying Lope de Vega when Rennert had already written all that could be said about him.) He worked also in the archives of the Royal Library of Escorial, a monastery just north of the city. Padre José María de Elizondo, who appears memorably in Canto LXXXI, helped Pound access a Guido Cavalcanti manuscript, and the American consul in Madrid enabled Pound to view an unpublished manuscript of Lope de Vega's in the royal palace's archives.[12] In addition to other scholars and translators, Pound also met the playwright José Echegaray, who had won the Nobel Prize for Literature in 1904.[13] Although he asserted to his mother that he "ha[d] my thesis so I can roll it out in one month's home work," Pound quickly drifted from his work on Lope de Vega; he was drawn instead to the Prado Museum, for instance, where he researched Velázquez.[14] When he returned to the United States, he would begin to translate Lope de Vega's 1633 comedy *El desprecio agradecido* (The grateful reject), but he never finished it, declaring instead that he did not want to bore contemporary readers with it.[15] He included his translation of Lope de Vega's "A Song of the Virgin Mother" (from *Los pastores de Belén*, 1614) in his *Exultations* (1909), in Christmas calendars for his father's business, and, later, in Mark Van Doren's capacious *Anthology of World Poetry* (1928).[16] And he even drafted in 1907 an incomplete and unpublished baroque-style play called "Quevedo," after Lope de Vega's rival Francisco de Quevedo.[17] He would discuss Lope de Vega's work in *The Spirit of Romance*, but his rejection of both Rennert's manner of academic investigation and Lope de Vega's aesthetics in his ensuing scholarship and poetics will prevent any sustained analysis of them.

While in Madrid, Pound happened to be in the crowd at the wedding of Alfonso XIII to Victoria Eugenie of Battenburg, a granddaughter of Queen Victoria. This wedding was supposed to heal longstanding rifts in Anglo-Spanish relations, but all hope was lost when a Catalan anarchist attacked the wedding party with a grenade. Pound quickly left Madrid to tour Spain; he claims that he boarded a train just as the authorities were rounding up anarchists and foreigners after the assassination attempt. In Córdoba, he wandered away from his guide and was pelted with vegetables for his odd dress and behavior (see Canto LXXXI). Most consequentially, he traveled to Burgos, the old capital of Castile and the historical home of El Cid.[18] Drawing on these experiences, he published his first three literary essays in *Book News Monthly* (Philadelphia) in the fall of 1906. In "Burgos: A Dream City of Old Castile," he lays out almost all of the elements of his engagement with the *Poema del Cid* that he will revisit across his career. The *Poema*, which he had studied extensively in school, tells of the heroic deeds of Rodrigo Díaz de Bivar (or Ruy Díaz of Vivar, ca. 1043–1099), called *El Campeador* (the great warrior) by the Christians and El Cid by the Moors. Repeating centuries-old Orientalisms as he imagines this past era in its present environs, Pound asserts that the "Spain of to-day" is an "inexplicable mixture of hell and paradise which no outlander can understand."[19] He believes, too, in an exotic and romantic vision, that the "dream Spain" of the country's "old song-glory" still existed in certain parts, without the "taint" of the "appearance of modernity" (B 91). When he arrives in "the Burgos of Myo Cid Campeador," Pound finds few signs of the Cid there, save the pillars of his ancestral home (Solar). But he also sees a number of "doorways in Burgos to which [the Cid] might have come, as in the old 'Poema,' battering with his lance butt at the door closed *por miedo del Rey Alfonso*" (B 91). Pound toured the fallen castles around the town in search of more signs of the Cid, who "never saw a barber through his long campaign," "embodied his Zeitgeist, and all the strife against Islam," and at the same time, was his era's "bandit Cassie Chadwick"—an allusion to the notorious defrauder of the late nineteenth century (B 92, 91).

In trying to walk the paths of the Cid quite literally, Pound was trying to replicate the sensations of the Cid's feeling of exile and foreignness, which registered for Pound both when he was mocked by the locals and, more symbolically, in his dream of becoming an exiled U.S. artist. Amid lengthy descriptions of the impressive cathedral at Burgos (greater than any in Paris, he insists), commoners and priests at worship, and a young tour guide who mistakes him for being French, Pound writes that he meets a "little maid of nine" who reincarnates the character who, early in the *Poema del Cid*, speaks to the Cid about his exile (B 92). He believes that he can capture, through her, "just how" the young girl in the *Poema* "fluttered over the centuries-old message, with little whirring sounds, and all the relative clauses out of place." In other words, he can use her voice to show the supernatural timelessness of the poetic qualities of the *Poema* itself, for this "little girl [who] is still in the capital of 'Castilla' . . . does not remember the Campeador" (B 92). Pound translates a few lines from her speech in the *Poema*, all of which will recur in several forms in his later works. The original is as follows:

> ¡Ya Campeador, en buen ora çinxiestes espada!
> El rey lo ha vedado, anoch dél entró su carta,
> con grant recabdo e fuertemientre sellada.
> Non uos osariémos abrir nin coger por nada,
> si non perderíemos los averes e las casas,
> e demás los oios de las caras.
> Çid, en el nuestro mal vos non ganades nada,
> mas ¡el Criador vos vala con todas sus vertudes sanctas![20]

Pound's translation:

> Aie Campeador, in good hour girt ye on your sword.
> The King hath forbidden it; last night came his letter
> With great escort, strongly sealed.
> We dare not open to you, nor in any wise give ye aid,
> For we would lose our havings and our homes
> And the eyes of our faces to boot.
> Cid, in our ill you will gain nothing;
> But the Criador (creator) avail you and all his holy virtues.
>
> (B 92)

With a mixture of English archaisms ("girt ye," "havings") and faux colloquialism ("to boot" is actually archaic, too, dating from the 1300s), Pound both offers a first sketch of his approach to the *Poema* and presages the Germanic/Romance-language collisions of his future poems and translations. The governing sounds of the original are the final -*os* across first-person plural verbs and masculine plural nouns (*osariemos, perderiemos, oios*) and the repeated -*ada* of *sellada, nada,* and a second *nada*. Pound instead uses several times the hard "g" of monosyllabic words mostly from Old English: "good," "girt," "great," "give." He then uses the English -*or* (also heard in the original) in "Campeador," "sword," "forbidden," "escort," as his repeating sound. This sonic element is present, too, in the doubling in Pound's parenthetical repetition: "Criador (creator)."

Evincing liberalism and misdirection in his translational style already, Pound minimizes the syllable count and sonic patterns of the original while also downplaying its exclamatory tone. He extends the final line to eighteen syllables, and the lowercase "creator" points anachronistically to a pre-Christian world. That is, both terms ("Criador" and "creator") come from the Latin *crear* ("to bring forth, create"), but the derivation is not straightforward in Spanish, as it is in most other Romance tongues. *Creador* (with an "e") is "Creator," meaning the Christian God; through a morphological branch, a *criador* is a guardian, a keeper, an educator (of knowledge and of manners both), a breeder of animals, a maid, a breast-feeder, and a grower of wine grapes. (In modern Spanish, a *cría* is a child, among other senses, and a *criada* is a child servant or slave.) This polysemy that developed in Spanish and Portuguese subtly points to a conception of diachronic linguistic indeterminacy that Pound, steeped in philological knowledge but rejecting philology's positivism, later will theorize and employ across the 1910s and, of course, across the *Cantos*. The Cid and the *Poema* have combined with Pound's studies of Spanish literature and national history to provide him an early font for his experimental poetics of translation and for his theories of the transtemporality of "song," as expressed and embodied in the *Poema*. Furthermore, before reading the *Poema del Cid*, Pound had read Corneille's play *Le Cid*, a French tragicomic farce based very loosely on the Spanish epic, and that had the effect of adding another layer of translated removal from the original to Pound's knowledge of the poem.[21] His encounter with the *Poema* is both a personal search for origins and a restaging and reimagining of the complex, often circuitous transmission of a late medieval song.

The End of Philology and National Traditions

In "Burgos," Pound frames the larger intellectual issues that governed his aspirations in professional academia. One of the other essays for *Book News Monthly*, "Raphaelite Latin," launched his assault on the "Germanic ideal of scholarship" and its excessive and misguided fixation on what the "author wore and ate."[22] Unlike Rennert, Pound could not stand for the "perversion of that primitive religion" of "hero-worship" that philology had made of literary study; philologists find themselves in Hell in Canto XIV.[23] Likewise, he could not sustain an interest in technical questions of historical syntax or in theater alone; Rennert studied both Castilian Spanish and Italian, but Pound was more intrigued by the reciprocal mutations and tensions among Spanish, Provençal, Italian, and more. Still, after a brief, disastrous stint teaching Spanish and French at Wabash College in Indiana in 1907–1908, Pound continued his increasingly vain pursuit of academic work. He turned material from Rennert's seminars into a series of lectures at Regent Street Polytechnic in London in 1909.[24] Those lectures would combine with his formation in U.S. universities and his research in Spain to compose *The Spirit of Romance: An Attempt to Define Somewhat the Charm of the Pre-Renaissance Literature of Latin Europe* (1910).[25] This extraordinary and sometimes strained text, which Richard Sieburth calls Pound's "first sustained archaeological excavation of the Tradition of the New," is something of a summa of Pound's intellectual development by age twenty-five and an inquiry into how national literary traditions gained political force.[26] Pound declares in the first words of his preface that "this book is not a philological work" (*SR* 5). He adds that he has "floundered somewhat ineffectually through the slough of philology" in his academic life and that he has acquired a particular hatred of the Germanic model of the discipline, which he saw as having no sense of comparative judgment and as being confined to "morphology, epigraphy, [and] *privatleben*" (*SR* 5). He later added bluntly that the "'university system' of Germany is evil" and also loathed what E. M. Butler would name in the title of a 1935 book *The Tyranny of Greece Over Germany*.[27] Philology had its golden age from roughly 1777 through 1872; it began to decline when Nietzsche renounced it in his *Birth of Tragedy* (1872), but in the early 1900s, Romance-language studies were still dominated by philologists who often had strong nationalist leanings.[28] Pound saw himself as rejecting the U.S. academic world of "men whose scholarship [was] merely a pasteurized, Bostonized imitation of Leipzig" (Shepard himself was trained at Heidelberg), and he paired his attacks on philology with his critiques of nationalism and "provincialism."[29]

Pound's university studies and his interventions beyond them occurred in a moment when philology and comparative literature were in an uncomfortable, estranging marriage and when philology more generally was becoming less an autonomous discipline than a set of practices diffused across the humanities. As Rebecca Beasley explains, the comparative literature that scholars such as George Woodberry and Arthur Marsh devised relied heavily on German philological methods.[30] For Beasley, the critical method that Pound was fashioning was a mixture of what he saw in this moment of American comparativism and in his own training in philology.[31] The advances in philology that Kenner claims catalyzed a generation of modernists, in short, were a divided legacy for Pound: his rejection of philology was strong but not wholesale—though he does carefully avoid addressing in *Spirit* the Grail Legend, a theme that preoccupied many philological studies of medieval literatures at the time and that would capture Eliot's imagination.

Long before he would found his own "Ezuversity," Pound was able to locate only pockets of support for this project in the United States' "institutions for the obstruction of learning"; neither Rennert nor Shepard published criticism, only scholarship and some conservative translations.[32] Pound claims in *Spirit*'s preface that "only by courtesy can [this book] be said to be a study in comparative literature" (*SR* 5). A synchronic, universalist approach to form and poetics would, for Pound, exceed the limits of diachronic, linguistically, racially, or nationally bounded studies that remain encased in linear histories. At times, he bristled at the very idea of national literatures as singular traditions; if one proposed to survey "American literature," he writes, "you may as well give courses in 'American chemistry', neglecting all foreign discoveries."[33] Yet, he used these traditions, as existing and intelligible conceits, when argumentatively convenient.

Pound hoped, against his Hispanist mentors, to show what readers and scholars alike could, as he would later write, "learn of comparative literature through translations."[34] The multilingual and transcultural roots of troubadour poetry defied the categories and developmental arcs posited by the brand of philology that Pound believed he could raze. His aim was to recreate in translation the aesthetic of his late medieval subjects, whom he saw as comparatists well versed in "several jargons."[35] Pound thus frames *Spirit* with an additional assault on the positivist and historicist assumptions of certain philologists who, by his account, had obscured the interconnections of a variety of late medieval literatures. The French scholar Gaston Paris, who had trained in Germany under the seminal figure Friedrich Diez, was a notable antagonist here.[36] Paris read such texts as an embryo of a national literary tradition that neatly cut out Provençal writing's divergent trajectories and assimilated them to a Parisian-centered French history. Pound acknowledges that the esteemed *Chanson de Roland* (*The Song of Roland*, ca. 1040–1115) is "quite interesting as a monument to 'la nationalité française'" but that "we, who have not had our literary interest in the poem stimulated of late by the Franco-Prussian war and the feelings of outraged patriotism attendant thereupon" cannot see the seeds of "what Paris terms the 'national style'" in the text (*SR* 75, 74). Pound refers here to a lecture Paris famously had delivered on the *Song of Roland* in December 1870, during the German siege of the city of Paris; in it, he argued that this ballad was the first piece of evidence of full French national consciousness, before any other European country had such a sentiment put into language. He thus turned his philological work into a wartime rallying cry.

By contrast, *The Spirit of Romance* ranges across hundreds of years of pre-Renaissance Romance and Latin literatures in several tongues in order to bear out its claim that "all ages are contemporaneous," meaning that the critic, Pound urges, must treat Yeats and Theocritus "with one balance" in order to find poetry that is "still potent in our own" day (*SR* 6, 5). Ovid and Apuleius stand next to Dante, Lope de Vega next to noncanonical figures such as Cavalcanti and François Villon, without chronology and without a singular argument.[37] Instead, *Spirit*, as a sourcebook and textbook—over half of it composed of Pound's translations, including at least one from his time at Hamilton—relies on Pound's claim that "poetry is a sort of inspired mathematics" that implicates a new scholarly method (*SR* 14). At once burnishing his credentials earned in conservative academic environments (the title page lists him as "Ezra Pound, M.A.") and radically transforming the practices he mastered there, Pound lays the groundwork for an understanding of Spain's literary past and El Cid's relevance to the twentieth century, when Spain seemed to have cordoned itself off from its formerly enriching international circuits.

Reconstituting the Life of Spain: Pound's *Poema del Cid*

Bound up with Pound's attacks on philology and his search for a new mode of comparative literature was the poet's own emerging translational style, which he developed by turning again to the *Poema* and by casting his translations against the methods and claims of his Hispanist forebears. Early in *Spirit*, Pound addresses at considerable length the medieval *Chansons de geste*, or "songs of heroic deeds" (from the Old French). These poems mix biblical stories, epics and myths from Troy and Rome, and Arthurian-style legends. Pound claims provocatively that the best of these long verse poems, which flourished in the twelfth century, come not from France—as scholars at the time almost univocally asserted—but from Spain. For Pound, in its "swift narration, its vigor, the humanness of its characters, for its inability to grow old, the Spanish 'geste' seems to me to surpass its French predecessor," the *Chanson de Roland* (SR 66). Pound relishes its "apparently crude rhythm" and irregular syllabics and caesurae that vary by line (SR 67). And like the Anglo-Saxon poetry that Pound would translate the following year ("The Seafarer"), it contains a great deal of assonance. Pound admits that he is "grateful for the refreshment of the Spanish *Poema*, and for the bandit Ruy Diaz [El Cid]. I perhaps profane the *Roland* . . . but the quality of eternal youth is not in it in such a degree as in the Spanish *Poema*," for the *Poema* eliminated the formalisms that Pound believed weighed down *Roland* (SR 78).

A summary of the entire *Poema*, which itself covers only part of the Cid's life, is not necessary here. It was composed between the late 1100s and early 1200s and drew on the same traditions of recycling previous texts and adapting them through performance and improvisation that scholars have noted across troubadour traditions. (We can see already that it resists what many philologists sought: details about an author's life that would help explain the text.) Pound focused, both here and in his poetry and translations, on an early section of the text: El Cid, a decorated military leader and nobleman in Spain, has just been exiled from his native Castile. Castile was arguably the heart of Christian Spain at the time; much of southern and eastern coastal Spain was in the hands of the Moors, and wars between the two kingdoms—and within them, as they unified and split internally—had been ongoing since the 700s. El Cid's banishment stems from several entangled alliances involving his loyalty to Prince Sancho (the future King Sancho II) and Sancho's fight with his brother, the future king Alfonso VI. When Alfonso takes the throne after Sancho's assassination, the Cid is exiled. He is told by a young girl that the king has declared that no one may aid him lest he risk losing his goods—and his eyes. Finding his personal castle all but demolished, he leaves town with his private army of sixty soldiers. The Cid's nephew Álvar Fáñez (whom he calls Minaya, "my brother") helps him deceive two Jewish moneylenders, Raquel and Vidas, by trading them chests full of sand in exchange for money to pay the soldiers and knights who joined him. The Cid then heads off to earn back his fortune and his name. He serves as a mercenary general under Moorish rulers in Zaragoza and eventually battles his way to control of the city-state of Valencia, where he becomes the ruler of a multiethnic, multireligious society. Finally, Alfonso relents in his hatred of the Cid and enlists him to free Castile from a recent siege by the Almoravids (Berbers) of North Africa; the Cid now gladly turns against the Moors and works his way back to becoming a legend for Castile. He dies, however, after the Almoravids once again sack Valencia.

The Cid, whom Pound twice calls approvingly a "bandit," is a complicated figure: he fought both for and against the Moors; he was a mercenary and a thief; he was exiled and redeemed; and like Odysseus, he was always *translated*: the name "Cid" itself is a transliteration of the Arabic *sidi* (or *sayyid*), the honorific mode of address variously translated as "Sir," "Lord," or "Master." Picking up on these themes and textual elements, Pound fashions a complex Cid into an emblem for his own designs. The *Poema* is also a hermeneutic model for Pound: he asserts that the text requires active participation on the part of the reader, who must complete the images and "tableaux" that it offers in order to understand fully its realism. Pound was most captivated by the opening scene of the Cid's departure from Burgos, when the exiled protagonist is refused hospitality by the locals and looks back desperately at his desolate castle at Bivar. Here, Pound writes, both "the scene and speech are not unworthy of Greek tragedy," for they give "the *Poema* much of its vitality; as the Spanish sense of tableau and dramatic setting give it so much of its charm," in "but a handful of lines in Spanish." The young girl that he discussed and translated in his "Burgos" article of 1906, too, appears in this scene amid the "crowded street, variegated trappings of the men, the armor and the pennants," where she is "lisping high words" (*SR* 67).

Pound then translates another key passage from the early part of *Poema* and stakes his more robust claim to a new reading of the text and its contexts. In the background were several other existing translations: Robert Southey's prose version in 1808, then the influential Hispanist John Ormsby's mixed verse and prose translation in 1879. (Pound was apparently unaware of Archer Milton Huntington's 1903 text.) Regarding an early scene that features a charge of lances (meaning both the weapon and the soldier bearing it), Pound compliments the version of Ormsby but adds with tongue in cheek, "not having Ormsby at hand, I have had to use my own translation, which, however, follows the assonance of the original" (*SR* 69n8). His choice of passages to translate, too, reveals his conscious debt not only to Ormsby but also to the greatest U.S. Hispanist to precede any of them: George Ticknor, who translated this same scene in his *History of Spanish Literature*.[38] The original reads:

> Trezientas lanças son, todas tienen pendones:
> sennos moros mataron, todos de sennos colpes,
> a la tornada que fazen otros tantos muertos son:
> Veriedes tantas lanças premer e alçar,
> Tanta adágara foradar e passar,
> tanta loriga falssa[r e] desmanchar,
> tantos pendones blancos salir vermeios en sangre,
> tantos buenos cauallos sin sos duenos andar.[39]

Ormsby's version is as follows:

> Three hundred lances down they come, their pennons flickering white;
> Down go three hundred Moors to earth, a man to every blow;
> And when they wheel, three hundred more, as charging back they go.
> It was a sight to see the lances rise and fall that day;
> The shivered shields and riven mail, to see how thick they lay;
> The pennons that went in snow-white come out a gory red;
> The horses running riderless, the riders lying dead.[40]

Finally, Pound's version:

> Three hundred lances are they, with pennants every one;
> Each man kills his Moor, with single blows 'tis done,

And now at their returning as many more go down,
And ye might well have seen there so many lances press and rise,
And many an oval shield there riven lies.
The ill-forged coats-of-mail in sunder fly,
In blood there issue the many bannerets white,
And many a good horse runs there whom no man rideth.

(*SR* 69)

The original *Poema* repeats variations on *todos* and *tantos* (including *todas* and *tanta*), which respectively mean "all" and "so many/much." With an epic rhetorical charge, the poem is associating these repetitions with the number and immensity of the lances, the blood spilling, and the symbolic pennants. (*Lanza* is also, in verb form [*lanzar*], to launch or hurl.) It is full of internal rhyme and assonance, owing in part to the capacities of Spanish to contain these features in ways that English cannot (because Spanish matches the endings of nouns and adjectives, for example, almost always with *-o/os* or *-a/as*). Thus, the original is wound tightly around the letter "t" and a range of vowels before the internal *-n*; in the first line, for instance: **Trezien**tas lanças **son,** **to**das **tien**en pen**dones**. The second line uses *sennos* as a repeated element around the consonance of *moros mataron* and the assonance of the long *o* sound. The final line, on the other hand, couples a full rhyme between *buenos* and *duenos* while accentuating the disappearance of the riders (or "owners," the contemporary Spanish *dueños*) and concluding with the verb *andar*—to walk or go—as a slant rhyme with *sangre*.

Ormsby's translation is close to the traditional English Fourteener, a style of fourteen-syllable iambic heptameter with rhymed couplets that was popular among seventeenth-century poets, especially for ballads. His choice of a familiar, if not staid form for a text that he faults for sometimes being formless is crucial here. Ormsby captures assonance at times ("when they wheel," "shivered shields") and often divides his lines with a caesura as the original does. His language is contemporary, even colloquial ("It was a sight to see"). But Pound rebuked translators who imposed syllabic regularity and form on the *Poema* and even quoted Rennert in his defense of maintaining the "crude[ness]" of the original in translation (*SR* 67n5). Pound's translation deviates greatly from his predecessor's. Where the original used the assonant and half-rhyming *todos* and *tantos* as scaffolding for the passage, Pound employs variations on "there" and interlaces them with "their," "Three," "they," and the concluding "th" sound in "rideth." He moves from "Three" in the first line, to "their" in the third, and then to a string of "there" in the fourth, fifth, seventh, and eighth lines. The "th" sound both replicates the dental "t" of Spanish and moves away from it by drawing it nearer the Anglophone "th," a combination Spanish does not have. In an amalgamation of early modern English (ye, 'tis), Anglo-Saxon syntax, and Hispanicized grammar and diction, Pound inverts the subject-verb or subject-verb-pronominal antecedent order in many lines: for instance, "are they" in line one, "there riven" in line five, "in sunder fly" in line six, "there issue the many bannerets" in line seven. While Ormsby translates *premer* as "rise," Pound reaches back to the obscure sense of "press," which derives from the same Latin verb, *premere*. Rhyme is partial in Pound's version, ranging from the perfect rhymes of "one" and "done" to the half-rhyme of "fly" and "white." His syllable counts vary greatly: by line, they are 13, 11, 13, 15, 11, 10, 12, and 13. Similarly, the diversity of spondees, trochees, iambs, and other metrical devices in each line belies attempts to domesticate its rhythm into either ballad-like patterns or the iambic pentameter that Pound disdained.

In this way, the *Poema*—which, Pound argues, shifts from *geste* to romance when the Cid is in Valencia—is registering Pound's transition within *Spirit* as a whole and within his translational and critical practices, which move away from a philological or even scholarly approach to the text. For him, the *Poema* was a paradigmatically rough song, open and adaptable, mutable and messy in invigorating ways that the contemporary critic resuscitates by breathing life into them via translation. Elsewhere in his discussion, Pound alludes to other scenes and textual elements that he will recycle through his later poetry, such as the deception of Raquel and Vidas and the Cid's elegant beard, which he says is a memory of Charlemagne. He gives many prose paraphrases of short sections of the text and offers a poetic translation of its final lines. He also links El Cid, as he will in the *Cantos*, to Lope de Vega. But most of his chapter in *Spirit* on Lope de Vega, in another of Pound's efforts to distance himself from Rennert, is hardly enthusiastic. He compares Lope de Vega to Shakespeare but notes that a national theater never took hold in Spain, leaving the Spaniard a singular writer. Lope de Vega's "religious plays," he adds in brief dismissal, "scarcely belong to world literature" (*SR* 182).

In other words, Lope de Vega and the *Poema* belong to what has been configured as the same national tradition, but they lack a strong continuity. The poet-critic instead must fashion the "one balance" that places the *Poema* in its fuller comparative contexts. For Pound, the poem makes sense next to the *Roland* and other Romance-language works of its era: "Provençal, Italian, Spanish, French," and all Romance tongues were "ways of speaking Latin somewhat more corruptly than the Roman merchants and legionaries spoke it" (*SR* 12). And it also makes sense next to temporally and geographically distant figures: he later wrote, "Virgil is a man on a perch. All these writers of pseudo *épopée* are people on perches. Homer and the author of the *Poema del Cid* are keen on their stories. Milton and Virgil are concerned with decorations and trappings, and they muck about with a moral."[41] Pound's use of Anglo-Saxonisms and foreignizing inversions in translation extends this connective web. *Spirit* is thus both a channeling of the comparative practices that Pound saw in his late medieval subjects and an introduction of the "magnet[ic]" role of the critic who must impose order on the "heap of iron filings" of the undifferentiated mass of the literary past, pulling Spanish literature into previously unknown shapes across time and space.[42] Comparison can both restore and create the wholeness in fragmentation that Eliot valorized, and what Pound will call the method of "Luminous Detail" privileges insight, translation, and arrangement over the aggregation of facts and historical contexts.

Comparing Empires: Spain, the United States, and Beyond

By this point, Pound was more studied in Hispanist scholarship than any other U.S. modernist would be, and even after he abandoned his pretensions to the profession, he cited in his poems such as his "Epilogue" (1912) his previous "five books containing mediaeval studies, experiments and translations."[43] But Pound was doing even more with the *Poema del Cid* than he explicitly claims in *The Spirit of Romance*. He was both engaging a debate on empire centered on Spain and laying the groundwork for his own account of the U.S. empire. The *Poema* was seen (and largely still is seen) as the prophetic epic of what would become the imperial Spanish state; the text even concludes with the claim that "today the Kings of Spain are of [El Cid's] blood" (*SR* 73). In the tacitly fused national and imperial visions of early modern Spain, the Cid's service under Moorish rulers was expunged, and he became both an icon of the Reconquista and a model for the conquistadors of the New World. After 1898, as Pound knew, arguments in Spain about imperial decline and national regeneration often were attached to readings of such historical, legendary, and literary texts and figures. *Don Quixote* and its protagonist oriented these arguments, as did the more controversial El Cid, who saw a spike in popularity both in Spain and in the United States in this moment.[44] As an argument against neo-imperialism, for example, the reformist Joaquín Costa famously exhorted Spaniards to double-lock the tomb of the Cid so that he would not ride again. Tellingly, Francisco Franco took the Cid's ancestral home, Burgos, early in the Spanish Civil War and made it his base; he was proclaimed Generalísimo there, and he envisioned the city as the seat of a dream of Spanish nationalism that emphatically Christianized and lionized the Cid.

In Pound's time, the leading authorities in Spain, Britain, the United States, and beyond, all of them major voices in the *hispanista* project, read the *Poema* as the birth of an exclusively Castilian Spanish poetry forged in the incipient moment of empire. Just as Pound was writing *The Spirit of Romance*, Ramón Menéndez Pidal, the prominent philologist whom Pound cites for his work on the text of the *Poema*, was publishing *Cantar del mío Cid: Texto, gramática y vocabulario* (1908–1912), his monumental study of everything from the diction to the paleography of the poem. (He later served as an advisor during the filming of *El Cid* [1961], which starred Charlton Heston in the title role.) Menéndez Pidal affirmed the Cid's Castilian, Christian roots and used him as a cipher for his own claims that Castile had unified the peoples that became the Spanish nation; accordingly, the coastal provinces should drop their claims of autonomy and assimilate to the central government.[45] Ormsby agreed that the *Poema* "stands at the very threshold of the literary history of Spain,"[46] and the heir to Ormsby's mantle, James Fitzmaurice-Kelly, a member of the Royal Spanish Academy, confirmed that in "both thought and expression," the *Poema* was "profoundly national" and its hero an exemplar of the "knightly orthodoxy" that defeated the Moors.[47] Huntington published his own three-part version of the text: a facsimile of the original manuscript, his own translation, and his notes on the etymologies and histories of the words; it earned him broad distinction in U.S. and Spanish academies. For him, the *Poema* is the "grandest of epics—the Epic of Spain. It is the expression of his patriotic spirit; the embodiment of his memories of the Reconquest;

the first child speech of his nation . . . The bearded hero of the poem is the familiar type—the ideal type of a Spaniard *rancio*, warrior and leader of a faction."[48] Huntington's wife, the sculptor Anna Hyatt Huntington, soon erected a statue of the Cid in front of the Hispanic Society.

For all of these *hispanista* scholars, the *Poema*'s connections to a pan-Romance-language literary tradition were attenuated and conclusively downplayed in favor of a story of conjoined national and linguistic origins that laid the groundwork for the story of a Castilian-dominated empire that began with the Reconquista. Pound's methods aimed to cut through the literary histories assembled by critics from Ormsby to Paris and to employ modes of comparison and translation that the narratives of empire had resisted. Pound's Cid is poetic more than historical; in this poetic ambit, he is international—a product of the wide circulation of *chansons* and *gestes* for which Spain was one birthplace. Pound agrees that the *Poema* is "distinctly Castilian," meaning that it could not have come from León or from Valencia, but that because of this fact, readers are surprised to learn that "the actual Ruy Diaz of Bivar was not a drivelling sentimentalist, but a practical fighting man" (*SR* 73). So it is, he continues, that "some people speak of disillusion, and marvel (in print) that he came to be chosen the national hero of Spain" (*SR* 73). Channeling this disillusion and surprise into skepticism, Pound reminds readers that the Cid killed Moors and cheated Jewish lenders but that he also served Moorish generals; he was an angry and wronged exile with whom Pound identified in his poetic career. Where the *Roland* portrays a mostly one-sided battle against the Moors and casts its titular figure as a martyr, the Cid alternately absorbs and rejects the society and culture of the people who then ruled large swaths of Spain—especially in the parts where Pound located the greatest intermingling with southern European troubadour networks.[49] The Cid was not a hero of empire and the *Poema* not the origin of an imperial literary formation; rather, they represented together instances of Pound's unfolding theories of what Hispanism had misconstrued in the overlapping literary-political past. The *Poema*, furthermore, was authored anonymously and was derivative rather than original. Its only extant copy was written by a monk some years after it circulated popularly; that copy is missing its first page and is damaged at various points: all of this enabled Pound both to illustrate and to critique, as he does throughout the *Cantos*, the routes and ideals of literary transmission across history.

In *Spirit*, Pound has performed a double move. As he emplaced the Cid in Spanish history, he valued in the Spanish past a disaggregated, plurinational landscape. At the same time, his understanding of the Cid will allow him to remove the Cid from Spanish history and then to replot him in new poetic and comparative contexts, as he will do in the "Ur-Cantos." In Pound's works just after *Spirit* and leading up to the "Ur-Cantos," we find Spain's past and the questions Pound raised through it framing a series of essays on U.S. culture and its surging empire, published in the *New Age* in 1912–1913 (published in 1950 as *Patria Mia*). He opens:

> America, my country, is almost a continent and hardly yet a nation, for no nation can be considered historically as such until it has achieved within itself a city to which all roads lead, and from which there goes out an authority.
>
> After such city has arisen people forget that what seems one nation had aforetime been many. Only within the nation itself is there left any consciousness of its parts, of, for example, Castille, Arragon, Leon, of Valencia, of Navarre, or of Burgundy, and Aquitaine. We now say "Spain" and "France."[50]

"Spain" is thus shorthand for many historical nations in the Iberian peninsula, and Castile is only one of them. "Race after race has drifted into Spain" over time so that one can only describe a "national average"—despite the efforts of the Castilian crown to subdue the other Iberian nationalities it subsumed—when speaking generically of Spaniards; this stands in contrast to the wave of "Anglo-Saxon" identity overtaking the United States.[51]

Pound then turns this historical ethnography into a reading of the relationship between culture and empire, which he will soon attempt to work out more specifically through the Spanish example: "All the fine dreams of empire, of a universal empire, Rome, the imperium restored, and so on, came to little. The dream, nevertheless, had its value, it set a model for emulation, a model of orderly procedure, and it was used as a spur through every awakening from the eighth century to the sixteenth" (*PM* 49). That is, imperial visions can foster great literary periods, but great literature does not occur because writers realize that they are "living in portentous times" (*PM* 55). Pound would declare just a few years later that during the Renaissance, "never was the life of arts so obviously and conspicuously intermingled with the life of power."[52] But the golden ages of drama in England and Spain, he writes in *Patria Mia*, had "nothing planned and concerted" about them (*PM* 55). Rather, Pound develops—alongside another critique of U.S. academia—several seeds of his well-known theory of patronage when he holds that the arts flourish only when "men of a certain catholicity of intelligence come into power" and sponsor it, regardless of the condition of the empire (*PM* 56).

The *Poema* did not necessarily presage imperial greatness, and that the ambitions and even the *failures* of empires can produce great literary periods was something Pound had pondered since his interactions with the decadent movement in London. He compared London, which he saw as the dying center of a fading empire, to Rome in its final days, and he at once appreciated and lamented the decline of imperial ideals that had provided so much material for the decadents.[53] In essays and in texts like *Homage to Sextus Propertius* (1919), he ranged from attacks to satires of empire as the Great War among Europe's massive empires raged. Artists could—indeed, should—create "civilizations," he argued, and "a civilization was founded on Homer, civilization not a mere bloated empire."[54] Germany was an antithetical example, for "the hell of contemporary Europe [in 1917] is caused by the lack of representative government in Germany, *and* by the non-existence of decent prose in the German language."[55] The German Empire's *Kultur* was, for Pound, an awful congregation of state-sponsored scholarship and propagandistic arts. Similarly, "Italy went to rot, destroyed by rhetoric, destroyed by the periodic sentence and by the flowing paragraph, as the Roman Empire had been destroyed before her."[56]

What hope was there for the United States in its rising imperial moment, in Pound's mind? He hoped, briefly and intermittently, that there would be an "American Risorgimento" that would outshine the Italian Renaissance—and that he would be a central expatriate figure in it.[57] He argued that "America has a chance for Renaissance" despite what seem to be "symptoms of sterility or even of fatal disease" in its culture, but that "you will get no idea of America if you try to consider it as a whole" rather than as parts, like in the case of Spain (*PM* 11, 12, 41). Whistler—whom he compares to Velázquez—was, "with Abraham Lincoln, the beginning of our Great Tradition" (*PM* 35); Pound also had wished in 1909 that he could "drive Whitman into the old world," for Whitman "*is* America. . . . He *does* 'chant the crucial stage' and he is the 'voice triumphant.' He is disgusting. He is an exceedingly nauseating pill, but he accomplished his mission."⁵⁸ He compared Whitman to Dante—and to himself. Pound also saw glimmers from other contemporary writers who could improve upon Henry James's successes and "not bring [their] nation into world's eyes ridiculous." American literature could only cohere as a node in an immense, transcultural network spanning centuries. But Pound was dismayed by the "diseases of American letters" such as "dry-rot, magazitis," and the "poxes" of various poetic "school[s]" (masculinism, the cult of beauty, and sociology) that he groups together as "post-Whitmanisms" (*PM* 23).

Pound's ideas for reform looked back to the university system that had both nourished and alienated him. In the United States, one could find subsidies and fellowships to "make a commentary on Quinet" or "write learnedly on 'ablauts,'" but one could not find similar support for "literature and musical composition" (*PM* 52). He wished for new schemes for professorships, popular scholarship, artist fellowships, collaborative workshops, and more; he argued in 1914 that "the universities can no longer remain divorced from contemporary intellectual activity. The press cannot longer remain divorced from the vitality and precision of an awakened university scholarship. Art and scholarship need not be wholly at loggerheads."⁵⁹ He hoped to transpose the model of the American Academy in Rome to New York and Chicago, too. "When a civilization is vivid it preserves and fosters all sorts of artists," he believed, and "when a civilization is dull and anemic it preserves a rabble of priests, sterile instructors, and repeaters of things second-hand. If literature is to reappear in America it must come through, but in spite of, the present commercial system of publication."⁶⁰ But by the time he published his poem "L'Homme Moyen Sensual" in *Poetry* in 1917 (on the heels of his "Three Cantos" in the same magazine), Pound seemed convinced that the bland, profit-driven middlebrow publishing industry was intractable and impossible to defeat—both domestically and internationally. He noted that the United States' leading authors and painters ("Poe, Whitman, Whistler") all saw that their "recognition / Was got abroad," just as the Americans who renovated verse in English in the twentieth century were all expatriates.⁶¹ The best he could do, he wrote with resignation, was to "combat" the "facts" disseminated by texts such as "'Message to Garcia', Mosher's propagandas."⁶² Pound alludes here to Elbert Hubbard's patriotic, bestselling propaganda essay-story from 1899 ("Message to Garcia"), which praises the heroism of a Spanish-American War lieutenant, and to the controversial book pirate Thomas Bird Mosher.

The United States was globally dominant but was "too far from civilization and won't for a hundred years distinguish between the first rate and the second rate; she will always stay content with copies" and cannot be trusted to judge the greatness of its own artists.[63] The country's interest in translation, moreover, barely had a pulse, and exceptionalism overshadowed the promise of perspective that Pound saw in comparative analysis and in the value of translation as an internationalist practice. He argued that "the first step of a renaissance, or awakening, is the importation of models for painting, sculpture or writing," but the United States was now primarily an exporter of insipid, uninspiring literature.[64] As Pound later explained, translation "stimulates," "enriches," and "extends" a dominant language, but only because it "highlights the sound, the lazy spots in the receiving language," without which the target tongue "dies" and "remains a language [*idioma*] of the past."[65] Indeed, he later sounded like the propagandists for foreign-language study in his moment when he argued in an Italian newspaper that

> I have struggled against monolingualism in America and I think I have been right to do so. The stimulus from a foreign language [*lingua straniera*] depends upon its being different and its being felt as radically different. The external language [*lingua esterna*] should protrude beyond our customary categories of knowledge, as a different system, one that in many cases is not even comprehensible to the native. . . . One should read a foreign book [*libro forastiero*] with the suspicion that the author might think differently from us, that even when he speaks in familiar forms, he is perhaps concealing another color, another arrangement beneath it. To uncover such differences is to give value to the reading.[66]

Non-Anglophone literatures, in other words, are disorienting, dislodging, and suspicious for Americans. What damns the United States, for Pound, is its inability to see the weaknesses in its dominant literary tongue that translation exposes.

For the poet or reader to understand the literature of the U.S. empire in the modern world, she would do better to look back to antiquity: "the Roman poets are the only ones we know of who had approximately the same problems as we have. The metropolis, the imperial posts to all corners of the known world. . . . The Greeks had no world outside, no empire, metropolis, etc. etc."[67] The networks empires create, the translingual exchanges they facilitate, and the scattered and incompletely knowable—rather than singular or exceptional—patrimonies they leave: these are what must be realigned by the perceptive modern critic, against the academic and public forces that Pound constantly assailed. To ask how Pound judged empire, or whether he supported or opposed it, is to ask the wrong question, for the answer is mixed: he loathed some empires of his moment and of the past and praised others, historical and contemporary. The point is that the contemporary critic and the poet, not the fact-checking philologist or the scholar of political history ("So-and-So was, in such-and-such a year, elected Doge"), create through translation, as a practice and as a socioeconomic force, the contexts by which literature stays alive ("STAYS news") regardless of geopolitical conditions.[68]

The "Ur-Cantos" and Pound's Retranslation of the *Poema*: The Splintered Text

"A great age of literature is perhaps always a great age of translations; or follows it," Pound claimed, in a point he would make many times across his career.[69] He held, in another assault on the academic versions of literary history, that there was not "any point in studying the 'History of English Literature' as taught. Curiously enough, the histories of Spanish and Italian literature always take count of translators" whereas English literary histories "slide over" it out of fear of being labeled unoriginal.[70] As he moved to beginning what would become the *Cantos*, Pound would retranslate his Spanish engagements in ways that point toward his new readings of the country's literary past, couched in his own effort to launch an expatriate American epic. He had mostly retained in *Spirit* an exegetical or pedagogical style of translation, but he deviated from scholarly and translational norms that he had cited and analyzed by infusing them with liberal substitutions at pivotal moments. He still held on, at times, to a linguistic essentialism ("the cadence and rhyme of [Lope de Vega's] Spanish gives it a certain suavity which I cannot reproduce"), but when writing of Arnaut Daniel's difficult language, he notes that "very often a Romance or Latin word stands between two English words, or includes them" (*SR* 201, 26). He argued for a method of reciprocal, irreconcilable estrangement between source and target languages. *Spirit* contained "translations of Words," he felt, and "*I needed freer mode for translation of spirit plus expression of myself*" after it.[71]

"About 1911," Kenner writes, "Pound came to think of translation as a model for the poetic act: blood brought to ghosts," or in Pound's terms, "bring[ing] a dead man to life, to present a living figure," just as he had done with the Cid and the young girl who speaks to him.[72] This was no new or sudden revelation for Pound; it was the result of his attempt to extricate himself from the academic standards of translators by asserting that the translator was affected by the process too. In his series of *New Age* essays "I Gather the Limbs of Osiris" (1911–1912), he defended his antifluid, unnaturalizing translational method as one that "sought in Anglo-Saxon a certain element which has transmuted the various qualities of poetry which have drifted up from the south, which has sometimes enriched and made them English, sometimes rejected them, and refused combination."[73] His facing-page bilingual translations of Guido Cavalcanti in 1912 were followed by the more radical experiments of *Cathay* (1915) and his calculated affront to U.S. academia that infuriated the classicist establishment, *Homage to Sextus Propertius*. He believed that "metre is the articulation of the total sound of a poem" and remarked to William Carlos Williams that "sometimes I use rules of Spanish, Anglo-Saxon and Greek metric that are not common in the English of Milton's or Miss Austen's day" as a way of writing through translation.[74] Again in "Translators of Greek" (1918), he condemned both French and English translators of Homer for their use of ornament—a style that he was variously contrasting across the 1910s with the virile, masculine hardness and abstraction that he saw in T. E. Hulme.

Pound famously employed a combination of then-vilified modes of mistranslation, both consciously and unconsciously.[75] He places translation at the center of comparative literary history in order to invoke what he sees as the imbalances, distortions, multiple meanings, variant possibilities, and incommensurate points that inhere in the process of translation; this in turn preserves the divergent hermeneutic possibilities, and the literary richness through instability, of any text. Pound translated from at least thirteen languages that he knew to varying degrees, and in contrast to Spanish, his interests in several of them (Italian, Provençal, Chinese) have been examined at length. But more important for Pound than any relationship between two discrete languages was the interplay of multiple languages, including those that the translator brings to the text when creating "elaborate masks" by speaking through others' voices.[76] "[No] man in our time can think with only one language," he later asserted; "different languages—I mean the actual vocabularies, the idioms—have worked out certain mechanisms of communication and registration. No one language is complete."[77] Pound preferred partiality and, as he wrote to Shepard, "*unEnglish*" writing and translation alike; translation was a heuristic practice that always revised the original in its labor.[78] There was no possibility, that is, of carrying over intact a literary relic from Spain's past; translation was a pedagogical, scholarly, and poetic reformation of it, and the imbalance of political and literary relations always inflected it.

These expansions of translation, Pound argued, were "the absolute best among all forms of writer's training," and his use of Romance-language rhythms, meters, phrases, and personae as he shifted seamlessly to what is typically regarded as his own poetry has been documented widely.[79] When Pound began in earnest in 1915 a "really L O N G, endless, leviathanic" poem, he realized that it would only come into being through a constant process of translation, retranslation, and revision that he had been honing since 1906.[80] One of his concomitant goals in his epic was to embody the theories of literary periods, greatness, and "vitality" that he had been working out; an early draft worried that he was "too careful to tell you [the reader] / The how and why of my meaning, 'here was the renaissance.' "[81] At the start of this process, he looked back to the *Poema* and to the Cid's figure, and after a number of plans, false starts, missteps, and hesitations, he published the first three cantos, which are known with their revisions as the "Ur-Cantos," individually across three months in *Poetry* in 1917.[82] In them, Pound turns the montage of fragments, or "super-position," into a new mode of translation that traverses Greece, China, Egypt, Italy, "middle Indiana," Catullus, Noh theater, the occultist John Heydon, and a bewildering array of temporalities ("you mix your eras," he says approvingly to Browning).[83] Translation proves his primary mechanism for rearranging sites, texts, empires, experiences, and more.

Pound had not yet settled on what would become the opening structural device of the work: his version of Andreas Divus's *Nekuia* episode from Homer's *Odyssey* (an episode that, Pound wrote, was a metaphor for the process of translation itself) was at the end of the third "Ur-Canto" rather than the beginning of the first one, where it would settle after both Eliot and Joyce foregrounded Greek myth in their works in the intervening years. The unpublished drafts of the "Ur-Cantos" themselves contain even more allusions to Spanish literary history and to the Cid in particular; many would be cut before their publication in *Poetry*.[84] In the middle of the "Ur-Cantos" are what Pound describes, in a line that he will also cut between the "Ur-Cantos" and the first book of *Cantos*, "the gestes of war 'told over and over.'"[85] If *Spirit* placed the *Poema* in a trans-European and transhistorical comparative context, the "Ur-Cantos" began to situate the *Poema* in a universal schema of "gestes." Amid the imagist, vorticist, and Noh techniques that Pound was employing in the set of three poems, he shifts from—as Ronald Bush characterizes it—a narrative monologue in the first "Ur-Canto" to "a series of paratactically arranged but not unrelated vignettes" in the second. Here, he returns to the *Poema* and puts the Cid among the "joyless ghosts, each fixed in a type of spiritual blindness" that the poem portrays in a transhistorical inferno.[86] Pound then "stuff[s]" into his poetic "rag-bag" a mixture of translations, paraphrases, misdirections, and reinventions of the *Poema* that amount to a rereading of the text he had, by now, interpreted several times.[87] In the second of the "Ur-Cantos," we find the Cid once again next to the troubadours Joios (or Joyos de Tolosa) and Arnaut Daniel but also next to much more—including Pound himself:

> False arms! True arms? You think a tale of lances . . .
> A flood of people storming about Spain!
>   My cid rode up to Burgos,
> Up to the studded gate between two towers,
> Beat with his lance butt.
>   A girl child of nine,
> Comes to a little shrine-like platform in the wall,
> Lisps out the words, a-whisper, the King's writ:
> "Let no man speak to Diaz or give him help or food
> On pain of death, his eyes torn out,
> His heart upon a pike, his goods sequestered."
> He from Bivar, cleaned out,
> From empty perches of dispersed hawks,
> From empty presses,
> Came riding with his company up the great hill—
> "*Afe Minaya!*"
>   to Burgos in the spring,
> And thence to fighting, the down-throw of Moors,
> And to Valencia rode he, by the beard!
> *Muy velida.* [~~There was a tale of jingling chivalry~~

~~Of pennons and~~]⁸⁸ Of onrush of lances,
Of splintered staves, riven and broken casques,
Dismantled castles, of painted shields split up,
Blazons hacked off, piled men and bloody rivers;
[~~On to the treachery of Carrion~~
                    and to King Amfos' pardon in the end.
~~Or you'd have ballads? Hear Fernan Gonzalez?~~
~~Find~~] Then "sombre light upon reflecting armor"
And portents in the wind, when De las Nieblas
Set out to sea-fight,
Y dar neuva lumbre las armas y hierros." [*sic*]
Full many a fathomed sea-change in the eyes
That sought him with the salt sea victories.
Another gate?
    And Kumasaka's ghost come back to tell
The honor of the youth who'd slain him.
Another gate.
    The kernelled walls of Toro; *las almenas*⁸⁹

We could trace the origins of many of these lines in the *Poema*, and we could compare those to Ormsby's version, but more important, Pound's version here is a patchwork medley chosen from many different points in the *Poema*. Some lines are direct translations from the original: "My cid rode up to Burgos" is "Myo Çid Ruy Diaz por Burgos entraua," and "A girl child of nine" is "Vna ninna de nuef annos." Others are loose translations; the original "Alcandaras uazias sin pielles e sin mantos, / E sin falcones e sin adtores mudados" is roughly the basis for Pound's two lines that bring back the signal word "press" from the *Poema* translation in *The Spirit of Romance*, when he translated what is now "the down-throw of Moors": "From empty perches of dispersed hawks, / From empty presses." Others still are greatly paraphrased or condensed versions of the *Poema*, such as the description of the ride to Valencia to fight the Moors (which comes much later in the text). The majority of the section from "My cid rode . . ." through "up the great hill—" consists of lines mostly taken from the original, reordered and loosely translated. And as I have noted above, even more material from the *Poema* circulated in Pound's drafts only to be deleted by 1917: an allusion back to the "pennons" of the passage Pound translated in *Spirit*, others to the nobility of Carrión (a fictitious family within the poem) and to the twelfth-century Aragonese King Amfos, and a final one to Fernán González, the hero of a companion Spanish epic that came shortly after the *Poema*.

More intriguing are Pound's deviations and recreations of the text in this passage. The short lines "*Afe Minaya!*" (roughly, "Here's Minaya!") and "*Muy velida!*" ("very beautiful") are Old Spanish; the former is directly from the *Poema*, but the latter was invented by Pound. That is, *Muy velida* is not in the text; *barba velida* ["soft/beautiful beard"] occurs several times as a modernized Homeric epithet for El Cid. Pound's addition of *Muy* brings out the rhyme with *Ruy*, El Cid's name; in his revision for *Lustra* (1917), Pound changes and adds a phrase with the line, "Let no man speak to Diaz (Ruy Diaz, Myo Cid)," thus glossing his own reference parenthetically.[90] Announcing its error—its "wandering" (*errare*) from the original—Pound's scene blurs the lines between the "False arms!" and "True arms?" in a fog (Spanish: *niebla*) of linguistic heterogeneity in which his voice speaks alongside that of the Cid; the poem is at once his, Spain's, and many others'. The returns, in dramatically altered and truncated form, of the scenes from the *Poema* that Pound translated for "Burgos" and for *Spirit* open up and break apart the translingual crossings of this passage. Again Pound uses inverted syntax and a number of repetitions—"arms," "lances," "empty," "out," "up to . . . "— and again he conflates the girl of the *Poema* with the one he encountered in Burgos. Similarly, the line "A flood of people storming about Spain!" is both historical (the wars of the twelfth century, or troubadours coming from across Europe to learn Spanish songs) and personal (his memory of the royal wedding and the invocation of a "You" to open the scene). In the *Poema*, the young girl is the only one in Burgos who dares speak to the Cid, and she tells him of the king's warning, which the narrator has already outlined to the reader/audience. In Pound's earlier translation of her speech, he progressed line by line; in this new version, he adds a description of her walking to a "shrine-like platform" to address the Cid through the wall. This moment echoes not only Pound's own interest in Japanese culture but also a line from early in the first "Ur-Canto" when Pound himself recalls speaking: "I stand before the booth, the speech."[91] He gives her voice, as he did with the same vocabulary in *Spirit*, as "a-whisper" and "lisp[ing]," then condenses her eight-line speech to just three lines. The elements of his three lines are all present in her original, except for "His heart upon a pike."

The allusion to a "pike," furthermore, comes after the lines, "When I was there, *La Noche de San Juan*, a score of players / Were walking about the streets in masquerade, / Pike-staves and paper helmets, and the booths, / Were scattered align, the rag ends of the fair." *La Noche de San Juan* is both the title of a play by Lope de Vega and the Spanish for St. John's Eve, a summer-solstice festival during which Pound was in Gourdon, France—a scene he fuses with Lope de Vega's Madrid. At the "masquerade" he sees "Pike-staves and paper helmets," with the former (also known as "pikestaffs") bringing together two key words within the poetics of this passage—"pike" and "stave." The scene of slaughtering the Moors that he featured in *Spirit* now is mixed with the opening castle scene to become "Of onrush of lances, / Of splintered staves / Riven and broken casques, dismantled castles; / Of painted shields split up, blazons hacked off, / Piled men and bloody rivers." Retranslating himself, Pound repeats certain language from his previous version ("lances" and "riven," which now rhymes partially with "rivers") and rephrases and alters a great deal of the text ("An oval shield there riven lies" becomes "painted shields split up"). In what becomes a self-referential scene, the violence depicted captures the fragmenting, distorting violence of translation and poeticization that Pound enacts, and vice versa.

The diction here contains the clues of this loose translation's polysemy in an etymological polylogue that blends Germanic and Romance derivatives. "Splintered staves" alludes to more than the rods of the lances used in fighting. A "stave" is also stanza, quatrain, or verse of song; a musical staff (from the same root word); a book chapter; and an alliterating letter in a line of Old English verse. Pound used this term earlier in the same "Ur-Canto II"—referring to the fragment from the troubadour Joios, he writes, "There's the one stave, and all the rest forgotten"—and in his own previous poetry.[92] The poetic-musical meanings—a combination he most appreciated in the troubadours—cross in this scene because a stave is also a wooden strip used in making a cask for wine. To "stave" thus is both to hold off and to break a cask into pieces (staves); Pound is both pushing at a distance and breaking apart poetic-musical form, all while portraying destruction in this scene from a text he has partially "splintered" to his own ends. Similarly, a "casque" (a "heaume" in an earlier draft) is a helmet for battle, a "cask" holds wine, and to cask is to break into pieces. "Dismantle" is to raze, as Pound said of the "dismantled castle" in *Spirit*, where he also translates a war song of Bertran de Born that includes similar language: "And it pleaseth me to the heart when I see strong castles besieged, / And barriers broken and riven" (*SR* 47). And "dismantle" is also to denude—to pull down the cloak (mantle) of another, linking to the line from "Ur-Canto I": "Who wear my feathery mantle, *hagoromo*" (a reference to the Noh play *Hagoromo* [The feather mantle] that Pound had translated with Yeats).[93] The double, triple, and more meanings embedded in Pound's language in this revision of his own translations—from his notes in "Burgos" to his rewriting of Ormsby—is part of the process of linguistic destabilization, montage, and multiplicity. "Splintered staves," in essence, self-reflexively articulates the critical epic *poiesis* that Pound practices, one in which history is "included" by way of charged fusions and fragmentations. He has transported the Cid and the *Poema* to new contexts that even Spain's once vast empire could never reach and further fragmented its language in what amounts to an early modernist revision of his academic and critical practices of the previous decade. And "splintered staves" also points to the fragmentation and eventual loss of Spain's late medieval musical-poetic tradition in a critique that Pound will amplify in the following years—and to his "splintering" of his own previous translations of Spanish texts.

Pound therefore places the Cid and the *Poema* again in new contexts by following a course of Spanish literature for several more centuries, only to come to no vital end. The lines "Then 'sombre light upon reflecting armor' / And portents in the wind, when De las Nieblas / Set out to sea-fight / *Y dar neuva* [sic] *lumbre las armas y hierros*'" appear to continue the quotations and misquotations (and misspellings) from the *Poema*, but they actually come from the Spanish poet Juan de Mena's *Laberinto de fortuna* (1444) on the death of the Conde de Niebla at sea.[94] Mena, the crucial writer in the Spanish language's transition from medieval to early modern just as the Reconquista was nearing completion, wrote this highly pro-Castilian poem in a demotic that, at many junctures, employed Latinisms from Lucan and imitations of Dante in twelve-syllable lines. In *Spirit*, Pound mentions this Spanish line (*Y dar nueva* . . .) and translates it as "And the arms and irons give forth new (or strange) reflections" (*SR* 34). Pound's cross-linguistic method then creates a half-rhyme between *lumbre* and "sombre" and repeats the English "arms" in Mena's *armas*. (Indeed, the first three poems of the *Cantos* will contain three more allusions to "arms," even after Pound deletes "False arms! True arms?") The original passage relies on hyperbaton and complex metaphor, and Pound's new version—which is another retranslation of his own previous works—brings out different resonances: "sea-fight" resembles the kennings of his own Anglo-Saxonized translation of the *Nekuia* episode of the *Odyssey*, and "salt sea victories" points to its alliterative poetics and "rode he to Valencia" to its inverted syntax (compare, "Poured we libations").

As the passage then encounters "Another gate?", it turns first to Noh theater (Kumasaka) and then to yet "Another gate": "The kernelled walls of Toro; *las almenas*." This final allusion comes from Lope de Vega, whose 1619 play *Las almenas de Toro* (The battlements of Toro) Pound had studied years ago. This play concerns Sancho II and the treacherous infighting among the royal family. King Sancho and El Cid take the city in Lope de Vega's play, which is set just before the events recounted in the *Poema del Cid*. The turn to Lope de Vega, who made only an ill-fitting and almost obligatory appearance in *Spirit*, allows Pound to dismiss the figure he treated in *Spirit* and, through him, to critique further Camões's *Lusiads* as a failed epic. Lope de Vega then leads into the story of the Galician noblewoman that Pound revisits at the end of the passage, Inês de Castro ("Ignez da Castro" in the *Cantos*), a member of the Portuguese court of the early 1300s, the secret lover of Pedro I of Portugal, and the subject of Lope de Vega's lost play *Doña Inés de Castro*. The Portuguese king Alfonso IV, who disapproved of Inês and Pedro's relationship, had her murdered and dismembered. When Pedro ascended to the throne, however, he claimed that he had privately married her before her death, and so he had her corpse exhumed and brought before the court, where he forced all of the nobles to kiss her hand and swear allegiance. This story also appears in Camões's *Lusiads*, which Pound had discussed in *Spirit* but had grown to see as even more faulty than he previously recognized. And finally, the last word of the third "Ur-Canto"—"Argicida," which itself is a mistranslation—picks up the name "Cid" again. The Cid and the *Poema* thus stand, in the "Ur-Cantos," between Pound's own experiences in Spain and Juan de Mena, with Kamusaka and a brief allusion to *The Tempest* inserted just before the turn to Lope de Vega. In other words, they belong to a poetic universe that is still largely Spanish but that became a dismembered corpse in the baroque era—an era that failed to maintain the translational, international, polysemic potential that the *Poema* had endowed to Spain and that Pound himself was now reviving in new translational modes.

"Splintered Staves" 69

The Death of Spanish Literature

If we look back to *The Spirit of Romance*, we see that Pound already was unsure if Spain's Golden Age was truly golden. He noted there that Lope de Vega was a "prince of letters" and that a "great age of letters" in Spain was possible with Cervantes and Calderón, but even while praising the latter two figures, he hesitates and never concludes that this "great age" came to fruition (*SR* 210, 211). If Pound began to seal his critiques of postmedieval Spanish literature's wrong turns in the "Ur-Cantos," he presented them even more stridently in the following years. From here, we can understand why the intellectual project that had preoccupied him through to the first draft of his *Cantos* was now being pushed aside and why Spanish literature had to be relegated to the margins for him. By 1916, Pound's growing distaste for Spanish literature as a whole was becoming more apparent: his sense of "KOMPLEAT KULTURE" included from "Spanish, nothing. Italian, Leopardi splendid . . . but not essential as a tool. Spain has one good modern novelist, Galdos."[95] By 1920, when Pound corresponded with Miguel de Unamuno, his Spanish had grown nearly too rusty to be intelligible, and in the Pisan Cantos, most of Pound's fragments and phrases in Spanish are ungrammatical and misspelled.

This was the product of both disuse and—connected to that disuse—a theory of literary and political history that continued Pound's Hispanism in new modes. Always seeking to publish in international forums, Pound contributed two essays to a Spanish periodical in 1921. One is a short survey of contemporary literary movements in England, highlighting imagism, Eliot, Joyce, and Lewis. The other, much longer, is a caustic condemnation of Spanish literature that Pound wrote especially for the Spanish people—a condemnation not unlike his attacks on English literature that aimed to jolt public consciousness toward reenvisioning a more nourishing literary heritage. Transferring his and Eliot's theories of English literary history to Spain, Pound claims in "Some Notes on Francisco de Quevedo Villegas" that a rampant "Elizabethanism" is the "disease of Spanish literature."[96] And just as "the rhetoricians 'ruined the Roman empire,'" a love of "indirectness" overtook Spanish writing during the baroque era, when "ornament of detail" overwhelmed subject matter—even in Calderón's plays—and thereby removed writing from its public, living functions (SN 12, 13). What happened to Spanish literature? How did the country from which, Pound claimed, the early troubadour

Guillaume de Poitiers "brought the song up" and inspired the prose of the French Renaissance, the country Guido Cavalcanti visited on a pilgrimage, decline so far?[97] Even when Pound compliments Lope de Vega, his dismissals of the playwright are in the background and will become more apparent in the *Cantos*. He adds that Lope de Vega's rival Quevedo was the last great Spanish writer until Galdós, then adds that Quevedo did not deserve his reputation. (He soon would shift his opinion of Galdós, too.)

Pound ultimately argues that "the vitality of Spain runs in the Poema del Cid, the best, I think, of all chancons de geste, in Calisto y Melibea, in Rojas, in the invention of Lope, in Cervantes" (SN 13).[98] Spain's literary vitality, for Pound, began when it was a haven for translators and translation practices. To account for Spain's literary decline, Pound—who was beginning to consolidate his thoughts on empire, states, and patronage via Italian examples, with Sigismondo Malatesta his better-known rebellious soldier-for-hire figure—asserts that one must look also to political history.[99] He notes that "hard shell democrats will doubtless consider the decline of the Spanish *cortes*, the foreign relations of Charles V, and the 'Flemmings' to blame for the Spanish fading" (SN 13). The reasons Pound cites were common explanations: the turn away from liberalism in parliament (the *cortes*), the Counter-Reformation that Charles V pushed, and the costly and ill-advised Eighty Years' War (SN 7).[100] Pound then asks rhetorically, "did [Spain's] literature cease to be of international importance chiefly because of her obstination in mediaeval philosophy and religiosity?" (SN 16). Spain lost its greatness, in essence, when the fervor of the Reconquista, which alternately purged Moorish thought and assimilated parts of it to an exclusively Catholic, Hispanic nation, continued through the Counter-Reformation and the Inquisition.

This intolerant, singular consolidation cut off the circuits of translation and cultural import-export systems that fed the once-powerful literary tradition in Spain. It killed the transnational "spirit of romance" that Pound saw in the *Poema*; Spain's aspirations to a "great age" were doomed from its modern origins. This "disease," Pound notes, "is not geographically Spanish" (SN 13). "Other countries have recuperated" after closing off their borders to "the other world," and Spain had a chance to return to "the main European current" in the 1700s (SN 19). But Spain's writers chose to narrow their national culture rather than to recover the "meandering" and varied network of "castles" that made the Europe he analyzed in *Spirit* so full of life (SN 19). This "disease" he finds again in his own moment: "the disease of both England and America during the last century is due precisely to a stoppage of circulation" that cut off "the importation of models" for new writing. The Napoleonic Wars, he notes, kept England from translating Voltaire when the English public needed his works.[101] As he puts it in Canto LII, "Once only in Burgos, once in Cortona / was the song firm and well given / old buffers keeping the stiffness" (*C* 258). The baroque era—Spain's last influential era, he holds—had set the country on a course that caused a "great deal of Spanish poetry" to become full of "ornament," enslaved by imitation and unable to liberate itself from "time" as great literature does, as Pound noted in a 1929 postscript to *The Spirit of Romance* (*SR* 211). Even Camões was, in effect, trapped by his conception of time; "an epic cannot be written against the grain of its time," Pound wrote (*SR* 216). Thus, Camões failed to represent Inês's story and "the splendid horrors of the Spanish past" because he wrote them as a "mirroring" rather than as "the simplest narration of the events themselves," leaving only a corpse for Pound to "dig up" (*SR* 219, 218). By the twentieth century, Spain was for Pound "not a civilized nation" but a "damn'd nest of savages" that warranted the old European prejudice that "Europe ENDS with the Pyrenees."[102]

The *Cantos* and the Reduction of Spain

By the time Pound published *A Draft of XVI. Cantos* in 1925, the baroque era and its use of "ornament" were fully dismissed; most of the lines on Inês de Castro were cut, and Camões was only present faintly. There was a wholeness to the "song" in the Burgos of the Cid that has been irrevocably lost in Spain. As Pound further reworked the "Ur-Cantos" between 1917 and 1925, he greatly altered and truncated the Cid, who moves from the second "Ur-Canto" to Canto III.[103] In this version, Pound writes:

> My Cid rode up to Burgos,
> Up to the studded gate between two towers,
> Beat with his lance butt, and the child came out,
> Una niña de nueve años,
> To the little gallery over the gate, between the towers,
> Reading the writ, voce tinnula:
> That no man speak to, feed, help Ruy Diaz,

> On pain to have his heart out, set on a pike spike
> And both eyes torn out, and all his goods sequestered,
> "And here, Myo Cid, are the seals,
> The big seal and the writing."
> And he came down from Bivar, Myo Cid,
> With no hawks left there on their perches,
> And no clothes there in the presses,
> And left his trunk with Raquel and Vidas,
> That big box of sand, with the pawn-brokers,
> To get pay for his menie,
> Breaking his way to Valencia.
> Ignez da Castro murdered, and a wall
> Here stripped, here made to stand.
>
> (*C* 11–12)

First, the differences: the scene of the charging lances is now gone, yet the play on "there"/"their" that Pound employed when translating that scene returns as he changes the lines "From empty perches of dispersed hawks, / From empty presses" of the "Ur-Cantos" to "With no hawks left there on their perches, / And no clothes there in the presses." The "girl child of nine" of the previous version is now given in contemporary Spanish as "Una niña de nueve años," a modernization of each word in the original, and a line that carries over the sound of "nueva" from the previous version. The "shrine-like platform" of the earlier version is now retranslated, reaching back to the *Poema*, as "the little gallery"—a reference to the townspeople who view El Cid from their windows as he enters. Pound adds "voce tinnula," from Catullus, to describe her "ringing voice." The "pike" is now doubled via rhyme as a "pike spike," and most important, the only actual quotation from the girl (drawn also from the *Poema*) reads, "And here, Myo Cid, are the seals, / The big seal and the writing." The emphasis now lies on the king's seals and writing, which are beyond the comprehension of the young girl. As Pound mostly mutes the girl and narrates her voice, he doubles "seals/seal" where the original has only one, but he rhymes it (*sellada*) with *nada* ("nothing"). Her language is monosyllabic again, but here Pound breaks up the rhythm of her lines (and his paraphrase) with more internal commas.

The remainder of the short passage refers to the story of deceiving the moneylenders, Raquel and Vidas, with boxes of sand disguised as trunks full of gold so that Cid can gather a private army ("menie") to raid Moorish lands in Valencia. (Compare the line in Canto I: "Men many, mauled with bronze lance heads" [C 4].) The allusion from the "Ur-Cantos" to Spain's Islamic past—"Mohammed's windows, for the Alcazar / Has such a garden"—is also gone.[104] Whereas he formerly left the Cid as an ostracized exile, Pound now closes with his deception of lenders in order to critique what he sees as usury. (It is tempting to cite this as an instance of his burgeoning anti-Semitism, but whereas in *The Spirit of Romance* he identified Raquel and Vidas as Jewish, in the *Cantos* they are only called "pawnbrokers.")[105] From there, we move directly into Inês de Castro again. Pound has lost some of the referential instability of the "Ur-Cantos" version in revision, too: the play on "dismantled" has now been literalized as "no clothes there in the presses," connecting it to the ravishing of the queen-to-be Inês ("stripped"). But he adds an internal rhyme across two lines with "pay" and "way," then a half-rhyme of "menie" (which also points to the surname of Juan de Mena and to *Las almenas*) and "Valencia." The story of the Cid now rests between Pound's memory of the steps at Dogana and the murder of Inês de Castro, followed by a quick turn to Mantegna and Italian painting of the 1400s. In short, the *Poema* has been reduced to more of a mininarrative of history than an epic, to use Pound's own conceptions.

Spain's squandered cultural promise becomes a minor, scattered theme in the *Cantos*, where Spanish literature and cultural references appear only sporadically, colliding with a host of other literary histories, with Pound's personal experiences and interactions with Rennert and Shepard, and with readings of the fall of many empires. The early references, in Cantos V and VIII, characterize Spain as a site that exported "song" to the troubadours. In Canto XX, Pound revisits his graduate training and his critiques of philology. The opening lines, "Sound slender, quasi tinnula" echo the "voce tinnula" that described the young girl speaking to the Cid in Canto III. Throughout Canto XX, Pound endorses "sound" and song over linguistic certainty, and he aligns himself with the Cid ("My Cid rode up to Burgos") when he describes his trip to Germany in 1911: "And that year I went up to Freiburg." Pound's own frustrated epic journey was a visit to the renowned German philologist of Provençal Emil Lévy to inquire about a word (*noigrandres*) because, as Pound writes, "Rennert had said: Nobody, no, nobody / Knows anything about Provençal, or if there is anybody, / It's old Lévy." Later in the same canto, Niccolò III d'Este goes into a delirium and witnesses an execution from Lope de Vega: "And they were there before the wall, Toro, las almenas, / (Este, Nic Este speaking) / Under the battlement" (*C* 91). Pound explained to his father, "Elvira on wall or Toro (subject-rhyme with Helen on Wall)."[106]

Lope de Vega's play now allows a transhistorical restaging of executions against walls, colliding no longer with the Cid before the walls of Burgos: in Canto XXX, the scene of Inês's murder is cast amid allusions to Greek gods and scenes of the Borgias. In parallel, in Canto XXII Pound uses his brief experiences as a tour guide in Gibraltar and his exploration of Granada to reflect on the persistence of Islamic and Jewish cultures in southern Spain, but Spanish literature is suppressed from his portrait. In later cantos, Pound revisits his time in Spain from 1906, including his visits to Madrid, Córdoba, and Granada, with references to the Velázquez paintings at the Prado; Rennert appears several times, too. Canto LXXXI, for example, begins with a subject-rhyme in which Zeus, Taishan, and Cythera are mingled, then includes quotations that appear to come from Zeus but turn out to be Padre Elizondo speaking in poorly rendered Spanish. Elizondo says (my translation): "Here [in Spain] there is much Catholicism but very little religion" and "I believe that kings will disappear" (Pound gives the latter as "Kings will, I think, disappear"). Pound's reunion with Elizondo in London enters the scene, and even his young tour guide in Burgos, who mistook him for French, speaks: "We call *all* foreigners frenchies" (*C* 538). A poetic return is made later in the *Cantos* with the recycled phrase "nueva lumbre" from Juan de Mena; in Canto CVI, Pound writes, "deep waters reflecting all fire / nueva lumbre, / Earth, Air, Sea" (*C* 773).[107]

Most of these allusions and revised memories, however, are no more or less consequential in the *Cantos* than any other lines that we might trace. The structural and polymorphous roles that the Cid, the *Poema*, and Lope de Vega played in the earlier versions have been reduced, in a dramatization of Spain's decline, to little more than "footnotes." After the "Ur-Cantos" and Canto III, that is, Pound redirected his effort to craft a poetics around the translational, comparative, and critical encounters with texts like the *Poema* that once mattered greatly to him. The *Cantos* shift their focus to sites that produced what Pound saw as stronger poetic lineages—Italy, most of all—while relegating his encounters with Spanish to sounds, moments, and experiences that lack the polyphony and polysemy that he earlier had staged. The endpoint of what were Pound's robust engagements with Spanish in the 1910s might seem more a whimper than a bang, but it reveals a telling arc of the poet's thought on the effects of empire on literary histories. Spain lost its "song" when it became an empire of orthodoxy that would not tolerate linguistic heterogeneity and instead attempted to forge a government-sponsored and unoriginal cultural patrimony of "ornament." The implications for the United States are not far from the assertions Dos Passos will make and that I will discuss in chapter 2: America's headlong rush into an overseas empire of commerce and conquest forged by an increasingly narrow conception of Anglo-Saxon identity would provide the grounds for neither an epic nor a "great age" of translation, comparison, and arrayed fragmentation. Pound's failed projects of his early career and Spain's failed literary history would cross multiple times, figured by a monument, the *Cantos*, that itself would never cohere.

CHAPTER 2

Restaging the Disaster

*Dos Passos, Empire, and Literature
After the Spanish-American War*

News from America is rather two edged. At the same time as we seem to be shutting ourselves out for ever from the esteem of civilized people—if there are any—by the recrudescence of the Inquisition and by acts of the filthiest barbarity, there seems to be growing a realization . . . of what is going on. At least the period of tame acquiescence seems to be coming to an end.
—JOHN DOS PASSOS, Letter to Rumsey Marvin (Madrid, 1919)

If we could inject some of the virus of [Pío Baroja's] intense sense of reality into American writers it would be worth giving up all these stale conquests of form we inherited from Poe and O. Henry.
—JOHN DOS PASSOS, *Rosinante to the Road Again* (1922)

AS A BRASH, REBELLIOUS YOUNG WRITER OF THE AMERICAN left with a freshly minted degree from Harvard, John Dos Passos experienced a symbolically momentous day on October 14, 1916, when his first nationally published article, "Against American Literature," appeared in the *New Republic*. This essay was a linchpin in Dos Passos's burgeoning theories of why modern capitalism and creative freedom were fundamentally incompatible. On that same day, Dos Passos boarded a ship for Spain, which became a vital site through which he elaborated and developed his internationalist, often Leninist critique of capitalism—specifically, its manifestations in contemporary imperialism— just as he was embarking uncertainly on a career as a journalist, translator, poet, political agitator, and more.[1] This conjunction, furthermore, was the starting point of a quarter-century-long arc of Dos Passos's career in which his radical revaluations of U.S. literature and his politicized readings of Spanish literary and cultural history were promulgated together. Indeed, especially in the late 1910s and early 1920s, Dos Passos offered portraits and translations of Spanish writing that simultaneously advanced the aims of the modernists of New York's Greenwich Village left, all while he attempted to find a model of social realism adequate to the revolution that he saw coming in the United States and around the world. In the process, he not only countered yellow-journalistic portraits of Spain and his own father's celebrations of empire but also worked to overturn the influence of a leading authority on the U.S. novel, realism, and Spanish literature: William Dean Howells.

For Dos Passos, at stake was a troubling circumstance embodied in Howells's writings, despite his compatriot's anti-imperialist and socialist politics: the U.S. novel and the U.S. empire were expanding hand-in-glove, especially after 1898, even as "American literature" remained for Dos Passos a vacuous cultural formation. The "stale conquests of form" that he sees in Poe and O. Henry are symptoms of U.S. literature's growth during its ill-gotten "conquest" of the North American continent—a conquest that had now continued overseas and had elevated a banal, commercialized brand of U.S. writing globally by invading foreign markets. Dos Passos read 1898 as the marker of a new geopolitical-literary era, as he would confirm most famously in the opening pages of his *U.S.A.* trilogy (1930–1936), but his specific provocation is to suggest that the collapse of Spain's empire was a *good* thing—and that U.S. fiction finally would blossom were its empire to suffer the same fate.[2] That is, for Dos Passos, Spain came to life literarily when its empire died, and he offers in his comparative readings of U.S. and Spanish literature a theory of empire's effects on literary aesthetics through which he aims to reduce and ultimately unravel "American literature." Dos Passos, in his broad, semiprofessional work as a Hispanist, was intervening in a longstanding debate on U.S. literary culture, its imbrication in empire, and its relation to Spanish writing. Washington Irving, William Prescott, George Ticknor, and Henry Wadsworth Longfellow had been crucial voices here before Howells. Where Pound was butting heads with medieval philologists, Dos Passos—with a similar disdain for U.S. academies and for German *Kultur*—was engaging the overlapping but distinct branch of public intellectualism that Howells now represented, attacking the Spanish novelists Howells championed and praising those overlooked by or unknown to him.

In what became a protracted battle for cultural authority and for new aesthetic paradigms that even pitted Dos Passos against his fellow traveler Waldo Frank, Dos Passos restaged the War of 1898 and reversed its presumed cultural effects. He thereby idealized Spain as a space that resisted capitalism, homogeneity, centralized nationality, and the devastation of modern war, all of which he saw as ingrained in American culture. Dos

Passos saw Spanish literature as a diverse assemblage of styles and ideas rooted in preindustrial artisanship rather than factory-driven commodification. He profiled writers of the left from the country's coastal provinces (the Basque Country, Catalonia, Valencia, Andalusia) and not those from the dying metropolitan capital, Madrid. Dos Passos sketched Spain, in its moment of great instability and potential revolution, as a federation of autonomous, decentralized provinces of workers' states poeticized by a new generation of writers who scorned Madrid. "Great art is possible only," he remarked in 1917, "where individuals are full, consciously or not, of great longing, great discontent."[3] He argued that the Disaster in fact "fired a fresh crop of young men with a determination to renovate their country at any cost . . . [with] hopes for education, for social justice," and for much more.[4] Dos Passos met several writers who had just been grouped together in 1913 as Spain's Generation of '98, including the poet Antonio Machado, and he provided for U.S. readers some of the earliest and most important translations and accounts of their literary politics. Dos Passos took part in this rebirth and globalization of Spanish culture in the United States by romanticizing the country's old, sputtering, underdeveloped economy and its *pueblos* even more than some of the writers he profiled did. He politicizes Spanish writing, sometimes tendentiously and anxiously, and pushes to harness the country's leftist foment in ways that his predecessors would not touch. He essentially agrees with the nationalist line within Spain that '98 is an exceptional generation, but—bringing out a central dialectic in *hispanista* thought—he does so for politically opposed reasons.

In this way, in a formative moment in the development of international modernism, Dos Passos desired to break apart the United States' reigning practices and to reconceive national literatures for a late- and possibly postcapitalist sphere. To recover and recontextualize Dos Passos, his interlocutors, and his peers is to rethink the unexceptional emergence of U.S. modernism, whose domestic and often nativist components in the 1910s—from the founding of *Poetry* to the Paterson Strike Pageant to the Armory Show—also helped fashion the new aesthetics of an international left. Amid many competing voices and visions of the modern, whether feminist, ethnic, materialist, regionalist, avant-garde, or otherwise, Dos Passos, Waldo Frank, and others of New York's Lyrical Left saw in Spain the blueprint for an imperial collapse and a revolution that would lay the groundwork for a new literary organicism that would express "America" democratically. Paradoxically, and with a mixture of optimism and pessimism from Dos Passos, American literature could only become coherent by being fragmented: yet, if national arts flourish when empires decline, both the writer and critic can find inspiration in the fact that now "there are many Spains" linked together by geography as an anarchistic network of literary styles.[5] Dos Passos's series of magazine articles on these topics were collected, revised, and published as *Rosinante to the Road Again* (1922), his "revealing little travel book," as Alfred Kazin called this complex fusion of travelogue, literary criticism, translation, autobiography, fiction, propaganda, and sociohistorical commentary.[6] This loose rewriting of Don Quixote's journeys across Spain imagines a historical and contemporary depth unseen in what he called "our blessed Benighted States," where literature was produced in cities with similar, often uniform characters, leaving artists such as himself a "stale" and paltry cultural legacy.[7] A usable past could only be created out of materials such as those Spain offered.

Dos Passos therefore collapses and rewrites Spain's cultural history into a political formation that, rather than abutting and enriching the United States, becomes all the more powerful when viewed in a paratactic balance with the culture of his native country. He extends Pound's skepticism about the greatness of the Golden Age not by digging back to the medieval period but by understanding that greatness as premised on the faulty grounds of empire and conquest. Cervantes and Jorge Manrique now become, for Dos Passos, prompts for exploring the voices and crafts of Spain's contemporary peasants, whom he wants to channel. And if translation and poetry were one endeavor for Pound, they remain distinct but interconnected for Dos Passos, who instead issued his own portraits of Spanish life in his only collection of poems, *A Pushcart at the Curb* (1922), which he published alongside *Rosinante*. In his aspiration to translate Spain and to become a central figure in the movements that he saw internationally, Dos Passos attempts to imitate Machado and replicate the effects of the Spaniard's poems. (Indeed, he tried to have *Rosinante* printed with the Spanish words in plain type rather than in italics, hoping they would blend with his English prose.) He continued this work through to the decentered, disaggregating style of his novel *Manhattan Transfer* (1925) and his *U.S.A.* trilogy; the final of these, critics have argued, shows clear lines of Baroja's influence.[8] The high modernism of *Manhattan Transfer*, therefore, is not only an interpretation and critique of American capitalism; it is also a rewriting of texts such as Howells's

A Hazard of New Fortunes (1890) and a grafting of Spain—especially Madrid in decay—onto New York.

Much as I sought in the last chapter not to make Pound's *Cantos* the only possible site of meaningful rethinking of modernist literary history, I offer not a reading of *Manhattan Transfer* or *U.S.A.* as culminating points in Dos Passos's career but instead a narrative of the author's overarching critical program. This program, into which his novels fit, was grounded in his sustained translational efforts at comparing the U.S. and Spanish empires. Reassembling a diffuse and diverse array of Dos Passos's translations, political commentaries, literary histories, letters, fiction, and more, I show that what became his signature modernist techniques were crafted in his work as a public Hispanist, comparatist, and nonscholarly translator. Later, Dos Passos's shifting politics took their most significant turn during the Spanish Civil War in 1937, when he would finally repudiate his leftism and launch a new vision of conservative U.S. nationalism, once again routed through his understanding of Spain. Here, after years of failed attempts to "infuse" a disastrous but enlivening foreign energy into U.S. writing, all while watching the U.S. empire grow over time, Dos Passos would return to the aggressively nationalistic ideals of his father, completing his destruction and reconstruction of the sense of "American literature" that Spain's modern history clarified for him.

Spain and the Anglo-Saxon World System

Dos Passos's writings on Spain are inseparable from those of his father, who still towered over his life in the mid-1910s. Dos Passos was the illegitimate son of the high-profile Wall Street lawyer and man of letters John Randolph Dos Passos, who was the son of a Quaker mother and a father who immigrated to the United States from Madeira, an island in the north Atlantic colonized by Portugal. John R. Dos Passos was a staunch corporate industrialist and advocate of imperialism in his adult life. Excited by his country's triumph in broadening its empire overseas in 1898, he published a book, *The Anglo-Saxon Century and the Unification of the English-Speaking People* (1903), which argued fiercely for this "unification" by "steps natural and effective." Committed to an ideal of Anglo-American homogeneity and supremacy and echoing Theodore Roosevelt, Henry Charles Lea, and a number of popular figures of the moment, the senior Dos Passos proposed a plan of "common, interchangeable, citizenship between all English-speaking Nations and Colonies"—a union of the long-reigning British Empire and the expanding American empire that had just defeated Spain.[9] Britain and America must move beyond their adversarial moments of the last two centuries, he felt, and Canada should join this confederation, which would be based in Anglo-Saxon principles of individual liberties and laissez-faire government. According to Dos Passos Sr., this would enable the future "anglicisation of the world," where English will be the "universal dialect of mankind" (*AS* xi). His construction here—a universal *dialect* rather than a standardized language imposed by domination—strives furthermore to naturalize U.S. empire as organic, indeed somehow autochthonous, as authorities ranging from Henry Cabot Lodge to Brander Matthews to a new class of scholars of Old English and Anglo-Saxon texts would insist.[10]

John R. Dos Passos's book, which implicitly rewrites 1776 and thus the foundational myths of Americanness, was also prompted by the British Empire's winning of the Second Boer War. The "Anglo-Saxon" victories in these two conflicts were a signal, in a new racial fiction that appealed to Dos Passos Sr., that the world's two strongest empires, the United States and the United Kingdom, were prepared to join forces. To the "great race" of Anglo-Saxons was now "entrusted the civilisation and christianisation of the world," he argues (*AS* 3). The Spanish-American War revealed that the United States was "*the* leading power of the world," a center of "wonderful development, progress, and marvelous wealth" that "evolved out of a confluence of natural conditions"—the allegedly invisible forces of markets—rather than a belligerent aggression, as in the case of German expansion (*AS* 3, 4). In Dos Passos Sr.'s plan for Anglo-Saxon dominance, Spain is his stereotypical negative example, a country now "shrunken" and playing only "a subordinate rôle in continental politics." The elder Dos Passos writes that he "know[s] of no sadder picture in modern history" than the fall of Spain from its "greatness" and its position as the "first of powers," and that Spain's loss to the United States mattered little to the rest of Europe at this point in its decline (*AS* 34). "Her possessions, rights, and powers have been wantonly squandered," he argues, "a result of policies and acts which are utterly unreconcilable with rational principles of true government" (*AS* 34–35). The Spaniards and Portuguese are, he believes, "hardy rovers and adventurous colonists" like the Anglo-Saxons, but they are utterly deficient in the capacity of holding and uniting [their colonies] into a great and permanent empire. Individually, they possess all the qualities which excite admiration and respect; aggregately, they seem to lack those elements which so strongly typify the Anglo-Saxon people, whose glory and solidarity now completely overshadow them. . . . The dismemberment and decline of the Spanish has been in an inverse ratio to the progress of the Anglo-Saxons.

(*AS* 35)

This notion of an "inverse ratio" was common among American and English nationalists alike after 1898, when numerous historians and cultural critics attempted to explain the "decadence of Spain," and Dos Passos Sr. follows with his own account of the political, economic, and social decline of Spain. Monarchism and clericism, predictably, are the chief culprits. He urges the fractured nations of the Iberian peninsula (Spain and Portugal) to unify and then to unify their former republics in the New World. But he finally concedes that this will not happen; Spain and Portugal are too "disintegrated, without unity of thought, action, or association" (*AS* 34).

John R. Dos Passos then turns personal. He confesses,

I find it difficult, in discussing this subject, to separate my feelings from my judgment. Sentiment, and some national pride (for I am half Portuguese), struggle hard to impel me to paint a glowing and radiant picture of the future of this race; but the cold, hard facts of history confront me at every step, and it is idle to attempt to distort or juggle with them.

(*AS* 34)

Furthermore, in his domestic politics, the senior Dos Passos became increasingly antidemocratic. He spoke out against allowing immigrants the right to vote or, later, to become full citizens of the United States. Even more controversially, he argued that Southern blacks were unfit for citizenship: his remedy was "temporarily to deprive them of suffrage, to put them upon probation, to quarantine them, until such time as they demonstrate an ability to intelligently and honestly cast a vote."[11] The ironies of Dos Passos Sr.'s positions are multiple: for one, his own family never would have become citizens by his logic. But beyond that, his racism selectively incorporated and defied long-held stereotypes of Spaniards and

Portuguese as black, partially imbued with Moorish blood, and thus unfit for modernity. The elder Dos Passos saw himself as having erased whatever hint of "blackness" might have been in his genealogy and cleansed it with a supremacist's version of Anglo-Saxon ideology.

Dos Passos and the Depth of Spain

The younger Dos Passos, of course, rejected his father's celebratory faith in the new U.S. empire and his monolingual English vision. He was not only a product of both Portuguese and Anglo-Saxon blood but also one of uncertain parentage: because he was conceived out of wedlock, his father did not acknowledge him until he was sixteen. He led a peripatetic life in hotels across Europe until he was eleven years old, followed by stays in what he considered the artificial elite worlds of Choate and Harvard—the latter indicted in 1908 as "the factory of American imperialism" by Van Wyck Brooks—upon his settling in the United States.[12] He published several pieces in the *Harvard Monthly*, including a sketch, "The Evangelist and the Volcano" (1915), in which he argued that "we Americans are a great people. We have wealth, industry, splendid sanitation, and a will . . . to reform the earth. We are a sort of epitome of the Anglo-Saxon spirit." His faint praise quickly turns to condemnation: we have "the completest inability to see anyone else's point of view. That is probably why the Anglo-Saxons conquered the world; and why America and American business methods were well on the way to conquer it" before the Great War interrupted. Dos Passos's belief that the "Nineteenth Century has collapsed" points again to the influence of his father's thought on his, even as they stand diametrically opposed in their judgments.[13] The following year, consonant with Brooks's *America's Coming of Age* (1915), he wrote in "A Humble Protest" of the "ponderous suicidal machine civilization" embodied by wartime Germany, which was driving the world to "immolate" itself "before a new Moloch."[14]

In 1916, Dos Passos had wanted to join the ambulance corps on the side of the Allies in World War I, but he bowed to his father's wishes and went instead to a safer, neutral Spain for what became a transformative experience. His parting shot to the United States was the audacious article "Against American Literature." Here, he laments and critiques the prevailing trend of "gentle satire" in his native country, saying that this trait is the only one that stands out as distinctly (and sadly) American amid "the mass of foreign-inspired writing in this country." Edgar Lee Masters and Edith Wharton represent its "modern—and bitter—form." American writers are derivative on the whole, and the United States has not thought collectively about its "national soul[,] . . . leaving that sort of thing to introspective and decadent nations overseas." Its literature is therefore bland and "unstimulating"; like American cities, he adds, "our books . . . are all the same."[15] In other words, the purported shift from Boston to New York City as the literary capital of the United States was meaningless to Dos Passos. If anything, it only ensured that U.S. literary production would be dominated by the mass-market publishers now housed in New York. Dos Passos's remedy for assembly line–style American literature is to "give it body—like apple jack—by a stiff infusion of a stronger product. As a result of this constant need to draw on foreign sources, our literature has become a hybrid which, like the mule, is barren and must be produced afresh each time by the crossing of other strains" (A 587). Exhibiting a familiar preoccupation and tension in American modernism between nativist and internationalist aspirations, he paradoxically wants a literature that is genuine, refreshed originally by its own resources, not by capital—yet also able to absorb nonnative sources. What the United States lacks, he says, is the accretion of the "moulding fabric of old dead civilizations," the "artistic stimulus, fervid with primitive savageries, redolent with old cults of earth and harvest, smoked and mellowed by time, [that] is the main inheritance of civilizations" (A 588). (In other words, a version of what Eliot would produce just a few years later, in England and through European history.) It also needs fairy tales and stories of terror, spirits, ghosts, and sacred lands, none of which are incorporated in the writing he surveys. Beyond his metaphors of "barren[ness]," Dos Passos misogynistically links this banal American writing specifically to women writers, too, deploring their "niceness" and "affectation," which he says pales in comparison to the Russian novels (all by male writers) that are now in vogue in the United States.[16] And his prognosis is grim, for "an all-enveloping industrialism, a new mode of life preparing, has broken down the old bridges leading to the past" in the United States, leaving only capital and commerce, which can sponsor or own the art of the world but cannot produce it—or can only produce a flattened, forgettable form of it (A 590). The vision of "America" that he implies here is white, Christian, and located mostly in New England; whether the oversight of minority and indigenous cultures is a fault he finds in modern literature or is his own blindness remains unclear (though the latter is more likely).

Dos Passos's theory and its faith in a renovated, denaturalized mode of Whitmanian writing bespeak the paradox that Susan Hegeman has pointed out in the thought of Waldo Frank: "it took some kind of collective to change society, but of course, the absence of that kind of integrated collective was the problem to begin with. The only way out of this bind was either a 'faith' that was deeply pessimistic at its core, or a search for some collective outside of modern alienation itself . . . [for] 'buried cultures.'"[17] Spain and its writers, he believed, might provide the antithetical and inspirational model, and this belief was the impulse behind the articles that eventually became *Rosinante to the Road Again*. He wanted to see a European revolution in the making, and he thought Spain—still reeling from the Disaster and rife with violent separatist conflicts, labor strife, neocolonial debacles, and political turmoil—could lead the movement while the continent was engaged in internecine war. With introductory letters from his father's friend Juan Riaño, the diplomat who helped negotiate the peace between the United States and Spain after 1898 and the first Spanish ambassador to the United States in 1915, he met influential figures and gained access to prestigious institutions.[18] He first enrolled in Spanish language and literature classes in Madrid at the Centro de Estudios Históricos (Center for Historical Studies), the famous academy headed by Ramón Menéndez Pidal. His classes there with the esteemed linguist and phonetician Tomás Navarro Tomás, who later would teach in exile at Columbia University, helped train Dos Passos's "un-Iberian ears," and he understood spoken Spanish in almost no time.[19] He also worked out an exchange with a local sociologist in which he received Spanish lessons for helping him translate John Dewey.[20] Dos Passos then spent time at the Residencia de Estudiantes; both the Centro and the Residencia had been founded in 1910 in a moment of liberal educational reform in Spain, and Dos Passos was eager to absorb their zeitgeist as a representation of the energies of a dynamic, new Spain. Yet the impulse of national regeneration and the influx of foreign investment behind them would also discomfit him; so would the many pro-U.S. and pro-Wilson signs he saw across Madrid.[21]

These experiences and their institutional contexts led Dos Passos to explore the ways in which the sedimented layers of Spanish history manifested themselves, whether aesthetically or in daily life, in unique modes that global capital could not assimilate. "Do you know the wonderful feel of old old roads which have been worn to a sort of velvet softness by the feet of generations and generations and generations?" he asked Rumsey Marvin. "And at night," he continued, "they all seem to get up and follow you in a crowd—the Romans and the Carthaginians and the Moors and the mitred bishops going towards Toledo, and the mule drivers with skins of wine from the south."[22] Writing in tones similar to the many travelogues on Spain that he read, Dos Passos noted that "the wonderful thing about Spain is that it is a sort of temple of anachronisms. . . . Roman Italy is a sepulcher—Roman Spain is living—actuality—in the way a peasant wears his manta, in the queer wooden plows they use, in the way they sacrifice to the dead," with Greek, Semitic, "Phoenician Moorish," and even modern French, American, and German elements blended "all in a tangle together!"[23] Dos Passos is captivated by what he sees as a transhistorical precapitalist Spain: the habits of peasants, their handmade tools and pottery, their ancient multicultural heritage, dances, and rituals from "protohistoric Iberian . . . and Magdalenian" times were all alive in the present.[24] His language becomes repetitive and almost incantatory as he describes this culture whose layers are visible and differentiated, not commodified and mass produced. Fascinated by the "*strata* of civilization—Celt-Iberians, Phoenicians, Greeks, Romans, Moors and French have each passed through Spain and left something there—alive," Dos Passos reads the "wonderful jumble" of Spain's fragmented, multilayered history alongside its contemporaneous debates within Spain about whether the country's future lay in an industrialized, Americanized modernity.[25] Ancient history cannot be manufactured in the present, and for Dos Passos, Spain's history—as he collapses and reprojects it—evinces everything that America's does not, and it can produce the continually thriving art that he wished for in "Against American Literature."

Dos Passos believed that Cervantes's *Don Quixote* was the first text to bring all of this together, and the novel colored Dos Passos's perceptions of Spain from the start. "I jabber Spanish a little & read it a little," he wrote to Marvin, "have read *Don Quixote* vol 1 & 2 in original and I intend to study it violently in the near future. . . . I've always been mad to know a lot of languages—it's so humanizing."[26] He read the novel again and again in the following months. And because of it, he preferred the countryside of Castile (Spain's central province) to the urban environs of its hub Madrid, but he nevertheless believed that "I am quite settled in Madrid now, feel as if I'd lived here all my life."²⁷ All along, he wrote many florid letters describing the landscape and tried his hand at some poetic sketches of it. He had tea with Jiménez and, later, Machado, and he made two important friends: José Giner Pantoja and José Robles. The former, a member of the distinguished family of liberal education reformers in Spain, was his guide through Spain.²⁸ The latter, a leftist activist and later professor at Johns Hopkins, would become Dos Passos's first Spanish translator (*Manhattan Transfer*, in 1929). But this trip to Spain ended abruptly in 1917, when Dos Passos had to return to the United States because of his father's death.

"Young Spain" and the American Left

Back home and energized by his time in Spain, Dos Passos grew more radicalized by the moment, and he wrote to Marvin that "my only amusement has been going to anarchist and pacifists meetings and riots—Emma Goldman etc. Lots of fun I assure you. I am thinking of becoming a revolutionist!"²⁹ He quickly found an ideal outlet for translating his impressions of Spain: the short-lived magazine *Seven Arts* (1916–1917). Brooks, Frank, Randolph Bourne, James Oppenheim, and others used the journal to disseminate the newest and best "expression[s] of our American life" in their country's imagined "renascent period" and, characteristically, to link Anglo-Saxon assimilationism and U.S. imperialism in essays opposing U.S. entry into the Great War.³⁰ Anglo-Saxonism at this moment was shifting, in prowar arguments, from a theory of race and nationalism to a theory of democracy and, in accordance, the necessity of interventionism.³¹ The *Seven Arts* writers, generally speaking, instead celebrated the fact that New York's immigrant population was composed to a large degree of castoffs or victims of European nationalist movements and revolutions—leftists and peasants who could not be assimilated into the consolidating xenophobic empires warring across the Old World. Their shared ideal was, in effect, to return the United States to its pre–Industrial Revolution immigrant heterogeneity.³²

Brooks sketched out in his essay "Young America" (1916) a politicized utopianism that the magazine worked both to domesticate and to internationalize with a series of articles profiling the young minds and spirits globally.³³ The writer Seichi Naruse described "Young Japan," Padraic Colum offered "Youngest Ireland," and Dos Passos followed with "Young

Spain."³⁴ Other notices from Germany, Italy, Turkey, China, Spanish America, and India shored up these assertions.³⁵ Dos Passos, with his opposition to the war growing more fervent, held out hope that in Spain and in Russia, "the conquest is not quite complete," and he feared that (as he explained to Giner) in "my own poor country . . . the day of triumph for plutocracy has arrived."³⁶ Thus, in "Young Spain," he presents a portrait of Spain and those Spanish whom he saw as engaged in the early stages of a revolutionary political transformation. Appearing in an issue headlined by Bourne's and John Reed's antiwar articles, "Young Spain" actually glorifies a country in "atrophy," full of corruption, infighting, and separatism, all of which have accelerated since 1898. Stark divisions have emerged between the pro-German and pro-Allies groups: the former includes "reactionaries, the clergy, and the ignorant priest-ridden classes—the high aristocracy and the lowest peasantry"; the latter has "the most connection with the modern world" and includes "liberals of all colors, the intelligenzia, and the munitions manufacturers, who have been growing very wealthy in the North."³⁷ More important, however, because of the war, class tensions are high, and "under the surface the moment comes nearer and nearer when the tension will snap. Famine is the mother of revolutions" (YS 481–482). Dos Passos reorients his father's reading of Spain's decline by attributing it to exploitation and then revaluing it as laying the foundation for revolution; he notes, too, in a subtle rebuff to his father, the strong familial ties among Spaniards. Spain has resisted countless invasions and revolutions over time, he writes, and will continue to do so with a mystical, irrational, anarchistic, indomitable individualism—one that tends in the opposite direction as the individualism celebrated by Dos Passos's father—that makes it, in spirit, "the most democratic country in Europe" (YS 480).

The anticapitalist revolution Dos Passos envisioned would come from Spain's outlying provinces, which he profiles through their distinct languages ("Gallego-Portuguese," Basque, and Catalan), all of which have "strong literary tradition[s]" (YS 477). "There seems no solution," he believes, "to the problem of a nation in which the centralized power and the separate communities work only to nullify each other" and where the latter cannot have simple calls for peace, bread, and autonomy honored (YS 481). "On every side" of Spain, Dos Passos writes,

> in thought if not in fact, the ice of national stagnation is breaking. The war of '98, which to us was merely an occasion for a display of the school

history-book style of patriotism, combined with an amazing skill in sanitation, was to the Spanish people a great spiritual crisis. It was the first thorough unmasking of the hopeless atrophy of their political life. From '98 indeed has sprung the present generation[, which tends] . . . toward anarchism, toward a searing criticism of the modern world in general and Spain in particular, [toward] . . . piecing together the tattered shreds of national consciousness. Not national consciousness wholly in the present capitalistic-patriotic sense, however, but something more fruitful, more local.

(YS 482)

This is Dos Passos's vision of Spain: a federation of autonomous communities united by the bonds of labor, in provinces with strong connections between the people and the land. Where his father has seen "dismemberment" and "decline" in Spain, Dos Passos saw a "spiritual crisis" that had paved the way for anarchist collectivism in a country where "unity of population is hardly to be expected" (YS 478). This rereading of Spaniards and this revaluing of the "disintegration" his father lamented allows him to idealize their incipient process of "piecing together" the remnants of a broken nation. What seemed like a triumph to Americans was merely an occasion for vacuous manifestations of commercialized nationalism; what seemed like a defeat to Spaniards was a revelation that their "national consciousness" could not be reformed through a capitalistic patriotism but would only come about through alliances of "local" interconnectivity.

Dos Passos then profiles three writers from the country's provinces who embody the spirit of this "younger generation" that the American wished to see; these writers were over two decades older than he, but their embodiment of "youth" superseded chronological time. The first is the Basque Pío Baroja, whose novelistic trilogy *La lucha por la vida* (The struggle for life, 1904) he had just read. Baroja resembles Henry James at first blush, Dos Passos argues, but in reality, there is "no comparison between them. The Spaniard has a sense of life, a buoyancy, a power to tell a story that make sickly beside them the pale artifices of the Anglo-American novelist. Far different, too, from James's quiet dissent from ideas American is Baroja's burning criticism of his country's inaction" (YS 482–483). But Baroja's politics, which were shifting from a youthful anarchism toward an antihumanist nihilism, fail to satisfy Dos Passos at this time. He argues—again returning to his father's worldview—that through Baroja, "Nietzsche has reached the present generation," as has "a worship of things Anglo-Saxon, of the efficient Roosevelt virtues, which sounds strangely in the ears of Americans used to reacting in the opposite direction from their red-blooded national ethics" (YS 484). Dos Passos then half-heartedly and briefly lauds the Valencian socialist writer Vicente Blasco Ibáñez, mostly for his radical politics, not for his writing, and for his opinions against the "Anglo-mania" that is becoming pervasive in Spain (YS 483). Dos Passos respects above all the Andalusian Antonio Machado, who, along with Baroja and Blasco Ibáñez, will receive extended treatment in *Rosinante*. Furthermore, he praises Rubén Darío's "call to the Spanish peoples to unite, to build a new ideal of life that would defeat what he called the *Yanki* ideal of dollars and steel," and Jiménez's ability to represent "his province [Andalusia], . . . his *pueblo*" to Madrid (YS 483, 484). Together, these writers all prove that "in literature the triumph of the commune over Madrid is near at hand" (YS 484). Connecting these politics to those of his compatriots, Dos Passos quotes a Spaniard who told him, "It is you in America . . . to whom the future belongs; you are so vigorous and vulgar and uncultured" (YS 487).

For Dos Passos, Spain is being almost geographically pulled apart from the margins, and thus the country cannot be reduced to its primary metropolis and national seat. As he later wrote to John Howard Lawson, "I am in a state—Spain is delectable, preposterous, decorative, everything—but in Spain is Madrid. It seems impossible to be in Spain without being in Madrid. I am bored with Madrid. I abominate Madrid. . . . I have been, am and shall be in Madrid."[38] Madrid represented the former Spanish Empire, the last vestiges of the Castilian plan to consolidate the disparate early modern republics of the Iberian peninsula into a single Catholic state, as Ferdinand and Isabella had named it. It was the collapsed center of the Spain that Dos Passos wanted to see diffused and refracted, and it was also full of connections to Euro-American capital and similarities to New York, the heart of what he called his "type-ridden country" and its culture that was "bunk" and "not so amusing."[39]

Howells, Spanish Writing, and the Literary Politics of Empire

In circulating these works, Dos Passos was contesting the power and legacy of William Dean Howells, whose essays published in the intervening years between "Young Spain" and *Rosinante* would force Dos Passos to recast his critiques, much as the end of the Great War would. Howells, one of the most influential critics in the United States in the late 1800s and early 1900s, had championed certain Spanish authors and their modes of realism, encouraging U.S. writers to follow their model treatments of the picaresque, among others. In his *Familiar Spanish Travels* (1913), he recalls his infatuation with *Don Quixote* as a young boy, which led to his lifelong romanticization of Spain's literary history and indeed its empire. As the book's title indicates, Howells reads Spain sympathetically as different yet knowable, similar to the Ohio of his youth in many ways. At the end of the text, he concedes, "If the reader asks how with this gentleness, this civility and integrity" Spaniards have earned such "repute for cruelty, treachery, mendacity, and every atrocity . . . I answer frankly, I do not know." In the closing line he adds, "I do not know how the Americans are reputed good and just and law-abiding, although they often shoot one another, and upon mere suspicion rather often burn negroes alive."[40] In a stark reversal, Spain's intimate goodness is, for Howells, to be set against the evils of U.S. society.

Howells assiduously studied the accounts of Spanish literature by Irving, Ticknor, and Longfellow, and in his essays, he attempted to characterize himself tentatively as an heir to their authority on both Spain and the United States. While searching the international literary landscape for a realism that was "nothing more and nothing less than the truthful treatment of material," Howells looked to Benito Pérez Galdós, Emilia Pardo Bazán, and Armando Palacio Valdés to provide models for his own compatriots (indeed, he was discussing Palacio Valdés when he gave this famous definition of realism).[41] He praised these three and attempted to capture a Spanish literary scene in which realism triumphed with novels that "are intense and deep, and not spacious," and he even tried to translate some Spanish texts.[42] "No French writer," he wrote in a moment when either the French or Russian realists appeared to many Americans to be the greatest, "has moved me so much as the Spanish."[43] In counterpoint, in his writings on the novel in the United States, Howells claimed that he could

> not believe that the novel of the United States ever will be, or even can be, written, or that it would be worth reading if it were written. In fiction, first the provincial, then the national, then the universal; but the parochial is better and more to be desired than either of the others. Next to the Italians and the Spaniards the Americans are the most decentralized

people in the world, and just as there can never be a national Italian fiction, or national Spanish fiction, there can be no national American fiction, but only provincial, only parochial fictions evermore.[44]

This version of provincialism from which "the national" and "then the universal" may expand struck the younger generation of U.S. writers to which Dos Passos belonged as simultaneously promising in its disavowal of nationality and hopelessly narrow in its conception of localism.

In an imagined conversation in one of his "Editor's Easy Chair" columns for *Harper's New Monthly Magazine* in November 1915, Howells argued against the need for a German-style "solidification" of immigrant groups in the United States in order to lay the foundation for great fiction, instead praising Spain's internal diversity ("the Basques, the Galicians, the Catalans, the Aragonese, the Castilians, and the Andalusians") with a benign naturalization of imperial histories. Howells adds that the United States is still undergoing its "solidification," which takes centuries, and thus, despite insisting elsewhere that realism sprang up universally, he holds that "in four or five hundred years we shall have simmered down sufficiently to produce a national novel of the quantity and quality of the great Russian, English, and Spanish novels."[45] He continues by reviewing the exemplary career and successes of Blasco Ibáñez, whose ability to capture "the likeness of the thing as it is" is, for Howells, unequalled anywhere in contemporary fiction, now that Tolstoy has died.[46]

The politics that underlay Howells's criticism were deeply and intimately, if sometimes unconsciously, connected to U.S. imperialism. When the Spanish-American War broke out, Henry James wrote to Howells that "I hate & loathe the war & have an ineradicable pity & tenderness for poor old proud, plucky, ruined Spain—so harmless & decorous, so convenient & romantic in Europe, with all her ruin & her interest . . . so continentally appealing & irresistible. I wish we had waited to pitch in to some one of our size."[47] Howells, who had been active in the Anti-Imperialist League, also attempted to dissociate himself from the ugliness of the U.S. actions that vaulted its writers into the same conversations as those from Old World empires. He believed that "our war for humanity [in Cuba] has unmasked itself as a war for coaling stations, and we are going to keep our booty to punish Spain for putting us to the trouble of using violence in robbing her."[48] But he also believed that this "stupid and causeless war" was nonetheless carried out by a "kindly and sensible nation," an apology for an empire that the young left could not stomach.[49] James, furthermore, confessed that "I have hated, I have almost loathed [the war]; and yet I can't help plucking some food for fancy out of its results—some vision of how the much bigger complexity we are landed in, the bigger world-contacts, may help to educate us and force us to produce people of capacity greater than a less pressure demands."[50] After the war, Howells wrote that if the United States "by any effect of advancing civility could have treated with Spain for . . . [those] three novelists [Galdós, Pardo Bazán, and Palacio Valdés] . . . I, for one American, should have been much more content than I am with Cuba, Puerto Rico, and the Philippines."[51] Sharing with James a belief in the connection between the war and its possible benefits for average Americans, Howells's substitution here articulates the links between the rising U.S. empire and the increasingly international scope and presence of the U.S. novel that Jonathan Arac has demonstrated.[52] As the novel achieved a new global dominance in this moment, Howells praised its universality and saw the similarities among U.S. writers, Spaniards, and masters such as Zola, Balzac, Turgenev, and Verga as actualizing an international cultural movement in novelistic realism. And Howells finally saw U.S. writing in this moment reaching the European bar in a way that his peer and interlocutor in England, Arnold Bennett, had come to acknowledge in 1912: "a few years ago the English author dictated the terms to the American publisher as a conqueror dictates terms to the defeated host"; now the U.S. novel "has acquired a future, a gem of brilliant water whose rays have dazzled the eyes of England."[53]

Howells conceded that he was "not a Spanish scholar, and can neither speak nor write the language," only read it.[54] (Indeed, when he met Palacio Valdés in Spain, the two spoke Italian.) He was committed to Spain and to Spanish novels in a manner that was outmoded and apolitical—no doubt undermined by his incomplete fluency in the language—by the terms Dos Passos sets forth. Galdós, for example, was an author who had become commercially popular in the United States by the 1910s, related often in middlebrow and popular media to Sir Walter Scott. (Pound, who had praised Galdós previously, defended him faintly by this point, and the *New Age* did not hesitate in 1910 to call him "old and rather stupid.")[55] Dos Passos will condemn viciously the nationalism and national iconography, and the easy adaptability to the U.S. markets, of Galdós's and Blasco Ibáñez's novels.

Dos Passos's Claims to Spain

Both politicizing Howells's localism and rewriting his familiar yet abstract portraits of Spain—along with those that circulated popularly in the United States—were key aims of Dos Passos's next journey. While new critics such as H. L. Mencken and Sinclair Lewis were working to dismantle Howells's authority on different terms, Dos Passos—whose politics were closer to Howells's than either of those two—was actually continuing in the line of Howells's Hispanophilia as a means to assert his own new authority. A brief stint in the Red Cross in France and Italy, where he met Hemingway, ingrained for Dos Passos the condemnations of the Great War as an imperialist debacle that he would depict in *Three Soldiers*. He then returned to Spain in August 1919 with his Harvard friends Arthur McComb and Dudley Poore. He immersed himself further in Spanish culture during this trip and contributed dispatches to a socialist paper in London. The journey resulted in some of his most profound and personal writings on the country—and on Portugal, which he also visited this time. Further investigating racial typologies, he wrote to Stewart Mitchell from Lisbon,

> Here I sit upon the soil of my ancestors. . . . The Portuguese, I find, are a good people, somewhat dirty, somewhat thievish, somewhat humble, lacking that superb haughtiness which seems to be the heritage of the Arabs to Spain, but a people full of goodness. Their main vice is their language, of which I disapprove entirely.[56]

Dos Passos both embraces and rejects his Portuguese heritage, and he overlooks its Arab history by restricting that—and the "superb haughtiness" he ascribes to it—to Spain. While in Portugal, he also found hope for his leftist ideals, writing that "the giant stirs in his sleep": against a fading monarchy, communists have proclaimed a new republic in a rural province, railroad workers have been on strike, and the Young Syndicalists have organized.[57]

Dos Passos's writings from this trip would eventually appear, alongside many of the articles he had published on Spain in the *Liberator*, the *Freeman*, and the *Dial*, as *Rosinante to the Road Again* in 1922. The title evinces the effect *Don Quixote* still had on his journeys—Rocinante [*sic*] is Don Quixote's horse—and Dos Passos's fictional traveling companions Telemachus and Lyaeus embody (and discuss) Don Quixote and Sancho

Panza, respectively. But they are also two sides of Dos Passos himself: one was the wandering son in search of his father (Telemachus, whose name means "far-fighter"); the other was an epithet for Bacchus, who releases humans from worries and anxieties (Lyaeus, a traveling bard and troubadour, whose name comes from a Greek word meaning "to loosen" or "to ease"). He uses these two figures in interchapters to expound impressionistically, and with a version of aesthetic fragmentation that he will push further in *Manhattan Transfer*, upon the themes he discusses in the descriptive and narrative sections of the text: Spain's multilingual and palimpsestic history, its landscape, its conviction of the absurdity of the Great War, the left's rise, and the possibility of a Spanish Arcadia.[58] Telemachus and Lyaeus meet a businessman who wants to become as wealthy as a Rockefeller or a Carnegie, and they meet villagers who echo Thorstein Veblen's readings of U.S. labor and consumption. Spaniards manage to ventriloquize and critique the contradictions of U.S. capitalism from afar.

The book is framed by its opening presentation of a moment that remained in Dos Passos's mind for decades: he interlaces the verses of the fifteenth-century poet Jorge Manrique's "Coplas por la muerte de su padre don Rodrigo" (Verses on the death of his father Don Rodrigo) with a flamenco dance performed by the renowned dancer Pastora Imperio. The former, cast in an old, popular style, was topical for Dos Passos because his father had just died and because his own middle name was Roderigo; the latter embodied all that made Spain stereotypically un-European, weird, strange, and impure. But more important, the poem and the dance captured what now enabled great art in Spain, in Dos Passos's mind: a deep, layered history of foreign cultures, such as the gypsy origins of the flamenco. Together, this transhistorical song and dance prompt Telemachus and Lyaeus's journey from Madrid to Toledo, the city where Spain's Islamic, Jewish, and Christian pasts are woven together in medieval architecture and arts.

In his book, Dos Passos expands several sections of "Young Spain" into a new chapter, "The Baker of Almorox" (a small village west of Toledo). The unnamed narrator studies the baker and writes, "in him I seemed to see the generations wax and wane. . . . Everywhere roots striking into the infinite past" (*R* 48). In the baker—in the many histories and peoples that he channels—Dos Passos sees in an Orientalist vision a "changeless Iberian mind" in the face of countless invasions and conquests. Evincing that Spain's balance of labor and leisure is better than the wealth-driven model of the United States, the baker embodies Spain's "strong anarchistic reliance on the individual man" that has persisted for centuries to become both "the strength and the weakness of Spain" (*R* 25). Dos Passos, after rendering several lines of Spanish speech phonetically in order to capture dialects, concludes that "in trying to hammer some sort of unified impression out of the scattered pictures of Spain in my mind, one of the first things I realize is that there are many Spains" (*R* 25). These many Spains, evoked in the music and painting that he treats too, show that a single Spain as "a modern centralized nation is an illusion." Many languages and dialects are spoken "in this country where an hour's train ride will take you from Siberian snow into African desert"—where even the landscapes and climates cannot unify (*R* 26). Spain's politics since the days of Ferdinand and Isabella's forced unification of the country have "corroded into futility all the buoyant energies of the country. I mean the persistent attempt to centralize in thought, in art, in government, in religion, a nation whose very energy lies in the other direction" (*R* 28). Now, Spain has nothing but "a deadlock, and the ensuing rust and numbing of all life and thought, so that a century of revolution seems to have brought Spain no nearer a solution of its problems" (*R* 28–29).

At this point, Dos Passos inserts several revisions of his earlier article, rethinking Spain much as Pound did. "Young Spain" had addressed the effect of the Great War on the country; *Rosinante* moves instead to a discussion of ancient Spain, the crafts of sculpture and watch making, and a multitude of "traditions: the tradition of Catholic Spain, the tradition of military grandeur, the tradition of fighting the Moors, of suspecting the foreigner, of hospitality, of truculence, of sobriety, of chivalry, of Don Quixote and [Don Juan] Tenorio" (*R* 30). Rewriting his earlier claims, Dos Passos now sees that

> the Spanish-American war, to the United States merely an opportunity for a patriotic-capitalist demonstration of sanitary engineering, heroism and canned-meat scandals, was to Spain the first whispered word that many among the traditions were false. The young men of that time called themselves the generation of ninety-eight. According to temperament they rejected all or part of the museum of traditions they had been taught to believe was the real Spain; each took up a separate road in search of a Spain which should suit his yearnings for beauty, gentleness, humaneness, or else vigor, force, modernity. . . . The problem of our day is whether

Spaniards evolving locally, anarchically, without centralization in anything but repression, will work out new ways of life for themselves, or whether they will be drawn into the festering tumult of a Europe where the system that is dying is only strong enough to kill in its death-throes all new growth in which there was hope for the future. The Pyrenees are high.

(*R* 30)

The Disaster, that is, gave the lie to Spain's "museum of traditions." It spawned a generation of writers who reject the legacy of Spain's national icons of the nineteenth century and are steering the country away from the fate of the ruined continent. What had been presented as "the real Spain" was a tool of centralized oppression, Dos Passos now notes in the wake of the Great War.

Dos Passos is optimistic that a current workers' strike represents, in metaphors often used in Spain at the time, the coming of an anti-European "New Spain, a prophecy, rather than a fact," but he cautions that "Old Spain is still all-powerful" (*R* 32). A local man tells Telemachus and Lyaeus that after the eras of "Torquemada, Loyola, Jorge Manrique, Cortés, Santa Teresa," and others, the youth of Spain are "working to bury with infinite tenderness the gorgeously dressed corpse of the old Spain" (*R* 37). He sees in his travels across Spain and in his studies of elections in Andalusia a country on the brink of agrarian revolts in its outer provinces, where the people suffer from malnutrition and starvation. A syndicalist summarizes for him, "we are being buried under industrialism like the rest of Europe. Our people, our comrades even, are fast getting the bourgeois mentality. . . . It is a race as to whether this peninsula will be captured by communism or capitalism. It is still neither one nor the other, in its soul" (*R* 122).

Translating Spain's Writers and Prospects

In this comparative and often estranging reading of modern Spanish literary history, the writers who had prophesied the New Spain were those whom Dos Passos had met and read and whose politics he admired. His translations of parts of their works were often new to English, too. He profiles Baroja at greater length in *Rosinante*, describing the Spaniard's literary world as "dismal, ironic, the streets of towns where industrial life sits heavy on the neck of a race as little adapted to it as any in Europe. No one has ever described better the shaggy badlands and cabbage-patches round the edges of a city, where the debris of civilization piles up ramshackle suburbs in which starve and scheme all manner of human detritus" (*R* 41). Comparing him to Maxim Gorki, Dos Passos claims that "outside of Russia there has never been a novelist so taken up with all that society and respectability reject" (*R* 42). Baroja, furthermore, "refuses to be called a Spaniard. He is a Basque," a part of an alternative "Spain" that was unwillingly engulfed by Castile during the industrializing wave after the Carlist Wars (*R* 39). Dos Passos offers translations of several paragraphs from Baroja's trilogy as evidence of his style, focusing on a passage in which the protagonist of Baroja's *La lucha por la vida*, the orphan Manuel, admits to being an anarchist; "Spain is the classic home of the anarchist," Dos Passos adds (*R* 44).[59] Manuel represents that revolutionary "spirit that, for good or evil, is stirring throughout Europe to-day, among the poor and the hungry and the oppressed and the outcast, a new affirmation of the rights and duties of men" (*R* 46). The Basque Baroja then went to live in and study Madrid, "febrile capital full of the artificial scurry of government," in order to undermine it (*R* 40). Returning to the ideals of "Against American Literature," Dos Passos declares that Baroja's writing is the cure—seen as a "virus," a threat—for the diseases of U.S. literature. These diseases follow a pattern of taming rogue aesthetics first put in place, he argues, by George Eliot. Where Mencken contemporaneously saw U.S. literature as being enriched and indeed consolidated around the contributions of foreign tongues and contact-zone dialects, Dos Passos wants the destabilizing effects of Baroja's writing to disaggregate the very notion of "America" at the core of such theories.

Returning to Blasco Ibáñez, Dos Passos notes that his naturalist novels, previously known only in Spain, now have a "European reputation," and his *Four Horsemen of the Apocalypse* (1916) has "capture[d] the Allied world" (*R* 63). This is a worrisome phenomenon for Dos Passos. Blasco Ibáñez was a political radical, an antimonarchic and anticolonial Republican who was imprisoned and exiled on multiple occasions. In his life in translation, however, he is the prime exemplar of American consumer culture's ability to defang politics and repackage them as banal melodrama and popular romance, especially in Hollywood adaptations. This, for Dos Passos, is a condemnation of both his writing and American tastes: "it is unfortunate too that Blasco Ibáñez and the United States should have discovered each other at this moment. They will do each other no good" (*R* 63). Instead of this "inverted Midas" who does not put sufficient thought and labor into his writing—he is just "one more popular novelist"—Dos Passos tells his American readers to look for Baroja, Miguel de Unamuno, Azorín, Ramón del Valle-Inclán, and above all, Machado (*R* 62, 63).

Dos Passos's encounter with Machado affected him for some time, and here his translations are most extensive. He saw that Machado's verse was, as he explains to his Anglo-American readers, "particularly original and personal. In fact, except for the verse of Juan Ramón Jiménez, it would be in America and England rather than in Spain, in [Richard] Aldington and Amy Lowell, that one would find analogous aims and methods" (*R* 71). Machado writes in ordinary speech, he incorporates folk ballads, and he paints poetic landscapes in a manner that "marks an epoch in Spanish poetry" (*R* 71). He achieved this by recasting his own Andalusian origins into a subtly ironic hyper-Castilianism that, like Baroja's work, critiques Castile from within. Dos Passos then prints ten of his translations of Machado's mostly bucolic poems. They are primarily about the rural landscapes of Soria in northeastern Spain, along with a moving poem on the burial of a friend and a tribute to an "Iberian god" who is also a "God of ruin" (*R* 77). But they also paint Castile as the site of a "Dead city of barons / and soldiers and huntsmen / whose portals bear the shields / of a hundred hidalgos," a city "swarm[ed]" by "hungry greyhounds" (*R* 76). With this allusion to *Don Quixote*, Machado conjures a Spain that, as Dos Passos translates, "neither is the past dead, / nor is to-morrow, nor yesterday, written" (*R* 79). Dos Passos's translations are very literal—at times awkwardly literal—with the exception of some small creative changes, such as his converting "casas denigradas" to "blackened houses" and his substitution of words such as "outlands" for specific place names (Extremadura) in Spain. Where Pound sought to recreate his own poetic voice and the *Poema del Cid*'s together, Dos Passos sees translation as a means of channeling bleak description *as* critique in Machado as in Baroja—something he will soon attempt to imitate.

Dos Passos's panorama of literary Spain concludes with portraits of the poet Joan Maragall and the playwright Jacinto Benavente. Maragall, a language reformer and intellectual, was central to the rebirth of the Catalan language after its "nearly four centuries of subjection to Castile," and Dos Passos believes that his verses make it hard to explain "how all our desires lay towards the completer and completer affirming of the individual, that we in Anglo-Saxon countries felt that the family was dead as a social unit, that new cohesions were in the making" (*R* 87). Benavente's plays exude the pure essence of Castilianism known as *casticismo*, embodying an arrogant, elitist claim to represent "all that is acutely indigenous, Iberian, in the life of Castile," a "refuge" from the country's homogenizing industrialism (*R* 94). In the contrast that Dos Passos draws between Maragall and Benavente, it is clear which he prefers: the regional poet who took part in a provincial rebirth by reaching back to the "Langue d'Oc" is better than even the anti-industrialist playwright in Madrid. Here again, we see him implicitly rebutting Howells, for the novelists that Howells admired were also provincial—Galdós was born in the Canary Islands, Pardo Bazán was a Galician aristocrat, and Palacio Valdés was Asturian—but they had assimilated, in Dos Passos's eyes, to a centralized national Spanish culture. Dos Passos's regionalist writers aimed to disintegrate that culture from within it.

Dos Passos, who continues by describing the funeral in Madrid of Fernando Giner de los Ríos and by profiling Unamuno briefly, had stumbled upon one of the great ironies in critical elevation of the men (all men) of Spain's Generation of '98: the term was coined and most often circulated by writers with conservative or even protofascist convictions, yet the writers that it encircled, as often as not, ranged anywhere from radical leftism to liberal humanism. Four years later, Waldo Frank, who had outlined his own plan for U.S. regeneration in *Our America* (1919), would grapple with these same questions in his *Virgin Spain* (1926), which profiles many of the writers and intellectuals that *Rosinante* featured. Frank, who believed that the War of 1898 had given "birth to a new spirit in Spain, and to Imperialism in the United States," offered more of a Blakean, prophetic, and mystical vision of Spain that largely accepted Spanish critics' emblems of organic unity couched in sublime rhetoric.[60] He treats politics very little, and when he does, he encourages Catalans, for example, *not* to separate from Castile: in the "Spanish drama of which the Catalans, even in their apartness, must be part," he writes, "Spain has a dawning will to break from the unity which its will created: her atoms, anarchic but pregnant, stir to be loosed and to begin again. . . . Now [the] resistance of the Catalans, even if it disrupts, may serve to create Spain again."[61] Dos Passos refined and reinforced his own portrait of Spain in his objections to Frank's, which he believed turned Spain into a "static elaborate monument." Frank's "psychological phraseology" was nothing but "mere ornamental verbiage" that reduces Spain to an ahistorical abstraction instead of conveying the "confused and confusing tragedy of the Spain of our day." Instead, Dos Passos insisted, Frank should have discussed the "whole tangled welter of industrial and working class politics through which Spain . . . is being tricked, seduced perhaps, into the howling pandemonium of the new world" of Euro-American commercialism, along with the "bloody farce of the Moroccan war" and Spain's divided internal politics.[62] To defend his version of Spain's fragmented wholeness was, for Dos Passos, to defend his self-crafted mantle as authoritative voice on Spanish literature and politics against Frank's increasing respect as a leftist Hispanophile.

Spanish Fragmentation and the Reassembly of Dos Passos's America

Dos Passos's clearest creative attempt to channel his vision of Spain was his volume of poetry *A Pushcart at the Curb*, which appeared in 1922 as an unstated companion volume to *Rosinante*. Here, Machado's influence, and to a lesser degree Baroja's, is visible, and the book features a sequence called "Winter in Castile" that bears a number of similarities to Machado's seminal collection *Campos de Castilla* (*The Landscape of Castile*, 1912).[63] Dos Passos later reflected (and revised his own history), in a foreword to a volume of English translations of Machado's poetry, that when he was learning Spanish, he "carried Machado's *Campos de Castilla* with a dictionary around in my pocket for months. Even today [in 1957] when I try to dredge up some Spanish, it is Machado's Castilian that I remember."[64] Machado's portraits of Spain's central, dominant province of Castile are brutal. He writes in "Along the Banks of the Duero River":

> Wretched Castile, once supreme,
> now wrapped in rags, haughty in her ignorance. . . .
> Castile, no longer the generous state of old
> when Rodrigo of Vivar, el Cid, rode triumphant.[65]

Across dozens of poems that depict the poverty of ordinary Spaniards and the betrayals of the peasantry by the government in Madrid, the Andalusian Machado (who himself was a translator of English literature) elevated the rural Castilian town of Soria, on the banks of the Duero, as a true center of human power and potential. He asks,

> Vigorous Castile, austere land,
> Castile which scorns luck,
> Castile of grief and of war,
> immortal land, Castile of death! . . .
> Like you, Duero, will Castile,
> perhaps, flow forever down toward the sea?[66]

The downfall of Castile is linked, for Machado, to the possibility of multiple Spains that Dos Passos carried further. In terms that would characterize early twentieth-century Spain for a generation of his compatriots, and that marked Dos Passos's sense of Old and New Spain too, Machado writes:

> Now there is a Spaniard who wants
> to live and is beginning to live
> between a Spain that is dying
> and another Spain that is yawning.
> May God keep you, little Spaniard,
> just now born into the world.
> One of these two Spains
> will freeze your heart.[67]

Machado's works, in effect, poeticize the internal ruptures and fragmentation of Spain that he witnessed, and they find their unity in a spiritualized, naturalistic power he sees in rural spaces. Through archetypal, folkloric, and biblical figures, he recounts a national history that becomes a universal leftist and populist critique. The dichotomies he sketches became personal when the Spanish Civil War broke out in 1936: Machado was an icon of Republican culture, while his brother, the poet Manuel Machado, sided with the Nationalists.

With a similar spirit but without the stark language, Dos Passos's poems in *Pushcart* are mostly brief portraits of scenes of rural Spanish life. The subjects include farmers, mule-boys, beggars, milkmen, plowmen, a "scissors grinder," a sailor with "scarred brown cheeks," and "women with market-baskets / stuffed with green vegetables, / men with blankets on their shoulders / and brown sunwrinkled faces."[68] Village plazas with music, sausages, and old women selling chestnuts populate the series of impressionistic scenes, and they are juxtaposed with descriptions of ceremonies, funerals, and age-old rituals. The poems have no narrative but rather function by emplacing these quotidian traditions in Spain's history by way of allusions to the sites in Spain where, for example, "knights" fought the "darkskinned Moors" in language replete with Dos Passos's signature compound words (*P* 47). Dos Passos recalls the "strata" of civilizations and the "layered ages" of Spain that fascinated him when he speaks of

> the old strong towers that the Moors built
> on the ruins of a Roman camp
> have sprung into spreading boisterous foam
> of daisies and alyssum flowers.
>
> (*P* 47)

In Spain, he believes, Greek gods inhabit modern life next to beggars and prostitutes; the "bells of Castile" sound across millennia of cultural mixing that modern nationalism cannot contain (*P* 30). His portraits of Castile do not approach the critiques that Machado lodged; rather, they ambivalently acknowledge the state's enduring symbolic power. Castile's bells still sound strong, without a voice against them, from "unshakeable square towers," while the towers built by the Moors whom Castile pushed out are "crumbled and doddering" (*P* 30, 47). Nor does Dos Passos's poem on the Tagus River imbue it with the power of Machado's Duero. Dos Passos does attempt, however, to compose briefly in Spanish in "Nochebuena" (referring to the night of Christmas Eve). This poem captures the cadences and frenzy of a festival in Madrid by repeating "*Esta noche es noche buena / nadie piensa a dormir*" ("Tonight is *nochebuena* / Nobody thinks of sleeping") (*P* 45).

The effects of Dos Passos's experiences in Spain on his prose were less straightforward and more diffuse. During his time abroad, Dos Passos revised his antiwar novel *Three Soldiers* (1920), whose controversially gritty, realistic, and antiromantic portrait of modern warfare, while not tied to Spain, evinces the military side of his critique.[69] More famously, the narrative shape of *Manhattan Transfer* (1925) manifests what Dos Passos praised in the aesthetic practices of Spanish writers of the left. As Frank's *City Block* (1922) undertook on a smaller scale, it disaggregates the metropolis of New York, rendering it in parts often inhabited by unassimilated immigrant laborers who relish their native cultures, languages, accents, and practices beneath the homogeneity of the city's capitalist culture. Thus, while *Manhattan Transfer* continues the manner of social realism that Dos Passos had been crafting in his prose for nearly a decade, its form and structure owe something to—and bear distinct similarities to—both *Rosinante* and *Pushcart*, alongside its more frequently commented similarities to cinematic montage. The novel is full of characters who, like the *golfos* (rogues, scoundrels) of the Baroja trilogy that Dos Passos praised, are scarcely able to make a living, turn away from or are ruined by financial success, or, in the case of Jimmy Herf, ultimately leave New York. Dos Passos employs what became identified as a signature modernist fragmentation of plot and narrative alongside distorted dialogue and revolutionary politics, all in the hope of superseding the works of the previous generation of realists—in the United States, in Spain, and around the world—that Howells had characterized. Emblematically, when several characters discuss the Great War and cast it as a battle among plutocrats and their empires, Congo Jake, a nomadic peg-legged sailor, remarks that he "wont go" to fight for the United States because a "workingman has no country." He explains, "I'm going to be American citizen. I was in the marine once but . . . Twentee tree. Moi je suis anarchiste vouz comprennez monsieur." In a mixture of pidgin English and pidgin French, Congo Jake argues that "You know why they have this here war[: . . .] So that workingmen all over wont make big revolution. . . . Too busy fighting."[70] Bearing out a position that fuses Baroja's politics with those of the Lyrical Left, Congo Jake both resists the homogenizing effects of New York City capitalism and, in the end, accepts them: he becomes wealthy as a bootlegger during Prohibition, changes his name to Armand Duval, and adopts a new life with a starlet wife.

As Dos Passos continued agitating and advocating for the international left, he returned, in scattered places, to the topics this chapter has addressed. After a trip to Mexico in which he met awkwardly with the country's vanguard writers, for example, he briefly revived his work as a Spanish translator with a version of Manuel Maples Arce's "Urbe: superpoema bolchevique en cinco cantos" (Urbe: super-Bolshevik poem in five cantos, 1924).[71] Tying it to his own fiction, Dos Passos titled the translation "Metropolis" (the same as the title of part 2 of *Manhattan Transfer*).[72] He felt little had changed in U.S. literature by 1931, when he translated and illustrated Blaise Cendrars's *Panama* from the French; in his foreword, he noted that "in America . . . poetry . . . has, after Masters, Sandburg and the Imagists, subsided again into parlor entertainment for high-school English classes."[73] He answered a questionnaire the following year, "Whither the American Writer?", by delineating a new genealogy of "proletarian literature in America" through Dreiser, Anderson, London, and even Walt Whitman, all of whom he cordoned off securely from the field of what he saw as increasingly oppressive Communist Party aesthetic dictates.[74] Several years later, in "The Course of Empire," the first scene of act 2 of Dos Passos's play *Fortune Heights* (1933), a "bum" takes a historical-prophetic view that returns to Dos Passos's earlier critiques: "We're headed for collapse. . . . There was the Egyptians and the Babylonians, and then there was Greece and Rome . . . the cyclic depressions got 'em and they went under. . . . Look at Napoleon and the British Empire, now; and now we're the greatest country in the world, but we're goin' under."[75] As an evolving answer to "Against American Literature," and one that contains plenty of untranslated Spanish and contortions of both English and other tongues around one another, the *U.S.A.* trilogy (1930–1936)—whose working title was *Course of Empire*—also contains conversations too numerous to detail among characters who believe that the United States is the new declining Roman Empire and not the heterogeneous Greek culture that Dos Passos idealized.[76] But where Dos Passos saw hope in the fact that "there are many Spains," his resigned, pithy comment on Sacco and Vanzetti—"all right we are two nations"—takes no solace in heterogeneity.[77]

Dos Passos, who loved to call himself "a man without a country" as he gained an international following, returned to Spain, with great optimism, in 1933 to observe the Second Republic, the liberal-leftist coalition government elected in 1931. His work had received a great deal of acclaim in Spain: in the much-debated issue of the leading journal *La Gaceta Literaria* in which Guillermo de Torre launched the debate on Madrid as the "intellectual meridian" of Spanish America, *Manhattan Transfer* was named "one of the best novels produced by the new North American literature [*la nueva literatura norteamericana*]."[78] Robles's translation of *Manhattan Transfer* was followed by *Rosinante to the Road Again* in Spanish in 1930, and the latter garnered its own notoriety; Dos Passos himself contributed a Spanish foreword to this printing.[79] Julián Gorkin's *10 novelistas americanos* (1932) described Dos Passos as one of the preeminent writers of the rising U.S. left and "one of the most modern novelists" in the world.[80] If he hoped that his own career would be part of the new version of "American literature" coming to life abroad, in politically charged and unfamiliar ways, Dos Passos had plenty of evidence to affirm that a new workers' state in Spain was reading and absorbing his aesthetics and critiques.

But on this trip, in which he interviewed both the Republic's first prime minister Manuel Azaña and Unamuno, Dos Passos did not find the inspiration he hoped for in the new Republic. Instead, in long articles that explored the history of socialism in Spain, he detailed the infighting and corruption that Stalin's interference only exacerbated.[81] His disillusion with the left, which had been festering for years, was finalized in 1937 when Robles, who was fighting for the Republican side, was murdered, allegedly by Stalin's agents.[82] Dos Passos backed out of his collaboration with Hemingway as a writer for Joris Ivens's *The Spanish Earth* (1937), a propagandistic film about Spaniards' suffering under Franco, and published an article, "Farewell to Europe!" (1937), in which he dismissed his earlier idealizations of Spain and placed his faith only in a conservative vision of America. He still believed, as he titled one of his dispatches from the civil war, that "The Villages Are the Heart of Spain," but his new politics were cemented. His father's ideals of Anglo-Saxon democracy are couched in slightly different terms here as Dos Passos, while arguing that the Communist Party betrayed the working class of Spain, sees the blueprint of a future of peace and individual liberty in "everything we have ever wanted since the first hard winters at Plymouth."[83] In other words, Spain's failure to become an ideal, stable leftist republic condemns all of Europe for Dos Passos, who then rewrites his own political past. His experiences in Spain therefore solidified both the leftism of his youth and the turn to the right that would consume the rest of his life. As Jon Smith argues, Dos Passos, across his mutable ideologies, "ascribed both his chief hate, the injustice of Anglo-American imperialism and capitalism, and his chief loves, the English language and the Jeffersonian system of democracy, to what he saw as his own and his country's Anglo-Saxon heritage and race destiny."[84] He never lost his conviction that the United States *was* an Anglo-Saxon empire—that this was more than a fiction of national mythology and that its exceptionalism was in some way legitimate—and he revaluated it against the course of Spanish political and literary history from the 1910s through the 1930s, in which Spain is alternately America's unamalgamated, aspirational, and cautionary forebear.

II
Spain's American Translations

CHAPTER 3

Jiménez, Modernism/o, and the Languages of Comparative Modernist Studies

> *When I came to the United States in 1916, I was writing my book of free verse* Diary of a Newlywed Poet *[1917], and I was still under the influence of a month of difficult navigation on the high seas and of my poetic memory of Unamuno. I had no idea that the New York that awaited me would have a stack of books also awaiting me, by poets who expressed themselves in forms analogous to my own: [Robert Frost's]* North of Boston, *[E. A. Robinson's]* The Man Against the Sky, *[Edgar Lee Masters's]* Spoon River Anthology, *[Vachel Lindsay's]* The Congo, *[Amy Lowell's]* Sword Blades and Poppy Seed, *[Edna St. Vincent Millay's]* Renascence and Other Poems, *and more. Being reborn [renaciendo] myself during those years, I felt this rebirth of American poetry as if it were my own—much as I did the rebirth of Spanish poetry in this moment.*
> —JUAN RAMÓN JIMÉNEZ, *Política poética*

JUAN RAMÓN JIMÉNEZ BELIEVED THAT THE MOMENT IN which he was "reborn" in American poetry in 1916 was but one point of intersection—though a very important one—in a centuries-old history of poetic innovation that crossed linguistic, national, temporal, and formal boundaries. He wrote himself into an English-language movement in the United States, one that he believed flourished symbiotically with Spanish poetry after 1898. In the experimental semiepic he composed during this trip, *Diario de un poeta recién casado* (*Diary of a Newlywed Poet*, 1917), he shifted among *modernismo*, U.S. modernism, Parnassianism, Spanish postromanticism, "mystical modernism," and more, in an attempt to make himself poetically a part of movements in several languages across time, not by imitating or by adopting foreign influences alone but by combining citations, allusions, translations, and translingual practices. In doing so, Jiménez both initiates and complicates some of the prevailing methodological and linguistic questions that have marked the critical histories of modernist studies in English and in Spanish. In his writings over the next four decades, Jiménez put "modernism"—as a term, a concept, and a historical or period designation—at the center of a centuries-old tension between the two languages. As he wove together expanded variations on *modernismo* and Anglophone modernism in translations and in classrooms, Jiménez formulated an idea of their imbrication and of the diverging, persisting gaps between them. Lamenting over a half-century ago that "*modernismo* has been studied in clichés, platitudes . . . with ideas accepted as conventional wisdom by critics too lazy to do the work of untangling them," Jiménez used the Spanish word *modernismo* to denote a polyglot genealogy of literature and thought that signifies something similar to what many Anglophone critics now mean by "modernism" as a worldly phenomenon.[1] He thus offers contemporary scholars both a way to address the familiar senses of the *modernismo* and modernism in correlation and an opportunity to recast them around one another in the dynamic, uneven spheres of international translation and circulation.

We can do so by framing modernism and *modernismo* through Jiménez's own career. He was one of Spain's leading poets for a majority of the 1910s and 1920s and was later a Nobel laureate, and he is traditionally seen in Spanish literary history as a bridge between the end of the *modernismo* of Rubén Darío and beginnings of the Generation of '27, which included Federico García Lorca, Jorge Guillén, and Rafael Alberti. His *Diary*, which was written in what he saw as the literary wake of the Spanish-American War, is an experiential, multigeneric text, a "provisional" work (as Jiménez calls it) that was also an early text in the archive of American literary studies in Spain. Jiménez, furthermore, was in a privileged position to think about modernism across English and Spanish: he began his career by helping spread *modernismo* across Spain in the early 1900s; he came to the United States during the formation of the poetic movement that soon would be named "modernism"; he collaborated with two of the most consequential thinkers on *modernismo*, Federico de Onís and Ricardo Gullón, between the 1930s and 1950s; he was a prominent *hispanista* who sharply critiqued the political grounds of *hispanismo*'s international project; and he was a professor and scholar in exile in the United States in the 1940s and 1950s, when the English term "modernism" was consolidated into a dominant conception and an emerging field that relegated *modernismo* (against Jiménez's understandings) to a restricted and minor movement in Hispanophone letters.[2]

This chapter therefore reconstructs three critical nodes in a historical network of modernisms: the early history and philology of *modernismo* in Spain between the 1880s and the early 1900s, the translational poetics of Jiménez's *Diary*, and Jiménez's theories of *modernismo* and multiple modernisms. Taken together, these nodes and their commerce prompt us to write, as Jiménez argues we must, literary histories of texts in motion, never settled, always translating and translated—histories *of* literary motion between languages and places (replicating the journey that *Diary* embodies), not histories of sites and productions alone. That is to say, translation here does not produce settled maps or chronologies of exchange but interlingual tensions that instead point up a diffuse schematic in which literature mediates geopolitics. Jiménez traces modernism, for instance, through French symbolism, but immediately argues that "symbolism is wrongly called 'French,' because France copied it from the United States [through readings of Poe], Germany [above all Wagner], and Spain. . . . St. John of the Cross in the great translation done by the monk of Solesmes."[3] In addition, Jiménez not only sees "Castilian mysticism" present in French symbolism but also asks if anything is "more symbolist" than the Arabic-Andalusian poetry of medieval southern Spain. Jiménez argues that *modernismo* and many other modernisms were continually reshaped together unequally and surprisingly, in ways that are ultimately impossible to assimilate across languages. He specifically presses on the theoretical and historical quandaries highlighted by leading Hispanists of his day in order to posit a broad, underacknowledged relationship between Anglo- and Hispanophone poetics that developed through the shared and paradoxically energizing post-1898 circumstances of Spain, the United States, and Spanish America.

With such thought, and with his poetry and translations too, Jiménez became a vital but often neglected Hispanist and Americanist. His idea of the *modernismo*/modernism conjunction in a shifting world republic of letters is potent in its comparativity, yet, toward the end of this chapter, I take up the drawbacks of his approach. Jiménez, for example, militates against the Anglophone critical impulse to assimilate the "modernisms" of diverse linguistic traditions but retains a faith in the explanatory power of notions of national races, linguistic heritages, and mutual compatibility. Elsewhere, he is variously familiar and routine, unexpected and defamiliarizing, Hispanophilic and sometimes plainly self-serving. In his case, empire—as we will see more pointedly in Unamuno (chapter 4)—is translated into a cultural patrimony forged by connections that often erase or repress political and social histories of domination, with war sublimated into cultural reciprocity. In reviving a term that was worn out almost before it had currency, rewriting Spain as an origin of a global movement that was predicated on Spain's status as a postimperial intellectual wasteland, and reconfiguring postcolonial movements to expand the cognates of "modernism," Jiménez offers a challenge to rethink modernism as constituted by never-completed, asymmetrical, and asymptotic processes of translation.[4] My aim, then, is not to recover a chapter in a history of transnational modernisms, nor to add Jiménez to a global modernist canon; rather, I use his work and his poetic figure to reconsider both the segmented and connected ways in which we historicize modernisms and the literary-geopolitical systems from which they appear to have emerged.

Naming *Modernismo*—in 1890 and in the Twenty-First Century

In the past two decades, the origins and the constitution of Hispanophone *modernismo* have been debated as robustly—and often with similar political stakes—as those of Anglophone modernism and many other roughly coeval movements around the world. Traditional literary histories suggest the following: *modernismo* was a movement originating in the Spanish American world of the 1880s, arguably initiated by the Cuban poet José Martí. It was crystallized in the Nicaraguan writer Rubén Darío's *Azul . . .* (Azure . . . , 1888) and given its name in an 1890 essay of Darío's, and then it faded in the 1910s with the rise of the avant-gardes and the death of Darío in 1916. It blended European and local sources to react against naturalism and positivism, and it was highlighted by writers such as Julián del Casal, Salvador Díaz-Mirón, Manuel Gutiérrez Nájera, and José Asunción Silva. Generally speaking, it privileged ornate, strictly rhymed, and formally complex verse, and its sensibilities were spiritualist, angst ridden, mythological, and escapist, full of ennui and enervation inherited in part from Verlaine and Baudelaire. After gaining momentum across Spanish America, it then spread surprisingly and against much resistance to Spain, where Jiménez and Antonio Machado, among others, adopted it.[5]

Despite their thematic, formal, epistemological, technical, and philosophical parallels, *modernismo* and Anglophone modernism have proven difficult to link discretely, and their relationship has remained a vexing issue for critics in both Spanish and English. Octavio Paz best framed the reasons why the movement has been elusive for historians, such as its peculiarly "antimodern modernity" and its cosmopolitanism blended with indigenous elements.[6] Gerard Aching explains that *modernismo* has been isolated amid the fields of modernist studies, comparative literature, and world literature often because of a lack of scholarly understanding of both its engagements with Paris—which embrace derivation while sometimes rejecting the Old World—and the politics of its New World elitist aestheticism.[7] Furthermore, *modernismo* was waning just as Anglophone high modernism, the movement that came to dominate the sign "modernism," was cresting, and contacts among writers from these movements were relatively sparse. As Alejandro Mejías-López and Mary Lee Bretz have pointed out, *modernismo* has been sometimes included, other times excluded from Anglophone accounts of (implicitly Euro-American) "modernism," or it has been described, in somewhat misleading terms, as "Spanish-American modernism" or "Hispanic modernism."[8] A quarter-century ago, Astradur Eysteinsson claimed on the first page of *The Concept of Modernism* (1990) that the differences between modernism and *modernismo* were "too many to warrant their critical coalescence."[9] The two-volume synoptic *Modernism* collection that he and Vivian Liska edited in 2007, however, devotes a chapter to it as a constituent international modernism.[10]

Meanwhile, a number of Spanish-language critics have resisted situating *modernismo* within paradigms of global modernisms that have been defined almost exclusively by their Anglo-American peers, worrying that the term loses its distinction in such an imperializing gesture.[11] *Modernismo*—both as a movement and as a term—predated the English-language modernism that, in its expanded definitions, has often tried to subsume it. Hispanophone critics have pointed out, too, the linguistic challenge that the *modernismo*/modernism question presents their scholarship. In English, it suffices to write *modernismo* (adding an "o" and using italics) to indicate a different object of study than the familiar (Anglo-American) modernism, but Spanish-language critics working in Anglo-dominant contexts must continually specify their references to *modernismo* as opposed to *modernismo británico, modernismo norteamericano, modernismo anglosajón* (literally, "Anglo-Saxon," but with the sense of "Anglophone"), or "modernism" (in quotation marks, with an explanation of the referent). The Brazilian avant-garde of the 1920s is also known in Portuguese and Spanish by the same polymorphous term, *modernismo*, while a related Catalan movement was *modernisme*, both of which prompt further investigation of its definitional divisions that I cannot address adequately here. More than a movement, then, a name and a conceptualization of literary history are at stake here.

Jiménez's early-career role as a Spanish *modernista* and his debt to Darío have been noted; likewise, he is known for having incorporated many foreign sources, Anglophone and otherwise, in his poetry.[12] In 1900, as a poet still in his teens, he received an invitation from Rubén Darío, who had just come to Madrid, to help "fight for the cause of *modernismo*."[13] Jiménez enthusiastically signed on; he called Darío "maestro" and "el modernista ideal," and he attacked the Madrileño press for its resistance to Darío's work.[14] He secured from Darío a dedicatory sonnet as prologue for his new collection of poetry, *Ninfeas* (1900); Darío asks him, "Do you have your armor, my young friend, / so that we can begin our courageous, divine battle?"[15] But what exactly was this cause he would fight for, and why was it called "*modernismo*," that name that still confounds its reception? And what did the term mean in Spain at the time?

Darío's work reinvented the Spanish poetic idiom by infusing it with foreign syntax and prosody, as Pound would do with English poetry two decades later, and by breaking the hendecasyllabic style popular since Garcilaso de la Vega in the sixteenth century. Elevating formal autonomy, he wrote, "I seek a form that my style cannot discover, / a bud of thought that wants to be a rose."[16] He called this form and this style *modernismo*: in a now-famous line from 1890, he wrote in the Barcelona-based review *La Ilustración* that the Peruvian writer Ricardo Palma "understands and contemplates with amazement the new spirit that, today, animates a small but triumphant and proud group of writers and poets of Spanish America: el *modernismo*."[17] Darío adopted the term from bohemian Parisian culture, where *modernisme* had been reappropriated in the 1860s and 1870s from a condemnation of faddishness to a celebration of antitraditional culture.[18] Soon, *modernisme* and its cognates were being applied to movements all around the world, from *art nouveau* and *Jugendstil* to the Catalan *Renaixença*, and to figures like Baudelaire, Wilde, and Sarah Bernhardt. Darío noticed that Spanish America had been left out of the discussion of what it meant to be modern—as had Castilian Spain. Here he found his entrée for critiquing what he saw as the highly academicized, worn-out version of romanticism that reigned at the center of Spain's decaying empire. Moreover, across the 1880s, the term *modernismo* had been used with great frequency in Spain, almost always pejoratively.

It was associated with both a growing heretical movement from within the Catholic Church and a blind following of all things chic in Paris, as the poet and journalist Eusebio Blasco lamented in his report *El modernismo en Francia* (1886).[19]

Modernismo, that is, gathered both the Spanish American challenge to Europe and Europe's internal challenges to reigning paradigms of art, philosophy, and religion—and including Spain's fears of France's aesthetic avant-garde.[20] As Matei Călinescu writes, for Darío, the "refreshing, 'modernizing' French influence (combining the major postromantic trends, Parnassian, decadent, and symbolist) was consciously and fruitfully played off against the old rhetorical clichés that prevailed in the Spanish literature of the time."[21] For Cathy Jrade, "in choosing this label, Darío . . . affirmed that what he and his fellow writers were attempting to do was to establish a mode of discourse commensurate to the new era that Spanish America had entered" and "to leave behind—either through their travels or their imagination—an anachronistic, local reality" and a vanished colonial history.[22] The bourgeois modernity that bohemian Parisians had mocked with *modernisme* now signaled what Darío saw as a claim to legitimacy to speak about the modern from sites deemed antimodern.[23] *Modernismo* invoked the creation of a tradition and the embrace of liberal, antipositivist, even sensual attitudes in a space—Spanish America—that was denied access to the traditions of the putative mother country. It was therefore both familiar and foreign, constantly unsettled and resisting attempts to imbue it with Old World historical prestige.

Darío's route to conquering literary Spain was through Paris, which already held cultural dominion over Madrid to a large degree. As Mariano Siskind argues, Darío controversially crafted a "deliberate and sophisticated construction of French universality as a cosmopolitan horizon of modernization for Latin America," one so invested in Paris that his Spanish American peers feared that he was further denigrating the New World.[24] Darío wrote that

> I, who know Baralt's *Dictionary of Gallicisms* by heart, realized that not just a well-chosen Gallicism but also certain particularities from other languages might be extremely useful, might even be of incomparable efficacy in a certain type of "transplant." Thus, my knowledge of English, of Italian, of Latin were to serve later in the pursuit of my literary ends.[25]

When Darío published *Azul*... in 1888, the Spanish novelist and critic Juan Valera wrote an often-cited and pivotal review in which he coined a term, "mental Gallicism," to describe the process by which Darío had fashioned his literary self. The title of the volume itself came from Darío's reading of Victor Hugo while in San Salvador: Hugo had written that "*L'Art c'est l'azur*," and Darío interpreted this as a claim for aesthetic autonomy: "blue, azure, was for me the color of daydreams, the color of art, a Hellenic, Homeric color, a color oceanic and firmamental."[26] "Azul" wasn't simply a translated term from French, though; it also signified in Spanish idioms. As Ilan Stavans points out, *cuentos azules* are "fairy tales," and a *príncipe azul* is a Prince Charming. This cross-linguistic synthesis ranges from the title to the syntax, prosody, prose grammar, and self-reflexivity of the collection itself. Valera's review, even though full of condescension, opened the door to *Azul*... 's overtaking Spain, and it was through an engagement with his Spanish reviewers, whose criticisms he would incorporate in prefaces and subsequent editions of his works, that Darío created his persona as chief *modernista*. Valera, with tongue in cheek, praised Darío's cosmopolitanism and noted that the Nicaraguan was "Parisian chic" but with a love of the classics and a knowledge of "all European modernity."[27] He addressed Darío personally and accused him, in essence, of wantonly raiding elements of European cultures, including Spain's, for his own poetic purposes, without a sense of their literary histories. Darío and *modernismo* also met with great resistance from a rearguard nativist reaction in Spain that attacked the movement as unrooted, pagan, mystical, and ahistorical.[28] The Royal Spanish Academy's dictionary dismissed the term as soon as it acknowledged it, calling *modernismo* an excessive "fixation on modern things with a disdain for the old, especially in art and literature."[29] Marcelino Menéndez y Pelayo balked at the movement's supposed ingratitude and irreverence toward Spanish culture. *Modernismo* was savagely ridiculed in the Spanish press. The writer Clarín (Leopoldo Alas) nicknamed Darío "D. Zabulón" or "D. Simeón" in his caricatures; others called him "Rubén Rubí" because of his interest in rubies and decadence. In his poem "El Modernismo. Fábula" (1902), Manuel del Palacio ventriloquized a *modernista* mockingly named Silvestre Boberías, who says that he cares not whether he is praised or censured, only that his name is known. In other words, *modernistas* were grubbing for cheap celebrity—a charge Darío embraced just as Baudelaire and Rimbaud had.[30]

The *modernistas* eventually won: Emilia Pardo Bazán's sympathetic criticism was instrumental, Pedro Henríquez Ureña explicated and defended the movement, and Amado Nervo declared convincingly that Spanish Americans were bringing fresh, superior literature to a stagnant Spanish scene. Soon, Spanish literary giants of the so-called Generation of '98, including Jacinto Benavente, Ramón del Valle-Inclán, and Antonio Machado, adopted *modernista* styles themselves. Thus, *modernismo* performed what Mejías-López has called an "inverted conquest": a postcolonial literature, arguably for the first time in history, swept across the former colonizer's literary world. (It was "the return of the galleons," one critic wrote in 1930.)[31] And it did so in a moment when Spain still dominated the literary markets of Spanish America—even while Spain itself was dominated literarily by France.[32] Darío was unabashed yet cynical: in 1905, he wrote that "the liberating movement that I happened to initiate in the Americas has spread to Spain, where . . . its triumph is assured, . . . [but] tomorrow we could all become Yankees (this seems most likely); my protest stands, regardless, inscribed on the wings of immaculate swans, illustrious as Jupiter."[33]

As Darío's fear of the "Yankee" indicates, he saw *modernismo* as partly a response to an altered geopolitical landscape. His and the movement's victory in Spain depended crucially on Darío's reading of the Spanish literary scene as the expression of a dying, blind empire. Darío himself did not spend much time in Spain until 1898, a decade after *Azul . . .* , when he was sent by an Argentine newspaper to write on the aftermath of the Spanish-American War. (His previous trip had coincided with the celebrations of *raza* in 1892.) He published a collection of articles and studies for the newspaper *La Nación* in Buenos Aires, *España contemporánea* (*Contemporary Spain*, 1901), in which he characterized the "atmosphere" in Madrid as "the last sigh of a decomposed organism" and enumerated its leading writers and intellectuals as variously "dead," "blind," "ill," and "disillusioned."[34] Darío also lamented the barriers to foreign literature that remain high in Spain: traditionalism and nativist Hispanism, he believed, have resisted "the inflowing of any cosmopolitan breath, and have also prevented any individual broadening, or liberty, or . . . anarchism in art—which is the foundation of the modern or modernist evolution."[35] He went so far as to ask his fellow Spanish Americans to pity Spain's decline as sympathetic Hispanic brethren. Darío noted in an article, "El crepúsculo de España" (The twilight of Spain, 1898), as he "watched the Yankees tear [Spain] apart," that

> Spain no longer has even a handful of dirt in the Americas, and she came very close to being forgotten by the American nations of her own blood and tongue, which now speak with one common voice. There is an experience common to these nations that the impoverished motherland must take into account beginning today, and which, in this twilight moment, will make her fix her eyes and place her hands on the cold, hard truth. Spain has wanted to remain enclosed within its many Great Walls. . . . A blind megalomania has influenced its spiritual leaders and the majority of its intellectuals, who have preserved the ancient armor without putting any bodies inside it. . . . Now is the hour of Twilight.[36]

He argues that it rests with the youth of Spain—poets such as Jiménez—to regenerate the country through "contacts with the universal breath" of foreign peoples and languages, which will allow the "Spanish spirit" to persist and then grow within the "light of the world."[37]

Furthermore, what is called *modernismo* came from the New World, Darío writes, because unlike "Castilian Spain," he argues, "our immediate material and spiritual commerce with the many nations of the world [produced it], and there is, in the new Spanish American generation, an immense desire for progress" since "the living force of a continent" is triumphing over tradition.[38] Where Valera had mourned that New World independence movements had broken up the Spanish Empire and had caused Spain's internal decadence, Darío countered and celebrated that "our modernism, if it can be called that, is beginning to give us a place apart, a place that is independent of Castilian literature," a spirit that is felt even in Catalonia, home to *modernisme*, but distinctly not in Madrid, which was a site of only "Silence. Stagnation."[39] Here, Darío bequeathed an ambivalent legacy to his fellow and future *modernistas*. Indeed, he asserted that the movement itself, *as* a movement, did not even matter that much to him. Only its "anarchic aesthetic" did, and he warned that "whoever obsequiously follows in my footsteps will lose his personal treasure."[40] His pan-Hispanism, which at once affirmed and denied the centrality of his Spanish American origins—he was even charged by his fellow *modernista* José Enrique Rodó with being anti-American—and his bifurcated thoughts on the United States, Whitman, and Theodore Roosevelt did not make him an easy forebear to adopt. With an understanding of the death of Spain, the interconnections of Spanish America, and the entwined rise of the United States, Darío effectively left a productively unstable signifier of *modernismo* that Jiménez would pick up in both his poetry and his critical writings and would manipulate for decades.

From *Modernismo* to Tagore to New York

Jiménez, in joining the *modernista* fight in Spain, was signing on just as the movement was waning and changing course, even as it was realizing its victory in Spain. He believed that he was destined to be the "successor of Rubén Darío, just as Darío was the successor of [Gustavo Adolfo] Bécquer."[41] His narrative of succession is telling: through Bécquer, he shifts the seat of Spanish poetry's historical course of development from Castile and Madrid to Andalusia (his native province), and through Darío, he acknowledges the conquest of Spanish poetry from abroad.[42] He soon spearheaded the founding of the *modernista* periodical *Helios* in 1903, and after he feverishly published eight books of poetry between 1908 and 1912, he became one of the premier poets in Spain. Still frustrated with what he saw as the insular and isolated literary cultures of his native country, he desired a larger, more variegated cultural atmosphere for his work—and like Darío, he wanted to disseminate foreign literatures further in Spain. In *Helios* and in other media, he and his peers published translations from the Anglophone world, whose poetry Jiménez found to be more "concentrated, natural, and everyday"; for him, "English romanticism is the greatest moment of universal romantic poetry."[43] He would seek to extend and historicize the pan-American links between Hispanophone and Anglophone literatures that his *modernista* colleagues had made by linking Spain to the United States, adding to both of them the emphasis on popular, vernacular poetic forms and simplified prose poetry.[44] He abandoned the octosyllabic verses and *romance* styles of his early work in favor of the "denuded" or "pure" song and free verse he would launch in *Diary*.[45]

Despite his successes in Spain, Jiménez's translational poetics only found expression, he felt, once he left his country; he railed, in a critique similar to Dos Passos's: "SPAIN. No more Madrid. In the United States and in Italy—one country Saxon, the other Latin . . . a poet, a scientist, a man can live in Chicago, Boston, New York; Rome, Florence,

Milan . . . But Spain, and France: countries of sad and absurd intellectual centralism!"[46] The "obliged deserter of Andalusia," as he called himself when referring to his marginalized province within Spain, soon found an ideal opportunity for renovating his career: in 1913, he met his future wife Zenobia Camprubí Aymar.[47] The Barcelona-born Camprubí came from a wealthy, distinguished family with roots in Spain, Puerto Rico, and New York. She was fluent in both English and Spanish, studied at Columbia University, and spent a great deal of time at her family's home in New York. Their courtship and relationship was marked by a love of Anglophone literature and the practice of translation. In 1914, as they were collecting English-language books, Jiménez and his "americanita" Camprubí translated Yeats, Blake, Frost, AE, and a great deal of Rabindranath Tagore into Spanish.[48] Here, Jiménez's synthetic revision of *modernismo* took another turn in the 1910s that made his intervention that much more diverse and perhaps surprising to contemporary eyes. His discovery of Tagore was electrifying; he and Camprubí obtained permission from Tagore to become his exclusive, authorized Spanish translators, and Jiménez slowed his own poetic production for the moment. Working from Tagore's own English translations and consulting Gide's French versions at the same time, Jiménez and Camprubí produced an astounding fifteen volumes of Tagore in Spanish in three years and a total of twenty-two volumes between 1914 and 1922.[49] (Jiménez found time, too, to continue his work as a French translator with a Spanish version of Romain Rolland's biography of Beethoven in 1915.) In essence, Jiménez's "rebirth" in U.S. poetry was simultaneously a rebirth through his engagements with Tagore, through a vicarious inhabitation of Tagore's fantastic stardom in the world of Anglophone poetry, and through a practice of translation that saw a universal poetics that superseded any poet's origins. Tagore, in turn, became in translation an important hinge in the post-*modernismo* transitions of Spanish poetry, even beyond Jiménez.[50]

Jiménez's trip to the United States in 1916 to marry Camprubí extended the dynamic of a relationship in which romance, translation, and poetic production were inseparable: much of their honeymoon was spent voraciously collecting and translating books by Poe, Keats, Whitman, Dickinson, Amy Lowell, and many others. They traveled along the East Coast, from Boston to Philadelphia to Baltimore to Washington, and visited the homes and graves of famous American authors; they also frequented places such as New York's Authors' Club and Cosmopolitan

Club, where Jiménez met a number of American poets. This trip took place just as Jiménez's interest in *modernismo* was waning (and, unbeknownst to him, Darío was nearing his death in February 1916) and as he was searching for new modes of expression. At the same time, *modernismo* was being discussed and its writers reviewed in U.S. periodicals with increasing frequency across the 1910s and 1920s, when translations of their works became more widely available. Darío was profiled in the *New Age, Others,* and various academic journals; was treated at length in *Poetry* in 1916; and he gave a powerful antiwar lecture at Huntington's Hispanic Society, where he was awarded a medal.[51] Solidifying his preference for English-language poetry over French, Jiménez veered away from *modernismo* and toward poets ranging from Francis Thompson to Robert Browning to Edna St. Vincent Millay, all of whom "appeared to me more direct, freer, more modern—some in their simplicity, others in their complexity," with what he called a "Northern" musicality and psychological exploration in verse.[52] He later spoke of his 1916 experience:

> And now I understand the benefits of that voyage for me. . . . I was a Platonist, a symbolist, an idealist since childhood, but I wanted to be mature with my current idiom, without Greco-Latinism, without the Italian Renaissance, without French symbolism. I wanted to be Andalusian, Spanish, and universal at the same time, but always of my moment. For this reason, it pleased me to publish my verses in daily papers, where they ought to have been published. In the United States I am always in my moment.[53]

In the United States, Jiménez claims, he seized upon a form and idiom between languages and between places, among his Spanish roots, the success of the poetic-prose minimalism of his popular works such as *Platero y yo* (1914), and his English-language and "universal" preoccupations.

Diary of a Newlywed Poet, *Modernismo*, and Reading U.S. Modernity

The result was a multigeneric and anthological registration of shifts such as these and of his slow release of *modernista* styles. While *Diary of a Newlywed Poet* is credited with having developed a new mode of

Spanish-language symbolism, its internationalist contexts and poetics remain underexplored. The collection of over 240 formal and free-verse poems, prose poems, impressionistic journal entries, aphorisms, reflections on literary histories, imagined dialogues, citations, commentaries on contemporary letters, notes of cultural anthropology, and translations is far from a typical *modernista* work, especially one of the character of the 1890s. It stands at the chronological, generic, and formal edges of *modernismo* and, at the same time, on several borders of Anglophone modernism's then-prevailing trends. The work spans the ten months of Jiménez's transatlantic voyage, his stay in the United States, and his return to southern Spain. His developing poetic being becomes the site of translingual poetic exchanges initiated by the book's Sanskrit epigraph. *Diary* is at different moments linear or recursive, spontaneous or molded into intricate shapes, fluid or fragmented, formal or experimental, with poems titled "No!", "Yes!", and " . . . ?" and with copies of advertisements from American buildings and signs. Some titles are in English; some quotations are given in English and parenthetically translated into Spanish by the poet himself. Its movements across literary history are heterogeneous, too: formal and affective traits of *modernismo* stand next to updated English romanticism.

The schematic structure of *Diary* clarifies some of the ways in which Jiménez sought simultaneously to continue and to renovate the vast, multilingual poetic heritage that was at his back. The first five parts of the book follow his actual journey, the sixth his mental wandering back to the United States; thus, his "rebirth" in U.S. modernism seems presaged from the very start of the book. From the opening section "Hacia el mar" ("Toward the Sea"), set in Jiménez's native Andalusia, we are led to expect a formally conservative collection of poems—simple rhymes, naturalistic imagery. But an anxiety jolts the poet-narrator when (at poem 20) the New World first appears through technology, conjuring for him both excitement and longing: "Two cablegrams: 'Mother, Fiancée: Moguer, Long-Island; Flushing: I am shipwrecked on land in a sea of love'" (*D* 116). Here, Jiménez casts his poetics across languages and geographies with techniques he will employ throughout the collection. The Spanish original includes both a loose sonic turn between "Flushing" and "Naufragué" and a half-rhyme around the consonant "m" in Spanish with "en mar de amor." As he boards the ship in part 2, "El amor en el mar" ("Love at Sea"), he initiates a transatlantic voyage that allows his feelings of love to turn to paralysis in a manner that might seem to move the text toward an established *modernista* existentialism, even nihilism:

> The water, steely gray,
> resembles a harsh stretch of earth
> of mineshafts long dug dry,
> in a devastated area
> of ruins.
>   Nothingness! Here for me today the word
> has found its resting place,
> like a verbal cadaver
> that has laid itself out in its
> natural sepulcher.
> Nothingness!
>
>   (*D* 144)

But just after this seamless shift from a familiar romantic yearning and despair to doubt and anguish, Jiménez can no longer find poetic inspiration around him.[54] He sees no Cervantine "La Mancha of water," only a "desert of liquid fictions" as he imagines Don Quixote trailing into the sunset on the sea. He complains, in late *modernista* language, "What malaise, what thirst, what harsh stupor / amidst this turbulence of sun and cloud, / blueness and moon, of dawn / delayed! / Severe chills. Sharp pain . . . " (*D* 110). The narrative approaches the United States primed for an injection of new material, new forms, new life.

The monotonous voyage finds its contrast in what he calls his "Ideal Arrival" in America, where it "seems like Turner is viewing it alongside us." Here, Turner's name is partially rhymed later in the line with the keyword *venir*, to come. Jiménez's series of poetic masks and morphing voices light on the sublime as the British Turner's watercolors are transported here in the book's first extended prose poem to become the American melting pot, then are blended with symbolic colors of racial diversity. This vision jars him, for it "resembles a song emerging from a dream, with us as its heroes," and it takes him back metaliterarily to romantic poetry, with an allusion to Keats:

> Yes, we are the truth, the beauty, the eternal strophe that endures, captured in the rhyme scheme, in the most beautiful perceived center of an

eternal poetry that we have always been aware of, and with which, anew, we eternally hope to be conversant—is it the second quatrain of a pristine aquatic sonnet?—. Where are we? In what period of time? Out of what novel have we come? Are we a painting? Are we landing?

(*D* 170; translation modified)

The recourse to English romanticism here is not merely an indication of Jiménez's predilections. Spain had only a faint romantic poetic tradition; such allusions fill this gap for Jiménez and inscribe his Spanish verses into a transnational history that he will continue to expand in his critical writings. Form is dominant for him, as it was for Darío; life imitates art, and his poetry arises through the constant sense of being *in* his own art.

This imagined union of life and art is the key to Jiménez's effort to emplot himself into literary history. The union is not easy; he remains disoriented. Lost in his art and in his arrival, he concludes, "my sheet of paper falls from my hand. . . . I don't know how to write any longer" (*D* 172). The wordplay here lies in "*papel*," which is both "a piece of paper" and "a role": he is a poet lost in time and space, without direction, newly arrived in America. These visions of a poetic/fictional self merging into an infinite world continue when Jiménez writes, "I am part of everything, and nothingness is still / only the port of dreams. . . . I am already at the center / in which whatever comes and whatever leaves / combines disillusionments / of arrivals and departures" (*D* 182). Upon arriving in the United States in part 3, he also learns that his one-time mentor Darío has just died in France. Darío's imprint remains large in *Diary*: the word "*azul*" ("blue" or "azure"), which points to Darío's *Azul* . . . , occurs some thirty times. In one prose poem, Jiménez takes up directly his own appearance in English for the first time, when he criticizes the Hispanist James Fitzmaurice-Kelly—the same scholar Pound engaged—for his poor translations of six of Jiménez's poems in the popular *Oxford Book of Spanish Verse* (1913). (Four titles were rendered badly, in fact, and one was changed without consulting the author.) Fitzmaurice-Kelly "baptized me in chromium blue," Jiménez writes, by reducing his complex meditations on color and emotions to a ubiquitous, bland, and misrendered "blue" at every turn, missing the nuances of his allusions to Darío's work (*D* 290).

But Jiménez must now forge his post-Darío reputation, must reconstruct his poetic genealogy, one distinct from his early means of "expressing the crisis of personality through symbolic vocabulary" that was indebted to his forebear.[55] He would differentiate himself by poeticizing his new set of experiences and literary readings—the two remain inseparable for him—in the eastern United States. The hints at a parataxis and blending of Anglo- and Hispanophone worlds that *Diary* has granted thus far will now be fleshed out in his text as more quotations and literary voices merge on the page. This process begins with an exploration of "Physical Culture" and decay among the gritty, smoky landscapes of the American metropolises. In keeping with the literal and figurative transitions that characterize the text, many of the poems in this third section are written from carriages, trains, or taxis. The poet describes an "Urban Tunnel" in Boston as "White and black, but without contrast. Dirty white and dirty black, in a brotherhood of the shabby. . . . Everything is confusion, diffusion, monotony, barren, cold and dirt at one and the same time, white and black, which is to say, black, timeless and incommunicable" (*D* 194). Far removed from the princesses and swans of *modernismo* or Parnassianism, he sees cemeteries, advertisements, and landfills, and his mind turns to Anglophone poetry. While on a train from Boston to New York, he thinks of the "false" and artificial poetry of the "New England poets" whom he did not appreciate: "Longfellow, Lowell, Bryant, Aldrich—a cloudless green sky. Without trees." They were the poets, in other words, who could create nothing from the barren American landscape. Jiménez calls to mind instead those who can; he quotes (in English) Amy Lowell's imagistic "A Winter Ride," "'Who shall declare the joy of the running!'" (*D* 202), and cites as a predecessor of hers Francis Thompson's "To a Snowflake." In between, he alludes obliquely to Poe with "no crow in sight. Painting, nothing more" (*D* 202). As he looks upon a "desert of rose-colored sand" and "strange shadows," he asks himself, "Emily Dickinson?" The sand and desert, the shadows and light blend together as he falls asleep on a train and the disorientation deepens. He believes for a moment that he is back in Spain: "Seville? Triana? Ah . . . no! . . . Cadiz? . . . New London! / Huelva? . . . New York, marvelous New York! In your presence, I forget everything else!" (*D* 200, 204). The juxtapositions and lines of connection among these poets and places will be elaborated in his critical outlines of modernism; *modernismo* and modernism, reconfigured as they both are in *Diary*, will find their dialogic expression in his own poetic idiom, he believes.

"One Book": On Being Spanish and American

For Jiménez, the only way to make sense of American modernity and to craft his transnational poetic persona is to immerse himself in the clash of the new and the ancient—of life, death, blood, phantasms, and love—that he finds in New York. New York is his inroads to American modernism and the dissimilar sources he sees in its texts. He asserts that to live in New York "is for me to live in the most complete place of our day . . . the city which, with all of its defects, and because of them, corresponds most to the actual man that I always wanted to be and which I could never be, because of my exterior/interior imbalances."[56] Seeking perspective, he first climbs to the top of the new Woolworth Building (completed in 1913), the tallest building in the world at the time, and writes the poem "New Sky," which he dedicates to José Ortega y Gasset. Here, he looks back at Europe from the New World and imagines a "new sky . . . / even without names!", a land "sin historias" ("without histories," with the additional sense of "without stories") (*D* 211). He looks back to Spain again several times, then looks to Asia, then imagines characters from Goya's paintings coming alive in New York and ponders a Velázquez at the Metropolitan Museum of Art. In "Garcilaso in New York," dedicated to Archer Milton Huntington, Jiménez places the famed sonneteer in modern-day New York. As he reads his distant compatriot's works while looking at a city street, his realization arrives: "Yes! I am whole! I am whole! I am whole!" (*D* 258). In other words, what makes him "whole" is that he has transported his Spanish poetic heritage to the United States and merged it with the modern chaos he sees around him, initiating what Lorca will do more famously in *Poet in New York* (1929–1930). As for Dos Passos, the U.S. literary heritage offered by Boston and New York is a double-edged and, at best, partially fulfilling "usable past." Spain's past literary empire and the effects of the United States' global capitalism must be yoked together poetically but in reconfigured and translated forms.

The backdrop for these insights and these sometimes frenetic alternations between Spanish and American literature is, at the same time, an otherwise tranquil spring day. This spring brings to mind for him a "Calling Card in Springtime from a Bibliophile Friend," a two-line work with Kurtz's exclamation from *Heart of Darkness* ("Horror!") interjected mid-poem and a vision of "one book" across languages at the end. The ideal of "one book" that combines the various cultures in which Jiménez was actually and mentally circulating—and which were overwhelming him, too—leads him to blend Spanish and U.S. literary worlds further. He looks out his window on Eleventh Street, and seeing "such a vast sea with a yellow moon / between us both, Spain!", he thinks of "the solitary moon," which "is dying, shattered, oh Poe!, over Broadway" (*D* 218). Here again, his Spanish "¡oh Poe! sobre Broadway" presents a sonorous long "o" across two languages and a slant rhyme on the third and fourth words, linking his debt to Poe and to New York (Poe's home for a brief time) through subtle cross-linguistic play. Later, he ponders, "The sky? One colorless color more to fabricate a flag with even fringes—the emblem of mortality—with the blue curtain over a third of the window, and two-thirds up, the yellow curtain. / Quoth the raven: Nevermore" (*D* 294). Jiménez's fixation on cemeteries—"The most attractive thing about America for me is the charm of its cemeteries," he writes—brings to mind Edgar Lee Masters for him, and as Graciela Nemes de Palau notes, he fuses this meditation with the oceanic themes of the book in a manner that resembles his interpretations of Valéry's "Le cimetière marin."[57] He sees a "cheerful cemetery" that is "like the one in Spoon River, it is situated on a hill that spring is just touching, on the other side, the most beautiful side, the side toward the river" (*D* 286). Epigraphs from Lope de Vega and from Shakespeare appear pages apart as literary histories collide in the present.

Just as these spheres seem to be merging, however, Jiménez abruptly sails back to Spain. The return trip in part 4 presents a different, unfamiliar sea with a "strange unformed language" (*D* 355). He again dedicates many poems to it and to the night, adding in several nocturnes, but the mood is altered. When he finally sees "Golden Iberia," he seems to find himself whole again, and he declares, "Yes. Now we are! Now I am!" (*D* 406). His poetic repertory has indelibly changed, however; as he feels the temporary thrill of "My fatherland and my soul!", his instinct the following morning is to translate not a Spanish poem but Robert Browning's "Parting at Morning" (*D* 414). He says that he places it "here, at this point on the planet," because it "persists in my mind and in my heart." Jiménez renders the final line of Browning's original ("And the need of a world of men for me") as "Y un fatal mundo de hombres para mí," nihilistically shifting the "need of a world" to a sense of an "awful," "dire," or "mortal" world that his Spanish "*fatal*" implies. Feeling alien in his native land, Jiménez takes a lengthy mental voyage back across the Atlantic for the final section, "Memories of the Eastern United States Written in Spain." He returns to Dickinson now, translating stanzas 2, 27, and 55 of her "The Single Hound." He chooses three stanzas that fit his journey and themes, highlighted by lines such as "The Soul that hath a Guest / Doth seldom go abroad—" (which he translates as "El Alma que tiene Huésped / rara vez sale de Sí") and "The Gleam of an heroic Act / Such strange illumination / The Possible's slow fuse is lit / By the Imagination" ("¡Resplandor de un acto heroico! / ¡Qué extraña iluminación! / —La mecha lenta del Puede / prende en la Imaginación.—") Throughout the translations, Jiménez attempts to replicate Dickinson's idiosyncratic capitalization and alliteration.

Soon after, his poem "Boston on Sunday" has distinct echoes of Dickinson in its punctuation, as he describes "the flowers all in order—tulips, jonquils, azaleas—look—through the purple windowpanes, as though on altars outside—to see the statues—what horror!—, the squirrels, the sparrows, the pigeons and the two of us" (*D* 452). At the same time, his memories of the United States are not all positive, especially when he asserts that his American peers are overlooking the best writers among them. He mocks the Cosmopolitan Club and the National Arts Club, and he reserves his greatest contempt for the stuffy pretentions of the Authors Club. He is appalled at his contemporaries in the Authors Club: half-rate, nameless poets who believe themselves to be modern-day versions of Poe and Whitman while they disparage Robinson, Frost, Masters, Lindsay, and Amy Lowell. His idea just before leaving is to burn the place to the ground. This mixture of registers and sites, bordering on a cacophony, will conclude the book. Presaging his later theories, Jiménez describes Whitman's birthplace and copies the plaque at the house. He also copies a "For Sale or Rent" sign in Philadelphia and a bulletin from a church service led by a disciple of Billy Sunday, the baseball player–turned-preacher who weaves baseball metaphors throughout his sermons. His last task is to find Poe's house, but "there is no guide." He cannot find it; he knows that it exists somewhere in New York—"I see it, I have seen it in a street"—but he will have to remain content, in keeping with the premise of part 6, with its existence in memory (*D* 486). He ends with an author's note that states that "this *Diary*, more than any other work of mine, is provisional" and will be altered in the future. "I don't know what it will become. I do know that today this book of mine seems like a rough draft of itself," he confesses, one that was written "to free myself from this side of my soul and body, of the recent me, troubled and without changes for now, of only a year ago" (*D* 492). The text never was significantly revised, but rather, it was extended and explicated through Jiménez's criticism.[58] His critical writings that followed constitute an expansion of the open-ended text that he abandoned in 1916–1917, paralleling in this way Pound's publications in the decade following *The Spirit of Romance*.

Jiménez described his *Diary* as a book of "surprise and skepticism," and the phenomena that "surprised" him in the United States were ones that he found anew, across the Americas and in Spain, for decades.[59] But the effects of Jiménez's American journey on his subsequent writings—especially in its journeys across literary traditions—are difficult to judge. He did move increasingly toward what he called *poesía pura* ("pure poetry"), which was similar to imagism in its distilled, concentrated simplicity. But from 1923 to 1936 (when the Spanish Civil War forced him to flee the country), he published no books of new poems, only individual verses in periodicals or collections, along with many translations. His relationship with Spain's younger poets, for whom he represented what Darío did for him, was ambivalent and sometimes contentious. His influence on the Generation of '27 was nonetheless visible, and he was not bashful about claiming that "modern symbolism in Spanish poetry begins with the *Diary*."[60] *Diary*'s place in international literatures of its moment, however, remains as ambiguous as that of *modernismo* itself.

Jiménez's History and Genealogies of Modernism(s)

If we look for similarities, the connections between *Diary* and the works of English-language American modernism that Jiménez cites—especially imagist texts—are readily apparent. One could find parallels to Frost, Millay, even Eliot, Toomer, and Williams, with equal ease. But that manner of comparison, as I have argued, is limited and overly simplistic. More intriguing and critically dynamic is the sweeping version of literary history through which Jiménez created his sometimes unexpected international repositioning of his own work from the American East Coast in 1916, through which he created a modernist triangle of Spain, Spanish America, and the United States. *Modernismo* and modernism were always paired for him; he reflected, "what good fortune I had to witness the arrival of Spanish American *modernismo* in Spain in the person of Rubén Darío, and then, some fifteen years later, to be present for the great success of the fundamental works of the greatest American modernists" whom he will treat in his criticism.[61] Conveniently, Jiménez himself was born squarely between these two generations of Spanish poets—younger than the *modernistas* and the Americans but older than the latter Spanish American writers he mentions. He combines this circumstance with his momentary location in the United States in 1916 to expand, around the poetics he was developing in *Diary*, his translinguistic figuration of *modernismo*/modernism as an interrelated phenomenon.

Jiménez's critical expositions come primarily in two sets of writings that he left behind: one for Spanish-speaking U.S. audiences in the 1940s and one for a course on *modernismo*/modernism at the University of Puerto Rico, Río Piedras in the 1950s. The lectures were to become a book that he left unfinished; it was to be called either *El siglo modernista* (The modernist century) or *El modernismo*. In all of these texts Jiménez intervenes in debates that prevailed in Anglo- and Hispanophone criticism alike for some time. Ultranationalist and Francoist critics in Spain had distinguished clearly between *modernismo* and the peninsular Generation of '98, continuing the turn-of-the-century denigration of the former as excessively hybrid, cosmopolitan, and peripheral and elevating the latter as a serious, uncontaminated, proudly national project.[62] In these debates, Jiménez sided with and revised the work of his friend Onís, an authoritative theorist of *modernismo* from his position at Columbia and the critic who first used the term "postmodernism" with regard to literature. For Onís, *modernismo* was "the Hispanic form of the universal crisis in letters and in spirit" that dates from 1885, reached across the arts, science, and religion, and continued into the 1930s, though with interruptions.[63] We must pause here to note that Jiménez and Onís—who later invited him to Puerto Rico for his lectures—both use the Spanish term "*modernismo*" in broad, less conventional ways. For my purposes, instead of moving back and forth constantly between "*modernismo*" and the Anglophone sense of "modernism," I will use, in my own capacity as translator, the word "modernism/o" to indicate that Jiménez, who never composed in English, is using the Spanish word *modernismo* to refer to something that does not settle in either Spanish or English.

For Jiménez, modernism/o variously was a "tendency" or "attitude," a "movement," a "mentality," a "wealth of ideologies and sensibilities," even a "cosmo-vision," all of which, he signals, stretch beyond the traditional sense of a literary "school" or group of figures. It flourished beginning in the late nineteenth century and dominated the twentieth, which he calls "the modernist century." But for Jiménez, modernism/o's roots are diverse and arose in separate places at separate times; for him, it was, as Richard Cardwell writes, not only a "*literary* problem" but also a "watershed in the development of the *history of ideas* in Spain."[64] Its theological origins in the Catholic Church's debates over "modernism" around the turn of the twentieth century, to which Jiménez often alludes, point to the common link: it is a reaction against dogmas of all types. "Modernism/o was to Romanticism what the Renaissance was to the Middle Ages," he writes; "it is a new Renaissance," much like the "renacimiento" that he described experiencing personally when he was reborn in U.S. poetry. In lieu of a definition, he contends that modernism/o is a constantly shifting "new form of expression."[65] Yet modernism/o is not a complete rupture with the literary past; Baudelaire, for instance, combined romanticism, Parnassianism, and symbolism, and all of these coexist in parts of Jiménez's works. Modernism/o both carries forward the romantic celebration of "the living, the free, the authentic: a mixture of beautiful form and great spirit" and evinces "a great movement of enthusiasm and liberty toward beauty."[66] Bécquer's postromanticism launched this current attitude in Spanish, for Jiménez, because he broke with aristocratic and courtly writing. Poe, Baudelaire, and the sixteenth-century Spanish mystic St. John of the Cross all performed similar roles in their times and places.

The true modernists were the mystics, in a secular, individualistic sense, he writes; Romain Rolland was exemplary. "Modernism/o is the same for the theologian as for the artist," he asserts.[67] In this formulation, Jiménez is giving a genealogy of his own liberal secular thought, honed during his time at the Residencia de Estudiantes and in conversation with Spain's leading Europeanizers, Krausists, and *heterodoxos* who challenged national myths. Where Darío only saw Spain as an empty field conquered by the cosmopolitan, foreign world, Jiménez restores Spain to the map of modernism. He wrote during his exile with an increasing sense of separation from Spain and from the Spanish language—"mi español perdido" (my lost Spanish)—as he called it in an article from 1943, and thus he is envisaging a coherent genealogy of modernism/o onto the same Spain that he "deserted." But Jiménez focuses more precisely on the cultural traffic that, over the centuries, produced modernism/o. In all of the great literary movements of the world, Jiménez believes, there is a fundamental interchange of foreign influences, as Pound would argue.[68] This admixture, achieved through translations and exchanges such as the Venezuelan poet Juan Antonio Pérez Bonalde's version of Poe's "The Raven," combined with French symbolism, exoticism, the gothic, and national traditions (especially those of Whitman, Dickinson, and Poe) to give rise to *modernismo* in Spanish America and Spain and to modernism in the United States. The poetry of New England and of the "Boston Brahmins" was too derived from England for Jiménez. Poe, by contrast, incorporated everything from African American spirituals to Southern lyric forms to incongruous rhyme schemes in his writing. He "purified romanticism" like Baudelaire and Bécquer did by getting rid of its exorbitance, anachronistic neoclassicism, and the "general vice of its epoch."[69] Whitman and Dickinson, meanwhile, both broke the paradigms of form and enabled American free verse. Continuing to make cross-cultural and cross-linguistic connections, Jiménez claims that the effect of Dickinson's persona and her work is comparable to that of Sor Juana Inés de la Cruz, the baroque poet and nun of colonial Mexico; he claims that Dickinson was, in effect, a neobaroque modernist who wrote poems that were "short, complicated, and full of ideas."[70]

As his paratactic and comparative history moves forward, Jiménez turns to the still-growing American West, which inspired writers such as Bret Harte, Joaquin Miller, and Edward Rowland Sill, who saw in the new West a "pueblo . . . a coming democracy, not the social decadence of the East" and the Boston Brahmins.[71] Jiménez was often keen, too, to champion lesser-known modernists he considered undervalued by national and international audiences, and his canon includes figures who are now seen by many critics as *anti*modernist but are yoked to names like Pound and Lowell by the populist mysticism he adumbrates. The "North American poets of the West" inherited sensibilities from Twain and Sidney Lanier also and took from Whitman "a popular, mystical, and democratic" style that did not simply mimic the American East. In this way, he adds, in an argument much like Dos Passos's, that Twain's legacy has been analogous to that of the non-Castilians Unamuno, Baroja, and Ramón del Valle-Inclán upon Spain's central province. And because the literary establishment of the United States was disconnected from the *pueblo*, Americans didn't appreciate the popular idioms of Whitman, Dickinson, and Poe fully during their lifetimes.[72] Jiménez's contemporary poets of the West then brought these styles to the East "by way of the path that

Spaniards opened some four centuries ago, from Saint Augustine, Florida, to California," just as Spain linked the two Americas.[73] Next came the first true American modernists, the "mystics of the Midwest," especially William Vaughn Moody and Edwin Markham.[74] Like their counterparts in Spain's coastal provinces (Eduardo Marquina, Jacint Verdaguer, Manuel Curros Enríquez) and Spanish America (Martí, Darío, Silva, Salvador Díaz-Mirón), this intergeneration turned against empire and toward quotidian life, symbolic exploration, and inner worlds. Both *modernistas* and U.S. modernists declared their literary independence from European derivation and metropolitan centers around the same time, in movements that began to peak, without a great deal of contact between them yet, during the same "epoch" of modernism/o. The movement from a semiperiphery to a center, whether within a country or in a global context, defines the contours of modernism/o for Jiménez, who himself had made both such journeys.

All of this paved the way for the U.S. modernism of the 1910s, which is also the most internationalist of U.S. movements. Prompted by the war of 1898, Americans revived their country's literature beginning in 1905, Jiménez writes. He asserts that the effect of modernism/o—the literary fellow-feeling and sympathies that it inspired—was to bring Spain, Spanish America, and the United States closer together, despite their political antagonisms. In part, this arose out of a shared predicament: after the war, all three regions needed to reintegrate themselves "morally and materially."[75] While some writers became enamored with imperialism, others, such as the war veterans Sherwood Anderson and the Cuban revolutionary Martí, turned their writing against the spirit of expansionism. In both cases, the war energized each country's otherwise languishing creative spirit. In the United States, it fostered a return to the "gran trío" of great poets that led to a modernist revival, Whitman, Poe, and Dickinson, who appear repeatedly in *Diary*. What may appear to be the consolidation of a national poetic identity around the canonical poets of the nineteenth-century United States, he argues, was actually a sign of a reenergized internationalist movement appearing simultaneously in Spain and Spanish America. The universal flourished homologously across national fields, he held. The unconventional circuits and configurations into which he plotted American literature thereby amplified the importance of his own career.

He most often lists his own contemporaries as "modernistas de tipo inglés y norteamericano," and many of them he discovered by reading

Poetry: Frost, Robinson, Masters, Amy Lowell, J. G. Fletcher, Vachel Lindsay, Sandburg, Millay, Pound, Eliot, and the imagists.[76] In his attempt to move across languages in his critical history, Jiménez notes the terminological problem. Writing from within the United States but in Spanish, he adds that these writers and their movements "are called here also 'modernism'; the critics use this word."[77] Expanding "modernism" as a word as much as a concept, Jiménez notes that these Anglophone writers, along with Stein and Joyce, constitute a "great, universal generation of this era."[78] And he includes elsewhere the Fugitives and their *Sewanee Review*, comparing their exaltation of the region to the work of Azorín, Machado, and his own. All of these writers, he insists, speak "not of poetic nationalism" but rather, speak to their nation—its literature and its history—by adapting foreign styles to their native tongues.[79] In this sense, his declarations of cross-cultural affiliation encapsulate the revisionary national lineage that *Diary* offers. He intertwines them constantly with such *modernistas* as Martí, Casal, Silva, Storni, Díaz-Mirón, Manuel Gutiérrez Nájera, Leopoldo Lugones, and María Eugenia (he includes Spanish American but not Spanish women) and with other poets including Yeats and Rilke.[80] Jiménez furthermore asserted in the 1950s that "modernism/o is not finished: it has been exaggerated, transformed, has gained liberties" in the works of Pablo Neruda and César Vallejo.[81] This contentious conception of modernism/o as spanning several more decades, beyond World War II, is one that he would carry into his own exile in the New World as he rethought his life in this "epoch."

The Afterlives of Jiménez's Crossings: Then and Now

As critics including Manuel Pedro González and Bernardo Gicovate claimed almost immediately upon the publication of Jiménez's lecture notes, Jiménez becomes haphazard at times and labels almost everything "modernist"; a similar criticism of contemporary Anglophone modernist studies extends the affiliations I have been tracing.[82] His critical writings are not only self-promoting, but they also reinscribe a type of colonial domination and elision onto a movement that was strongly Spanish American—often *anti*-Iberian and often pre-Hispanic, as Paz noted—in its origins. Spain, for him, differentiated *modernismo* from its Spanish American origins by adding its unique and stereotypical mysticism; otherwise, he follows Onís in seeing *modernismo* as evincing the shared racial and linguistic heritage of Spaniards and Spanish Americans. We can read this sensibility back, then, onto Jiménez's claims to see a precursor to symbolism in the cross-lingual Arabic-Andalusian poetry of medieval southern Spain, whose multiple cultural roots prefigure those of French symbolism. (Here again, his slights to Castile are apparent.) And when discussing the arts of mid-nineteenth-century France, he argues that Parnassianism was indebted to Spanish romanticism; impressionism to El Greco, Velázquez, and Goya; Baudelaire to José de Espronceda. Political and cultural history, temporal conjunctions, or formulations of modernity are not as vital to Jiménez's theories as they are to those of contemporary critics. Rather, he celebrates international exchange across uneven power relations—among states and literatures alike—in a manner that dilutes the very peripherality that key figures of modernism/o integrated as critiques in their works and their idioms. He also marginalizes or leaves aside writers in nonhegemonic languages: modernism's many dialects, or its manifestations in Yiddish or Galician, for example, in fact disoriented some of the bearings that he posits.[83] Which is to say that, even when decentering the Paris-London-Berlin axis and theorizing a flourishing of modernisms globally, Jiménez's criticism relies on the paths of empire that still trouble contemporary Anglophone modernist critics who seek to extricate literary history from imperial legacies.

The task remains to explore and to make sense of the intersections of global literary history and translingual modernisms in a text such as *Diary* on the terms that writers such as Jiménez offered. Jiménez used this long vision of modernism/o as a tool for reading Euro-American modernists, too—most pointedly, Eliot, whom he saw as his Anglo-doppelgänger and whom he both translated and (later) rejected for his politics. This poetic self is one he would refine for several more decades after the Spanish Civil War, when he was back in the Americas, now as a professor at the University of Miami (Florida) and the University of Maryland, among other places. (Some of his thoughts on modernism/o, in fact, were developed as part of his series of Spanish-language radio broadcasts for the American government during World War II.) He visited Pound at St. Elizabeths and taught Spanish to Henry Wallace. But, despite his efforts, he would not achieve recognition in the Anglophone world until 1951, when the scholar J. B. Trend published his *Fifty Spanish Poems* in English. Two years later, *Poetry* dedicated an issue to him, and in 1956 came the

Nobel Prize. Though poets such as Tagore are understood to have been parts of more than one modernist movement across borders and languages, Jiménez was not (and still is not) widely known to Anglophone readers. Spanish literary scholars, too, tend to read him almost exclusively in national contexts.

Anglophone scholars of modernism have become increasingly aware that the term so intelligible and familiar to them for decades—"modernism"—has had little purchase in other languages. I have attempted, by way of the networks reconstructed in this chapter, to suspend the ontological or definitional questions about modernism and *modernismo* while tracing instead their entwined and diverging histories across several languages. Other maps of modernisms caught between languages also might account more fully for such theorizations of *modernismo* and other terms for which "modernism" was, in actuality, a belated and sometimes outlying cognate. These maps will point to new temporalities and geographies that more familiar maps of colonialism and migration cannot explain: Kelly Washbourne notes, for instance, that both Ezra Pound and the Mexican poet José Juan Tablada both translated the Chinese poet Li Po (Li Bai).[84] Or, to return to Tagore, Pound collaborated with the Bengali poet's pupil Kali Mohan Ghose in 1913 to translate the fifteenth-century Hindi poet Kabir into English. Translation, as a lens, has the potential to preserve the asymmetries and the irreconcilable elements that characterize the multiple emergences of movements that insist, however ambivalently, on being called by the congeries of cognates gathered as "modernist."[85]

CHAPTER 4

Unamuno, Nativism, and the Politics of the Vernacular; or, On the Authenticity of Translation

> *As for many years my spirit has been nourished upon the very core of English Literature—evidence of which the reader may discover in the following pages—the translator in putting my* Sentimiento Trágico [The Tragic Sense of Life] *into English, has merely converted not a few of the thoughts and feelings therein expressed back into their original form of expression. Or retranslated them, perhaps. Whereby they emerge other than they originally were, for an idea does not pass from one language to another without change. . . . Hence this English translation of my* Sentimiento Trágico *presents in some ways a more purged and correct text than that of the original Spanish.*
> —MIGUEL DE UNAMUNO, author's preface to the English translation of *The Tragic Sense of Life* (1921)

THE NATIVIST VIEW OF AUTHENTIC NATIONAL LITERATURES hinges on a resistance to translatability. A national tradition emerges, this view holds, when a language fully incorporates its autochthonous resources, vernacular and local idioms, and other such materials connected to its land—a mapped area that, in turn, delimits and naturalizes the literature. These texts are not translatable, in the conventional sense: they can only be approximated by analogy in another tongue. As the influential linguist Antoine Berman put it, "a vernacular clings tightly to its soil and completely resists any direct translating into another vernacular. *Translation can occur only between 'cultivated' languages.* An exoticization that turns the foreign from abroad into the foreign at home winds up merely ridiculing the original."[1] By "cultivated," Berman means languages that are spoken and intelligible in many places; he laments the fact that dialects are forever doomed to localism. In other words, linguistic and literary nativism—grounded in the idea that the essence of a people, nation, or race is expressed organically in demotic language and its poems, ballads, and more—claims the irreducible singularity of a *Volk* (however heterogeneous the population may be) and its speech and writing. Every country, every culture, every language, even every village theoretically can have its *Nibelungenlied*, its *Huckleberry Finn,* or its *Divina Commedia*. Untranslatability becomes a sign of authenticity; to speak in a non-native tongue is to speak insincerely, impersonally, outside of one's innate linguistic sphere.

Such assumptions were crucial, as we saw in previous chapters, to branches of romantic philology, to the modern origins of comparative literary studies, and to monolingual formations of national literatures. Indeed, literary nativism, though critiqued for decades by academics, still reigns in popular U.S. culture, in undergraduate curricula, and in many global critical traditions. The roots of this thought lie in a brand of nationalism that exhibits a "literary xenophobia" (to use Lawrence Venuti's term) and "a fear that foreign literatures might contaminate native traditions." But at the same time, Venuti notes, history shows that "nations do indeed 'profit' from translation. Nationalist movements have frequently enlisted translation in the development of national languages and cultures, especially national literatures. . . . Nationalist translation agendas depend on . . . circularity: the national status of a language and culture is simultaneously presupposed and created through translation."² This might occur in many ways: a nation's scholars might translate the texts of their distant linguistic, religious, or ethnic ancestors; a government might support translation as a project of Westernization that augments its own international standing; an internally dominant literature might enrich itself by gobbling up texts in minor languages produced within the state's boundaries; a culture might use translation of the texts of one language as a collective form of protest against the domination of their occupier; or even individual translators might alternately domesticate or foreignize texts from abroad in order to affirm the naturalness and superiority of their nation's primary tradition.

This problem—the simultaneous utility, if not necessity, and putative impossibility of translating foreign literatures—stretches beyond the nativist view of imported texts to its treatment of exported ones. What happens when the authentic national literature leaves its soil and is reformulated in translation, in dialectal shifts by creole or colonial populations, or in its absorption into a pidgin, patois, and hybrid tongues in a contact zone? The presumptive answer—it loses its authenticity—did not fit Miguel de Unamuno's Spanish nativism, and the philosopher's controversial and sometimes contradictory theories of how literary expression became *more* authentic through translation in particular are the starting point for this chapter. At first blush, Unamuno looks like a classic nativist. With a debt to Johann Gottfried Herder, Wilhelm von Humboldt, and Friedrich Schleiermacher, he held a romantic notion of the intimate connection between a *pueblo* (in Spanish, both a "village" and a "people") and its tongue. "I am a patriot; to each his own *patria*," Unamuno wrote.[3] But Unamuno was a heterodox and prolific master of translation between the 1900s and 1930s. He read thirteen languages beyond Spanish and translated everyone from Demosthenes to Walt Whitman, Giacomo Leopardi to Humboldt himself. Most often, he translated figures known for having poeticized their local vernaculars.

As intellectual projects, nativism and a commitment to translation are compatible in an anthropological or ethnographic sense, as if Unamuno were compiling an encyclopedia of distinct cultures (the "United Nations model" of world literature). "In each country," he wrote, "what interests me the most are those things that are most authentic [*castizos*] and characteristic, the least translated and the least translatable."[4] But as the epigraph above and a number of Unamuno's writings indicate, he went farther in his claims, asserting that parts of his best-known work were, in his mind, composed in English and translated internally into Spanish. Bringing out this paradox, Unamuno noted that translations had "ultimately influenced me in the formation of my native thought [*pensamiento patrio*]."[5] Furthermore, and not unrelated, Unamuno held that José Hernández's Argentine gaucho epic poem *Martín Fierro* (1872), which clearly drew on resources disconnected from the Iberian soil, was counterintuitively more *Spanish* than Argentine. In other words, for reasons opposed to those Dos Passos offered, Unamuno circuitously posited that Castilian Spanish literature actually grew with the end of the Spanish Empire in the New World: the seeds it planted in Spanish America flowered into vivid new variations on a common tongue. In extensions and revisions of this logic, Unamuno claimed that he discovered his own vernacular in Spanish through English—specifically, through translating Thomas Carlyle. In short: translation *becomes* his original.

To make sense of this, and to understand why it mattered so much after 1898, we must examine Unamuno's vision of a country whose governments kept him in exile for large parts of his adult life and its relationship with the United States in the new century. Scholars of Hispanophone literature are familiar with his often-critiqued cultural imperialism and Iberian chauvinism. But scant attention has been paid to his theories of literature in English and, in particular, to an Anglophone U.S. tradition that, as it differentiated itself from England, became a key point of contrast to his theories of Spanish American writing. The United States was an intriguing case for a thinker who normally studied national literatures with medieval or classical roots. Against the Spanish example, he held that English in the United States did not expand the linguistic empire of Britain but, rather, became autonomous and authentic in Whitman. American literature, for him, was emergent in Whitman and then only a few decades later was *divergent*, dangerously splintered as it rose globally in ways that the literatures of Argentina or Uruguay, for example, did not. The United States' leading authors had divagated from the country's natural path of development and evolution and turned American English into an Esperanto of commerce after 1898, much as Dos Passos feared, or into an unrooted cosmopolitan hodgepodge, as in Eliot's and Pound's poetry.

Unamuno might appear something of an outlier in this book's structure, except that within this work, he attempted to transfer America's lost poetic tradition to Spain. He wanted to resuscitate Whitman in translation, then to point to the regional poets, such as Carl Sandburg, Sidney Lanier, and William Vaughn Moody, who might preserve the "authentic" course of U.S. literature in the twentieth century. As he advocated the study of foreign literatures as a means to *enhance* the autochthonous language and literature of Spain, Unamuno also became a leading figure in founding contemporary American studies in Spain. Most important, the United States became for him a critical meeting point of English and the persisting presence of Spanish, one that he elaborated in his writings for the New Orleans–based Spanish-language periodical *Mercurio* (1911–1927). Unamuno aimed to revive connections between Spain and the United States after 1898 and to create an intellectual circuit, composed largely of the U.S. Hispanists whom he befriended and who translated his own work into English, of which he would be a crucial part. His publications and his authorial reputation in English would circulate in this network, too, and the latter part of this chapter reconstructs his foreign presence. He saw himself, an exiled icon of dissidence for many writers and cultural critics beyond Spain, as a part of a growing English-Spanish global union—an heir to Whitman—translating across the two languages and even inserting Anglophone U.S. poetry into his own highly personal *Cancionero*, a poetic diary that he began in his final exile in 1928. In short, Unamuno's attempts to consolidate Spanish national identity after the empire's collapse unraveled his own nativist propositions in favor of a new outline of global English and global Spanish within a field of translation governed by the clashes between commerce and "spirit."[6]

As he became an apologist for U.S. empire and a critic of Spain's decline, Unamuno thus imported to Spain a literary tradition with no roots in Iberian soil but one that itself had been enriched by its contact with Spanish cultures, much as Whitman himself believed. Such parts of his career highlight broader issues that, beyond Unamuno's strange turn as a bilingual pastoral modernist or his international reputation, open up important questions in translational and comparative literary studies: what happens to vernaculars as they become the dominant languages of expanding and contracting empires? And were the booming print landscapes of English and Spanish writing in the New World of the early twentieth century consolidating or fragmenting the languages of the Old World? This chapter traces the ways in which Unamuno's social theories of language are modified and often undermined—though productively—by his own literary practices, all in order to understand how a translated vernacular became the vehicle for reading one empire and its literary history from the near-vacated shell of another. The renovated configurations of Spanish and American literatures that his theories and his work create through registers of translation become complex models of cultural historiography that challenge still-pervasive approaches to the literary past.

From Nativism to a Literary Empire

Unamuno's thought, from the start, was framed by his understanding of language as an evolving collective organism. Before his debut as a public intellectual, he wrote a doctoral dissertation on the language and people of the Basque Country, where he was born. Following theories from Humboldt's study of the Basques from 1821, which Unamuno would translate into Castilian, the young scholar became convinced that languages followed different evolutionary paths and that Basque had become stifled by separatist movements that sought to protect the language from outside influences. Castilian, on the other hand, was transformed more rapidly and robustly with the spread of the Spanish Empire. As the crisis of empire was peaking in Spain in 1895, during the Cuban Revolution, Unamuno published a provocative series of articles, later collected and revised as *En torno al casticismo* (1902), in which he attempted to understand the historical destiny of Spain's Castilian essence.[7] He was entering an intellectual and literary environment that, as José-Carlos Mainer and Stephen G. H. Roberts have shown, was becoming increasingly professionalized and politically polarized.[8] As he aimed to make himself the iconoclastic voice of a national upheaval grounded in organicist populism—and, in his youth, socialism—Unamuno urged a widespread deprofessionalization of intellectualism, a process that would return intellectuals to the *pueblo*. (He once proposed that university professors and secondary-school instructors should be sent to impoverished, rural parts of Spain in order to teach basic literacy skills, among other things.) His diagnosis of the "Spanish problem" and of the country's entrenched political factions resonated even before the War of 1898—a war that he opposed and that, in turn, amplified his own voice in the wide-ranging debates on *regeneracionismo*.

Harnessing the spirit of the celebrations of the Hispanic *raza* commemorated in 1892, Unamuno relied on what was a common reading in late European imperial settings and reinterpreted empire as *spirit* rather than as a political project. Especially in his revisions of *En torno al casticismo* after 1898, Unamuno focused the fraught questions of Spain's imperial decline on the domestic concept of *casticismo*, which both signifies untranslatability and is itself difficult to translate. The root word, *castizo*—from *casta*—means "pure" (chaste) or "genuine," and "caste," as in "pure breeding" or lineage. (The book's title is, roughly, *On Pure Tradition*, or *On Spanish Authenticity*.) While the word *castizo* can be applied to that which is considered authentic in any culture, it has a long history in Spanish culture of signifying an antiforeign stance in language, bloodlines, knowledge, customs, religion, and more. It was the central term in the centuries-old debates in Spain over whether the solutions to the country's perceived decline since the 1600s should come from a revival of Spanish traditions alone or by turning to outside sources. Unamuno vacillated and sometimes contradicted himself, but most generally, he favored a version of the nativist solution to the rejuvenation of Spain, but with qualification: there was more to "Spain" than most Spaniards recognized, including the sedimented layers of other cultures (European and African alike). Only "Europeanized" Spaniards could "discover" and "make" Spain, he argued, but they must channel what they learn from foreign sources into a national project.[9] In looking to build what he called "la otra España" ("the other Spain"), he argued that "one must make the foreign familiar" and, by doing so, defamiliarize one's native surroundings at the same time.[10] Instead of becoming rootless cosmopolitans, then, Spaniards should "be what we in ourselves are, seeking our permanent essence and ground, de-Latinizing ourselves, too, until we get back to our Iberian, Moorish, Berber, or whatever, inmost beings."[11]

Spaniards should "Spanishify" (*españolarse*) themselves, that is, and must guard themselves against faddish foreign movements such as *modernismo*.[12] At once naturalizing and rewriting the history of Spain's dominant identity, Unamuno writes that he cannot understand either why Spaniards and Spanish Americans are enamored of "Neo-Góngorists, Latinists, Local-colorists, Decadents, Parnassians, Victor-Hugo-ists and other fads from overseas, with their shipments of Quechua, Guaraní, Araucanian, Aztec, Toltec, or Chichimeca monstrosities."[13] Only what was buried in Spain's soil should be excavated and brought to light, and that soil was made of words. Indeed, in his own text *Vida de Don Quixote y Sancho* (1905) he included a "Vocabulario" as an appendix. He explained that any words in his text not found in the dictionary were "taken from the mouth of the *pueblo* of the Salmantine region" or from *Don Quixote* itself, for in order to "enrich the language [*idioma*], it is better to fish in the tomes of old writers for words that are dead today, or to pull them from the guts of popular speech."[14] Unamuno's case, therefore, was not grounded in a theory of racial purity but in biological *convivencia*; he held that Spaniards themselves were descended from a mixture of Iberians, Celts, Romans, Visigoths, Semitic peoples, Berbers, Arabs, and others. Rather, language was the great universalizing and profoundly historical bond for his holistic, melting-pot nativism—his assimilationist narrative that glorifies Spain's internal racial mixing over time. (The parallels here to Whitman's thought in essays such as "Slang in America" [1885] and to Mencken's effort to catalog the "American language" will resurface momentarily.)

Thus, Unamuno developed his conception of "intrahistory." He thought that history could best be understood by looking at the discrete, interpersonal histories of anonymous people realized in the products of popular culture—especially linguistic ones—rather than in state structures or political histories. Life, he believed, lay in a vast communitarian sea of which most historians see only the surface. Unamuno argued that "what happens to individuals happens also to the people [*pueblos*]. Their collective spirit, the *Volkgeist* of the Germans, has a subconscious base, below the public consciousness that we know and that history shows us."[15] He calls for the properly attuned folklorist to recover "the social protoplasm, the germinative plasma, the eternal *Pueblo*, the perdurable primary material from which the temporary *pueblos* arise."[16] *Literatura* and *pueblo* remained connected for him in a Humboldtian manner—especially in its emphasis on the evolutionary, unstable nature of language, tied to environments and human creativity—a connection that was reformed famously in the early twentieth century by figures such as Franz Boas, Edward Sapir, and Benjamin Lee Whorf, for whom language was both a conceptual, structural agent and a limit for human thought.[17] Unamuno's study *Vida del romance castellano* (The life of the Castilian romance) included a bibliographic essay on the history of the Spanish language for which he chose a line from Shelley's *Prometheus Unbound* as the epigraph: "He gave man speech, and speech created thought, / Which is the measure of the universe." Esperanto, having no roots in a defined culture or its authentic soil, was an abomination to him.

In keeping with this thought, Unamuno held that the true *casticismo* had been appropriated and distorted by a state-created xenophobic, cultish nativism of his moment; it had been turned into naïve patriotism and base jingoism. He wrote that "Spaniards go on repeating time and again the same ineptitudes and the same lies [or 'fairy tales': *patrañas*] about our old tongue and our race [and] . . . our history."[18] *Casticismo* had excluded popular history and daily life, he felt, and had ossified it into a tradition commensurate with the vision of the monarchic state. Nobles, monarchists, and oligarchs, with a top-down portrait of Spain embraced by the nationalist bourgeoisie, had narrowed *lo castizo* and had stacked the cultural institutions, academies, and universities with ideologues who invented neat lineages to justify their social positions; they had even transformed Don Quixote from a mad knight errant into a rational conquistador. Thus, Ramón Menéndez Pidal could claim that Castilian, "this Hispano-Roman language, continuous in its natural evolution, is the same found as a literary language in the *Poema del Cid*, the same brought to perfection by Alfonso the Sage, and essentially, the same in which Cervantes wrote."[19] At their core, Unamuno's nativism and even his nationalism were a *critique* of Spanish nationalism as it was conceived and disseminated at the time. (Later, he called the hypernationalist regime of Miguel Primo de Rivera that exiled him in the 1920s "pornocratic" and replete with "rapacious tyranny" that was busily "fool-making" and "bleeding" its people—a regime of "sluts, thieves, and troglodytes.")[20]

Unamuno shared plenty of sympathy with Menéndez Pidal and with the reigning imperialists, but his understanding of the Castilian tongue came from other sources and helped compose a distinct political vision that valorized translation as the instrument of evolution and exchange. Through folkloric study, new dictionaries and glossaries, and most important, translations of a wide range of texts that reveal *casticismo* by way of comparative contrast, the state must become an organic expression of the culture of average Spaniards, he argued. José Luis Venegas adds that Unamuno saw literary creation itself as fundamentally social, making the "process of authorial self-discovery" through inventing fictions a parallel to the "principles of collective identity" that he advocated.[21] Academic scholarship—especially philology—froze and finished this process: "What a cemetery a dictionary is!" Unamuno wrote in a poem.[22] In another, he asserted his dedication to "Lengua, lengua, no lenguaje"—"Tongue, tongue, not language"; the latter term also signifies style and jargon, removed from the organic embodiedness of the "tongue."[23]

Average Spaniards, Unamuno asserted, had fundamentally anarchic, mystical, and irrational souls that the state had tamed into an artificially rational order. To discover this lost Spain, Unamuno elaborated a new theory of Hispanicity (*hispanidad*)—not "*españolidad*"—because he wanted to "attach himself to the old historico-geographic concept of Hispania [the Roman province], which included all of the Iberian Peninsula," not simply the modern state-formation of Spain (*España*).[24] His romantic sense that races and languages were natural and timeless while states were historical and contingent ("only the human is eternally *castizo*") led him to elevate Spain's unique contributors to intellectual and religious history—the mystics, such as St. John of the Cross, Teresa of Ávila, and Fray Luis de León.[25] In order for Unamuno's claims to cohere, "Spain" first had to be delimited to a renovated Castilian essence and then had to be expanded to include the imperial and international contacts that had caused the Castilian tongue's evolution over time. The philosopher therefore railed against regional separatist movements and applauded the historical assimilation of tongues such as Leonese and Aragonese into Castilian during the Reconquista, when Isabella and Ferdinand united both crowns and tongues. (He even urged Castilian Spaniards to learn to read the languages of their provincial neighbors such as the Catalans and Galicians in order to absorb and assimilate their influences in making a single Iberian community that coalesced from the periphery toward the center.)

And though he called the "lengua castellana" his "intimate coat [*íntimo abrigo*]," he believed that the tongue needed to be "Europeanized" and "modernized," to become "at once lighter and more precise; it needs some disarticulation, because of the present tendency to anchylosis. . . . Our language tells us things from across the great sea that it never told us here."[26] He believed that the "spirit" of the Castilian language that existed in the blood of Spaniards could be carried abroad and enriched, whether by *criollos* in Spanish America or by exiles and omnivorous readers such as himself.

With these theories, Unamuno was intervening in the debates over race, language, and nation that had been fermenting in Spain and in Spanish America at least since the 1830s; in the second half of the nineteenth century, Domingo Faustino Sarmiento and Juan Valera had become leading public voices on these matters.[27] Unamuno's chauvinist, paternalistic assumptions and his cultural imperialism are clear and have been noted by many contemporary scholars. But rather than embracing the material politics of Spanish Empire—he opposed the neocolonial invasion of Morocco too—he translated, as Joan Ramon Resina writes, "the end of political empire [into] the founding of a language empire and the achievement of linguistic supremacy over historical and geographic contingencies."[28] The losses in the Spanish-American War could only be compensated by gains within Spain in order to exercise "spiritual" authority over the cultures of the New World, in what Robin Fiddian calls an "illustration of the metropolitan intelligentsia's reluctant adjustment to the postcolonial realities of *fin de siglo* Spain."[29] Unamuno saw a threat: the former colonies were not sites where *casticismo* was evolving and progressing; in fact, they were fragmenting Castilian and fusing it with indigenous, black diasporic, or other elements that had no roots in Iberian soil or being. Thus, he launched a project of unifying Spanish-speaking peoples around the world, not only in Spain. Unamuno was at pains to praise the fact that the Spanish language had been reconstituted and manifested in so many colorful modes in the New World—rather than confessing that it had variously conquered, absorbed, and wiped out many local tongues. Unamuno desired to see a number of distinct dialects of Spanish all bound together by an "habla común" (common speech), a core of Iberian Castilian. The resulting tongue would be "sobrecastellano" ("Super-Castilian"), which had absorbed and purified elements from abroad and vernacular variations on Iberian Spanish.[30]

While dismissing writing by German or Italian immigrants to Latin America, Unamuno celebrated the "Americanization" (referring to Spanish America, not the United States) of Spanish and the poetry of Peruvian and Uruguayan Spanish vernacular traditions. In his early, much-debated 1894 article on *Martín Fierro*, Unamuno called the poem "the flower of *gaucho* literature, that literature which is so unknown here [in Spain] . . . the consecration of [Argentina's] independence, the flower of the *criollo* spirit."[31] The poem was, for him, at once Argentine and "deeply Spanish . . . Spanish in its language . . . Spanish in its soul."[32] Indeed, he even held that *gaucho* idioms are a "resurrection of our adventurers from the earliest times of the Reconquest."[33] This work, whose idioms and dialectal terms are ultimately "of the pure Spanish race" (*españoles de pura raza*), was Homeric for him, and it carried forward a tradition seen in the *Poema del Cid* and *Chanson de Roland*. But, he added, for the poem to be "propagated in Spain, it will have to be accompanied by a short glossary and notes for explication."[34] He illustrates this program for how to study the demotic and to make it intelligible abroad by including notes on words like *chacras* (small farms) and *boliche* (grocery store), calling them the "breath of the Pampa," formative parts of the "lengua nacional argentina."[35] (However, he undermines his own celebration of *Martín Fierro* by claiming that its non-Spanish words derived mostly from indigenous terminology, not from words used by *criollos* or settlers of Spanish origin.)[36] The colonial hegemony of the past was, for Unamuno, now multicultural unity-in-diversity, and he propagated this thought not only in Spain but also in over four hundred publications in Spanish American media in the first quarter of the century.[37] Moreover, technological modernity, rationalism, science, and commercial expansion were symptoms of Europe's disease, for which Spain, after undergoing its own indigenous version of a Reformation, held the cure in its global linguistic empire of irrationality and mystical mythology.

The Dialectics of Translation: English Literature in Spain

Unamuno's dynamic inward/outward process for recovering and reconstituting Spain and for ensuring its cultural supremacy in Spanish America relied crucially—and paradoxically—on his own work as a translator. Translation was a hermeneutic, poetic, and ethnographic process for him:

one could understand another nation, as it expressed itself in literature, by attempting to translate its key works—and by failing. "There is nothing like [translation] to set oneself to carrying out," he wrote of translating Greek, for "to have to pour [*verter*] a thought from one language to another, one must penetrate both languages and the thought itself."[38] At the same time, he argued that no language was immune to the corruption that any translation brings: "I challenge anyone to translate Hegel or Schleiermacher into correct and clean Castilian without disfiguring its thought or killing its nuances.... In reality, there is nothing perfectly translatable." "Languages," he added, "are, strictly speaking, untranslatable but not impenetrable; there is commerce between them."[39]

Here we return to a paradox of nativism and, indeed, to many versions of exceptionalism: Unamuno himself claimed that he searched out the "least translatable" in each culture and felt that languages had "commerce between them" yet resisted successful translation, so what ends does translation serve other than affirming the foreignness of the Other, rendered in necessarily inadequate Spanish? Unamuno used his own Spanish existence as an example of how to approach the foreign, claiming that he "felt" the many parts of Spain's intrahistorical past in himself, including its "Africanism" and "Europeanism" alike. But he could only feel them through an "intimate relationship" formed by "oppositions" and internal dialectics: "When I was a child, my mother, who had studied in France, had me learn French; I read German at twenty, English at twenty-five, and I've scarcely read in Spanish. I have lived outside of Spain in spirit—and that is what has made me Spanish."[40] When giving his own literary-philosophical lineage, he wrote that "I can point to Hegel, Spencer, Schopenhauer, Carlyle, Leopardi, Tolstoy, as my main teachers, and along with them the thinkers with religious concern, and the English lyric poets.... As regards Spaniards, I can affirm, for sure: none, nobody. I scarcely have been influenced by any Spanish writer at all. My soul is not very Spanish."[41] By "discovering" his Hispanicity through foreign-language contacts rather than through the supposition of a mother tongue, he hopes to revive what had become a stale heritage of Spanish literature. Translation and native-language enrichment, in other words, were impossible but nevertheless mutually beneficial projects. When he composed his experimental novel-essay *Cómo se hace una novela* (How to make a novel) in Spanish, Unamuno had it translated into French in 1926 before it appeared in Spanish, then published it in Spanish in 1927 by retranslating the French version back into Spanish, with annotations on the French. He similarly refused to read works in translation, devoting himself instead to learning the original language and then pairing it with his own work.

Turning back on himself in his own poetry, Unamuno writes, "Translators, traitors! / Fathers of Esperanto, / bricklayers of Babel!" He calls upon translators—framed with an allusion to the Italian play on words *traduttore, traditore*—to look not only to other languages but also "below ground," to the "singular tongue, the untranslatable, / eternal, universal."[42] His first major collection of his own poetry, *Poesías* (1907), included translations of Carducci, Leopardi, Coleridge, and his Catalan friend Joan Maragall at the end. In a note to that volume he wrote that he saw no point in trying to render Italian free verse, for example, in Spanish syllabics. He explained, too, that he used in one of his own poems a word, "enlojada," that "is not found in the Royal Academy's dictionary, but that I have gathered"—returning to his familiar phrasing—"from the mouth of the *pueblo*."[43] As in the case of Pound, the line typically drawn between translation and original poetic production was constantly crossed and blurred, and as did Pound, Unamuno valorized discovery and creation by error rather than by mastery in the process of translation.[44]

A voracious reader and autodidact, Unamuno knew French, Italian, Portuguese, Greek, Latin, German, English, Swedish, and German well enough to translate from them. His publications for the journal *La España Moderna*, a review of European thought, brought dozens of new works to Spanish readers.[45] These included translations of Schopenhauer, Hegel, Leopardi, Herbert Spencer, Carl von Lemcke, Karl Kautsky, and Karl Larsen. He soon began contributing translations to other prestigious magazines such as *La Revista Internacional*. Briefly under the spell of Hippolyte Taine's work, he also translated more foreign views of Spain, including the German Ferdinand Wolf's *Studies in the History of Spanish and Portuguese National Literature*. In the final years of the 1800s, he translated Shakespeare, Shelley, Spencer, and Carlyle, among many others, and he published versions of English tracts on political economy. All told, he produced more than one thousand pages of translations from English between 1893 and 1900.[46] Translations of Coleridge, Wordsworth, and Whitman would follow soon after.

In the early 1900s, an appreciation of English literature was in vogue among Spanish intellectuals, and Unamuno idealized it. For him, English was "the richest and most complete" language because of its three distinct historical sources (Anglo-Saxon, Franco-Norman, and Latin), making it the "omnivore of languages." (Castilian, however, had "double" the resources, he held, only they were as yet untapped.)[47] He believed that "English literature is, without a doubt, the least monotonous, has better variety of tones and accents to offer us and above all that in which we find more men who have written and fewer professional *literatos*." Unlike French and its rootless cosmopolitanism, as he saw it, "English literature has become superior to all other literatures because it has been one of aficionados and not professionals."[48] Furthermore, England's political life was, for him, the "the most translatable," and it exhibited the best reciprocal expressive relationship with its literature.[49] But among common Spaniards, a "xenophobic . . . Anglophobia, an artificial and artificed product" of political cultures, remained in place. This fear was the "product of bad education and a systematic falsification of past history" born of the myth that English literature presented a threat to the "fragile . . . traditional *castizo* education."[50]

He warned, however, that English was potentially suffering by way of its homogenization through commerce—that it was becoming, in effect, an argot of international business. Just months after the War of 1898, Unamuno published "The English-Speaking Folk," an article in which he claimed, with an eye to Anglophone U.S. writing, that English was becoming "a *Volapük* of business and *Sabir* of the uncouth."[51] Under the "banner of divine conquest through industrialism," he writes, English is now the "most advanced language [*idioma*] among the developmental courses of our tongues [*lenguas*]," removed from any single, knowable *pueblo*.[52] English has been "enriched through derivation, through metaphorical translations of meaning, and greatly through the pressure of foreign terms. It is, like the people who speak it, a predatory language; it takes words where it happily finds them and appropriates them simply by saying them in its own way."[53] This market-driven assimilative process will eventually impoverish English to the point of linguistic death, he holds.

English could be recovered through the same internal/external mechanisms that held promise for reviving Spain: indeed, English could be deepened and made more complex by translations by Spaniards. Blake, H. G. Wells, and above all, the lyric poets—Wordsworth, Coleridge, Burns, and Keats are often cited—influenced him, and he appreciated the challenge their uses of English presented: "writers in Southern [European] countries . . . ought to immerse ourselves sometimes in Northern fogs. . . .

Our own depths are spread out fully through contact with the foreign [*lo extraño*]. . . . Usually what is most untranslatable in foreign literatures is poetry, and within it, the lyric tradition . . . especially the English lyric," which he saw as "the purest expression of a national culture."[54] He found "national culture" in lesser-known works, too, such as William Cobbett's *Rural Rides* (1822–1826), a series of portraits of bucolic and pastoral life in the English Midlands. Drawing a parallel to the Spanish romantic poet and dramatist José Zorrilla, who collected national and folk legends and revived forgotten plays, Unamuno insists that such works are nearly untranslatable because of their reliance on localism, yet they must be translated. (Unamuno's notes from his readings in foreign literatures are full of marginal comments on words he discovers in them that are local, vernacular terms not found in dictionaries.) Unamuno then continued his own studies of folktales with essays on the Welsh romance legends, and he wrote both on England's cultural historians who took an interest in Spain, such as George Borrow, and on contemporary Hispanists such as Martin Hume.

In his first major translation, Unamuno published the entirety of Carlyle's *The French Revolution: A History* (1837) from 1900–1902, just as he was revising and reissuing his own *En torno al casticismo*. Carlyle famously wrote with extensive use of the first person, in the present tense, as an imagined eyewitness to the French Revolution, and with an epic, metaphorical, novelistic, multiperspectival, and rhetorically rich style. This literary combination, Unamuno suggested, was necessary for Spain to digest in this moment, just after the Disaster: Carlyle was an intrahistorian of a foreign culture, a disseminator of foreign (German) thought and literature domestically, and a foreigner (a Scot) within a homogenizing empire. Unamuno praised Carlyle's prose as a Scots-inflected blend of English's Germanic and Latinate roots executed with authorial personality, not with the artificial detachment that Unamuno associated with academic historiography. Carlyle also spoke to Spaniards because, Unamuno wrote, "we lack that which Carlyle called the heroism of the *pueblo*."[55] Unamuno nicknamed him "Maese Pedro," after the puppet-show director in *Don Quixote*, for "his way of 'making' history"—his pulling the strings of farce, comedy, tragedy, and more at perfect moments.[56] When Unamuno's translations were presented to Spanish readers, the editor of the journal *Advertencia* wrote that "Carlyle, the prince of English writers, is unknown in Castilian. All that has been published is one treason [*traición*] of *Heroes,* incomplete."[57] This note was followed by a letter from Unamuno himself, saying that his translation was "crude, because I have proposed to reflect the very peculiar and not always clear style of this eloquent Puritan."[58] He wrote that his "great feat in translating *The French Revolution* into Spanish was simply to take the same liberties with Spanish that [Carlyle] did with English, and where he forged an English word I would forge a Spanish one . . . [in order to capture] the specific Carlylean rhetoric," which required "abusing Castilian Spanish."[59]

Translating Carlyle contributes to the reformation and renovation of Spanish. Carlyle became an ambassador of Anglophone literature for Unamuno, and so it was that, in the same moment in which he was arguing that Spaniards must recover only what was buried in their linguistic soil, he was establishing himself as one of the chief importers of works whose "Anglo-Saxonism" was far removed from anything Spanish. He realized later that he chose "Carlyle, not for his ideas, which strike me as very sparse and not at all original, but for his exposition of them, his impetuous style"; he declared that "it was Carlyle who perhaps contributed most to my finding my own style."[60] Carlyle had provided a path for literary English that Unamuno would synthesize with his own Spanish *poiesis*. But the preservation of a lyric tradition and the literary witness to political change, Unamuno saw, were more active in the United States—a country that, unlike England, was a postcolonial empire that also had a still-visible Hispanophone presence.

The United States and the English-Spanish World

What intrigued Unamuno most was not just the monolingual English canon of American literature, which he did not find furthered England's linguistic empire, but also the growing Hispanophone world of the United States—and the new class of mostly academic Hispanists. Unamuno saw here the grounds for a reciprocal circuit of intellectual exchange between two nations that had just been at war. He befriended a number of Hispanists, translators, and expatriate American Hispanophiles: Warner Fite, Everett Ward Olmsted, Royall Tyler, Rudolph Schevill, Homer Earle, Raymond Weaver, and Archer Milton Huntington. At the same time, Unamuno's students Federico de Onís and Ángel del Río became leading Hispanists in the United States, and Unamuno himself contemplated leaving Salamanca for a teaching post in the United States as early as 1903.[61] Turning away from British Hispanists, he concluded that by 1906, "the United States now is the nation in which Spain is studied better and more extensively. All of its great universities now have Spanish literature and language courses."[62] Unamuno believed that the U.S. interest in Spain was a boon for his own *casticismo*. Addressing a Spanish audience, he acknowledges that politics bear on his own account of U.S. Hispanophilia, and he acknowledges the local fear of an ulterior motive on the part of the "anglosajones" to dominate Spanish America politically and economically. But Unamuno repudiates this by saying that the American Hispanists do not seek material gain or domination; instead, they desire to "penetrate the spirit" of Spanish America by way of Spain—to understand their neighbors to the south by understanding Lope de Vega and Cervantes better.[63] Again relying on a nostalgic impression of spirit dubiously separated from the material effects of imperialism, he reads this through the reigning philosophical discourses in the United States—especially positivism and what he sees as its connections to global capitalism—but claims to see an antiutilitarian thrust behind this U.S. intellectual enterprise. Spain and its former republics, on the other hand, are consumed and ripped apart by a brand of positivism that has killed their imaginations.

Shortly after 1898, Unamuno began staging a series of U.S./Spanish juxtapositions:

> When Spain was forced in war with the United States, the daily press let loose a flood of ineptitudes when talking about the butchers—other times they would call them, with a little more finesse, "pigs"—the barbarous Yankees who thought of nothing other than amassing millions. A chorus of proud and presumptuous ignorance. One could talk of Emerson or of Longfellow, of James or Channing, but it was useless. And later, when they defeated us, one could hardly recognize the spirit of Emerson, for instance, in the portraits of our conquerors.[64]

Broadening his reading of the effects of U.S. interventionism over the next two decades, Unamuno celebrated the entry of the United States into the Great War and regretted that Spain was nearly absent from the world stage by then. He hated the "pagan imperialism" and destructiveness of the German Empire and declared, "the country of Washington and

Lincoln will not fail in this great Revolution"; Germany, he writes, had "Kultura with a K"—culture as a war machine of corrupted Christianity.⁶⁵ Meanwhile, "here I am [in Spain], with pen in hand, fighting a brave quixotic battle against our reactionaries, almost all of them Germanophiles (without knowing Germany, of course)," while Spain fragments internally in its provinces.⁶⁶ The Americans, for Unamuno, are joining English and Jewish peoples as the "most active workers for a future international society—diligent, antimilitaristic, without ignorant notions of pride," despite the motivations for the Spanish-American War.⁶⁷

Unamuno's apologetic tone after 1898 would resonate with the U.S. audiences that had begun to read his works in English translation in the early 1900s, when academic, literary, and popular writers—from Havelock Ellis to Ford Madox Ford—frequently discussed him. (He also corresponded with figures ranging from Pound to Frank to Lewis Mumford, and he met Dos Passos, Hemingway, and others personally.) In 1909, Unamuno published a series of essays, entitled "The Spanish Spirit," in the London weekly *Englishwoman*, in which he argued that Spanish was becoming, with English, "one of the two great Indo-European languages of the world" but that these two tongues would soon find a unique union.⁶⁸ Unamuno was happy, for instance, to see the signal term "Yankee" absorbed into Spanish as *yanqui* rather than importing the "exotic" letter *k* to Spain.⁶⁹ He added contributions to the *Independent* and the *Saturday Review*, then wrote several book reviews for the British academic journal *Hispania*.⁷⁰ These engagements with the Anglophone literary and professional world took place just as Unamuno was composing what would become his most discussed work beyond Spain, *The Tragic Sense of Life* (*Del sentimiento trágico de la vida*, 1913)—a text he claimed to have written with a volume of Keats in hand.⁷¹ The English translation of *Tragic Sense* proved to be the culmination of a broad-ranging English-Spanish synthesis that Unamuno had been theorizing and working to enact across the first two decades of the twentieth century.

The book, a philosophical meditation that Unamuno conveys through interpretations of his own international precursors in thought and literature, is antisystematic and thrives on a resistance to form and rational articulation. Indeed, Unamuno quotes Whitman in the middle of the text in defense of his method: "that tremendous Yankee poet [wrote that] . . . 'I charge that there be no theory or school founded out of me.' "⁷² Rather, the text implies a theory of translation that encapsulates Unamuno's debts to Carlyle and his approach to native languages. By claiming in his author's preface to the English edition that his translator, the British Hispanist J. E. Crawford Flitch, had "merely converted not a few of the thoughts and feelings therein expressed back into their original form of expression," Unamuno binds his own authorial capacities to a non-Spanish language that happens to dominate the globe in the moment.[73] He adds that he has revised the translation extensively in collaboration with Flitch, so much so that it is now "a correction, in certain respects, of the original." Moreover, the necessary changes and cuts "perhaps compensate . . . for what [they] may lose in the spontaneity of my Spanish thought, which at times, I believe, is scarcely translatable."[74] The text includes myriad allusions to, citations from, and discussions of Anglophone figures, from Arnold and Bacon to Oliver Wendell Holmes and William James. Unamuno characterizes Spain, furthermore, through quotations from Huntington.

Unamuno's claims to have composed *through* English are difficult to verify with textual evidence. What is certain is that his international career, and particularly his importance in the United States, almost immediately ascended. When *The Tragic Sense of Life* appeared in English in 1921, it garnered over twenty reviews, and the praise landed Unamuno a "translation package" to bring his complete works into English.[75] Unamuno found himself treated, as his peer Ortega soon would be, as a global voice representing Spain in the interwar period. Beyond his work he became known as a "spokesman for social justice and intellectual freedom" after he was dismissed from his rectorship in 1914, tried in 1920, and exiled in 1924. The British *Athenæum*, which commented regularly on his works, cited him as a voice for "intellectual progress" who was being victimized by a "militarist government" and added that "if he has a weakness, it is his passion for Englishmen."[76] The Hispanist Aubrey Bell called him a "modern Don Quixote, tilting against the windmills of every rigid and stilted system," and the *Encyclopedia Britannica* and *London Mercury* alike averred that he was the greatest living Spanish writer.[77] Unamuno's banishment to the Canary Islands soon became an international cause célèbre for intellectuals and writers, even eliciting condemnation from T. S. Eliot, who typically refrained from making such statements in *Criterion*.[78] Unamuno's own caustic letter that blasted the Primo de Rivera regime circulated in translation across a number of media globally.

Seeking to capitalize on Unamuno's growing name, Ezra Pound wrote him in 1920 and sent him a copy of his *Quia pauper amavi* (1919) with an inscription, then followed with several more letters. Pound had just become the foreign editor for the revamped *Dial*, and he wrote to Scofield Thayer that Unamuno "is accepted as the most important Spanish writer," so that if the magazine wanted to convey "what the outer world ought to know about Spain" and to gain the "respect of [the] Hispanic world . . . a monthly Unamuno wd. be a good start."[79] Pound asked Unamuno for some "literary studies or 'recuerdos' [memoirs]" for the *Dial*, hoping that he would "make *The Dial* your representative organ in the United States."[80] An advertisement for the new *Dial* in the *Nation* named Unamuno as part of the review's staff covering "The Continent," but the Spaniard eventually published only one piece in the *Dial*, a short, enigmatic parable of literary philosophy called "The Cavern of Silence" (1924).[81] Unamuno also wrote for other Spanish-language media in the United States, such as the New York–based *El Gráfico* in 1917 (where he urged Spaniards again to "Spanish-ify" themselves), and he dedicated a poem to the first issue of the *Revista Hispánica Moderna*, founded in 1934 by Onís. He added to this bilingual and translational work by writing prologues and epilogues in the 1920s and 1930s to Spanish translations of English-original works, including W. H. Hudson's *The Purple Land* (1885), the novel about an Englishman in Uruguay that memorably figures into the plot of Hemingway's *The Sun Also Rises* (1926).

Unamuno's ties to Onís and other U.S. Hispanists ensured that he was discussed often in *Hispania*; his works made their ways into classrooms and graduate seminars, and his name was mentioned frequently in the new academic journals of modern languages in the United States in the 1920s. Intellectual and middlebrow media discussed him, too, and by 1924, the imagist poet John Gould Fletcher would even use Unamuno's work to reread Whitman.[82] That same year, the *International Book Review* (New York) named *Tragic Sense* one of the ten greatest books of the century (though the century was not even one-quarter finished), and later, Unamuno wrote for journals such as *Books Abroad*, was reprinted in the *Living Age*, and, finally, contributed to the *New York Times*. His exchanges with Waldo Frank then solidified his relationship with the United States. In 1927, Unamuno published in the Argentine *Síntesis* his touchstone article "Hispanidad," which was partially a review of Frank's *Virgin Spain* (1926)—a text that, in turn, includes a discussion of the "strictly modern . . . radical mystic" Unamuno.[83] Seeing Spain in mystical, organicist terms that converge neatly with Unamuno's, Frank calls the philosopher "the strongest moralist of our day," adding that "Wells and Shaw have thin voices beside his well-aimed uproar" (*VS* 282). Unamuno in turn praises Frank's portrait of Spain and then translates the final chapter of *Virgin Spain*, "The Port of Columbus." The chapter is an imagined dialogue between Cervantes and Columbus in which the writer has the explorer look upon the chaos and Babel of the land he discovered. Columbus confuses it with Spain—"Are you looking at America, or Spain?"—and sees that the New World has been nothing but the "Grave of Europe" (*VS* 296, 298). And when "Modern Europe flourished," Spain was busy playing mother to a new world: "She bore America" (*VS* 299). Columbus finally prophesies that Spain will endow its eternal "spirit" upon "the north: they whose speech is English" and who have ruined the world with global capitalism (*VS* 300).

The fusion that Frank sees between Spain and the United States appealed to Unamuno: for both of them, Spain could be the spiritual leader of a commercialized, Americanized globe. Unamuno believed that his own career could forge such U.S.-Spanish bonds, much as Jiménez hoped to do poetically. He collaborated robustly with the U.S. journal *El Mercurio*—a vital and emblematic source of the Spanish language in the English-dominated country, as he saw it. The review listed him on the masthead as its correspondent-editor for sociological issues and, at one point, offered him the editorship. With its simultaneous international focus and dedication to the local growth and dissemination of Hispanophone cultural life in the United States, *El Mercurio* stands as a vital record of Spanish intellectual debate of the moment.[84] In an early issue, Unamuno published one of his own seminal essays, "Lengua y patria" (1911), in which he lauds Argentina for having resisted an English invasion and defended its Spanish linguistic traditions.[85] He sees language as the "currency" in the "commerce of ideas," for "today, language [*lengua*] is the principal patrimony of all Hispanic *pueblos*, it is our fortune, the banner that our merchandise must display." To conserve the Spanish language, he writes, is to conserve the "individual spiritual independence" that it brings, and without that, political independence is meaningless. Turning to the Anglophone world in which his readers mostly lived, he writes that

> when one of the proponents of the supremacy of "English-speaking folk" repeats, referring to England and the United States, that blood is thicker

than water, alluding to the consanguinity that unites more than the sea separates ... he forgets that the blood of the spirit is language, and that the North American of Polish, German, Italian, or Irish blood, if he speaks and thinks in English, feels in English, whether he wishes it or not, English is the blood of his soul.[86]

English, therefore, has performed the linguistic-racial union that consolidates the United States, yet it has only done so in tension with many other languages. Spanish, meanwhile, is the language of some twenty nations without being the monopoly of any one of them—not even Spain—and he now tells his Hispanophone audience that it "is the language that will one day share with English global dominance."[87] The "international tongue [*lengua*]" of Castilian "will come to be the second, and perhaps the first, tongue in the world," he prophesies.[88] This triangulated circuit—the United States, Spanish America, and Spain—maps an evolving "spiritual" world in which Unamuno sees a global future of vernaculars forged by linguistic extensions of English and Spanish.

Unamuno, Whitman, and the American World

Unamuno ultimately searched, as he did in all national literary traditions, for the organic, authentic spirit of this country—the United States—in which he himself was now a literary voice in two languages. He read Emerson, Thoreau, and Poe, then many works by William James. Soon his library contained books by writers ranging from Franklin to Pound.[89] But for Unamuno, the English-language literary production of the United States was summed up in the work of Whitman, who was then being translated more frequently in Spain. He had written several essays on the poet; one of the first was "Adamic Song" (1913), in which he characterizes Whitman as "that American, enormous embryo of a secular poet."[90] Whitman was an American master of the lyric poetry that Unamuno appreciated in England's history. In another article, "Abraham Lincoln and Walt Whitman" (1918), written during the Great War, Unamuno praised Whitman for having juxtaposed an opium eater, a fishpacker, and a prostitute with the president and his cabinet, all as a means of capturing the entirety of the *pueblo*. In his poems on Lincoln, "Whitman gave to the world his poems to define America, its athletic democracy . . . he left us a book that is a man, a mirror of this most overflowing collective life. . . . He was not a politician in the specific sense of the word . . . but contributed more to the formation of the civil soul of the Great Democracy of North America than most of the politicians of his day."[91]

Whitman furthermore appealed to him as a Hispanophile who recovered Spain's presence in the United States. Whitman's poem "Spain" (1873) recycled a number of persisting tropes for Spanish decay, feudalism, immutability, and syncretism—Spain was the dying mother of the New World, a fallen monument frozen in time and immobile. Yet Spain's vitality in the history of the United States was key to Whitman: Spain's death and life in the New World were entwined. Returning to his poetic tropes in an essay-letter "The Spanish Element in Our Nationality" (1883), Whitman writes that, against the overemphasis on the United States' English and German roots, "no stock shows a grander historic retrospect—grander in religiousness and loyalty, or for patriotism, courage, decorum, gravity and honor" than Spaniards.[92] Whitman urges Americans to "dismiss utterly the illusion-compound" portraits of Spaniards that he claims are stereotypes invented from *The Mysteries of Udolpho*, and he even asserts that the "cruelty, tyranny, [and] superstition" found in Spanish history is equivalent in the "corresponding *résumé* of Anglo-Norman history."

This romantic melting pot became for Unamuno an ideal figuration of the United States and its Spanish roots: Whitman, who had a prominent name in Hispanophone letters by the turn of the century, was for Unamuno the bard of a shifting, bilingual U.S. tradition. First, Unamuno imitated some of Whitman's prosody in his own works.[93] Then, alongside verses addressed to Melville and Poe, he wrote a short poem to Whitman in 1929:

> Walt Whitman, you who said:
> this is not a book, it is a man;
> this is not a man, it is the world
> of God to which I gave a name.[94]

Whitman's popular embrace of America's diverse immigrant populace was the most elemental piece for him to translate, Unamuno believed. Thus, after having translated the entirety of "O Captain! My Captain!" and the first part of "When Lilacs Last in the Dooryard Bloom'd," he rendered in Spanish the eleventh section of "Salut au monde!" (1856)—the section in which Whitman shifts from a poetic "I" to an internationalist "You." In Whitman's original, he catalogues capaciously and with exclamations the new citizenry of America with an globalizing purview that, as scholars have noted, he widened on revision—when he also changed the title from "Poem of Salutation" to a French phrase:

> You, whoever you are!
> You daughter or son of England!
> You of the mighty Slavic tribes or empires! you Russ in Russia!
> You dim-descended, black, divine-soul'd African, large,
>   fine-headed, nobly-form'd, superbly destin'd, on equal terms
>   with me!
> You Norwegian! Swede! Dane! Icelander! you Prussian!
> You Spaniard of Spain! you Portuguese!
> You Frenchwoman and Frenchman of France![95]

Whitman's list begins in England, and it begins with the female subject, not the male; he repeats this order with "Frenchwoman and Frenchman." And perhaps most famously, he spends the most time describing his peer of African origin, elevating him romantically and invoking the first person to place him "on equal terms with me!"

Whitman's spiritual populism was, for Unamuno, a version of humanistic socialism rooted in Christianity, and Whitman presented for him a lyrical portrait of heterogeneity contained under the aegis of a single national destiny. His translation from 1930, which is mostly literal and attempts to replicate Whitman's cadences in Spanish, begins as follows:

> ¡Tú quién quiera que seas!,
> tú hijo o hija de Inglaterra,
> ¡tú de los poderosos imperios y tribus eslavos!, ¡tú ruso de Rusia!,
> ¡tú oscuramente descendido, negro africano de divina
>   alma, grande, de fina cabeza, noblemente formado,
>   soberbiamente destinado, en iguales términos que yo!,
> ¡tú noruego!, ¡sueco!, ¡danés!, ¡islandés!, tú prusiano!,
> ¡tú español de España!, ¡tú portugués!
> ¡vosotros francés y francesa de Francia![96]

Unamuno converts the opening line, which Whitman builds around the repeating "oo" sound, into a "que" sound that he repeats in three consecutive words. He also shifts the repeated "you" into a subjunctive clause that will not be repeated throughout as the "you" (*tú*) will be. Unamuno reverses the gender order of Whitman's list: for both English and French subjects, he places the male ("hijo" and "francés") first, undoing Whitman's gender politics. By a similar measure, he emphasizes the Slavic "poderosos imperios" before "tribus"—a political construction precedes tribalism here. Whitman's extended line on the "black, divine-soul'd African" provides Unamuno a creative opportunity for cultural translation, too. Whitman's "dim-descended" becomes "oscuramente descendido"; the Spanish root here, *oscura*, means "dark, gloomy," and secondarily, "black," allowing Unamuno to double the racial metaphor. "On equal terms with me" becomes a somewhat awkward "en iguales términos que yo!"—literally, "on the same terms as I [am]." The conjoining "with me" is subtly altered to create a slight distance between speaker and subject; "términos" (like the English "terms") signifies both "criteria" and "words" or "vocabulary." It plays also on "terminación" as "destiny" (linking to "destinado" in the previous phrase). Unamuno ambivalently embraces, in translation, the African pasts within Spain, even as he did little to recover African contributions to Spanish culture and, at times, disparaged Andalusia's Bedouin elements. He suggested instead (though with vacillations) that European environments and climates had produced the greatest thought.[97]

More important, Whitman's poeticized America ("the United States themselves are essentially the greatest poem") and Unamuno's intellectualized, spiritualized Spain converged in the early 1930s. The Spaniard believed that Whitman had founded a line of poetry that was being continued by certain U.S. poets who rejected the commercialized flattening of English internationally. Paralleling Dos Passos's reading of Spain, Unamuno immersed himself in the works of three regional American poets whom he saw as modern heirs to Whitman—the "Poets to Come" whom Whitman himself addressed in his own imagined future. They were the Chicagoan Carl Sandburg, Sidney Lanier of Georgia, and William Vaughn Moody of Indiana. Unamuno's readings of them inspired not translations but poeticizations in his own neoromantic, pastoral verse. That is, he composed *through* English much in the way that he claimed to have thought and articulated *Tragic Sense*, as he had done since reading Carlyle, and he characterized his own poetry as a mixture of Italian form and English lyric. Even when looking to vernacular poets, he rarely tried to translate dialect; instead, he relied again on glossing and adaptation. He dedicated a poem to the occasion of the baptism of his first grandchild after reading Sandburg's "Haze," for instance, and quoted the line, "Why do the cradles of the sky rock new babies?" Unamuno appreciated the ways in which, in the opening section ("Sunrise") of Lanier's "Hymns of the Marshes," the land and language are fully entwined:

> As a lover in heaven, the marsh my marsh and the sea my sea.
>
> Tell me, sweet burly-bark'd, man-bodied Tree
> That mine arms in the dark are embracing, dost know
> From what fount are these tears at thy feet which flow?
> They rise not from reason, but deeper inconsequent deeps.[98]

He responds with a poem called "Remembering Dante While Reading 'Sunrise (Hymns of the Marshes)' by Sidney Lanier."[99] Here, as Unamuno fuses his own voice with two foreign ones separated by six centuries, he writes of a "celestial shore on the river of the dead" in which he sees a mythic boat. This vision carries him to a place where "eternity fell / (in a single moment, / and I heard in the darkness / —God lay in its center—) / to the past, the grave / of the whole future [*porvenir*]." Unamuno appreciated Lanier's archaic diction and Anglo-Saxon sounds—like Unamuno, Lanier had written scholarly works on Welsh romances and Arthurian legends—finding them a Whitmanian version of a vernacular threatened by modernity. Lanier, however, went too far for Unamuno by writing in the dialectal voice of illiterate Southerners: dialect must remain linked more closely to the "core" language, he believed, as Sandburg's use of slang did.[100]

Unamuno's closest identification came with Moody. In his notes on Moody, he sees that this poet's sources are "his pueblo, [which allow] his I's . . . [to] come about by con-versation, not dia-logue. All poets are one, one collective poet. . . . [Even if in] auto-dialogue."[101] After reading Moody's "Road-Hymn for the Start," Unamuno wrote a new poem subtitled "*Errand-goers who forget?*—William Vaughn Moody." The line he cites comes from the following sequence in Moody:

> What we are no tongue has told us: Errand-goers who forget?
> Soldiers heedless of their harry? Pilgrim people gone astray?
> We have heard a voice cry "Wander!" That was all we heard it say.[102]

Moody's poem plaintively relishes a rustic life that had not been led "astray" by the "errands" of modern life. Unamuno's poem rewrites him:

> Forgotten errand-goers
> Of the errand; the stars
> Tell us nothing, we do not know how
> To read their footprints. . . .
> Errand-goers without errand
> —being forgotten means not being—
> our lost life escapes us,
> along with our future life.[103]

He concludes his poem inspired by Moody with the same word ending his Lanier poem: *porvenir* ("future," but also literally *por-* + *venir* [to come, to pass]). This subtle signal of an American future returns us to the legacy of Whitman that Unamuno sees not in the industrial world power that the United States had become but in the recovery of a *Volk* and their vernacular variations on English. Unamuno desired to foster contact for Spaniards with a certain part of the United States: the bucolic, socially diverse conglomeration of regions, vernaculars, and intrahistories that he saw as authentically American—and in danger of being wiped out by the dominant culture. (He even attempted, briefly, to capture in Spanish the rhythm of Langston Hughes's poetry: a poem written on Unamuno's copy of *Fine Clothes to the Jew* reads: "Ríe, briza, arrulla, llora, / cantando sobre la cuna" ["She laughs, rocks, coos, cries / singing above the cradle"].)[104] English and Spanish, he presumed, would unite and cover the world but would not produce hybrid tongues such as Spanglish. His own work—in English translation, as a translator of English, as a Spanish poeticizer of English, and more—would exemplify this revised Hegelian course of entwined "spirits." Whitman had no poetic lineage in the Spanish language in the United States that Unamuno had explored; rather, his own writing carried Whitman's legacy, in translation and *poiesis*, to Spain.

Thus it was that Unamuno became, across the interwar period, one of the first leading authorities in Spain on Anglophone U.S. literature through both his commentaries and his poetics. By contrast, his position in English-language literary history remains uncertain.[105] Even in Spain in 1930, just when his work was being appropriated by the burgeoning fascist and Falangist movements, *La Gaceta Literaria* devoted a special issue to his internationalism, featuring essays from writers around the world (including Dos Passos) titled "Unamuno and France," "Unamuno and England," "Unamuno and Judaism," and so forth.[106] He was called by the *New York Times* in 1932 "the greatest living philosopher among the world's hundred million Spanish-speaking people"; only four years later, when his engagements with U.S. culture were peaking, he died while under house arrest just after the outbreak of the Spanish Civil War.[107] In an obituary, the Hispanist and translator Walter Starkie dubbed him "the most important Spaniard that has ever lived since Goya," but he lost favor with other liberal intellectuals for having briefly backed the Nationalists in the war.[108] This disparate legacy—Unamuno as archetypal nationalist and cultural imperialist, Unamuno as cosmopolitan mediator of international exchange—bespeaks the central paradox of nativism's problem with translation. Unamuno is both Spanish and un-Spanish, a figure who, when seen through translation and as a translator, cannot be resolved or made authentic in the ways modernist historiography seems to demand.

III
New Genealogies

CHAPTER 5

Negro and *Negro*

Translating American Blackness in the Shadows of the Spanish Empire

> Led by American Negroes, the Negroes of the world are reaching out hands toward each other to know, to sympathize, to inquire. There are few countries without their few Negroes, few great cities without its groups, and thus with this great human force, spread out as it is in all lands and languages, the world must one day reckon. We face, then, in the modern black American, the black West Indian, the black Frenchman, the black Portuguese, the black Spaniard and the black African a man gaining in knowledge and power and in the definite aim to end color slavery and give black folk a knowledge of modern culture.
> —W. E. B. DU BOIS, "The Negro Mind Reaches Out,"
> in *The New Negro* (1925)

THE BLACKNESS OF SPAIN, HOWEVER OBSCURED, TRANSFIGURED, or distorted over time, was apparent to W. E. B. Du Bois, for whom the "black Spaniard" was part of the global battle for racial justice. Du Bois's journal *Crisis* pointed in a variety of articles to the hidden vitality of "black Spain," to its "black madonnas," even to Picasso and Gris as having come from "Afro-Celtiberian Spain."[1] As neocolonialist ambitions in Spain and Italy cast new "African shadows," Du Bois exhorted an expanded range of "black Spaniard[s]" to see their own implication in the struggle against capitalist imperialism and for an international black "modern culture."[2] Langston Hughes also theorized the blackness of the country that "once belonged to the Moors, a colored people ranging from light dark to dark white."[3] Hughes asserted that "many Spaniards are quite dark themselves, particularly those from the South, where the sun is hot and Africa not far away. Distinct traces of Moorish blood still remain," making Spain a European state in which race relations should be renovated paradigmatically.[4] In his poem "Letter from Spain" (1937), Hughes has an African American soldier from Alabama fighting for the Republic in the Spanish Civil War ask a dying Moorish soldier why he had joined Franco's legions. Johnny, the U.S. soldier, believes that the "Moor" was "just as dark as me" and thus is incredulous that he would give his life for a fascist cause that would only exacerbate the worldwide oppression of black peoples. Like Du Bois, Hughes saw a racist manifestation of Western imperialist ideals as inhibiting average Spaniards from embracing both their African roots and the tropes of blackness assigned to them by other Europeans for centuries; indeed, as inhibiting them from realizing their own black modernity, which had been fissured and left unrecognizable by the categories of race advanced by contemporary empires.

As they variously search out blackness in overlooked sites, Du Bois and Hughes employ a strategy common among several modes of claiming diasporic solidarity in the early twentieth century—a strategy that throws into relief some fundamental but confounding elements of modern Spanish history. The "Moor" that Johnny meets (most likely a Berber from Morocco) may well have been surprised to learn that he was "black," as Picasso would have been too. In fact, many of the crucial commonalities posited by the overlapping movements of the New Negro, *négritude, negrismo*, and various forms of pan-Africanism were complicated in Spain in the 1920s and 1930s. For that reason, Spain has remained a peculiar, often unintelligible space on the maps of global blackness, and contemporary critics have had little more success in grasping how it functioned in the cultural networks of this era. That is, Brent Hayes Edwards, Michelle Ann Stephens, Michel Fabre, Carrie Noland, and others have shown how black writing reached across languages and across the African diaspora to nearly all corners of the world.[5] Paris, where black arts found a wave of popularity in the *vogue nègre* during an idealistic moment of imagined racial reconciliation after the Great War, has long been understood as a central node from which this network also extended to France's colonies and dependencies.[6] The strong links between Harlem and the Anglo-, Franco-, and Hispanophone Caribbean have been recovered, too. But Spain's stereotypically recalcitrant and self-defined exceptionalism seems to be powerfully at work in resisting legibility in the dynamic spheres of international black culture.

These complications and aporias can be explored fruitfully by thinking about a single word and the concepts that coalesced around it: Negro. In the 1920s, Spaniards found that a word from their own language (*negro*)—one that had been used infrequently and unsteadily to denote race for centuries—had made an uncanny return in translation as an Anglophone formulation (Negro) that was a new marker of the quest for political, social, and cultural rights in the United States and across the globe.[7] "Negro" had acquired dignity and both symbolic and practical purchase in these campaigns, and it now had a broad-based literary movement—the New Negro Renaissance—attached to it. The translation of this keyword back into Spanish became a process in which critics and writers negotiated not only their national anxieties about race but also the contemporary politics of Spain's literary and imperial histories. The history that Du Bois, Hughes, and many others elicit dates back to the eighth century AD, when the Moors invaded the Iberian peninsula, and follows through to the fifteenth-century enslavement of West Africans in Spain just before the conquest of the New World. It continues through the racial theories that undergirded the Reconquista and the expulsion of Moors and Jews, through the transatlantic slave trade and the creation of theories of mixed blood, and, indeed, through to the 1920s and 1930s. Spain's attempt to colonize Morocco was met by a guerilla insurgency, led by Berbers in the Rif region, that shocked the invading army and triggered events leading to the Spanish Civil War, in which Franco enlisted "Moorish" soldiers for his cause. In short, Spain's uneasy relationship to blackness, and its concomitant modern reformulation of the Hispanic *raza* in this moment, made "Negro" / *negro* privileged terms for a variety of provocations and positions that shook the core of Spanish national mythology.

This chapter traces the ways in which a host of competing and conflicting voices and agendas attached themselves to a critical formation that crystallized these issues: *literatura negra* (black literature), which itself reframes New Negro, *negrista*, and other formations through imbalanced circuits of translation. I delineate first the fiercely contested emergence and coherence of *literatura negra* as it was understood as an aesthetic field, a political critique, or some combination of the two, all in the contexts of the revisions of the fields of Hispanism and American studies that this book has outlined. In part, these differing understandings were enabled by a paradox, as Spanish writers and critics saw it, that drew much commentary: the writers of the New Negro Renaissance had achieved international recognition because of the global rise of the same U.S. empire that they turned their pens against and exposed as a hypocritical beacon of freedom. This duality, along with the introspection prompted in Spain by modern American blackness (especially in literature), meant that more was read onto and through *literatura negra* than racial sympathy or aesthetic evaluation. An unexpected array of critics and poets, including key voices of Hispanophone Afro-Antillean literature, offered unorthodox synthetic genealogies of *literatura negra* that cited Spain as the origin of this mode of writing. Beginning in the mid-1930s, a spate of anthologies—themselves both manifestations and archives of literary community-making endeavors—sought to demonstrate that the roots of black writing lay in baroque Spanish poetry that had adapted the cultures of African slaves in early modern Spain, when the country's literature was great, as it was implied to be again in the contemporary moment. The experience of slavery became aestheticized, and empire was translated into a neutral set of geographical connections.

Translation enabled yet continually undermined or threatened such claims, and this chapter uses a combination of translational analysis, media history, and philology—zooming in and out at various moments—to tease out how *literatura negra* functioned as a multifarious complex. As translators, comparatists, critics, and writers sought to stabilize the still-shifting notions and terms for contemporary black writing, they aligned and separated Seville and the U.S. South in order to project a new, trans-historical collision of the present U.S. empire and the past Spanish one. The theoretical and translational pathways of *literatura negra*, which simultaneously carried Hispanism and American studies into new popular and leftist territories, included claims that Hughes and Lope de Vega, for instance, belonged in a single, synthetic, bilingual (English/Spanish) genealogy that often excised Paris, rendered Africa only a source from the past, and flattened the Americas into one unit. The converging and often exceptionalist conceptual and material histories I reconstruct here, that is to say, are concerned less with producing or theorizing a black modernity or Afromodernism or with the ontology (even the explanatory potential) of race or of terms like "America" / *americana*. Instead, they employ *literatura negra* as a means to reconfigure the relationships among poetry that resulted from slavery and its legacies, the primitivist aesthetics of white European writers, the patterns of blackface in early modern Spain's arts, the international stardom of Federico García Lorca, the reigning narratives of white U.S. exceptionalism, and the diasporic poetics of the Caribbean in ways that yoke the trajectories of imperialism to distinct aesthetic innovations.

In the second half of this chapter, I turn to two black U.S. writers, Hughes and Richard Wright, whose writings on Spain and translations of

Spanish literature reinterpret the processes that the first half of the chapter adumbrates. As he was in many international circuits, Hughes is the link here—he was both an emblem and a conduit of *literatura negra*—as he channeled to U.S. culture Spanish Republicanism, poetry (especially Lorca), and racial ideologies in his work as an unacknowledged, unofficial Hispanist. But his own collaboration on translations of racist propaganda for the Spanish Republic complicates what might otherwise seem like a fortuitous fusion of aesthetics, politics, and the fluid ideals of blackness that he represents. By concluding with Wright's ethnographic narrative of race relations in Franco's state, *Pagan Spain* (1957), I point to a still-germane critique of the benign nostalgia about the Spanish Empire's glory and the persisting attempts to reread racial conflicts brought about by imperialism as forerunners of multiculturalist aesthetics. Both Hughes and Wright seek to denaturalize and disorient Spain rather than to add it to a map of black literary production—to turn Spain's proclamations of exceptionalism in race and in literature against themselves. "Negro" and *negro* therefore highlight, in this chapter, not a bilingual fusion and an corollary attachment between U.S. and Spanish modernisms, but rather, an incommensurability, skepticism, and questioning of the legacies of black modern writing, through to Wright's recasting the terms again in Spain with his paradoxical formulation, "white Negro."

Conceiving *Literatura Negra* and the Politics of Translating Claude McKay

Spanish conceptions of race had been tethered to empire for centuries, whether in the obsessive theories of castes and gradations of blood in the New World or in the blood-purity norms established in Spain itself, where African slaves were imported from the mid-1400s.[8] As it did across Europe and the United States, racial taxonomies saw a resurgence of study and debate in Spain beginning in the late 1800s. Madrid held a colonial exposition in 1897 that replicated those seen in Paris and London; anthropology, the human sciences, and several pseudosciences were consolidated as academic disciplines; the fervent arguments for regional separatism in Spain's provinces, such as Galicia, the Basque Country, and Catalonia, now used biology to justify their claims; and at the same time, Jews and Gypsies were often depicted in blackface-style caricature. For Spanish thinking about blackness,

Cuba and Morocco were the two constant, quite dissimilar coordinates; the Disaster of 1898, the ongoing race rebellions, and the new invasions of North Africa kept them in focus. In 1914, Julián Juderías coined a term that would be used all around the world, *la leyenda negra* (the Black Legend), to refer to the demonization of the Spanish, through tropes of Africanness, as cruel barbarians in the New World conquest (see introduction). Juderías's book went through numerous editions and unified the knowledge on what was often called *España negra*, a term that had circulated for centuries. Its effect was to make *negra*, as a conception of race, something that was applied falsely to Spaniards in the propaganda of imperial competition and in the pseudoscience of race theory that was popular in "Anglo-Saxon" locales. Juderías thus erected a clear boundary between the Spanish *raza* and notions of blackness that were tied to Africa. Moorish blackness, the nationalist mythology held, had been absorbed and assimilated into the Hispanic *raza* and purified by the Catholic spirit over centuries, leaving Spaniards a unique and securely nonblack race.[9] This *raza* was celebrated with the new *Fiesta de la raza* in 1913; official investments in *raza* increased when the fiesta gained a royal decree in 1918 and was marked by King Alfonso XIII on October 12—the day of both Columbus's landfall and the appearance of the Virgin Mary to Saint James, the patron saint of Spain.[10]

As Spaniards across the political spectrum paid close attention to the battle for civil rights in the United States, the work of Marcus Garvey, the terrorism of the KKK, and the Scottsboro case, they largely understood American blackness as racially distinct from Spanish identities.[11] The popular phrase *hermano negro* (black brother) became a sign of sympathy for international black causes, especially those in the United States, and most often to the scene of distinctly male black suffering. The translation of the French communist Magdeleine Paz's wide-ranging study of black life in the United States *Frère noir* as *Hermano negro* in 1931—just months after the proclamation of the Second Republic—put the term and its political attachments in greater circulation. With quotations from Du Bois, she speaks of the "línea de color," she explains the term "nigger," and she reprints in her text Hughes's "I, Too," with the line "I am the darker brother" translated as "Soy el hermano negro."[12] (I will return to these translations momentarily.) With *hermano negro*, something of a meme in its moment, Spaniards could now affirm both their solidarity with oppressed blacks in a foreign country and their distance in race and citizenship from U.S. Negroes.

At the same time, Spanish interest in black U.S. writing spiked. By contrast, there was very little interest in Spain in Moroccan, African, or "Moorish" literature—only politics—at the time, and black writers were routinely excluded from any general discussion of literatures of North or South America. Almost no black writing from anywhere in the world had been examined, and certainly not *as* black writing. *Literatura negra* and *poesía negra* had denoted, at the turn of the twentieth century, a type of writing that depicted poverty, deprivation, death, and morose topics; Spanish critics most often associated it with French naturalism and decadentism.[13] Spaniards then watched the craze for all things black in Paris; soon Josephine Baker, the *revue nègre* and the *danse sauvage*, and jazz all received coverage in Spanish media.[14] For some, this signaled a new era of multiculturalism in Europe; for others, it was simply neocolonial domination exoticized; others still participated in the avant-garde appropriations of black cultures for aesthetic ends.[15] Regardless, the rising profile of U.S. black arts began to embody a new sense of *literatura negra*. By 1926 a leftist journal could proclaim that "la literatura negra," led by U.S. writers, was flourishing and that it represented a new confraternity of all races.[16] The Argentine journal *Caras y Caretas*, which had significant Spanish circulation, ran a feature that same year called "La literatura negra en los Estados Unidos" (1926). McKay, Hughes, Paul Lawrence Dunbar, Jessie Fauset, Georgia Johnson, Countee Cullen, Walter White, and Joel Rogers are named as the leading literary "negros de Yanquilandia."[17] Print media such as the *Chicago Defender*, the *Baltimore Afro-American*, *Crisis*, *Opportunity*, and *Negro World*, along with the Pan-African Congresses in Paris and London, also were credited with putting black writing on the map for European readers.

Across the 1920s, other critics aimed to show how, for instance, "the historical life of the black race [*raza*], from savagery to civilization, through slavery and peonage to the torture of the ergastula, has become the subject of the first theatrical production performed exclusively by Negros" in New York, or that in the wake of Josephine Baker's fame, a "black literature [*literatura de negro*] has invaded" the elite realms of aesthetics.[18] By 1929, the critic Antonio Marichalar, who was arguably the most vital disseminator of Anglophone literature in interwar Spain, would affirm that black American writing is neither a "flash in the pan" nor a craze, like jazz, in Europe. "This is not a token Goncourt Prize; it is not Dumas's curly hair," he notes. "It is an important constellation [*pléyade*] of Negros . . . and *negristas*."[19] Others followed Marichalar by proclaiming that a "gran poesía"—"la poesía negra"—is now part of a "gran poesía negra norteamericana" that transforms the experiences of life in the Caribbean and Ethiopia alike.[20] Leftist publications praised and quoted Hughes, tying his racial politics to the global socialist struggle. His "I, Too," for instance, was printed in full in translation within an anti-American screed by Esteban Pavletich in 1930.[21] The journalist Vicente Carreras would argue that "from Phyllis Wheatley, the first black poet in the United States, to Paul Lawrence Dunbar, in North America and in Cuba, Mexico, and other countries of the new continent, poets of color" such as Hughes and William Waring Cuney are capturing a uniquely black American experience now crystallized in the arts of Harlem.[22]

On the heels of this growing consensus, one of the most important and provocative representations of black American literature, Claude McKay's *Home to Harlem* (1928), was translated into Spanish in 1931 as *Cock-tail negro*. McKay was already known in literary circles in Spain for *Banjo*, both in its English and French translations, and for his politics, which resonated with the leftist ideals of the newly elected Second Republic. While Hughes was cited often and would become the bigger star in Spain, McKay was the first to be translated in full. Here, *Cock-tail negro* evinces the dilemmas that Spanish translators encountered when approaching the terms "Negro" and "nigger" and when moving between *negro* as adjective and noun. The very title of the translation is indeterminate, possibly meaning a black cabaret scene or a black person (a "Negro") that one might find at such a scene. The title, in other words, manifests the instability, in English-Spanish translation, of the term *negro* that it seeks to fix as a coherent ontological unit. The norms for translating U.S. terms for race were constantly shifting at this time, as a broader range of black U.S. works were translated, often published by new leftist presses. Most often, "Negro" was rendered simply as *negro* and "mulatto" was easy to render as *mulato*, but "darky" was *morenito*. *Moreno*, the root word, means "brown skinned" and could denote color regardless of race in a way that *negro* did not. The same problem obtained with the often-used *oscuro*, which literally means "dark" and thus implies a relational rather than ethnic trait. For the majority of the first half of the novel, McKay's translators seem puzzled and at pains to avoid using *negro* to refer to a person. A line like "He had made a popular Harlem Negro manager" becomes "Se había convertido en una figura popular en el Harlem negro," or "He [the manager] had become a popular figure in black Harlem."[23] At one point, the translators even wildly substitute "negra" for "ugly," when the protagonist Jake refers to a woman as "fat and ugly." Other terms abound—"morenito" for "darky" rather often—but when a line in the original includes both "Negro" and "nigger," the translation freezes and uses "negro" for both, losing the stigma of the latter.

The translation, then, not only flattens McKay's phoneticized dialect into natural, idiomatic speech but also precludes itself from accounting for the racism *within* international black cultures, as McKay depicted it. For example, McKay writes of Jake that "as an American Negro, he looked askew at foreign niggers. Africa was jungle, and Africans bush niggers, cannibals."[24] The translation reads, "como negro americano, miraba de soslayo a los negros de otros países. El África era la selva, y los negros africanos de los bosques, caníbales" (*C* 128–129). Thus, Ray's assertion that "soy un negro" is impossible to understand as a statement of pride, self-loathing, or realization of how he is seen by racist whites (*C* 125). By contrast, in this and other translations, *blanco* and *raza blanca*—although not concepts that had much purchase in Spain otherwise—are consistently translated with the same words, providing a surprising stability to a foreign fiction of race.[25] In short, *Cock-tail negro*, far from standing as a document of certain political and racialized solidarity, is fraught with internal translational contradictions.

Cock-tail negro, nevertheless, was understood both as a literary landmark in international black culture and as a political manifesto.[26] "All of the anguish, all of the painteresque quality, all of the drama of Negro life in North America is gathered in the pages of this novel," wrote one reviewer, who added that the translation has "conserved in Castilian Spanish all of the verbal expressionism of the original English, which is constantly sprinkled with the slang of the poor black world of Harlem." Turning immediately to a comparison with Spanish history, the reviewer notes that "among other differences the Negro Yankee has with the Negro of our colonial epoch is that the former belongs to a splendid material civilization that now endorses his smoking and cabaret and dancing"; in contrast, such behavior was always repressed by the Spanish Empire.[27] The critic Adolfo Salazar contrasted the authenticity of McKay's "novela negra" with the superficial "art nègre" of the French cultural scenes that he dramatizes in *Banjo* itself. The desire for black culture in Paris, Salazar insists, is nothing more than an extension of the ethnographic projects that have brought Africans to France in grotesque pavilions and expositions. Toomer, Johnson, Hughes, Du Bois, and McKay together have made a new base in Harlem, Salazar insists, from which they prophesy a "Zionism of color" to make a new black world, one opposed to assimilation and advocating instead for larger-scale change. He concludes, with masculinizing metaphors, that "the dark masses are awakening from a sleep cycle and a robust, muscular movement is coming with an affirmative attitude, if not one of conquest [*conquista*], liberation, and pacts," then one that addresses, as *Banjo* does, "the most profound question of humanity."[28] McKay's novel was also excerpted in translation in Julián Gorkin's *10 novelistas americanos* (see introduction), and it was reviewed alongside Paz's *Hermano negro*, which appeared that same year. Paz's book was characterized as telling the backstory to McKay's, as it explained the origins of the "línea de color" that created a racialized consciousness that now allows *Cock-tail negro* to stand in for the lives of millions of black Americans.[29]

Across the 1920s and 1930s, then, "Negro" in translation did a great deal of work, both as a binding agent and as a complication. By the mid-1930s, most critics pointed to coextensive contexts and to leading U.S. figures in the international movement of *literatura negra*, even if the significance of the texts was unsettled. Then, in 1936, just days before the civil war began, the famed writer and chronicler of the avant-garde Guillermo de Torre contributed the most broad-ranging history of black U.S. expression yet seen in Spain.[30] Torre's article is skeptical—he believes that black American writing has attracted global attention because of the ascent of the United States as a superpower (the United States has otherwise only exported cinema and jazz, he says); this, in turn, now shines a light on the country's internal problems and has undermined its prophetic, white narratives of progress. But Torre sees true innovation in *literatura negra* and seeks to connect that achievement to Spain, so he locates its origins in modernist primitivism—in Picasso's masks—and thus introduces the idea that Spain not only participated in the movement but perhaps played an originary role. Yet he "deplores that in our own [Spanish] literature there is not even an echo" of this movement right now. Spain has gained no knowledge of black aesthetics from its colonies in Africa, he laments, only political and economic reports. Moreover, even the Afro-Antillean ethnic groups of Spain's former colonies are joining in this new movement that is known as *negrismo*, an ambivalent term to which Marichalar and others had alluded and that will preoccupy the anthologists that I treat in the following section as they inscribe Spain into the capacious formation of *literatura negra*.

Anthologizing the *Negro* World: The New Geographies and Aesthetic Genealogies of Black Writing

In this moment, as Spanish critics only recognized intermittently, an interconnected movement in black writing had been developing in the black Caribbean. When this movement found global popularity in the early-to-mid-1930s, *literatura negra* shifted again—this time, by way of what Edwards has called the "multilingual, Western rush to anthologize blackness" through new vocabularies and modes of reception.[31] The collections gathered by Alain Locke, James Weldon Johnson, V. F. Calverton, and Nancy Cunard in English; by Blaise Cendrars in French (*Anthologie nègre*, 1921); and by Leo Frobenius in German (*Der Schwarze Dekameron*, 1910) all found their ways to Spanish readers, both in the original language and in translation.[32] But the anthological consolidation and expansion of black literature in Spain had little of the ethnographic focus on African culture that Cendrars's and Frobenius's landmark volumes had, and the connections to Africa generated in Spanish texts were faint compared to those made by the writers of the *négritude* movement. Instead, a competition materialized among visions of modern black writing as essentially diasporic and New World, often spelled out polemically in the prologues and introductions to these anthologies and then affirmed by their contents. Surprisingly, McKay—despite his Caribbean roots—was connected more often to European and especially Soviet leftist writing, and Hughes would become the greater emblem of a *literatura negra* understood as primarily a pan-American phenomenon specifically in English and Spanish. Poetry also fit more easily in anthologies and was cheaper to translate (often anonymously) and to publish than entire novels were, so the conversations on *literatura negra* tilted toward poetics as anthologies began to proliferate. Perhaps even more surprisingly, editors ranging from the Cuban Emilio Ballagas to the Spaniards Julio Gómez de la Serna and José Sanz y Díaz worked, despite their differences, to make Spain a vital source of the contemporary production of black literature. To understand the logic of these anthologies, we must first trace out the motivations for the imaginative literary and linguistic geographies that they charted.

The connections within the "Harlem–Havana axis" of black writing and music were not apparent to most Spanish critics prior to the 1930s.[33] The U.S. New Negroes had found European fame first, and the critique of international race relations and imperialism that they shared with their Afro-Antillean counterparts largely was read as a national (U.S.) or as a generically political (leftist) argument. The mixed-race poet Nicolás Guillén, who was the face of the new *negrismo* movement in Cuba in the early 1930s on the heels of his *Motivos de son* (1930) and *Sóngoro cosongo* (1931), had cautioned, however, against such easy links to Harlem. In his famous article "El Camino de Harlem" (1929), he worried that Cuban society was seeing the birth of an Afro-Cuban arts movement that would lead onto a path toward segregation and ghettoization, as exemplified by New York City. Afro-Cuban and black Caribbean *negrista* poetry mixed Orientalist primitivism, European forms, and both African diasporic and indigenous elements to produce a syncretistic version of black vernacular expression in the New World.

At times converging with the New Negro and *négritude* movements, at other times diverging, *negrismo* brought success for the Cubans Guillén, Ballagas, Ramiro Gómez Kemp, and Ramón Guirao, the Puerto Rican Luis Palés Matos, and others. Black Cuba was its center of gravity, but Ballagas insisted that *negrismo* and black writing in general remained open fields in which Europeans and white Americans could participate.[34] The porous borders and shifting definitions of blackness or Africanism with *negrismo* explain its terminological overlap with European negrism (also *negrismo* in Spanish), which signified the aesthetic experiments with black figures and dialects by white authors. Picking up on these trends, the journalist Victor de la Serna (no relation to the brothers Gómez de la Serna) argued that Harlem and Havana's Jesús María barrio (a neighborhood settled by former slaves) were separated only by "the difference between a dark-skinned [*moreno*] Spanish-speaker and a black [*negro*] English-speaker."[35] Evincing his uncertainty about how to understand the movement's racial capacities, Serna alternately labels Guillén a "poeta negro," "mozo moreno" ("dark-skinned boy"), and a "moreno latino" ("dark-skinned Latino"). And for Serna, Guillén notably "aligns himself with the great Spanish poets of our day—who also show a great taste for him. This great current beneath the ocean connects one continent to another, carrying a message of affection."[36]

Serna thereby points, with a benign metaphorization of the history of slavery, to the third node in this new triangulated network: Spain. The most visible Spanish writer to attempt to follow this transatlantic pathway was Lorca, who traveled that very route (Madrid–New York–Havana) in 1929–1930 and became the cipher through which these movements were understood in Spain. (Lorca's voyage was not uncommon, however: some three-quarters of a million Spaniards immigrated to Cuba in the first three decades of the 1900s during a push to "Hispanize" the lost colony.) Theorizing the shared roots of flamenco, *duende* (roughly, "soul"), the blues, and Cuban *son*, Lorca gave a new voice to this growing international body of work. In his famous lecture "Play and Theory of the *Duende*," Lorca called the Andalusian *duende* a "black sound" and explained that "black sounds are the mystery, the roots fastened in the mire that we all know and all ignore, the mire that gives us the very substance of art."[37] Lorca connected the *duende* of gypsies and Arab Spaniards to the "most delicate and spiritual element" of U.S. black aesthetic and cultural worlds, which he poeticized in his *Poeta en Nueva York* (1929–1930).[38] Completing the circuit imagistically, he sees New York as "Senegal with machinery"; in the poem "Dance of Death," he writes, "*The mask, look at the mask! / How it comes from Africa to New York!*"[39] He then arrives in Cuba and asks, "But what's this? Spain again? Universal Andalusia?" In Cuba, "the blacks are here, with rhythms I discover typify the great Andalusian people—little blacks without tragedy who roll their eyes and say, 'We are Latins.'"[40]

Enacting these connections as a new hybrid Anglo-/Hispanophone aesthetics, Lorca blends his own signature incantatory and repetitive style with what he sees as the African-rooted rhythms of life in Harlem in his well-known poem "The King of Harlem." Thus, the opening line (repeated as the fourth line, and repeated again later) reads "Con una cuchara" ("With a spoon"), which divides neatly—*Con una | cuchara*—into two amphibrachs, both beginning with a hard *c* and ending with a soft *a*. As he builds the primitivist musical cadences of the poem, he sighs, "¡Ay Harlem! ¡Ay Harlem! ¡Ay Harlem!", invoking the neighborhood's name through his own poetic voice, as in his signature forlorn cry, "¡Ay de mí!" Lorca sees Harlem as a modernized mythical site, where there are shamans, "oppressed reds" (invoking both the color of blood and the left), "mulattos," and, in another twice-used repetition, "Negros, Negros, Negros, Negros."[41] Blackness in Harlem, for Lorca, is both an essence and a sound embodied in the quasi-spiritual term "Negro"/*negro*. *Poeta en Nueva York*, which also includes his celebrated ode to Walt Whitman, ends with his Cuban poems, dedicated to the Cuban ethnographer and theorist of blackness Fernando Ortiz; the second of the two, "Son de negros en Cuba," will be reprinted in a number of anthologies.

Lorca's successes enabled more Spanish critics to begin including their country on the map of *literatura negra*. Enrique Díez-Canedo compared Ballagas's *Cuaderno de poesía negra* (Notebook of black poetry, 1934), which received significant press in Spain, to the Andalusian Spanish writer José Carlos de Luna's *El Cristo de los gitanos* (The Christ of the gypsies, 1934). He acknowledged, though, that the stronger links were between Ballagas and those "poets of the [black] race . . . who can also say 'I, too, sing America.'"[42] Elsewhere, Spanish poets like José Méndez Herrera capitalized on this trend in a manner similar to their Parisian counterparts—ventriloquizing blackness through a host of stereotypes such as the "sleeping black continent," the employment of "primitive" rhythms, and alluding to the "*tam-tam* and Gambia." (Méndez Herrera's collection *Ébano al sol* [Ebony sun, 1941] included an encouraging prologue by Manuel Machado, who said to him: "let yourself live, poet / in your gold and black world.")[43] Spain was now being affirmed as the source of historical and contemporary black writing (and still—in keeping with the notion of *raza*—the poetry of the *andalucismo* movement remained unconnected to *literatura negra*).[44] As the powerful critic Guillermo Díaz-Plaja put it, "the first poems of Negroes are found in the greatest classics of the Spanish language." Now that the "marionette has cut the threads that were held by the pious white hand" of colonial rule, "he has his own voice . . . and a real accent, vibrating between African nostalgias of the past and white paradises of the future."[45]

At the same time, even Caribbean voices offered apologetic visions of Spain's role in these aesthetic genealogies. Summoning the power of the anthology to curate and package a movement still in the making, Ballagas gathered his *Antología de poesía negra hispano-americana* (Anthology of black Spanish American poetry, 1935) and published it in Madrid. Ballagas, who had established himself as an authority on Afro-Antillean writing, maintained his conviction that black writing did not depend on the poet's ethnicity. Indeed, his *Antología* includes biographical notes on the contributors, and many of them are listed by race as either "raza blanca" (such as Ballagas himself) or "raza negra." Nearly half of the contributors are white, by the book's own measures, and the Chinese-Afro-Cuban writer Regino Pedroso is peculiarly called "raza negroamarilla (sin otra mezcla)" ("black-yellow race [with no other mixture]").[46] This taxonomic collection of "Black Spanish-American" figures includes well-known writers such as Lorca (his Cuban-inspired "*Son* de negros en Cuba"), Guillén, Palés Matos, Alejo Carpentier, and Ballagas himself, alongside lesser-known names such as Marcelino Arozarena. And, as Frobenius's anthology had, this collection features a glossary that Ballagas will expand in his new collection *Mapa de la poesía negra americana* a decade later.[47]

In his introduction to his *Antología*, Ballagas declares that there are three distinct directions in contemporary "world poetry" (*poesía universal*): they are *poesía pura*, *poesía folklórica*, and *poesía social o política*. While the majority of works bind themselves closely to the doctrines of one of these three movements, he writes, black writing crosses all three. The denigrating, imperialist version of black writing appears in Cendrars, Ramón Gómez de la Serna, and Paul Morand, and like jazz, it only indulges the fantasies of these European writers who have created "touristic African art" that exists outside of historical time and space (*A* 14). Against these "carved idols" and exoticisms, Ballagas argues, his anthology taps into "other deep currents in which the Negro can be seen from within, from his deeply human workings" (*A* 14). Paradoxically, he claims that all of the poems in the *Antología*, despite their authors all being contemporary and many of them nonblack, derive in some way from the experience of slavery, which is the defining condition of black life outside of Africa.

To capture this condition, he turns to Hughes, a "poeta mulato" from the United States, and reprints in translation the "I am a Negro" section of *The Weary Blues* (1926). Hughes is the greatest "dark [*oscura*] lyric voice of North America" and represents an Anglophone blackness seen also in Cullen's poetry, and his work is intimately connected across languages to the Cuban "poesía obscura" (*A* 16). This Cuban poetry, Ballagas notes, is created by white poets, too, who are able, "although white in race, to cultivate and to translate faithfully the black art [*arte negro*]" of the island's Afro-Cuban life (*A* 19). Ballagas concludes, in a note on the process of gathering his anthology, that his very title *poesía negra* is not "completely right," for it is also *poesía mulata* and *poesía blanca* that result from engagements with *el tema negro* ("the black theme") (*A* 20). *Literatura* and *poesía negra*, for Ballagas, come to mean everything from specific aesthetic forms to general imaginative sentiments. Black writing is, for him, an open field through which he can promulgate a vision of racial solidarity grounded in English- and Spanish-language exchanges. His anthology centers on poems in black dialects, taken from carnivals and ceremonies, and it points constantly, through various allusions, to black life in Africa—even as it includes no works by African writers. The white Uruguayan Ildefonso Pereda Valdés's "El Candombe" employs an imagined African essentialism of drum-driven frenzy and primitivist howls "that the blacks make even blacker, / with African sadness transplanted to America" (*A* 28).

Pereda Valdés's line "that the blacks make even blacker" ("que los negros ponen más negra") is one of many to include often cadence-like repetitions of the term *negro*, which Lorca had employed. Such moments are telling: much of the anthology's effort to delineate *literatura negra* would strike a contemporary reader as a borderline-demeaning exoticization. Ballagas even intercalates images such as a stereotypical African "tribal" woman dancing and a caricature of a thick-lipped black face in a top hat overlooking New York City. The putative dichotomy between "genuine" black writing and white negrism has been deconstructed by a number of critics, however, and more intriguing in this case is the genealogy that Ballagas envisions but does not articulate fully at this point. He includes Lorca's poetry as a Spanish representative of the open field of participation that *poesía negra* offered, and he publishes Pedroso's "Hermano negro" as a tie to the now-familiar phrase of solidarity. Pedroso writes, "Negro, hermano negro, / tú estás en mí: ¡habla! / Negro, hermano negro, / yo estoy en ti: ¡canta!" To translate this poem into English is to ask what the cross-linguistic valence of "Negro" is in this situation: whether the English equivalent is "Negro, brother negro" or "Black man, brother black man" depends on how one interprets Pedroso's employment of a word that now signified across two languages. "You are in me: speak!" and "I am in you: sing!" follow each repetition, and the claim "¡También yo soy tu raza!" ("I too am your race") resonates across the stanzas (*A* 155). Furthermore, the explicit anti-imperialist politics of Pedroso's poem, with its repeated references to Scottsboro, militate against the mostly apolitical, open configuration of black writing that Ballagas proposed.

Taking up the questions that such poems raise, Ballagas would extend and revise his positions on black writing in his new anthology, *Mapa de la poesía negra americana* (Map of Black American poetry, 1946). He admits in his introduction that he "does not treat black poetry in all of its purity, mythology, and African originality" but instead searches for "an integration of the racial in the plenitude of man," and he sees that in the "mixed blackness" of the New World—especially in North America—the "black accent of the black poet and of the white poet in uniting synthesis, a fraternal colloquium."[48] Again extending the reach and purchase of *negro* as an aesthetic descriptor, he attaches his work to the successes of the New Negro literature and holds that "poesía negra norteamericana" uses different slang words than the patois of "poesía mulata," yet the two are expressions of the same universal "tema negro" (*M* 10, 12). Ballagas reminds his readers that "there were Negros in Spain before they were in the Americas, thus they appear in the *negrista* references in Cervantes," and that the "presencia negra" in the works of contemporary poets like Lorca, Rueda, and Alberti is "of American provenance" (*M* 12). The dialectics of racial categorization and mixing that pressed upon baroque writing were revived and energized in this moment. As he argued in his enlarged article version of this introduction, Góngora, Sor Juana, William Blake, and Countee Cullen all channel blackness in their writings, even if they had no experience of slavery. His claims for an Iberian origin for black writing, moreover, stem from the fact that "the first Negro [slaves] brought to the Americas did not come from Africa, but from Spain." Spain actually gave black writing its original "creative impetus," and because of Spain's universalist cultural patrimony, the senses and capacities of *negro* can be expanded.[49]

Ballagas's new arrangement begins with bilingual editions of Longfellow's and Whitman's poems that center on black subjects ("The Slave's Dream" by the former and "Ethiopia Saluting the Colors" by the latter, for instance). They are juxtaposed, in the "U.S." section, with James Weldon Johnson and Langston Hughes; Countee Cullen closes the section. Cuba receives the lion's share of space in the anthology, from "Anonymous Songs" to José Martí's "Versos sencillos," up to poems by Guillén, Carpentier, and Ballagas himself. McKay appears later as the sole representative of Jamaica—not with one of his poems in Jamaican dialect, but with "The Harlem Dancer." Most every other country and region in the Americas finds space, from the Argentine José Hernández to the Brazilian Jorge de Lima. Ballagas concludes with a section called "Poesía de motivo negro escrita por españoles" ("Poetry about black themes written by Spaniards"). Here, he reaches across four centuries to gather works by the baroque writers Lope de Vega, Góngora, and Simón Aguado; by writers of Spain's recent past (Unamuno, Lorca, and Salvador Rueda, all of whom died in the 1930s); and by Spanish contemporaries such as Alberti and Alfonso Camín. These exoticized, often minstrel-like depictions of putatively "black" rhythms in poetry are, by Ballagas's account, a foundation for modern black poetics.

In keeping with Ballagas's views, the Spanish word *negro*, both in the original and in translation, works across a host of figurations of race in the collection, but variations on racial terminology continually modify it. The subject in Hughes's "Song for a Dark Girl," for instance, is "joven negra"; a possible parallelism with Hernández's "Canta el moreno," which translates almost literally as the masculine version of Hughes's title, is foregone in favor of the kind of taxonomy of skin color that Ballagas used to frame the collection. Cullen's "To a Brown Girl," by contrast, is "A una muchacha morena," and in McKay's "The Harlem Dancer," even the color of a "black" neck becomes "cuello moreno." The most profound shift comes, then, in the publication of Pedroso's "Hermano negro," now in Spanish, English, and Portuguese. These multiple versions of Pedroso's poem, which had just appeared in English in the United States, extend the titular note of solidarity across languages. But the English version includes a twist. The original Spanish line, "Negro en Haití, negro en Jamaica, negro en New York, negro en La Habana," repeats *negro* as a catch-all term for blackness no matter the language, and the Portuguese maintains *negro* in all cases. The English rendering confuses this: "Black man in Haiti, Jamaican nigger, black man / in New York, nigger in Havana." Here, "*negro*" is a "black man" in New York yet a "nigger" in Havana (almost certainly a Hispanophone context) and in Jamaica, where the language was most likely English; furthermore, there is a "black man" in Francophone and/or Kreyòl Haiti. The term "nigger," which had seemed untranslatable, is now transposed onto a Hispanophone environment where it becomes even more foreign, estranged.[50]

Modifying Ballagas's claims, a new collection, *Lira negra: selecciones afroamericanas y españolas* (Black lyre: Afro-American and Spanish selections, 1945) was assembled and published in Madrid during the Second World War, and its editor, José Sanz y Díaz, framed the war as its defining condition. He writes in his prologue that "amid the disoriented anguish of the world at war, a new and authentic literature is being born: that of the Negros.

It has its roots in remote, eradicated civilizations" of sub-Saharan Africa of the fourteenth through sixteenth centuries.[51] Following one line of ethnographic thought, Sanz y Díaz believes that the "antecedents of this flourishing of Negroid letters [*letras negroides*]" are the oral and popular cultures of Africa—its many legends and myths (*L* 15). This "prehistoria de la literatura negra" was transmitted into dialect across generations, but only after centuries did black writers, educated in modern universities, transfer it to "learned languages: Spanish, French, Portuguese, and English" (*L* 15, 16). In a new, starkly ethnocentric account, Sanz y Díaz sees *literatura negra* as emerging only in the twentieth century, when "millions of men of color" with newfound access to the world's greatest schools and academies of art began to create syncretistic music, art, sculpture, and more.

This institutional theory leads him, like Ballagas, to find *literatura negra*'s most vital modern origins in the works of Spanish writers. The early seventeenth-century dramatist Antonio Mira de Amescua of Granada wrote about black figures and Lope de Vega published works that featured conversations with black characters, he notes (*L* 11,12). Others such as Juan Bautista Diamante, Simón de Aguado, and Góngora highlight a history in which an "infinite number of Spanish authors populated our literature with Negroes" (*L* 12). His genealogy—controversial then as now—therefore includes the claim that, until the twentieth century, the Negro himself did not produce any significant works, despite isolated texts such as Daniel Alexander Payne's "poema negro" of 1841 (*L* 12). "For a century," Sanz y Díaz argues,

> poets of color tried to imitate whites, to copy as closely as possible European forms and thought. But now, in the apogee of what is called *arte negro*, with the craze for African jazz, with *negrista* painting, with the song and the *son* of Afro-Spanish America, *literatura negra* is born, the *poesía negra* of Spain and of the Americas. It was a phenomenon that began in the United States. . . . with Hughes, Dunbar, Corrothers, Alexander, Cullen, and McKay. . . . Later, the Antillean *rumba* lent its rhythm to poets of black blood and Spanish tongues.
>
> (*L* 13, 14)

This occurred, he writes, when the prosody of the Spanish classics combined with *cabildo* chants, which were the "first rumblings in Spanish of a theme and a soul completely African still" (*L* 14). This blending is made possible not so much by slavery but by the capacious Spanish tongue, which "embraces these manifestations of a *pueblo* sheltered by its culture. Spanish lends its astonishing ductility, its riches, and its harmony. . . . The *poeta negro* perfectly embroiders, like a fine tapestry, his poetry, with colored threads around exotic gems, sparkling jewels, and mysterious and deep notes of Africa" (*L* 14). Thus have "poetas negros de Hispanoamérica y de los poetas blancos españoles" collaborated to make contemporary black writing, forged in a cauldron of bilingual tension between the two tongues (*L* 14). Regarding themes, "the bush and the cloister—Africa and Spain—bring to the *lírica negra* a sensual freshness and a mystical moan that is deep, ancestral, and totemic," Sanz y Díaz concludes, so that "the ascetic Hispanic voice is mixed with the pagan breath of the forest" (*L* 19). Only in the final line of his prologue does he mention slavery: "And without a doubt, the most heart-rending black poems have been produced in the South of the United States, because there we find the bottomless font of the bitterness of ancient African slaves" (*L* 20).

Black writing here is cross-racial and simultaneously Spanish and African—though its Africanness is only apparent when filtered through Europe. *Lira negra*'s contents are therefore expansive: almost every country of the Americas is represented. Many of the names were by this point familiar to Spanish readers: Guillén, Carpentier, Ballagas, Hughes, McKay, Cullen, and Bennett are the headliners. But in searching across the New World, Sanz y Díaz brings together less familiar and non-Anglo- or Hispanophone names from Brazil and Haiti. Under "French Congo," he includes both René Maran and Blaise Cendrars. He reproduces anonymous Negro spirituals, finds a poem from "Guinea española" (now Equatorial Guinea, one of Spain's few African holdings at the time), and in keeping with the claims of his prologue, includes a number of Spanish poets. Lope de Vega, Manuel Machado, Lorca, José Méndez Herrera, Alfonso Camín, Antonio Maciá Serrano, Isidoro Martínez Alonso, Rafael Duyos Giorgeta, and José María Uncal are all included; Uncal in particular attempts to channel Hughes's jazz-inspired poetics. The anthology is primarily from the Americas, but when one looks beyond the Americas, there are five poems from colonial Africa compared to thirty from Spain. Spain produces black writing not because of its Moorish past but because of its imperial encounters with Africa. Like other collections, this one also offers a "léxico negro" that explains hundreds of terms and a bibliography that ranges from portraits of Harlem by black U.S. writers to histories of Spain's African relations. All the while, even as these anthologies posited that black writing originated in Spain, they never linked it to the claim that Spaniards themselves were black or partly black, as many Europeans and Americans still saw them. Blackness was not connected to the Moors of the past or to the Morocco of the present either.

Ballagas's work had changed the framework for understanding black literature and its internationalism—so much so that in 1942, an anthology of distinctly U.S. black writing even had to explain why Spain was absent. In that year, Julio Gómez de la Serna (brother of Ramón) published *Constelación negra: Antología de la literatura negroamericana* (Black constellation: Anthology of black American literature). The collection is based on V. F. Calverton's *Anthology of American Negro Literature* (1929), but from Calverton's some hundred selections there are only several dozen translated. Calverton's own essay, "The Growth of Negro Literature," traces the roots of "Negro art and literature" to pre-1500 African empires and arrives at the claim that blues, jazz, spirituals, and black folktales are superior to the European-derived white American culture, which "has not developed a culture that is definitely and unequivocally American."[52] He adds, "indeed, we may say that the contributions of the Negro to American culture are as indigenous to our soil as the legendary cowboy or gold-seeking frontiersman. . . . In fact, they constitute America's chief claim to originality in its cultural history."[53] Gómez de la Serna carries over this essentialism and writes that "black poetry . . . is pure, simple, of a direct and authentically new lyricism."[54] In his exoticized reading, the "tragedy of the race" is always latent in the *humorismo* of black poetry, and through his art, "the Negro is *naturally* loving, without our *cerebral* complications, with that hypocritical and conventional false modesty of European love—Saxon love, more than anything— . . . he loves woman *as* woman" (P 11).

Once again, Hughes, here called a "mulato," is central. But despite Hughes's success, Gómez de la Serna writes, black literature is not sufficiently known to Spanish readers; still, Spaniards are not "blind to the light" of these "authentic darker *brothers*" ("auténticos *hermanos* oscuros") (P 12). Black poetry is "new" and "bright," he says, inspiring an "irrepressible attraction" of racial sympathy, much as the poetry of Rabindranath Tagore stirs anticolonial sentiment (P 15). Of his own translations, he writes that his "method" is

> *literalism*, the most *adherent* as possible to the Black American text. At times I have reached an assonance on my own, without rules or poetic norms. . . . The reader will keep in mind the enormous difficulty to translate [*trasladar*: carry over] to Castilian, to Spain—language [*lengua*], idiosyncrasies wholly distinct to the Negroes—this special language [*lenguaje*] of theirs, with an orthography which flouts all of the rules of English, and in whose language flourishes, abundantly, the slang terms of the Negro argot.
>
> (P 14, 15)

Gómez de la Serna admits that he is happy to be "defeated" by black poetry—that he aimed to bring to life its "tone" even when its music has been lost. In this anthology, Hughes's "I, Too" again has "darker brother" rendered as "hermano negro" (P 11).[55] The phrase is repeated in the translation of James Alexander's "The Dark Brother" as "El hermano negro," and the phrase "brother race" is "raza Hermana." But the Spanish "*negro*" once again levels semantic differences: Countee Cullen's "To a Brown Boy" is "A un muchacho negro," and "To a Brown Girl" is "A una muchacha negra," but Gwendolyn Bennett's "To a Dark Girl" is also "A una muchacha negra." The nuanced differences within blackness that poets such as Cullen and Bennett explored, and with them the internal debates among New Negro writers over racial terminology and ontology, are subsumed by the singular term "negro." Then, one of the most provocative pieces in Calverton's anthology, Frank Horne's "Nigger: A Chant for Children," undergoes an even more dramatic flattening in translation. First, "black" is rendered as "negro," as when Othello is described as a "negro varón" ("black man" or "black boy," without the sense of *hombre*). But the shocking, repeated line at the end of each stanza, "Nigger . . . nigger . . . nigger," becomes "Negro . . . negro . . . negro." While echoing Lorca's "Negros, negros, negros, negros" from "The King of Harlem," the translation fails to capture the force of the epithet and instead normalizes and naturalizes it. The ambivalence of *negro* as a term used in solidarity—*hermano negro*—and as a faint effort to denote foreign racism underscores what remained a persistent anxiety about translating blackness in Spain. Anthologies consolidated certain maps of black writing but translation constantly threatened to make the routes the anthologies claimed to have uncovered as obscure as they had been previously.

Hughes and the Moors: A Wartime Ethnography of Race and Culture in Spain

Meanwhile, as all of these anthologies circulated, their mostly aesthetic claims about *literatura negra* were countered by a distinctly political vision outlined in the most influential collection of black writing in the Spanish Americas for nearly three decades: the *Antología de la poesía negra americana* (1936), edited by the leftist Pereda Valdés, published in Chile, and distributed in Spain too.[56] This volume, which drops the "*Hispano-*" qualifier of Ballagas's title, validates the links among U.S., Caribbean, and Spanish American poetic blackness that figures such as Guillén and Hughes had advocated while also excluding Spain. It also brings to the foreground the dialectic between Hughes as cipher and as interpreter of these very cultures and politics, something that Vera M. Kutzinski has explored in Spanish American contexts but that remains unexplored with regard to Spain. Pereda Valdés, who had published a book of poems called *Raza negra* in 1929, takes a longer, politicized view of what is now called the Plantation South: he begins with Phyllis Wheatley, then jumps directly to the turn of the twentieth century in black U.S. writing with James Corrothers, James Weldon Johnson, and then Hughes, Cullen, Dunbar, McKay, and Sterling Brown. Notably, he also includes a number of contemporary female poets such as Carrie Williams Clifford, Angelina Weld Grimké, and Gwendolyn Bennett. These names all appear alongside some of the same Spanish-language figures that Ballagas gathered—the Cubans Guillén and Pedroso, for instance—and also Lusophone writers from Brazil (Luis Gama, Francisco Octaviano, João da Cruz e Souza), the Francophone Haitian Jacques Roumain, and a collection of spirituals and slave songs from across the Americas. But the U.S. poets (fifteen of them) far outnumber those of any other country (Brazil is next, but with only five), and Spain is excluded.

The book gathers "the principal poets, black, white, or mestizo, who have made black poetry," which Pereda Valdés's introduction describes as arising from the "suffering" of a "damned race" ("raza maldita"), the descendants of Ham who were exploited in Africa and enslaved in the Americas.[57] "Black poetry has borne its best fruits in the lands of the North" (referring to the U.S. South), Pereda Valdés claims straightforwardly; "there, life is harder, the battles are bloodier, filled with the cries, moans, and dying gasps of the lynched" (*AP* 13). The Negro spirituals of the American South, he argues, bespeak suffering best, inspired as they were by the realization of Christ's suffering. Pereda Valdés divides contemporary U.S. black poets, all of whom he sees as working in a black religious tradition, between those who use biblical sources to advocate rebellion (Hughes, Cullen, McKay) and those who draw on the same sources to advocate "submission" (Corrothers, Felton, Johnson). His sympathies are clearly with the rebels, who reveal their spiritual heritage poetically as (in clearly Marxist terms) "a base of economic suffering and a superstructure of mysticism" (*AP* 12).

Hughes is now the "gran poeta" of his race, and this "poeta tan auténticamente negro" ("truly authentically black poet") is the poet of the "revolution" (*AP* 13). Later, in his capsule biography within the text, Hughes is called the "most universal of the poets of his race," the "universal poet of all oppressed races," and the one who sings the "sorrow of the exploited—black or white, red or yellow—he is the poet of social revolution" (*AP* 32, 33). Pereda Valdés quotes "The Weary Blues" at length, and the translation of "I, Too" that he prints breaks with the previous versions published in Spanish America by turning "darker brother" into the familiar phrase, "Soy el hermano negro," connecting it to the popular phrase of sympathy with the black struggle (*AP* 35). Blackness, for Pereda Valdés, is first and foremost a political formation, and Ballagas's universalism reaches for a cross-racial spiritual commonality where it should instead seek a socialist one. Accordingly, *negro* is used far more in the anthology's translations than any other term such as *moreno*, thus casting a wide net for blackness as a singular bond. Expanding these views in his collection of essays *Línea de color: Ensayos afro-americanos* (1938), which he dedicated to Hughes and Cunard, he outlines *literatura negra norte-americana* from Phyllis Wheatley to Booker T. Washington, James Weldon Johnson, and Hughes.

This anthology and those analyzed above unfolded two lines of reading black U.S. poetry in its Hispanophone orbit: an aesthetic one historically bound to Spain and a politicized one that cordoned off Spain. These two would remain in dialogic tension for several decades, even across the changing visions of blackness brought about by the Spanish Civil War and World War II.[58] The bridge between these lines was Hughes. Hughes's involvement in Hispanophone literary culture and his many translations of writers ranging from Lorca to Guillén have been well documented, and they contributed to his recognition by Spanish editors.[59] The poet's relationship to Spain was informed both by his friendships with anticolonial writers in the Hispanophone Caribbean and by his readings of the Spanish Civil War as more than a proxy battle for the global tides of communism and fascism. The war, for Hughes, was an central theater in the international campaign for racial equality. He had watched "black" Berber rebels in Morocco deal the Spanish colonial army a stunning defeat in 1921 in what became known as yet another "Disaster," the Disaster at Annual.[60] Fifteen years later, General Franco, when he launched his rebellion against the Spanish Republic from his base in Morocco, used both calls for "Hispano-Arabic brotherhood" and bribes to convince tens of thousands of local "Moors" that they were part of Spain and that the Republicans were "foreign infidels" because they were godless.[61] (Yet a Nationalist poet popularly characterized the war as a "new *Reconquista*, a new expulsion of the Moors!")[62] Franco's Moors were shock troops popularly known for terrorist-style tactics that brought back the images of Moorish bogeymen from Spanish fairy tales.[63] Franco meanwhile glorified the historical mixture of the Spanish *raza* even while remaining a paranoid anti-Semite, too; he wrote the screenplay for the propaganda film *Raza* (1941), which affirmed the theory of Catholic-racial fusion. All the while, a leading fascist theorist warned that a "certain danger, of Africanization in the name of progress, is clearly visible in Spain. . . . We can state categorically that our Marxists are the most African of all Europe."[64]

These developments gave Hughes his entrée to reread Spain. When he traveled to Spain during its civil war as a reporter for the *Baltimore Afro-American*, he was captivated and perplexed by Franco's Moors. He first saw in Madrid,

Spain's besieged capital . . . wide-awake Negroes from various parts of the world—New York, our Middle West, the French West Indies, Cuba, Africa—some stationed here, others on leave from their battalions—all of them here because they know that if Fascism creeps across Spain, across Europe, and then across the world, there will be no place left for intelligent young Negroes at all.[65]

For Hughes, Franco was one with Hitler and his policies of ethnic cleansing. Indeed, one could "give Franco a hood and he would be a member of the Ku Klux Klan, a kleagle."[66] This leads to Hughes's horror when he discovers that "on the opposite side of the trenches with Franco, in the company of the professional soldiers of Germany, and the illiterate troops of Italy, are the deluded and driven Moors of North Africa. An oppressed colonial people of color being used by Fascism to make a colony of Spain."[67] Blacks from around the world are fighting for the Loyalist cause in Spain, he writes, yet Moors, "who are my own color," are fighting with Franco for a white supremacist state.[68]

The circumstance affected him greatly; two decades later, Hughes reiterated in his autobiography *I Wonder as I Wander* (1956) how the people of Madrid were shocked at "that rebel Franco bringing Mohammedans to Spain to fight Christians! The Crusaders would turn over in their graves. The Moors are back in Spain."[69] During his time in Spain, he absorbed this aura of surprise from the locals: "now, here I was—a Negro myself," he writes, "suddenly frightened by another dark face!" (*W* 350). He notes with fear the "strange union of the Cross and the Crescent against Spanish democracy" (*W* 351). And so, while he was in Spain in 1937, Hughes spent much time trying to understand the complexities and ironies of this battle in which color lines were dramatically blurred: "I knew that Spain once belonged to the Moors, a colored people ranging from light dark to dark white," he wrote.[70] Hughes notes that white Spaniards are partially black themselves and thus are relatively free of racial prejudice; the Republic has created a colorblind workers' paradise. Because "Negroes were not strange to Spain," he adds, "most Spaniards had seen colored faces." One could also find "colored Portuguese" throughout the country, and "in both Valencia and Madrid I saw pure-blooded Negroes from the colonies in Africa, as well as many Cubans who had migrated to Spain" (*W* 351). Hughes believes that Spaniards are naturally hospitable to peoples of African descent but that Franco has politicized Africa in a way that makes that hospitality currently impossible. His celebration of Spanish blackness even becomes an identification when he takes pride in being mistaken for a "Moor who had got lost and had accidentally run across the line somewhere."[71]

Hughes's survey of race in Spain also aimed to explore his own presence there as an emblematic black author.[72] He laments that "the least representative of the books on colored people seem to be the only ones translated into Spanish—or rather perhaps I should say, the most sensational and exotic. [William] Seabrook's *Magic Island*, [Julia] Peterkin's *Scarlet Sister Mary*, Paul Morand's bad short stories of stavism. And nothing by colored writers themselves." Incompletely aware of what had been published in Spain by this time, he argues that "Walter White's *Fire in the Flint*, for instance, or James Weldon Johnson's *Along This Way*, would be of greatest interest to Spanish readers just now, struggling as they are with tremendous social problems of their own."[73] Extending this point, he notes the shared roots of aesthetic forms across Spanish and U.S. black cultures: "Flamenco is to Spain, I suppose, what the blues are to America—I mean the real Negro folk blues. And the flamencos seem to have the same effect on their audiences as blues do when sung in the Negro theatres of the deep South."[74]

Hughes accordingly attempts to meld black American and Spanish forms and topics in his own writing. In his "Letter from Spain," the poetic narrator, Johnny, writes to his fellow black American correspondent that "We captured a wounded Moor today."[75] Johnny argues that Franco has "nabbed" Africans, in a modern form of slavery, and conscripted them for the fascist cause. But Johnny and the "Moor" cannot communicate with one another—they speak different languages. Their imagined solidarity, however, frightens not only Franco, but also England and Italy: a "free Spain," Johnny asserts, will lead to revolts in the English and Italian colonies in Africa.[76]

This understanding of the Spanish Civil War as a race war was controversial and surprising to U.S. readers, no doubt, but prevailed among the Spanish left, whose leading poets he befriended. With "Letter from Spain," Hughes was participating in an established tropology within Spanish poetry of the moment, and in his translational work, he would implicate himself in an ongoing anti-African iniative.[77]

Carmen T. Sotomayor writes of this theme in Spanish Republican ballads that Moors—almost always named as such, rather than Moroccans, Berbers, or Arabs—were constantly labeled "traitors" and were seen variously as deceptive and deceived. They were both traitors to the international black cause and, more pointedly for the Republicans, they were traitors to Spain. Indeed, the Republicans who embraced black American literature used the same racist propaganda against Franco and his African troops. One popular, nativist war ballad declared emblematically that "Moors and foreign armies" have "swept across Spain / in the blackest invasion [*la más negra invasión*]," headed by Germans, Italians, and other unwanted foreigners.[78] Resulting from the contacts with Republican writers that Hughes made in 1937 were at least three of his translations of Spanish poems, recently recovered from the archives by Evelyn Scaramella, that treat the theme of Franco and the Moors: Juan Gil-Albert's "Lamentación por los muchachos moros, que, engañados, han caído ante Madrid" (Lament for the deceived Moorish boys who died before Madrid), rendered by Hughes as "Lament for the Young Moors"; Rafael Alberti's "El moro fugado" (Hughes: "Moorish Deserter"); and Emilio Prados's "El moro engañado" (Hughes: "The Moor Betrayed").[79] All of the Spanish versions were included in the widely circulated *Romancero de la guerra civil* (Ballad book of the Civil War, 1936), which Hughes brought back to the United States with him. This collection features a section, "Romances de Moros" ("Ballads of Moors") in which Moors are depicted as thieves, traitors, believers in a "false promise," and above all, "black."

In Alberti's pseudonymous "El moro fugado," he stresses the "black beard, black eyes, / black" visage of the "stealthy" Muslim, and Pascual Pla y Beltrán envisions "the reconquest of Granada" in which the Spaniards will once again expel the Moors from southern Spain.[80] Prados's venomous poem uses variations on a repeated refrain, "Go back to Africa, Moor" (as Hughes translates it), throughout its otherwise loose structure. The Moor is told "Spain is not for you," to flee before "your dark skin is chapped" by the "cruel" cold of Spain. Retracing the Reconquista, the poem tells the Moor to flee through the cities of southern Spain and to swim across the Strait of Gibraltar, then adds, "if in crossing you are lost, / it is better to die living / than to live a wicked death. Go back to Africa, Moor." The Moor is unwanted also because the "black poison of your hate / is bitter with deception." Hughes's translation then invokes language from his own poetry, too, when he writes, "They're making fun of you, / darker brother," for an original that only says "hermano" (without any term for "darker"). Hughes has inserted his own famous line ("I am the darker brother") into the translation. With this, Hughes aims to make the poem more sympathetic: "Fight, fight, fight . . . / for the freedom you will have / when the arms you carry today / are turned against those who now bribe you." The Moor is duped, having been "bought" and "sold" as Africans were in the slave trade. He is both victim and aggressor.

Hughes never published these translations; he had to gloss over the fact that while he was calling for solidarity among Moors, Spaniards, and American blacks, the Loyalist ballads characterized Franco's armies as invading African hordes best repelled back to their home continent. Instead, Hughes used his own Spanish Civil War poems, which became increasingly bilingual and included lines in Spanish from texts such as *Don Quixote*, to show translational solidarity. In language, geography, translation practices, and form, Hughes was, in effect, what we might characterize as a transplanted Spanish poet for a brief period in 1937–1938. Indeed, his "Song of Spain" was published next to a poem of Lorca's in Nancy Cunard's trilingual anthology of poetic defenses of the Spanish Republic in 1937. The Loyalist journal *El Mono Azul* (Blue overalls) printed four of his poems on its front page, in translation by Alberti, during the war, and his anti-imperialist pro-Republican Second International Congress of Writers for the Defence of Culture in 1937— where he again linked the U.S. South and Franco—resonated widely.[81] He would develop his extended relationship with Lorca's work over the following decades; the translations of Lorca's *Romancero gitano* and *Bodas de sangre* that Hughes began during the war would finally be published in 1951.[82] Hughes, as a poet and as a figure received and interpreted in Spain, thereby bespeaks the paradoxes of race that Spain's ambivalent relationship to Africa brought back into focus in the 1920s and 1930s.

Wright and the Races of Franco's Spain

The reconceptions of race in Spain brought about by Franco's victory and by his regime in the following decades suppressed the racial politics that had cohered and splintered over the period of writing and reception that this chapter has traced. This history became the premise for a later work by Richard Wright, himself the heir to the legacies of black writing that Hughes and others had forged in the interwar period. Wright, who had become a French citizen in 1947, traveled to the Gold Coast in 1953 and to Indonesia for the Bandung Conference in 1955. In between those two journeys, he visited Spain in 1954–1955, fifteen years after Franco's victory in the civil war. In the opening of his critical travelogue *Pagan Spain* (1957), whose title signifies on Waldo Frank's romanticized portrait *Virgin Spain* (1926), he asks himself why, despite the "admonitions of my friends to visit Spain—the one country of the Western world about which, as though shunning the memory of a bad love affair, I did not want to exercise my mind"—he was so "scared" to witness "the reality of life under Franco."[83] After all, he writes, "totalitarian governments and ways of life were no mysteries to me. I had been born under an absolutistic racist regime in Mississippi; I had lived and worked for twelve years under the political dictatorship of the Communist party of the United States; and I had spent a year of my life under the police terror of Perón in Buenos Aires" (*PS* 1). The equations that Wright makes here between the absolutisms of Mississippi, the Communist Party, and the Perón regime frame his understanding of Spain as a country in the grip of a dictator. The transatlantic network of the South, Spain, and Spanish America that had been theorized variously as the aesthetic and political grounds for *literatura negra* was now a triangulated connection of authoritarianism.

Wright's blackness becomes a central issue almost from the moment he enters Spain. He is greeted with a "knowing smile" by a Spanish woman, causing him to wonder, as Hughes did before him, "Did I remind her of Moors?" (*PS* 6) He discovers, however, that Spaniards have "no racial consciousness whatsoever"; the youth are "cut off from the multitude of tiny daily influences of the modern Western world" and so the movements that he had covered as a journalist had little resonance to them (*PS* 11).[84] Instead, Spaniards now know themselves through the catechism-like nationalist tracts produced by the fascist government, which Wright translates and reprints verbatim across scattered parts of his text.[85] As he "replays some of the main tropes of the Black Legend against Spain" (in María DeGuzmán's words) by pointing up to Spaniards their repressed black heritage, Wright sees a postimperial nation struggling to redefine itself with a willful blindness to the pressing issues of geopolitics: namely, race and decolonization.[86]

Wright's attempt to understand the mechanisms of the Franco regime's internal controls leads him, not surprisingly, to center on the question of race; this book is dedicated to Alva and Gunnar Myrdal, after all.[87] Wright explains the distinct understandings of race and blackness—especially Africanness—held by Spaniards and recounts an almost comic scene in which he is mistaken for an African pimp who has come to take Spanish prostitutes to brothels in Morocco. Confused and unable to grasp blackness in familiar terms in Spain, Wright instead argues that Protestants are the "*white Negroes*" of Spain because they are "*treated* as Negroes" (*PS* 138).[88] This paradox provides Wright with what he sees as his moment of enlightenment in Spain, where he is marked less as a "Negro" and more as a "heathen": Spain remained stuck in the Inquisition (*PS* 16, 162). No secular life developed in Spain, leaving it on the sidelines of what Wright sees as the determining development of the modern West. Spain was "not the West. Well, what then was it?" (*PS* 192). Spain, he concludes, is "a holy nation" and "a sacred state—a state as sacred and irrational as the sacred state of the Akan in the African jungle" (*PS* 192). It is a pagan, mystical, primitive state, but one *without* a future; one that is comparatively African even as it resists such identifications.

Wright's depiction of Spain as claustrophobic and irrational was borne out, he believed, when Franco's government censors banned many New Negro writers. Wright nonetheless claimed to have found *Black Boy* in a pirated edition there. *Pagan Spain* was proscribed in Spain and was only translated into Spanish in 1970 in Argentina; an edition produced in Spain followed much later, in 1989. History suggests, then, that Spain could only acknowledge its versions of blackness in a new, multicultural light after the end of the Franco regime, when a modern marketing campaign ("Spain is different") coincided with the country's return to the global stage, marked by the 1992 Barcelona Olympics. Now, one finds Spain celebrated by María Menocal, in a contemporary version of the Arabist theory that nationalists once promulgated, for its purported culture of tolerance during its Christian-Jewish-Islamic medieval period, with Toledo billing itself as "la ciudad de las tres culturas" of *convivencia*.[89] Such narratives—which reinscribe Spanish exceptionalism—overlook or naturalize the racially driven violence, enslavement, and fractures that defined Spanish imperialism and modernity, offering instead a mode of historiography that sees enrichment and connectivity rather than devastation and disconnection. In other words, these contemporary stories obscure the ways in which a falling empire and its rising foil in the first half of the twentieth century produced a controversial, paradoxical, yet stimulating understanding of the complex modern literary inscription of blackness in translation.

CHAPTER 6

"Spanish Is a Language Tu"

Hemingway's Cubist Spanglish and Its Legacies

IN A LETTER FROM KENYA IN 1954, ERNEST HEMINGWAY WRITES to the art collector Bernard Berenson:

> I have many funny things to tell you and you alone. How you say that in W'Kamba [the Kamba language] is with one word *Tu*. This means you alone, you only, you who I love, you who I see again, you with who I share a tribal secret.... It is strange that you should say it the same way in Spanish the only language I really know. If I had been born in Spain like your defunct friend [George] Santayana I would have written in Spanish and been a fine writer I hope. As it is I must write in English, a bastard tongue but fairly manoeverable [*sic*]. Spanish is a language Tu.[1]

Hemingway is rarely, if ever, discussed as a practitioner of the crosslinguistic wordplay associated with high modernism. His spare, minimalistic English prose seems far removed from Ezra Pound's rhyming "τροίη" and "lee-way" or from James Joyce's multilingual portmanteaux in *Finnegans Wake* (1939). But in this letter, he speculates on a word in Kamba and its homophone in Spanish and on the similar concepts that they encompass, all of which are grounded in intimacy and secrecy between an "I" and a "you." English, by contrast, is for Hemingway born of infidelity; it violates a sacred I-you bond that he sees in other tongues. Yet its "bastard" nature, its ability to be manipulated, makes it a generative font for him: at the end of this passage, Hemingway plays on the English "too" in order to bring his native language into this interlingual network. The Spanish word *tu* (*you*—Hemingway tellingly forgets the diacritical mark here) and the topics that this letter highlights also lie at the center of *For Whom the Bell Tolls* (1940). Hemingway's novel of the Spanish Civil War famously employs nonidiomatic English dialogue full of *thee*s and *thou*s to create what Edmund Wilson called a "strange atmosphere of literary medievalism."[2] As a group of Spanish-speaking Republican fighters and the Anglophone protagonist speak lines such as "What passes with thee?" or "Go and obscenity thyself," they have alternately absorbed and alienated generations of critics and readers. The implications of the novel's complex linguistic experimentation have been overshadowed, however, by a focus on Hemingway's personal politics, obscuring its place in the histories of modernism, of the twentieth-century novel, and of the English/Spanish language politics of its era. To bring together and revise these histories and to recover the rich estrangement and the subdued formal artifice of *For Whom the Bell Tolls*, this chapter reads it as a work *of* and *about* translation that disorients the very "round and whole and solid" style of writing that Hemingway helped conceive.[3]

To consider *For Whom the Bell Tolls* as a translation of any sort might seem strange: it is not a translation of a preexisting foreign-language text, and Hemingway, unlike most of his modernist peers, never published such a translation in his entire career. But in fact, from its composition and its narrative operations to a pervasive web of symbolic scenes, historical allusions, and thematic strategies, *For Whom the Bell Tolls* posits and reforms a capacious theory of translation in need of delineation. Combining techniques of the Poundian "beauty of mistranslation" with his sense of the Gallicized Russian that Leo Tolstoy fashioned in *War and Peace* (1869), Hemingway produced at nearly the same moment as the publication of *Finnegans Wake* a radical experiment in linguistic synthesis in a superficially realist novel.[4] My understanding of the text as an exploration of translation—and its failures—is borne out by a crossing of actual and fictional worlds that Hemingway stages. The protagonist, Robert Jordan, an American volunteer in the brigades of the Spanish Republican army, has been sent to blow up a bridge near Segovia, and his literal and symbolic capacity as translator hinges on the prior death of one "Kashkin." Kashkin, a Russian dynamiter who previously served Robert's role, never appears in the novel except in other characters' discussions of "the other one." Robert initially tells his Spanish comrades simply that Kashkin is dead; later, he says that Kashkin had committed suicide rather than be captured by the enemy. Only later still does Robert confess to his fellow fighters that, in truth, he shot Kashkin at the Russian's own request (to spare him his suffering, he says) and that he kept his comrade's gun and felt "absolutely no emotion" over the killing.[5]

Such a revelation would seem typical enough in a Hemingway novel were it not for one detail: Kashkin was the name of Hemingway's real-life friend Ivan Kashkin, a leading figure in the Soviet era of socialist realism who translated many of Hemingway's works into Russian. Hemingway called him "the best critic and translator I ever had"; one who "knew what I was trying to do better than I did"; one with whom he corresponded on his plan for the brand of multiperspectivalism that he crafts in *For Whom the Bell Tolls*; and one who translated, while Hemingway was composing the novel, his germane report "On the American Dead in Spain" (1939).[6] Robert has killed off the namesake of Hemingway's translator and placed himself in the role of cultural mediator and translator only to fill this role poorly, even disastrously— and at times, he is suicidal himself. Furthermore, Hemingway's familiar realistic narrator turns out to exercise a peculiar mode of self-censorship, which becomes its own version of unreliable translation and miscommunication. The narrator can no more stabilize a "corrupted" wartime Spanish language than can the archetypal Hemingway hero Robert, originally a college Spanish instructor in Montana, exert any real impact on the civil war.

Reading *For Whom the Bell Tolls* through its alienating collision between English and Spanish, set against a backdrop of a war involving soldiers speaking Russian, French, and other tongues, makes it less the gripping, realistic wartime epic or call to arms that it was proclaimed to be in the 1940s and more a cacophony full of ironies, misdirections, false cognates, mistranslations, and heteroglossic ploys too extensive to catalogue fully here. In a veiled effort at becoming a "fine writer" in Spanish, Hemingway offers, in short, a text suspended *between* languages in an era in which English was simultaneously expanding globally and homogenizing. *For Whom the Bell Tolls*'s willful distortions further complicate Hemingway's signature style, a style that has been shown in recent scholarship to be "actually highly idiosyncratic, highly *stylized* . . . a particularly mannered version of experimental modernism" and not "an especially 'natural' brand of literary realism."[7] *For Whom the Bell Tolls*, moreover, merges two evolving strands of cubist and translational practices that stretch across Hemingway's career. While Hemingway's literary cubism, rooted in his plan to translate Cézanne's revolution in visual arts into literature, has been noted often, it has rarely been mentioned outside of his early works such as *In Our Time* (1925) and *The Sun Also Rises* (1926), and it has not been considered in translingual contexts. *For Whom the Bell Tolls*, as a work of cubist Spanglish, culminates an arc of Hemingway's stylistic trajectory in which his incomplete knowledge of Spanish combines with his serious study of Spanish literary history to become a theory of novelistic narrative, censorship, and epistemology that approaches a Beckettian version of writing. He buries affect and depth in language with formal experiments in translation as a register of oscillating linguistic movement. His Spanglish, that is, enacts a reading of Spain's literary past and political present during the Spanish Civil War. The alternative portrait of Hemingway as a maker of a minoritizing literary dialect—a Spanglish produced by deep, historical linguistic structures rather than traditional linguistic contact zones—diverges from his well-known legacy of influence from Harlem to Moscow, and it opens new ways of conceiving of late modernism's responses to both high modernist experimentation and the specter of total war, in the contexts that this book has adumbrated.[8]

As Hemingway constructs what is also an unorthodox response to the presence of the United States in Spain during the civil war, he points also to what was effectively a multinational invasion of Spain in the late 1930s and, thus, a counterpoint to the era of Spain's own imperial ventures, to which he often alludes. Toward the end of this chapter, I consider this reading of Spain as a transtemporal contact zone and of the war's literary-linguistic legacy in several other varieties of literary Spanglish that are tied to Spain: those created by Felipe Alfau, Malcolm Lowry, and Ben Lerner. Where the last chapter focused on a poetic past, this one traces out a network of affiliations to sketch a sample genealogy of English-through-Spanish in the novel, from late modernism through to postmodernist and contemporary literature.

On Not Knowing Spanish: Hemingway's Experiments in Illiteracy

Hemingway put not "just the civil war [but] everything I had learned about Spain for eighteen years" into *For Whom the Bell Tolls*, producing a text that he defended as the greatest he wrote in a style that he abandoned afterward (and he did not publish another novel for ten years).[9] But despite all of his time in Spain and his exotic romanticization of the land and its people; despite his writings on bullfights and wine, his Orientalist infatuation with the rich nobility and crude barbarity of Spaniards; and despite his absorption in the country's literary history, Hemingway was at best semiproficient in Spanish. He could read well and could converse (with great struggle) but could hardly compose at all. He suffered from what he called, with some nativist pride, "analfabetismo agudo con derrame" (acute, overflowing illiteracy), yet imagined himself to be an American author only by accident—a Spanish writer expressing himself in English.[10] Spain was, for him, "the best country in Europe" and "the most Christ wonderful country in the world," and he believed that his "future may yet lie in the Peninsula."[11] But his experiences indicated otherwise. Indeed, Hemingway attempted to insert himself into Spanish literary history by proclaiming the influence of Pío Baroja's realist novels on his own works. But when he made a pilgrimage to see Baroja on his deathbed, Baroja shouted dismissively in Spanish, "What the fuck is this guy doing here?"[12]

Despite these limitations, Hemingway used Spanish to varying degrees in a number of his works, all the while imagining that he would never be able to access parts of the language. He reflected to Edmund Wilson that Spanish

> is easy to learn superficially. But there are so many meanings to each word that, spoken, it is almost double talk. In addition to the known meanings of a word there are many secret meanings from the talk of thieves, pickpockets, pimps and whores, etc. This occurs in all languages and most of the secret language is very ancient.[13]

As in the letter to Berenson, for Hemingway, the inaccessible part of a foreign language is that which is buried by time ("very ancient") and which encodes "secret," contraband, and intimate words or topics in "double talk"—a version of intralingual translation. Spanish is, for him, "the roughest language that there is," one that accreted mystery and unintelligibility simply by way of aging in one place, contrasting what he imagines the "bastard tongue" of English to have lost in the course of its global spread.[14] He plays with this liberty and openness that he sees in Spanish and meditates on the effects of translation in his semiprofessional Hispanist study *Death in the Afternoon* (1932), which also includes a glossary of Spanish terms:

> Suerte is an important word in Spanish. It means, according to the dictionary: Suerte, f., chance, hazard, lots, fortune, luck, good luck, haphazard; state, condition, fate, doom, destiny, kind, sort; species, manner, mode, way, skillful manoeuvre; trick, feat, juggle, and piece of ground separated by landmark. So the translation of trial or manoeuvre is quite arbitrary, as any translation must be from the Spanish.[15]

Hemingway's notes on the necessarily "arbitrary" nature of translations from Spanish, as he perceives it, and on the endless multiplicity of meanings attached to *suerte* indicate both a broad exploration of the depth of particular words and a resignation to their untranslatability—their bottomlessness.

Rather than translating anything from Spanish, Hemingway began developing in the 1920s a theory of the incomplete Spanish language as a tool and a foil for his manipulations of English. He experimented with his mannered illiteracy both in private (in letters and in conversations, the latter of which he often mentions in his correspondence) and in published works. His letters reveal his dialectal and multilingual experiments in development—everything from fanciful phoneticized spelling to cross-linguistic doggerel to calques—in a way that resembles the practices of Pound, Eliot, and Stein, practices that Michael North has highlighted in their correspondence.[16] He employed broken Spanglish with the painter Waldo Peirce, for instance: "Querido Valdito mio: ?Que tal hombre? lo siento un barbaridad no to see you anymore."[17] And in a revealing letter to Arnold Gingrich in 1933, Hemingway details what he learned from his modernist predecessors and peers, then concludes with a self-consciously garbled Spanish-Italian "confession." Here, he acknowledges learning some "technical" elements from Joyce, a great deal from Stein "before she went haywire," little from Ford

Madox Ford and Sherwood Anderson, and "how to say what you felt about [your] country" from D. H. Lawrence. Abruptly, he stops and writes, "What the hell is this, confession, "benedeteme parde porque ha aprendido."[18] The phrase means, roughly, "Bless me, father, for I have learned," but the misspelled "padre" becomes "parde," doubling the request for "pardon" that is implied in the blessing, and "ha aprendido" is actually in the third-person singular ("he has learned"), distancing Hemingway from the "I" who seeks forgiveness in the already incorrect "benedeteme."

His first significant public laboratory for crossing Spanish and English was *The Sun Also Rises* (1926), in which a number of sexual, religious, and even racialized anxieties surface through figurations of "translation." In Spain, amid the fervor of the holy *fiesta*, the lapsed Catholic Jake Barnes notes that "San Fermin was translated from one church to another," referring to the obscure ecclesiastical sense of "translation"—the transfer of holy objects and bodies of saints.[19] Moments later, his friend Bill Gorton repeats the term when he urges, upon hearing that Brett Ashley wants a bath, "Let's translate Brett to the hotel" (*S* 163). This meaning—to move or transfer—is retained in the Spanish *trasladar*, the false cognate that Hemingway uses to "infect" English with the Spanish of the setting, as he will throughout *For Whom the Bell Tolls*. In contrast to these awkward uses of the word "translation," the critical Spanish term *afición* (and *aficionado*) remains only vaguely translated. It is clearly meant to signal homosexuality but is given by Jake only as "passion"—specifically for bullfighting. In the novel's climactic scene, Jake serves literally as a translator for Brett and the bullfighter Pedro Romero, who share a sexual passion for each other. Pedro admits here that he knows English but says that he cannot speak it in public, for that would tarnish his image as a matador. Jake's successful translation makes him—as Robert Cohn charges—a "pimp" (*S* 194). Throughout the novel, then, translation binds and occludes the intimate, the sacred, and the profane.

Hemingway refracted this dynamic, in part, into the wartime pidgin Italian of *A Farewell to Arms* (1929), and in *To Have and Have Not* (1937), the American smuggler Harry Morgan operates between Florida and Cuba, prefiguring Robert Jordan as a mediator between Anglophone and Hispanophone cultures.[20] But he was disappointed with the latter book, which includes only bits of Spanish. Instead, he built up his experiments across his non-novelistic works in the thirties, often around similar themes. In his short story "A Clean, Well-Lighted Place" (1933), for instance, Hemingway once again turns to religion and mixes the Spanish "nada" throughout the Lord's Prayer in English: "Our nada who art in nada, nada be thy name," and so forth.[21] His Spanish Civil War play *The Fifth Column* (1938) and the short stories from Spain that he published alongside it contain many characters speaking broken English and Spanish with various accents, alongside bilingual characters who turn out to be untrustworthy. Most notably, a "Moorish Tart" named Anita speaks a pidgin English that she learned in Gibraltar, the primary contact zone in Europe for English and Spanish. Throughout all of these works, Hemingway was engaged in a protracted effort to wrest and employ a language that he knew partially as the grounds for his practice of creative translation and composition. As he wrote part of *For Whom the Bell Tolls* in an Anglophone setting (the Rockies) and part in the Hispanophone Caribbean, his limited grasp but thorough exploration of the irreconcilabilities that exist between the Germanic tongue English and the Romance language Spanish became the springboard for his uncommon entry into the field of modernist mistranslation.

The Unfamiliar Familiar and the Failures of Translation

Many novels in English, such as *The Sun Also Rises*, that are set in non-Anglophone locales drop hints—foreign words in italics, untranslated phrases with explanations in English of their meaning—to indicate to the reader that the text is an imagined translation, but rarely is this foreignness a premise for estranging the dialogue of the entire novel, as it is in *For Whom the Bell Tolls*. The dialogue in the novel exists primarily between Robert and a group of Loyalist fighters with whom he is encamped for three days. This group includes Robert's self-absorbed nemesis Pablo; Pablo's outspoken wife, Pilar; and Maria, the Spanish gypsy with whom Robert immediately (and without explanation) falls in love. All of them, it is implied and sometimes stated by the narrator, are speaking Spanish nearly all the time. The source from which the novel unfolds its brand of interlingual defamiliarization into a sphere of irreconcilabilty, mistranslation, and unknowability is the familiar second-person-singular form of address. In English, the pronoun "thou" (with "thee," "thy," and "thine") was predominant until roughly the seventeenth century; forms of "you" were used for the plural and for formal address.²² Forms of "you" overtook "thou" across almost all contexts: both the familiar and the formal, the singular and the plural. "Thou" became associated with elevated, rare literary language; in contrast to its roots, it appears to contemporary readers (as it did to Hemingway's) to be *more* formal, associated with Shakespeare or with Donne's Meditation XVII (1623), which supplies Hemingway's title. Like other Romance tongues, however, Spanish preserves with more regularity forms of *tú* as the familiar and *usted* for formal discourse. Linguists call this the T-V distinction (from the Latin *tu* and *vos*); the historical correspondence between Spanish and English thus would be *tú*–thou and *usted*–you.

Most critics have assumed that the T-V distinction in the novel follows a logical pattern of grammatical translation.²³ For instance, in an exchange between Robert and Pilar, we read, "'You please me, *Inglés*,' Pilar said. Then she smiled and leaned forward and smiled and shook her head. 'Now if I could take the rabbit [Maria] from thee and take thee from the rabbit.'" After beginning with the formal "you," she leans in closer and establishes familiarity with Robert before switching to "thee"; an uncomfortable Robert replies formally, "You could not" (*FW* 156). But the exchanges are actually far more confused than this. Robert and Pablo converse as follows:

> "Thou," he said to Pablo. "Do you think this snow will last?"
> "What do you think?"
> "I asked you."
> "Ask another," Pablo told him. "I am not thy service of information. You have a paper from thy service of information. Ask the woman. She commands."
> "I asked thee."
> "Go and obscenity thyself," Pablo told him.
>
> (*FW* 211)

Here, Pablo would presumably be switching from the familiar to the formal within one sentence ("Thou . . . you think") not once but twice ("thy service . . . You have"), and Robert would refer to him as "you" and "thee" just seconds apart. In other words, the shifts between "you" and "thee" do not have the logic of intimacy and familiarity that they should were the novel a direct translation of dialogue that was originally in Spanish. By a similar token, the verbs that accompany "thee" and "thou" are sometimes archaic ("canst") and sometimes contemporary, with little consistency. It is not simply that the novel is estranging readers by using "you" formally, then; it is muddying the very possibility of a translated Spanish grammar and suggesting that the process of translation somehow has been distorted. As Edmundo Desnoes put it, the novel's English is "españolizado"—"Hispanicized," or in a more appropriately awkward formulation, "Spanished."[24]

Most pointedly, this vacillation occurs in Robert and Maria's intimate conversations, which jump illogically between "you" and "thee." Indeed, just lines apart we find "I love you" and "I love thee," thereby implying as its original the bizarre, almost comical Spanish construction *La amo*, or *Le amo*, for the common sentiment "I love you."[25] The novel employs these missed correspondences between English and Spanish grammars and registers them as a template for making camaraderie or love of any type linguistically unutterable. Intimacy is not an alignment of like points or emotions but an irreconcilability that the novel will transfer to multiple scenarios. (Indeed, in another moment, Robert tells Maria that his father and grandfather were "Republicans" in the United States. Maria, relying purely on a transliteration of the sense of "Republican," is surprised to hear that such an allegiance did not result in their being shot, as her Spanish Republican father was.) The shifting language and grammar of *For Whom the Bell Tolls* allow no emotional depth; we have only a surface of words clashing and missing one another, even beyond Hemingway's likely intentions. The gaps between English and Spanish are evident even on the levels of spelling, typography, and orthography, which are inconsistent and riddled with errors throughout the text. The interplay between intimacy and translation that Hemingway employs here is as old as the metaphorical uses of "faithful" and "fidelity" to denote "accuracy" in translation. And so, a fabricated, multilayered foreignization projects a world in which the phrase "I love you" becomes an impossible, mistranslated statement.

Such confusion is present even in the opening scene of the novel. Here, Robert and his elder colleague Anselmo (both as yet unnamed) speak to each other formally as "you," and the English remains idiomatic, classically Hemingway, until "the old man" (Anselmo) says awkwardly that they might have to "climb a little in seriousness." Robert asks him formally, "How are you called?"; Anselmo's response switches to the familiar with

"How do they call thee?" (*FW* 2). The two characters then switch directly back to the formal "you" in conversation. Robert's answer ("Roberto") points to the fact that his appellation in the novel is inconsistent: some characters call him "Roberto," others "*Inglés*" ("English," which he protests, since he is from the United States and only *speaks* English rather than *being* English). The narrator only calls him "Robert Jordan"—always the full name, unlike any other character in the novel—a technique borrowed from Stein's "Melanctha" (1909).

Robert, after having disposed of Kashkin, assigns himself the role of cultural-linguistic intermediary only to become a victim of cross-linguistic interplay and irreconcilability. His sole, symbolic mission, after all, is to *destroy* a bridge. On one level, the novel's discourse replicates the setting and plot: thousands of foreign mercenaries from all political stripes have descended on Spain during the civil war, and within their own ranks, they are unable to communicate clearly. But more specifically, Spanish, in its collisions with English, Russian, French, and more, has become further fractured in ways that cannot be repaired by Robert, a mistranslator and a mistranslated figure himself ("*Inglés*" for "American"). Robert retains a naïve faith in English as a lingua franca and returns to it when he is frustrated with Pablo, admitting that

> "When I get very tired sometimes I speak English. Or when I get very disgusted. Or baffled, say. When I get highly baffled I just talk English to hear the sound of it. It's a reassuring noise. You ought to try it sometime." . . .
>
> "What do you say, *Inglés*?" Pilar said. "It sounds very interesting but I do not understand."
>
> "Nothing," Robert Jordan said. "I said, 'nothing' in English."
>
> "Well then, talk Spanish," Pilar said. "It's shorter and simpler[.]"
>
> (*FW* 180–181)

First using English to needle and tease Pablo, then to vent to Pilar, Robert finds himself both assured and baffled by English, which is reduced here to a defamiliarized and Steinian "reassuring noise" without content. Similarly, Robert thinks of his father, who committed suicide: "I'll never forget how sick it made me the first time I knew he was a *cobarde*. Go on, say it in English. Coward. It's easier when you have it said and there is never any point in referring to a son of a bitch by some foreign term" (*FW* 338). English has become uncanny—familiar yet estranged—for Robert. When thinking of Maria, his mind floats across languages:

> Now, *ahora, maintenant, heute. Now,* it has a funny sound to be a whole world and your life. *Esta noche,* tonight, *ce soir, heute abend.* Life and wife, *Vie* and *Mari.* No it didn't work out. The French turned it into husband. There was now and *frau*; but that did not prove anything either. Take dead, *mort, muerto,* and *todt. Todt* was the deadest of them all. War, *guerre, guerra,* and *krieg. Krieg* was the most like war, or was it? Or was it only that he knew German the least well? Sweetheart, *cherie, prenda,* and *schatz.* He would trade them all for Maria. There was a name.
>
> (*FW* 166–167)

The deficiencies of English, the gender misalignment in French with his invented, hoped-for rhyme (*vie* and *Mari*-a), and the putative gravity of German all converge here in a polyglot disassembly—a meditation on the failures of language across utterances and meanings. Robert is not a polyglot arranger, and he cannot, in Poundian terms, "make it cohere."

Perhaps the greatest irony in the novel is that Robert's many communicative failures occur despite—or because of—his imagining that his profession as a Spanish instructor and author of an ethnographical travelogue on Spain would aid him. (He imagines, too, that if he lives through the war, he will write a "good book" about it [*FW* 165].) He tells himself that his comrades "trusted you on the language, principally. They trusted you on understanding the language completely and speaking it idiomatically and having a knowledge of the different places" (*FW* 135). But in an emblematically confusing scene early in the novel, Robert meets with the comrade El Sordo (literally, "The Deaf One"), who initially speaks to him in a "pidgin Spanish" because he does not believe the American will understand him (*FW* 147). Elsewhere Robert's closest friend Karkov (a Russian) speaks a "strange Spanish" that discomforts him (*FW* 239). Even Robert's attempt to make jokes and puns in Spanish fails: when he plays on "huevos" (literally, "eggs" but slang for "testicles") in a jab at Pablo's manhood, his colleague Fernando asks, "What eggs?", and Robert hastily explains away his flop (*FW* 199). He is grilled by his comrades for being so "presumptuous" as to teach Spanish without being a native speaker (*FW* 209). In this capacity, he serves (poorly) an extratextual function as Hemingway's surrogate, answering the charge of presumptuousness in the way he has used Spanish and the war in his English novel. "That I am a foreigner is not my fault. I would rather have been born here" (*FW* 15), he says, echoing Hemingway's dream of being a "Spanish writer." This intra/extratextual boundary is blurred more explicitly here when Robert's stable source of pride emerges: his superiority to Kashkin. Kashkin is disparaged by Pilar for being "nervous" and having "spoke[n] in a very rare and windy way." Kashkin's failure, it turns out, was one of speech and language. Robert notes, too, that the "one great difference" between himself and Kashkin is that "I am alive and he is dead." When Robert fears that his comrades see him as too much like the "coward" Kashkin, he reminds them of this difference, in two languages: "'*Murio*,' Robert Jordan said into the deaf man's ear. 'He is dead.'" This translation is unnecessary: El Sordo speaks Spanish, so Robert is redundantly translating "He is dead" for his own purposes, just before he finally confesses, "I shot him" (*FW* 148). By contrast, in another real-life reference, Robert idolizes over against Kashkin his unseen comrade Duran, named for Hemingway's friend Gustavo Durán (*FW* 290). Durán, an artist turned soldier for the Republic, was Hemingway's unofficial consultant for the novel; he hastily proofread the novel's Spanish lines and accompanied Hemingway to New York to publicize the novel in interviews.[26] His presence and Kashkin's absence combine to suspend Robert, as a figure meant to cross diegetic borders, between the internal and actual worlds of the novel's translational engagements.

Moreover, the machinations at play here elucidate the role that Hemingway's idiosyncratic narrator plays in effecting them. Far from clarifying the disorienting dialogue, the narrator only compounds it with unnecessary repetitions, inconsistent translations, and nonidiomatic English borrowed from the characters' mouths. The narrator, for instance, begins to use awkwardly transliterated Spanish phrases such as "the woman of Pablo" rather than "Pablo's woman" or "Pablo's wife," makes obvious or redundant observations, and translates the same Spanish phrases differently while in the same contexts.[27] This provides, in turn, a hermeneutic lens for understanding the novel's notorious, bizarre excision of obscene words. *To Have and Have Not* was Scribner's first published title to include the word "fucking," which contributed to its low sales. Needing money for his impending divorce, Hemingway devised a strategy in *For Whom the Bell Tolls* that would allow this novel to enter the

Book of the Month Club—and it paid off, as the novel sold half a million copies in its first five months.[28] But this novel uses self-censorship less as a tool for propriety and more as a rhetorical and narratological strategy in a multilingual environment in which it is yet another type of translation. The self-reflexivity is apparent in the fact that "unprintable" is used rather than "unspeakable":

> "Go to the unprintable," Agustin said. "And unprint thyself. But do you want me to tell you something of service to you?"
>
> "Yes," said Robert Jordan. "If it is not unprintable," naming the principal obscenity that had larded the conversation. The man, Agustin, spoke so obscenely, coupling an obscenity to every noun as an adjective, using the same obscenity as a verb, that Robert Jordan wondered if he could speak a straight sentence. Agustin laughed in the dark when he heard the word.
>
> (*FW* 45)

Not only is the narrator an auditor and transcriber of the conversation; he is also an editor who understands the nonprintability of what he records in the actual world of the novel's circulation. When Agustin says to "unprint thyself," he is not simply having an obscenity removed by the narrator-editor; he is also telling a character in a novel to unprint himself from the page, to wipe his being—which only exists in print—out of existence. As the narrator claims, "there is no language so filthy as Spanish. There are words for all the vile words in English and there are other words and expressions that are used only in countries where blasphemy keeps pace with the austerity of religion" (*FW* 318). Yet, when the characters' insults reach "the ultimate formalism in Spanish . . . the acts are never stated but only implied" (*FW* 93).

Indeed, in his manuscript revisions, Hemingway replaced everything from euphemisms to outright profanities in English with Spanish words: "make love" became "joder" ("fuck") while Spanish phrases like "me cago" ("I shit") remained intact.[29] French obscenities are also printed, as when Marty says, "*Nous sommes foutus*" ("We are fucked") (*FW* 428). The narrator, in short, knows how censorial codes operate in a largely monolingual book market like that of the United States, and for him, translation is censorship, and censorship is translation, insofar as both bury the original.[30]

This explains, too, why Robert's relationship with Maria is marked not only by declarations of emotional intimacy that are depthless and nonsensical but also by sex that is rendered in prose in which formal artifice overtakes description ("the acts are never stated but only implied"): "one only one, there is no other one but one now, one, going now, rising now, sailing now, leaving now, wheeling now, soaring now, away now, all the way now, all of all the way now; one and one is one, is one, is one, is one, is still one . . . " (*FW* 379).

Hemingway thus rewrites, through Robert, Conrad's misplaced protagonist Marlow, who is a struggling narrator and reader of symbols and who replaces the unseen, dead Fresleven in the same way Robert replaces Kashkin.[31] Moreover, if Robert Jordan is a stand-in for "the American Dead in Spain" that Hemingway eulogized, he is an emblem of the failure of American volunteers (the United States refused to intervene militarily) to affect the war, for the war was over by the time the novel was published—indeed, Hitler had already invaded Poland, too. Rather, Robert, framed within the theory of language and translation that Hemingway implies, is more a combination and culmination of Hemingway's laconic American male protagonists whose speech and thought is betrayed by translation into foreign settings. Maria, in turn, first voices Molly Bloom when Robert asks if she would like to have sex: " 'Yes,' she said almost fiercely. 'Yes. Yes. Yes' " (*FW* 73). More broadly, she embodies the untranslatable and ineffable that Hemingway saw in all languages—her name encodes the reference to the Virgin Mary, even as Hemingway forgets the diacritical mark in the Spanish *María*—and that both fascinated and frustrated him in Spanish in particular. Maria is wise, then, in attempting to preserve what exists of their relationship by requesting, "Do not speak. It is better if we do not speak" (*FW* 379). Robert's dream of a life in the United States with Maria is a mixture of the idealized and the repressed: he imagines inviting his Spanish IV undergraduates to their home to smoke pipes and have "informal discussions about Quevedo, Lope de Vega, Galdós," then notes that "Maria can tell them about how some of the blue-shirted crusaders for the true faith sat on her head while others twisted her arms and pulled her skirts up and stuffed them in her mouth" (*FW* 164–165). The only way in which the romance plot, and the intimacy that inheres in it, could possibly succeed in this novel is through silence, not through translation.

Misreading Hemingway's Cubist Late Modernism

To account for Hemingway's project at a conjuncture of translation studies, modernist studies, and a formalist history that would include literary cubism, we must first look to the ways in which *For Whom the Bell Tolls* was initially received and misread some seventy-five years ago. "The novel that has something for everybody," as it was advertised, was a polarizing work.[32] Critics and reviewers in the early 1940s seized immediately on the novel's dialogue and treated it in moral and judgmental terms, praising or condemning Hemingway for the merits of his Spanish accuracies or inaccuracies and for the political allegiances he allegedly reveals. On one side, despite relying often on essentialist and sometimes incorrect generalizations about demotic Spanish, were powerful claims such as V. S. Pritchett's (himself a translator of Spanish works). He declared that "in his astonishingly real Spanish conversation, [Hemingway] has surpassed anything I have ever seen. Keeping close to the literal Castilian phrase with its Elizabethan nobility, he gets the laconic power of its simple statements and also the terrific rhetoric of its obscenity."[33] Joseph Warren Beach concurred, and Carlos Baker later asserted that Hemingway, through "Marlovian" idioms "'corrected' towards modernity by the intermixture of the contemporary *lingua communis* with the slang removed," captured something in Spanish that is more organic, with intermingled sacredness and profanity that belong to the "real" cadences of "real" Spanish peasants.[34] Howard Mumford Jones added that "the conversation is carried over almost literally from the Spanish, and it would appear that colloquial Spanish permits a combination of dignity, rhetorical precision, and wild poetry unattainable in a Germanic tongue. . . . An immense part of the vitality of *For Whom the Bell Tolls* lies in the imaginative force of its dialogue."[35] Others disagreed vociferously, calling the novel a betrayal of the Republican cause for which Hemingway was agitating (as Alvah Bessie, a veteran of the Spanish war, charged) or, in Gilbert Highet's case, a "bloody awful kind of unspeakable Spanish . . . [turned] into a far more unspeakable American language."[36] In a now-famous essay, Hemingway's Spanish friend Arturo Barea castigated him for his exploitation of obscenities and sexual innuendos in Spanish that impugned the virtuous character of Spanish women.[37] Both the anti- and the pro-Hemingway camps pointed to the transhistorical nature of Hemingway's experiment, though few pressed upon its implications; almost none related it to Hemingway's previous works or to other modernist texts, and most often, Tolstoy was the topical but not stylistic touchstone. In the decades since, these patterns have mostly held.[38]

Far from replicating actual speech, the novel in fact generates its dialogue between the poles of English and Spanish by restaging and distorting linguistic collisions across history. This process takes hold from the start, when Robert hears Anselmo speak "rapidly and furiously in a dialect that [he] could just follow. It was like reading Quevedo. Anselmo was speaking old Castilian and it went something like this, 'Art thou a brute? Yes. Art thou a beast?'" (*FW* 11). It is doubtful that Anselmo would speak like the baroque playwright Francisco de Quevedo, and Quevedo's Spanish was not "old Castilian," which was used from the tenth to fifteenth centuries. (Robert later confesses that Quevedo was "hard to read" and that Pilar was a better storyteller [*FW* 134].) The Spanish world Robert imagines throughout the novel with his stock of baroque-era references to Velázquez or Lope de Vega cannot align with the world of the war. Far from it, and from the ideals of Hemingway's glowing reviewers, the Spanish in the novel, which draws on both Quevedo and vernacular speech, is not the stable, uncorrupted, autochthonous tongue that even Hemingway himself dreamed at times.

Rather, in the 1930s, Spanish was undergoing dramatic changes in a time of political and cultural upheaval. There are some characters, like Fernando, who hinge their hopes for the Republic on its transformation of its registers of class in familiar address: "For me the revolution is so that all will say Don to all. . . . Thus should it be under the Republic" (*FW* 210). The praise bestowed on Hemingway for *capturing* Elizabethan or Marlovian or even contemporary Spanish speech is misleading, then, for this connection is something of a ruse. "What passes with thee?" was never spoken in any era in English but is entirely invented from a hodgepodge of translingual materials. Hemingway only *implies*, through the narrator and through Robert, the existence of an original Spanish text that appears realistic yet is linguistically impossible. To unpack this novel's linguistic world is to realize that Hemingway points to a Spanish ur-text that is as corrupted and contorted, if not more, than the English: an unlocatable original that is weird and inflected with pidgin English, French, Russian, and more and that yields a modified, laconic, rhetorically rich English. Hemingway told Ivan Kashkin of his plan for the novel, "I try to show *all* the different sides of [the war.] . . . So never think one story represents my viewpoint because it is much too complicated for that."[39] His observation that despite his own ardent Republicanism "the Spanish war is a bad war . . . and nobody is right" explains his determination here to avoid "writ[ing] like God"—from a single, omniscient viewpoint.[40] Indeed, Hemingway began his first draft of the novel in the first person, with Robert as the "I," but abandoned that by the third manuscript page.

Specifically, Hemingway's method is a version of cubism, a structural (rather than spoken or creolized) Spanglish that becomes a two-dimensional scaffolding for a wealth of strategies of mistranslation that the novel embodies, corrupts, and further confuses. One of the reasons that cubism in the visual arts was rarely translated successfully into literature was the difficulty of capturing in sequential words the simultaneity of multiple perspectives that Pablo Picasso, Georges Braque, and Juan Gris were able to fuse into one flattened plane with paint.[41] The sanctity of the single viewing plane of representation, grounded in realism's adherence to a singular version of human perception, was violated by cubism, which refashioned representation around artifice, antinaturalism, and a multiperspectival collage of object and conception. Stein, Wallace Stevens, and Hemingway had to rely on repetitions to create such effects; the multiple perspectives are thus only visible as the time of reading passes. Most other practitioners of literary cubism—Guillaume Apollinaire, Max Jacob, several Dadaists and surrealists—were poets, too, and could at least use fragmented lines, collages of images in material juxtaposition, and manipulations of the space of the printed page in ways that were less common in novels. Hemingway saw himself as translating Cézanne into literature; returning to his trope for translation, he noted in *A Moveable Feast* (1964) that what he learned from Cézanne's techniques "was a secret."[42] He cut from the original draft of "Big Two-Hearted River" (1925) a passage, known as "On Writing," in which Nick Adams aspires to write like Cézanne painted. But critics have assumed that Hemingway's cubism, filtered through Stein, dissipated or transmuted into other techniques roughly after the late 1920s.[43] Daniel Worden reminds us, however, that the frontispiece to *Death in the Afternoon* (1932) was Juan Gris's cubist painting *El Torero* (1913), which frames what Worden reads as a literary experiment in the synthetic cubism of the 1910s.[44]

Only a few years after the publication of *For Whom the Bell Tolls*, Joseph Frank would frame this dilemma and challenge in modernist literature, which he claimed sought to "undermine the inherent consecutiveness of language."[45] Hemingway's new cubism in *For Whom the Bell Tolls* not only moves beyond formalism and geometric abstraction in one language; it proposes to resolve the problem of the need for repetition and shifting perspectives by combining Spanish grammar and English content with no portmanteaux. The implied and buried translational referent—the semantic structures of the Spanish language and their verbal articulations—silently provides the backbone of an experiment that throws a light on, rather than glossing over or naturalizing, the process and limits of translation. The result is what we might call "structural Spanglish," as opposed to the better-known version of Spanglish that relies on code switching. The flatness of the canvas becomes the flatness of the fused linguistic unit, where "What passes with thee?" represents two linguistic "perspectives" that, alone, are incomplete, without semantic depth, never reconciled as organically whole "planes." Blending synchronic and diachronic approaches to translation, Hemingway uses these various planes to dig into and cut across the sediments of English and Spanish alike.

This novel thereby helps illuminate the stakes of several current conversations that originated in the field of translation studies. Translation has energized the transnational turn in modernist studies of the past two decades, for instance, by registering the scholarly shift away from analyzing modernism *in* various languages, nations, or regions (English modernism, Spanish modernism, Chinese modernism, African modernism, and so on) and toward the translingual networks of aesthetic practices, material objects, and writers themselves. Such approaches take up the implications of Pound's seminal struggles to dislocate and denaturalize English through translation. Pound wanted to condense multiple temporalities of languages into one compositional instant in the present. The effects of this revolution have been traced in poetry, from Pound's own "The Seafarer" or Canto I to Louis and Celia Zukofsky's homophonic translations of Catullus. Scholars have also brought fresh attention to the political or racial bonds effected through translation, as in Langston Hughes's versions of Nicolás Guillén's and Jacques Roumain's works. But such topics are rarely examined in Anglophone novels, with the singular exception of Joyce's works. Hemingway stands between and disorients both of these various modes of translation. While absorbing Pound's lessons and speaking *through* Spanish as Pound had, he chastised his one-time mentor for having "abandoned the English language for Unknown Tongue."[46] Hemingway's work instead aims to maintain, but to distort and deform, English around a foreign tongue, as Henry Roth did in an era of American nativism and as Conrad did while the British Empire worked to homogenize English globally.[47]

That is, Hemingway manipulates English around his imagined, unreal Spanish, ranging selectively across history to fashion a "translation without an original," as Emily Apter has characterized James Merrill's *The Changing Light at Sandover* (1980).[48] In this way, Hemingway looks toward the antiepistemology of the postmodern approach to the flatness of language. The dialogue is a depiction of multiple interruptions of what Roman Jakobson described as the transition from interlingual to intralingual translation, in which signs are rearranged into idiomatic order in the target language, leaving no residual trace of the source language.[49] But here the interstices of the translational process are highlighted, yet the illogical fusions and their subtle misdirections in Hemingway's novel are apparent only to readers who know both English and Spanish (or at least some Spanish) and can see the colliding linguistic planes. The result is the minoritizing of a dominant, native language akin to what Gilles Deleuze and Claire Parnet characterize as literary "bilingualism," which is "speaking in one's own language like a foreigner," as Kafka and Beckett do.[50] Hemingway's dialogic suspension between English and Spanish calls itself out *in* English but *through* Spanish, as literary, artificial, and dislocated, in contrast to the homogeneity and global power of his native tongue. The multiperspectivalism that prompts this effect and its force upon the characters, the dialogue, the narration, and the plot of this novel stands next to the works of the writers Deleuze and Parnet name—Kafka and Beckett—as forebears of the linguistic experiments best known in postmodernist novels.

To read Hemingway as a late modernist in literary history is to read him as a transitional writer who is commenting both on high modernism's multilingual architectonics and on his own reputation in novel history. *For Whom the Bell Tolls* blends third-person omniscient and limited narration; free indirect discourse and interior monologues through multiple characters; translated, mistranslated, transliterated, and half-translated (or semifluently translated) dialogue; self-conscious, self-aware, and/or self-censorial narration; false cognates, nonidiomatic expressions, and untranslatable jokes; linguistic misrecognitions; and often inaccurate or nonsensical varieties of Spanish and English across multiple demotics, registers, and time periods. Robert believes that "being in Spain was natural and sound"; even so, he acknowledges that "he never felt like a foreigner in Spanish and they did not really treat him like a foreigner most of the time; only when they turned on you" (*FW* 165, 135). The novel's mixture of languages and idioms replicates this dialectic of intimacy and foreignness—and finally, betrayal. Thus, it is only on the novel's final page that Robert is "completely integrated now," as he lies on the ground preparing to fire at enemy troops as he dies (*FW* 471). The many mistranslations and miscommunications of *For Whom the Bell Tolls*, however, remain impossible to "integrate," leaving us a late-modernist reading of linguistic collisions that face, as Robert does, the coming total war.

Alfau and the Americanization of Spain

I have suggested that Hemingway's novel not only marks a particular moment in late modernism and in the history of modernist translation more generally, but also constitutes a critical part of an arc of postmodernist writing visible through commonalities and shared techniques across a diffuse range of texts in postwar literatures. This disoriented Hemingway connects, through his specifically English-Spanish *ostranenie*, to poets such as Hart Crane, Federico García Lorca, Jack Spicer, and Salvador Novo, each of whom used one language's idiom to dislodge their respective native tongues. A broader web would extend to Zora Neale Hurston's twisting of African American idioms around Caribbean tongues or Anzia Yezierska's fusion of English and Yiddish grammars, the self-censorship in Peter Carey's *True History of the Kelly Gang* (2000), the stilted speech in Jonathan Safran Foer's *Everything Is Illuminated* (2003), many of the texts in collections such as *Rotten English* (2007), and even the invented tongue of Paul Kingsnorth's *The Wake* (2014).[51] I will chart here something specific: a mode of novelistic Spanglish as mistranslation, for which Hemingway's late modernism stands as a hinge from Pound to the present. The genealogy I offer looks back to Spain and its literary history as the motivation for its dislocations and hybridizations of English.[52]

Felipe Alfau, a contemporary of Hemingway's who was all but forgotten until recent years, was born in Barcelona in 1902 and immigrated with his family to New York City when he was fourteen. He published a volume of children's stories, *Old Tales from Spain* (1929), which was followed by a novelesque collection of short stories, *Locos: A Comedy of Gestures* (1936), which critics have seen as a combination of *Pale Fire* and *Six Characters in Search of an Author*. Alfau immersed himself in New York's Spanish expatriate culture, writing music criticism for the Spanish daily *La Prensa* and even taking a course at Columbia with Onís.[53] His masterpiece novel, *Chromos*, was in galleys in the late 1940s when he abruptly pulled the text from production. After abandoning the text, Alfau turned away from writing and disappeared from the literary world, becoming a translator of financial documents for Morgan Bank in Manhattan. *Chromos* was published in 1990 by the Dalkey Archive Press and was nominated for a National Book Award. That same year, *Locos* appeared in Spanish translation, and a Spanish version of *Chromos* followed in 1991; Alfau, who resisted efforts in either language to recover his seminal importance as a writer, claimed to have hated both of them. By the time the critic Ilan Stavans interviewed him in a nursing home in 1991, he was a bitter, racist, suicidal man who had spent three-quarters of a century living in the United States.

As an experiment with multilingualism and narration, *Chromos* shares much stylistically with the works of Alfau's Hispanophone near-contemporaries Borges and Cortázar and thus has drawn the inevitable comparisons, but Alfau almost certainly had no knowledge of their works. The novel follows a group of figures whom Alfau calls "Americaniards" (American Spaniards) through a narratorial voice of Spanish-inflected English.[54] Alfau himself believed that his "English is Iberian—an acquisition. It's half English and half my own creation."[55] Indeed, the very title of the novel looks like it is suspended between the two tongues: "Chromos" might appear to an Anglophone audience to be a Spanish word, much like the title of Alfau's first novel was (and *Chromos*'s epigraph is an untranslated misprint of the second line of *Don Quixote*), but, in fact, it refers to chromolithograph calendars that play a metaphorical role in elaborating the novel's formal structure. Similarly, the novel's opening lines make it sound as if it will be a familiar tale of immigrant life: "The moment one learns English, complications set in. Try as one may, one cannot elude this conclusion, one must inevitably come back to it. This applies to all persons, including those born to the language and, at times, even more so to Latins, including Spaniards" (*C* 7). But in the second paragraph, we leave behind the expected questions of assimilation for a less common speculation on the effects of English acquisition:

when we [Spaniards] enter the English-speaking world, we find the most elementary things questioned, growing in complexity without bounds; we experience, see or hear about problems which either did not exist for us or were disposed of in what he [the narrator's friend Don Pedro] calls that brachistological fashion of which we are masters: nervous breakdowns, social equality, marital maladjustment and beholding Oedipus in an unfavorable light, friendships with those women intellectualoids whom Don Pedro has baptized perfect examples of feminine putritude, psychoneuroses, anal hallucinations, etc., leading one gently but forcibly from a happy world of reflexes of which one was never aware, to a world of analytical reasoning of which one is continuously aware, which closes in like a vise of missionary tenacity and culminates in such a collapse of the simple as questioning the meaning of meaning.

(C 7–8)

The unnamed narrator of *Chromos* offers dozens of sentences like this: wandering, unexpected, and contorted by what we learn is a collision of languages with an allusive range that reaches from Cervantes to Ogden and Richards.

This and more goes into the making of what Jill Adams characterizes as Alfau's "Iberian English, which shows itself occasionally in the hyper-correct diction of the non-native user ('Therefore the nickname El Telescopio with which our same authority on the typical had baptized it.'); the awkward use of Latinate words ('isochronous steps'. . . .), unusual and often jarring syntax," and untranslated Spanish terms.[56] Within this version of Spanglish in interwar New York, the unnamed narrator conveys a mostly aimless and nonchronological plot that replicates the wanderings, physical and intellectual, of the main characters. As in *For Whom the Bell Tolls*, the majority of the dialogue originally takes place in Spanish—the narrator makes that explicit in *Chromos*— and is translated for readers by a figure who claims that his English is imperfect even though "translating" is his "business and means of livelihood" (C 51). The prose is pointedly ungrammatical and employs, perhaps more than any other "error," a lack of parallel structure in order to convey a sense of the two languages clashing: "Strong inclination to relive the past and he is the one who had got the tickets and had persuaded me to accompany him," he writes of his friend Garcia [*sic*], for instance (C 48).

The narrator's disclaimers about his English and his likely intentional errors are somewhat at odds with his career, in a doubling of Alfau himself, as a translator. This becomes clear through the long sections of the text that summarize the plot of an unremarkable soap opera, which becomes a novel within the novel, that Garcia describes in conversation to the narrator. The narrator constantly downplays his comprehension of English, writing that "I have it on good authority that [Don Pedro's] English was perfect, but he had nursed an invincible accent and an unassailable syntax" (*C* 14). The narrator also stresses his other limits: as he summarizes Garcia's story and dialogue, he writes, "I'll drop the quotation marks because I don't remember exactly Garcia's words" (*C* 53). Furthermore, the narrator creates multiple layers of translation within his narration. He notes, concerning a performance of *Don Juan Tenorio* that he and Garcia attend in New York, "as we Spaniards like so much to make puns, I had said something like this to Garcia: 'If we were speaking English, I could say that the drama was not ghostly but ghastly, get it?'" (*C* 48) The play on words only works in English, of course, so the implied original in Spanish is at once possible (he could be rendering a similar Spanish pun here) and inaccessible, thus unverifiable.

As the narrator and his fellow exiles wander—and as they praise "loitering" and lament that Americans do so little of it, even criminalize it—they discuss the decline of Spain, the transformations of Spaniards in New York City, and Spanish figures and tropes, from the Black Legend to *castizos*, from flamenco to Cervantes. Against the exhortations of his compatriots, however, the narrator attempts to rewrite the typology of Spaniards that was indebted to Cervantes: rather than the idea that Don Quixote and Sancho Panza represented the two types of Spaniards (idealist and pragmatist), he argues that his Americaniard friends Dr. de los Rios and Don Pedro represent a "national history and structure" that was "ethnological and racial within the same country, one showing the Visigoth and the other the Moorish influences" (*C* 11). For the narrator, Spain's two types are the two ethnic groups identified by contemporary Spaniards as the sources of *castizo* purity and black/Arabic contamination, as the popular mythology of the early twentieth century held. Such an understanding of Spanish existence, he suggests, is only possible within the United States.

The narrator ultimately becomes one of the few Spaniards who can accept the "complications" that American English imposes. Don Pedro ("the Moor") instead expounds a "theory of the Latinamericanization of the United States" through music and immigration, and the narrator asks, "But is this the new conquest of the Americas, by the Americas and for the Americas? This mutual transcontinental, translinguistic, transracial osmosis?" (*C* 16) The narrator sees an irony in the new U.S. imperialism: it imports cultures that it supposes to conquer and then makes those cultures—and, soon after, immigrants representing them—its own conquerors as white Americans become entranced by their music, languages, restaurants, and more. The narrator therefore concludes the novel by looking back to 1492 and asking "whether my ancestors were but immigrants disguised as conquerors, or whether all other aliens are but conquerors disguised as immigrants" (*C* 348). He continues on the final page: "To express this in my own language would be superfluous. To attempt to describe it in another's impossible. In Spanish I don't have to explain my nation or my countrymen. In English, I can't. It is the question of the synthetic method as opposed to the analytic. . . . As I said in the beginning, complications set in" (*C* 348). *Chromos*, in other words, relies on an unending and transtemporal oscillation between English and Spanish that never settles—"complications" riddle it from start to finish—and thus becomes a figuration of asymmetrical interlingual penetration since 1492.

***

Two other novels, separated by over half a century, help clarify further points in this genealogical line. At almost the same moment that *Chromos* was in galleys came a better-known text of late modernism, Malcolm Lowry's *Under the Volcano* (1947). At the heart of its sometimes hallucinatory, confused narrative, which rewrites *For Whom the Bell Tolls* in several ways, lie a number of Spanish/English mistranslations. The stumbling, drunken Consul Geoffrey Firmin is not only a debauched version of Robert Jordan displaced in Mexico but also an even clumsier Quixote figure. (Indeed, Lowry writes at one point, "The Consul shut the door behind him and a small rain of plaster showered on his head. A Don Quixote fell from the wall. He picked up the sad straw knight . . . And then the whiskey bottle: he drank fiercely from it.")[57] The novel is also a commentary on the Spanish Civil War: its action takes place on November 2, 1938, as the war was turning definitively toward the Nationalists; the International Brigades had disbanded and left the country in October. Hugh Firmin, the Consul's half-brother and foil, is active on the British left, has recently been in wartime Spain, and will leave Mexico soon on a ship carrying munitions to the Loyalists.[58] Hugh's connections to Spain even bring a version of Spanglish to the text when he reads a telegram, presumably botched by local agents, that the novel transcribes as "DAILY GLOBE intelube londres presse collect following yesterdays *headcoming anti-Semitic campaign mexpress propetition see tee emma mexworkers*" (*U* 98).

And thus, in his final, fatal encounter, the Consul is accused by the Mexican police, in pidgin English, of "mak[ing] the map of the Spain? You Bolsheviki prick? You member of the Brigade Internationale and stir up trouble?" (*U* 372). The officer's English is not merely inflected by Spanish; it also contains elements of French ("Brigade Internationale" rather than "Brigadas internacionales") and possibly Russian. The Consul is then mistaken for being "*Sr. Hugo Firmin*," member of the "*Federación Anarquista Ibérica*" just before he is killed (*U* 385). The last page of the novel reprints the sign that the Consul—our filter for much Spanish dialogue, however distorted—has misread throughout the novel:

¿LE GUSTA ESTE JARDÍN?
¿QUE ES SUYO?
¡EVITE QUE SUS HIJOS LO DESTRUYAN!

(*U* 134)

The Consul earlier had translated these "simple and terrible words" as "You like this garden? Why is it yours? We evict those who destroy!" (*U* 135). He incorrectly renders the sign into an English inflected with Spanish: *evite* ("avoid") becomes a false friend that he gives as "evict," which ties to the multilayered themes and metaphors of Eden, hell, and "eviction" that Lowry embeds in the narrative. But its meaning is lost on the misreading Consul, marking the novel's Spanish as an ur-text never translated or assimilated to its English narrative, but one whose mistranslation foretells his fate. Hugh therefore sees the sign later and correctly (to use the term provisionally) sees the Spanish as "¿Le gusta este jardín, que es suyo? ¡Evite que sus hijos lo destruyan!" He then translates—or the narrator translates through him, we are not certain: "Do you like this garden, the notice said, that is yours? See to it that your children do not destroy it!" (*U* 242–243).

Furthermore, this mistranslation is multiplied—and the terms "correct" and "incorrect" complicated—by the fact that Lowry himself originally mistranscribed the Spanish, and then his printer followed suit.[59] Lowry later claimed to have copied the sign from a public garden in Oaxaca in 1938 and insisted that it was grammatically wrong there. "But in one way," he wrote to his editor, "it is immeasurably more dramatic as it is, even though wrong.... Indeed 'Evite' does *look* as if it meant 'evict,' even if not in the first person plural."[60] Lowry postulates that Hugh should correct it but that "both the sign as it appears in the book, incorrect as it is, and the Consul's hallucinatory translation of it, are of the utmost importance," so Hugh's version cannot erase these mistakes. Lowry then wanted the sign transcribed correctly on the final page of the novel, where it appears again, alone and verbatim as before, but both the "correction" he sent and the resulting printed edition are still not idiomatic: "que es suyo" should not be set off as a separate question since it is a clause that modifies the phrase in the first line.[61] That is, the "correction" on the final page repeats both the Consul's and Lowry's errors. A compounded mistranslation that crosses back and forth between the fictional world of the text and the world of Lowry's own incomplete Spanish becomes more than a thematic development: again, it scaffolds and articulates the novel's very structure, its mode of narration and dialogue and its development of symbolism through hallucination and paranoia coded as translation. Accuracy and inaccuracy are built into the processes of translation—even transcription and printing—so fully that they become motifs rather than markers of actual linguistic transference.

More recently, Ben Lerner stages a clever comic scene early in his novel *Leaving the Atocha Station* (2011), in which his protagonist-narrator Adam Gordon attempts to translate Lorca. Gordon, a poet paralyzed by his fear of being outed as a fraud, is on a fellowship in Spain, has planned to "teach myself Spanish by reading masterworks of Spanish literature," and has "fantasized about the nature and effect of a Spanish thus learned, how its archaic flavor and formally heightened rhetoric would collide with the mundanities of daily life, giving the impression less of someone from a foreign country than someone from a foreign time."[62] When he comes to Lorca, he practices a mode of translation indebted to the aleatory experiments of Language poets:

> I opened the Lorca more or less at random, transcribed the English recto onto a page of my first notebook, and began to make changes, replacing a word with whatever word I first associated with it and/or scrambling

the order of the lines, and then I made whatever changes these suggested to me. Or I looked up the Spanish word for the English word I wanted to replace, then replaced that English word with a Spanish word that approximated its sound ("Under the arc of the sky" became "Under the arc of the cielo," which became "Under the arc of the cello"). I then braided fragments of the prose I kept in my second notebook with the translations I had thus produced ("Under the arc of the cello / I open the Lorca at random," and so on).

(*L* 16)

Lerner's character imagines himself to be brilliantly original by way of an exercise that is wholly unoriginal: the combination of literary Spanish and English in order to alienate and foreignize both. The poeticized Spanglish that results presages the linguistic combinations that characterize much of the novel. Moments after this, Gordon listens to his love interest Teresa tell a story about her past, which he likely understands but gives in the novel's narrative in translational indeterminacy: "The father had been either a famous painter or collector of paintings and she had either become a painter to impress him or quit painting because she couldn't deal with the pressure of his example or because he was such an asshole, although here I was basically guessing" (*L* 30). This unsettled reciprocity between originals and translations culminates the novel when, in the closing lines, Gordon and Teresa devise a plan in which "Teresa would read the [poetic] originals and I would read the translations and the translations would become the originals as we read" (*L* 181). The version of Spanglish in this novel is a formal artifice that stretches Hemingway's experiments in new directions while pointing to the embrace of failure, error, and unoriginality that I will explore in the conclusion.

CONCLUSION

Worlds Between Languages—The Spanglish Quixote

CONTEMPORARY SPANGLISH IS ONE THEORETICAL LINGUISTIC endpoint for the patterns of English/Spanish convergence that this book has examined. Spanglish has generated a great deal of controversy in the United States in recent years, though primarily in discussions of identities and linguistic patrimonies. Rarely have topics such as literariness and translation surfaced here. Spanglish, of course, is not technically a *language* into which one can *translate* something, in the traditional senses of either term. Rather, it is a vernacular amalgam of code-switching techniques that registers a continual transition and interplay between English and Spanish, as it developed with little standardization or rules in various contact zones. Despite this rather typical pattern of emergence in linguistic history—understood this way, it is the inverse of Esperanto—Spanglish has elicited outrage from many corners. Some of those reactions have come from predictable sources (the Royal Spanish Academy, nativist white Americans) while others are perhaps surprising, including Octavio Paz and a host of Latin American immigrants who want to forge cultural autonomy for Spanish in the United States.[1] For some, it signals another stage of the American English conquest of Spanish that has accelerated since 1898.

At a tangent to these discussions is the line of hyperliterary, mistranslational Spanglish that Hemingway created and that I noted in figures like Alfau and Lerner. Between the identitarian embrace of Spanglish and the literary poeticization of it lies an experiment carried out in 2001 by Ilan Stavans, a professor at Amherst College and a foremost advocate of "Spanglish" in the United States. Stavans produced a Spanglish version of the first chapter of Cervantes's *Don Quixote*, and it was immediately greeted with everything from raucous laughter to stunned horror. Integrating not only traditional and modernized Spanish and English but also a variety of dialectal expressions, idioms, loanwords, calques, neologisms, misspellings, mispronunciations, and more, Stavans's text uses Spanglish to do several things. First, it recreates the linguistic flux of Cervantine Spanish to defamiliarize what became a standardized language in the centuries that followed the original novel. Simultaneously, it points to the interpenetration of Spanish and English over time—a process for which the Anglo/Spanish exchanges of Cervantes's day was an impetus. Furthermore, it comments implicitly on the previous translations of *Don Quixote* into English by suspending the text between the Spanish of its day and the English of the present-day United States—in an invented form of Spanglish. Creating a text that inhabits multiple linguistic and novelistic worlds, both familiar and unfamiliar, Stavans thereby carries out a translation that never settles on either linguistic pole. Stavans sees Spanglish as an emblem of the latest chapter in the failed efforts of Hispanophone and Anglophone governments, institutions, academies, and cultural figures to standardize, police, and cordon off languages that have been entwined and colliding since Columbus. "Since 1492," he writes, "there have been two different stories cohabiting in the vast continent: the success of the north and the defeat of the south. That mere fact makes it even harder for Anglo-Saxon culture in New York to recognize as equal that of the inheritors of Luis de Góngora and Lope de Vega."[2] By recovering these collisions and the spaces between them, Stavans leaves the *Quixote* productively transposed between its Castilian world and a translated American English one. The text belies the naturalizing narrative of Spanglish's emergence in vernacular speech.

Why a Spanglish *Don Quixote*? Cervantes's novel has been an enormous, sometimes near-impossible historical burden for four centuries for artists of all types—not only Hispanophone novelists. Perhaps most famously, in Jorge Luis Borges's story "Pierre Menard, Author of the

Quixote" (1939), a contemporary author attempts to inhabit the life of Cervantes—to "*be* Miguel de Cervantes," Borges writes—so that he can reproduce *Don Quixote*.[3] He wants to prove that the Quixote is a "contingent" book, it is "unnecessary," and so he reproduces it verbatim; Borges's narrator is fascinated by the alleged differences between the two versions.[4] In a variation on this theme, Orson Welles's unfinished film version of *Don Quixote* from the late 1960s contains an incredible deleted scene in which the intrepid knight and his faithful Sancho Panza enter a movie theater in contemporary Spain. While Sancho, seated next to a young girl in the audience, enjoys the romantic Western film, Quixote, in a very Wellesian twist on Cervantine satire, draws his sword, rushes toward the movie screen, and rips apart the fabric as men on horseback ride by onscreen. There can be no artifice, then or now, that Cervantes has not already created and preemptively shredded, Welles implies.

The elevation of *Don Quixote*'s singular originality—its arguable status as the first novel—is ironic in light of Cervantes's own designs. His narrator claims that the story itself, beginning in the ninth chapter, is his retelling of an anonymous *morisco*'s translation of an Arab writer's account of the knight Don Quixote. This becomes something of a running joke in the novel itself, for Cervantes modeled the very world of his novel and of Don Quixote's quite unoriginal imagination on the artificial worlds of Spain's famous chivalric romances. What's more, the fictional world of the novel and its actual world of circulation blend hilariously in the second volume, when Don Quixote and Sancho Panza come across the spurious (and inferior, they assert) second volume of their own adventures—a volume that actually was written by a pseudonymous Avellaneda and printed during the ten-year gap between the publication of Cervantes's own two parts.

Thus, Stavans comes to the *Quixote* not to make it new and, indeed, at times not even to make it different, by rendering it in a Spanglish "translation"—a term I qualify shortly. Stavans has published the first chapter in several places, including in his book *Spanglish: The Making of a New American Language* (2003), alongside a six-thousand-word dictionary of Spanglish. Not simply a novelty or a predictable implicit attack on high culture, Stavans's text sees itself as part of a theory of languages and their morphologies, of signification and writing—a theory of translation itself as a never-complete process, a poststructuralist approach to it moving away from equivalence that he outlines in a series of critical writings spanning two decades.[5] (The text itself looks like a translation in process, and it requires bilingualism to grasp.) In his own role as Spanglish authority, Stavans dates the origins of Spanglish to the contact between English and Spanish speakers after the Louisiana Purchase and United States' westward expansion into Mexico, but his version of the *Quixote*—a text that predates this time by two centuries—calls up an even earlier moment of linguistic interchange between English and Spanish.

Stavans suggests that one of the only ways to make the *Quixote* "original" between its first language and a language into which it has been translated at least nineteen times (English) is by way of a Poundian project: to translate it into a language that is *not* a language, that is both and neither Spanish and English. In English versions, the knight Don Quixote has been everything from a sincere romantic to an ironic postmodernist, and every translator must contend not only with Cervantes's text but also with a history of succeeding translations of remarkable variety and quality spanning four centuries. The tensions between originality, creativity, fidelity, and replication are familiar in translation studies, as is the idea that each translator makes the original text into a unit of her contemporary culture, her zeitgeist, in some form or another. Stavans's aim, however, is to make the *Quixote* simultaneously recognizable and unrecognizable, domestic and foreign, vernacular and literary. His translation defamiliarizes the most familiar of Spanish texts, reclaiming what he sees as its unfamiliarity and innovation in its moment, when Spanish was being codified but was still greatly in flux (as it remains)—despite how ossified it might seem four hundred years later, after some seven hundred editions of *Don Quixote* in over 150 languages, including a controversial recent "translation" into contemporary Spanish by the scholar Andrés Trapiello.

The original *Quixote* played the major role in both transforming and solidifying the modern Spanish that was evolving from Old Castilian, which itself was an agglomeration of words acquired from vulgar Latin, Moorish Arabic, Celtiberian, Hebrew, Basque, Gothic, and more, and was rapidly being infused with borrowed words from indigenous New World tongues and from English. (Cervantes's family, furthermore, is speculated to have been *conversos*, and the name "Quixote" possibly has Hebrew roots.) Stavans celebrates the fact in his criticism that, to his mind, both *Don Quixote* and *One Hundred Years of Solitude* read better in English than in Spanish, and he asserts that García Márquez's masterpiece—even in Spanish—would be incomprehensible to Cervantes. His mixture of registers in the Spanglish *Quixote* is bewildering; he opens:

> In un placete de La Mancha of which nombre no quiero remembrearme, vivía, not so long ago, uno de esos gentlemen who always tienen una lanza in the rack, una buckler antigua, a skinny caballo y un grayhound para el chase. A cazuela with más beef than mutón, carne choppeada para la dinner, un omelet pa' los Sábados, lentil pa' los Viernes, y algún pigeon como delicacy especial pa' los Domingos, consumían tres cuarers de su income. El resto lo empleaba en una coat de broadcloth y en soketes de velvetín pa' los holidays, with sus slippers pa' combinar, while los otros días de la semana él cut a figura de los más finos cloths.

The syntax more closely resembles English, likely because the word order would not work in the opposite direction and because in English (unlike Spanish) there are more idiosyncrasies of pronunciation and spelling.[6] The rhythm, however, is closer to Spanish. Indeed, swaths of the original Spanish are untouched, intact: "de La Mancha," "nombre no quiero," but others are updated, modernized, or combined with English elements, such as "skinny caballo" for "rocín flaco."[7] Cervantes's parenthetical "que en esto hay alguna diferencia en los autores que deste caso escriben," on the other hand, is rewritten, entirely in Spanish with the same meaning, in a more modern register, "hay diferencia de opinión entre aquellos que han escrito sobre el sujeto." Here, it seems that a reading knowledge of Spanish is necessary for the reader of the Spanglish *Quixote*, whereas no such long strings occur in English in the chapter.

With a roughly equivalent balance between source languages, other words are translated straightforwardly into English—"grayhound" [*sic*] or "beef," for instance—and there are English idioms such as "high Heaven" and "early riser." But there are also English words spelled phonetically as if pronounced by a native Spanish speaker, such as "Livin," and others have been created by mispronunciation: the English "quarters," fusing with the Spanish "cuartos" in part, becomes "cuarers." Some are back-formations from English that have been Hispanicized, whether as new verbs or by adding a Spanish article: "remembrearme," "el chase," "choppeada," "la dinner." Word choices can be interchangeable, without regulation, such as "que" and "that." Cervantes's "Quieren decir" becomes a modernized slang, "La gente say," and the common "hermano" ("brother") becomes the slang "bró," evincing contact with U.S. English slang. African American slang surfaces when Cervantes's "yo señora, soy el gigante Caraculiambro" ("I, my lady, am the giant Caraculiambro") becomes "Yo, lady, soy el giant Caraculiambro," humorously playing on the crosslinguistic "yo." Stavans decides to have the narrator repeat and sometimes add words that are not in the original, such as "El pobre felo," where Cervantes omits descriptors and simply repeats the pronoun for "he." "Para" is often reduced to "pa'" and the formal "Usted" becomes "Usté," dropping the "d" as many Hispanic Americans do. Stavans draws on everything from Miami Cuban to Nuyorican to Tex-Mex from either side of the Rio Grande, though the center of gravity is clearly New York. Alongside his Spanglishisms, Stavans also invents words such as "forgetear" and "awakeado" that one reviewer, herself a New York Spanglish speaker, claims are not Spanglish at all.[8] Such a response signals one of Stavans's victories: a reader who looks for a singular Spanglish speaker or for a plausible, organic vernacular captured in the text will be disappointed, if not befuddled. This translation would be better called one of Spanglish*es*.

This multitude of shifts between Spanish and English language and rules, however, is not the most innovative aspect of the text. There are other signs only visible to the eye—belying the claim that Spanglish is only a spoken vernacular—the days of the week, for example, are written in Spanish but capitalized as they are in English. English spelling has influenced Spanglish orthography even when there is no audible consequence, as in the word "pearlas" for *perlas*. And other cues are subtler, such as "rasón." Castilian Spanish (that of Cervantes) pronounces "razón" with a "th" sound; New World Spanish, however, treats the "z" and "s" sounds as roughly interchangeable. Stavans reverses this later, misspelling "princesa" as "princeza" and accentuating the oral break with Iberian Castilian that his translation enacts. Stavans also misspells "promisa" for "promesa," indicating the degrees by which Spanish has been Anglicized with no change in meaning. There is a slight change in meaning, though, when he substitutes—and the word again is hardly accidental—"significante" for "significativo." The common "significativo" is "significant"; "significante" is the term in linguistics for "signifier."

Stavans takes steps to ensure that his narrator does not appear uneducated—as speakers of Spanglish often are stereotypically presumed to be—with some fascinating word choices. Stavans uses some obscure English words in place of obscure Spanish ones, such as "buckler" for "adarga" rather than the more common English "shield" or Spanish "escudo." (And in fact, an "adarga," like other pieces of equipment the knight uses, was outdated in Cervantes's time.) This term, like several others ("sally," for example, which many previous translators of the *Quixote* used), seems to indicate a deep fluency in English—in English *before* its contacts that created Spanglish. There are also words that have been adopted more or less into English, such as "hidalgo," that Stavans renders as "gentleman" (later "felo"), or "hacienda," which becomes "estate," demonstrating a comfort in English that exceeds the Spanish at these points. At the same time, all of Cervantes's words for various types of horses are reduced to "caballo." Our narrator furthermore knows, as both Cervantes's narrator and the English translator of the *Quixote* must, about other literary knights, such as Amadis of Gaul and Palmerín of England. And Cervantes's untranslated Latin "tantum pellis et ossa fuit" is given in Latin, followed by a parenthetical translation into idiomatic English, "all skin and bones."

The passages focused on domestic relations, however, include some of the more surprising word choices:

> Livin with él eran una housekeeper en sus forties, una sobrina not yet twenty y un ladino del field y la marketa que le saddleaba el caballo al gentleman y wieldeaba un hookete pa' podear. . . . But all this no tiene mucha importancia pa' nuestro cuento, providiendo que al cuentarlo no nos separemos pa' nada de las verdá.

In a sly and telling substitution, Stavans substitutes the word "ladino" for "mozo," a houseboy or errand runner. "Ladino," of course, comes from the Latin root for the word "Latin" itself, and over time it has accrued a multiplicity of different meanings in Spanish. It refers to several other linguistic worlds: Ladino is the language of Sephardic Jews created from a mixture of Spanish, Hebrew, and Arabic; it also refers to Old (Romance) Castilian. A "ladino" in the New World, however, is a person of mestizo (or sometimes indigenous) heritage who only speaks Spanish. And "Ladino" is the name that Mexicans give to a dialect of Spanish spoken in New Mexico and southern Colorado, a dialect that preserves or revives some archaisms from Old Castilian alongside its influence from New World languages and from English.[9] Stavans, whose own family is of Sephardic ancestry, thus reemploys the multiplicity and polysemy of this word. He ponders in his autobiography whether "Ladino—Judeo-Spanish, also known as *judesmo*—a dialect that recalls old Spanish and Portuguese but is written in Hebrew characters" had successfully traveled to the Mexican neighborhood of his youth.[10] The primary meaning of "ladino" in Spanish, in fact, is "skillful, crafty, or cunning"; Stavans, the translator, is implicating himself as the cunning, linguistically mischievous boy in the master's house. These layers of significance are amplified when we look back at the words that Stavans has replaced from Cervantes: while most of Cervantes's language comes from vulgar Latin, "mozo" is of unknown origin; "adarga" (which became "buckler") has Arabic roots, as does "hanega" (a measure of a land's grain), which becomes "acres." Cervantes's "pantuflos," which he borrowed from French, becomes the decidedly Germanic "slippers."

Rather than permitting transparent communication, Spanglish obscures the access to the original "place" or world of the novel because of its specific grounding in and constant allusions to actual worlds far removed from Cervantes's. Indeed, the first signal that Stavans gives of his plan to transport the *Quixote* comes, fittingly enough, in the third word, "placete" for "lugar," a back-formation from the English "place," which in turn came from a Latin root. He repeats this word later when he translates Don Quixote's moment of self-naming after his "linaje y patria" (lineage and country) as his "placete de origen." His "placete" is this text, Stavans indicates, much like the knight's place in Cervantes's text, is the text itself. He seems to be working to confuse what he saw in his own youth in Mexico, in a place in which Yiddish and Spanish collided and blended while still carving out a semiautonomous realm in private spaces. Stavans grew up in a Yiddish enclave of Mexico, the descendent of Eastern European Jewish immigrants, and he sees a number of continuities between Yiddish and Spanglish—only Yiddish went on to become a somewhat formalized language. He writes that Israeli Hebrew and worldwide Zionism have effaced the linguistic diversity of the Jewish diaspora and history, much as Castilian did with Spanish as Spain's empire grew.[11] Stavans's Spanglish captures a moment in the evolution of a language that is not yet a language, nor is it a creole or patois, nor may it ever become a language.

***

These separate yet intermingling worlds created and inhabited by different languages are at the heart of the disorientation that Stavans's Spanglish *Quixote* seeks to effect. "Translation" is not really the appropriate term for this textual/linguistic act. Stavans's note on the piece reads "Transladado al Spanglish por Ilan Stavans." "Transladado" is a fusion of the Spanish "trasladado" (with no *n*) and the English "translated." "Trasladar" is not the Spanish word for "to translate"; "traducir" is. "Trasladar" is "to move, to transfer," and its Latin roots branched into the *English* word "translate," not the Spanish "traducir." (This is the same difference Hemingway employed in *The Sun Also Rises* and that Pound played upon with his invented terms such as "traducer" and "transduction.") This simultaneous assertion of the impossibility of translation and the actual practice of it recalls a comment that Don Quixote makes in the second part of the novel. He says to Sancho, while they are at a printer's shop, that "translating from one language to another, unless it is from Greek or Latin, the queens of all languages, is like looking at Flemish tapestries from the wrong side, for although the figures are visible, they are covered by threads that obscure them, and cannot be seen with the smoothness and color of the right side."[12] The visibility of the threads themselves here among the "smoothness and color" of both the original and the English *Quixote* is exactly what the Spanglish version—which Stavans claims to be expanding into the entire novel—foregrounds. Its suspension between two languages, two literary systems and their histories, indeed between two imperial moments separated by four hundred years, makes it a resonant commentary on the many moments of incomplete coherence that this book has traced.

NOTES

Introduction: Modernism, Translation, and the Fields of Literary History

1. Juan Ramón Jiménez, *Política poética*, intro. Germán Bleiberg (Madrid: Alianza Editorial, 1982), 184. Whenever it is not unduly awkward, I have used the adjective "U.S." rather than the commonplace "American." Beyond the obvious benefits, this both helps clarify the confusion caused by the different points of reference of the Spanish *americano* (see chapters 4 and 5) and highlights the awkward lack of an English equivalent for the adjective *estadounidense* ("of the United States"), as is evident in the foreign formations I discuss below.

2. If we do not privilege poetic form in literary history, for example, we might see Eliot's *The Waste Land* (1922) as but one part of a larger program that included criticism, editorship, historiography, French compositions and translations from French, and much more, all held together by a core practice of translation. Historically, the field of translation studies has been more conservative, often for disciplinary reasons, in thinking of translation as distinct and autonomous. But to see the cultural past robustly through translation, I argue, affords an opportunity to move beyond the allusive range of even the most capacious poems or novels alone. This is not to label all practices "translation" or to reduce or flatten poetry into a version of translation; George Steiner's attempt to recast all communication as "translation," for instance, actually evacuates much of the concept's analytic potential. Rather, I aim here to level modes of literary production.

3. For the moment, I am using "modernism" in a way that Paul K. Saint-Amour terms "indexical": invoking a commonly held sense of the term, with a history behind it, while aiming not to reify it further; see Paul K. Saint-Amour, *Tense Future: Modernism, Total War, Encyclopedic Form* (New York: Oxford University Press, 2015), 40–43. Similarly, I will use "American literature" and "Spanish literature" in a historical, not ontological, manner, and I will not parse the overlaps or differences between "fields" and "disciplines" in this moment. See especially chapter 3.

4. Ezra Pound, "The Renaissance," in *Literary Essays of Ezra Pound*, ed. T. S. Eliot (New York: New Directions, 1968), 214. Hereafter cited in the text as *LE*. For an exemplary recovery of comparative practices from beyond Euro-American academies, see Nergis Ertürk, "Toward a Literary Communism: The 1926 Baku Turcological Congress," *boundary 2* 40, no. 2 (Summer 2013): 183–213.

5. Ernest Hemingway, Letter to Harvey Brett, November 5, 1956, in *Selected Letters*, ed. Carlos Baker (New York: Scribner, 1981), 873; Letter to Howell G. Jenkins, November 9, 1924, in *The Letters of Ernest Hemingway, Volume 2: 1923–1925*, ed. Sandra Whipple Spanier et al. (Cambridge: Cambridge University Press, 2013), 175.

6. Lawrence Venuti's *The Translator's Invisibility: A History of Translation* (New York: Routledge, 1995) is likely the best-known study to take such an approach, and its conception is very Poundian. The most familiar names in translation studies to argue for the centrality of translation in writing literary histories, especially comparative ones, are Itamar Even-Zohar, Susan Bassnett, Emily Apter, Gayatri Spivak, Natalie Melas, and Venuti himself. My thinking here is indebted also to Ignacio Infante's *After Translation: The Transfer and Circulation of Modern Poetics Across the Atlantic* (New York: Fordham University Press, 2013). Certainly, translation has stimulated everything from blank verse in English to Baudelaire's symbolism (via Poe), or even the Latin American Boom (via Faulkner), but my aim here is to hold such innovations and formations at a skeptical distance first rather than presuming their conceptual coherence as a historiographical starting point.

7. Ezra Pound, "Notes on Elizabethan Classicists," in *LE*, 232.

8. Exceptionalist thought has many sources, from Christianity to capitalism, that I do not have the space to treat fully here. David Shumway's *Creating American Civilization: A Genealogy of American Studies as an Academic Discipline* (Minneapolis: University of Minnesota Press, 1994) remains a valuable history of the discipline, but by focusing exclusively on the formation of American studies by Anglophone figures within the mainland United States (and by rarely mentioning empire), Shumway partially replicates the very logic he aims to critique. His work has been both extended and modified by Emily Apter, Arif Dirlik, Amy Kaplan, Leo Marx, and Donald Pease, among others. Nancy Glazener's *Literature in the Making: A History of U.S. Literary Culture in the Long Nineteenth Century* (New York: Oxford University Press, 2015) provides an excellent account of this topic in the previous century.

9. See George Steiner, "What Is Comparative Literature?" in *No Passion Spent: Essays 1978–1995* (New Haven, Conn.: Yale University Press, 1996), 142–59; and

Katie Trumpener, "Beyond Alsace-Lorraine: Collaborating with Comparative Literature," *ADFL Bulletin* 36, no. 2 (Winter 2005): 22–26.

10. Van Wyck Brooks, "On Creating a Usable Past," *Dial* 64, no. 7 (April 11, 1918): 337.

11. Rubén Darío, *España contemporánea* (Madrid: Visor, 2005), 29. "Inverted conquest" comes from Alejandro Mejías-López.

12. Richard L. Kagan, introduction to *Spain in America: The Origins of Hispanism in the United States*, ed. Richard L. Kagan (Urbana: University of Illinois Press, 2002), 2–3.

13. A different version of this book would include these and other figures, but they had alternative—and often less productive, for my argumentative purposes—sensibilities of translation and comparison, and different aspirations toward becoming a public authority.

14. Federico de Onís, "El español en los Estados Unidos," *Hispania* 3, no. 5 (November 1920): 275; Richard L. Kagan, "The Spanish Craze: The Discovery of Spanish Art and Culture in the United States," in Stanley G. Payne et al., *When Spain Fascinated America* (Madrid: Fundación Zuloaga, 2010), 27. For enrollment statistics, see Jamie B. Draper and June H. Hicks, "Foreign Language Enrollments in Secondary Schools," ACTFL (2002), http://www.actfl.org/public/articles/Enroll2000.pdf.

15. Qtd. in Ofelia García, "Teaching Spanish and Spanish in Teaching in the USA: Integrating Multilingual Perspectives," in *Forging Multilingual Spaces: Integrated Perspectives on Majority and Minority Bilingual Education*, ed. Christine Hélot and Anne-Marie de Mejía (Buffalo: Multilingual Matters, 2008), 33. See also Lawrence A. Wilkins, "Spanish as a Substitute for German for Training and Culture," *Hispania* 1, no. 4 (December 1918): 205–221.

16. Julián Gómez Gorkin, introduction to *10 novelistas americanos* (Madrid: Zeus, 1932), x.

17. The Spanish history is perhaps less familiar to some readers: Castile (Castilla) is the central (both in geography and in national mythology) province of Spain; its capital is Madrid. It gained its prominence in the late 1400s, when Isabel I of Castile and León married Ferdinand II of Aragón, thus uniting the crowns of Castile and Aragón and forming the basis for what became a rapid expansion of the Spanish kingdom across the Iberian peninsula by way of the Reconquista against the Moorish kingdom. Centuries of wars and treaties followed, in which the central Castilian kingdom annexed regions including Catalonia, Galicia, Asturias, and the Basque Country to constitute the modern Spanish state.

18. Djelal Kadir notes that literary histories still very often are "tautologically plotted by certain master narratives of historiography that claim total explicatory power over the fortuities of history and historical life," such as "narratives of imperial successions [and] providential history." Djelal Kadir, "What Does the Comparative Do for Literary History?" *PMLA* 128, no. 3 (May 2013): 644. My thinking throughout this introduction is indebted in important ways to Eric Hayot's "Against Periodization; or, On Institutional Time," *New Literary History* 42, no. 4 (Autumn

2011): 739–756; see also note 19, below. There are other implicit and fundamental questions, such as why we associate "great" literary periods with formal innovation and quantifiable influence, that I do not have the space to engage here.

19. Many such issues are also implicit in Ted Underwood's *Why Literary Periods Mattered: Historical Contrast and the Prestige of English Studies* (Stanford, Calif.: Stanford University Press, 2013). A good, though now dated, introduction to these matters is Douglas Robinson's *Translation and Empire: Postcolonial Theories Explained* (Manchester: St. Jerome, 1997). I mean to discount neither the proposition that literary and geopolitical histories can align nor the importance of considering their alignments by critics who study texts from emerging markets, for example, or who trace the correlation between the Russian Empire's growth and the spread of its novelists' influence.

20. On its face, it is unremarkable that modernist writers connected to one another, and to various people and sites, in a world that a number of global empires had worked precisely to connect in multiple ways. The question, rather, is the ends for which connection and comparison were employed. On this topic, see Harris Feinsod, "Vehicular Networks and the Modernist Seaways: Crane, Lorca, Novo, Hughes," *American Literary History* 27, no. 4 (Winter 2015): 683–716.

21. See Brent Hayes Edwards, *The Practice of Diaspora: Literature, Translation, and the Rise of Black Internationalism* (Cambridge, Mass.: Harvard University Press, 2003).

22. The groundwork for these claims was laid in the postcolonial critique of imperial temporalities. A locus classicus is Johannes Fabian's *Time and the Other: How Anthropology Makes Its Object* (New York: Columbia University Press, 1983). The bibliography in modernist studies is extensive; major contributors include Susan Stanford Friedman, Simon Gikandi, Jed Esty, Peter Kalliney, Jahan Ramazani, and Christopher GoGwilt.

23. Frederic Jameson, "Modernism and Imperialism," in *The Modernist Papers* (London: Verso, 2007), 155. By contrast, scholars of early modern literature such as Barbara Fuchs have seen imperial rivalry as an agent in making national literatures; see *The Poetics of Piracy: Emulating Spain in English Literature* (Philadelphia: University of Pennsylvania Press, 2013).

24. "Splendid little war" comes from John Hay, a diplomat and Hispanist in his own right, in a letter to Theodore Roosevelt, July 27, 1898, in *The Life and Letters of John Hay*, ed. William Roscoe Thayer (London: Constable & Co., 1915), 2:337; on the "Disaster" (*El desastre*), see below.

25. See the dossier "Reframing Postcolonial and Global Studies in the Longer Durée," ed. Sahar Amer and Laura Doyle, *PMLA* 130, no. 2 (March 2015): 331–438.

26. Within this framework, see Meg Wesling's *Empire's Proxy: American Literature and U.S. Imperialism in the Philippines* (New York: NYU Press, 2011) and Vicente L. Rafael's *The Promise of the Foreign: Nationalism and the Technics of Translation in the Spanish Philippines* (Durham, N.C.: Duke University Press, 2005).

27. See, for instance, Gail Bederman, *Manliness and Civilization: A Cultural History of Gender and Race in the United States, 1880–1917* (Chicago: University of

Chicago Press, 1995); and Susan Kirkpatrick, *Mujer, modernismo y vanguardia en España, 1898–1931*, trans. Jacqueline Cruz (Madrid: Cátedra, 2003).

28. Winfried Fluck's skeptical reading of the transnational trend in American studies provides a germane damper on the rush to reinvent "an America reinvigorated by an aesthetic plenitude made possible by cultural flow and exchange." Winfried Fluck, "A New Beginning? Transnationalisms," *New Literary History* 42, no. 3 (Summer 2011): 369. He points to the exuberance and exhilaration with which influential scholars like Shelley Fisher Fishkin have greeted transnational criticism. See her ASA presidential address, "Crossroads of Cultures: The Transnational Turn in American Studies," *American Quarterly* 57, no. 1 (March 2005): 17–57. Susan Stanford Friedman has been criticized on similar grounds for her work to expand the field of modernist studies; see most recently *Planetary Modernisms: Provocations on Modernity Across Time* (New York: Columbia University Press, 2015). As I explain below, this is not to discount these modes of transnational work; my first book, *Modernism and the New Spain*, relied on connectivity and collaboration for its structure and argument. And there are certainly ways to expand or reconfigure a field like modernist studies or American studies without replicating the expansionist logic of imperialism; see Christopher GoGwilt, *The Passage of Literature: Genealogies of Modernism in Conrad, Rhys, and Pramoedya* (New York: Oxford University Press, 2011). A balanced approach to these topics can be found in the essays in *The Oxford Handbook of Global Modernisms*, ed. Mark Wollaeger (New York: Oxford University Press, 2012); see especially Wollaeger's introduction (3–22). Sean Latham and I address these issues in the history of modernist criticism in *Modernism: Evolution of an Idea* (London: Bloomsbury Academic, 2015), 1–16, 153–161.

29. For a germane argument in favor of thinking through the partiality of "areas," see Christopher Bush, "Areas: Bigger than the Nation, Smaller than the World," http://stateofthediscipline.acla.org/entry/areas-bigger-nation-smaller-world.

30. See María DeGuzmán, *Spain's Long Shadow: The Black Legend, Off-Whiteness, and Anglo-American Empire* (Minneapolis: University of Minnesota Press, 2005), 187–241.

31. See Sebastiaan Faber, "Economies of Prestige: The Place of Iberian Studies in American Universities," *Hispanic Research Journal* 9, no. 1 (2008): 7–32.

32. These processes also resulted from numerous other effects that the Spanish-American War catalyzed and that I do not have the space to treat fully: the construction of the Panama Canal, the Jones-Shafroth Act, waves of immigration from Spanish-speaking countries, U.S. designs on South American markets, Iberian American and pan-American solidarity movements, and much more.

33. On the inherent ironies, see Djelal Kadir, "America's Exceptional Comparabilities: An Instance of World Literature," *Comparative Literature* 61, no. 3 (Summer 2009): 209–219.

34. This is the case despite the facts that exceptionalism and its legacies in American studies have been thoroughly historicized and discredited by now and that most Americanists acknowledge, after decades of resistance to the idea, that the United States is an empire. The closest works one can find would include Kirsten

Silva Gruesz, *Ambassadors of Culture: The Transamerican Origins of Latino Writing* (Princeton, N.J.: Princeton University Press, 2002); Laura Lomas, *Translating Empire: José Martí, Migrant Latino Subjects, and American Modernities* (Durham, N.C.: Duke University Press, 2008); Raúl Coronado, *A World Not to Come: A History of Latino Writing and Print Culture* (Cambridge, Mass.: Harvard University Press, 2013); and Kate A. Baldwin, *Beyond the Color Line and the Iron Curtain: Reading Encounters Between Black and Red, 1922–1963* (Durham, N.C.: Duke University Press, 2002). See also Jonathan Arac, "Imperial Eclecticism in *Moby-Dick* and *Invisible Man*: Literature in a Postcolonial Empire," *boundary 2* 37, no. 3 (2010): 151–165.

35. See *Comparison: Theories, Approaches, Uses*, ed. Rita Felski and Susan Stanford Friedman (Baltimore, Md.: Johns Hopkins University Press, 2013); the essays in the *PMLA* dossier on comparative literary studies (*PMLA* 128, no. 3 [May 2013]: 608–697); and the topic of "reciprocal defamiliarization" in R. Radhakrishnan, *Theory in an Uneven World* (Oxford: Blackwell, 2003), 82. Exceptions in literary studies are rare but include Karen Thornber, *Empire of Texts in Motion: Chinese, Korean, and Taiwanese Transculturations of Japanese Literature* (Cambridge, Mass.: Harvard University Asia Center/Harvard University Press, 2009); and Eiichiro Azuma, *Between Two Empires: Race, History, and Transnationalism in Japanese America* (New York: Oxford University Press, 2005). Rebecca Beasley has noted, in a classic example, that British writers and critics around the turn of the century felt they must devalue Russian and German literature; see "Modernism's Translations," in *The Oxford Handbook of Global Modernisms*, ed. Mark Wollaeger (New York: Oxford University Press, 2012), 551–570. For comparative studies of U.S. empire by historians, see Charles S. Maier, *Among Empires: American Ascendancy and Its Predecessors* (Cambridge, Mass.: Harvard University Press, 2006); Jane Burbank and Frederick Cooper, *Empires in World History: Power and the Politics of Difference* (Princeton, N.J.: Princeton University Press, 2010); Thomas Bender, *A Nation Among Nations: America's Place in World History* (New York: Hill and Wang, 2006); and *The Age of Empires*, ed. Robert Aldrich (London: Thames and Hudson, 2007). Kathleen DuVal's many works on Spanish/U.S. relations in the early republic bear notice here too. See also Ann Laura Stoler, "On Degrees of Imperial Sovereignty," *Public Culture* 18, no. 1 (Winter 2006): 125–146; and Anthony Bogues, *Empire of Liberty: Power, Desire, and Freedom* (Hanover, N.H.: University Press of New England, 2010). While valuable for having energized debates on empire, Michael Hardt and Antonio Negri's *Empire* (Cambridge, Mass.: Harvard University Press, 2000) is beyond the scope of this book. I do not engage here the definitional questions about empire or about whether the United States is an empire (and, if so, what kind). Rather, I take as established that empires are always shifting and renarrating themselves, constantly fragmenting and cohering into new shapes, often in multidirectional and anarchic ways, and that empires rely on mimesis, on accruing everything from material wealth to aesthetic forms from other empires and from diverse societies.

36. Some exceptions include the works of critics such as César Domínguez, Domingo Ródenas de Moya, Juan Herrero-Senés, Luis Cifuentes, Brad Epps, and

Joan Ramon Resina, who have also rethought Spanish literature in comparative Iberian contexts.

37. See *Cultures of United States Imperialism*, ed. Amy Kaplan and Donald E. Pease (Durham, N.C.: Duke University Press, 1993), esp. 3–21; and a number of works by Pease. John Carlos Rowe's *Literary Culture and U.S. Imperialism: From the Revolution to World War II* (Oxford: Oxford University Press, 2000), Paul Giles's *Virtual Americas: Transnational Fictions and the Transatlantic Imaginary* (Durham, N.C.: Duke University Press, 2002), and Amy Kaplan's *The Anarchy of Empire in the Making of U.S. Culture* (Cambridge, Mass.: Harvard University Press, 2005), while important for their treatments of U.S. empire, focus almost exclusively on U.S. texts—many of them canonical and almost all of them originally in English—and U.S. national formations. While they use the responses to empire to rethink U.S. cultures, their approaches ultimately enrich the United States without a sufficient eye to the relative effects of such a project. The same is true of recent studies such as Andy Doolen's *Territories of Empire: U.S. Writing from the Louisiana Purchase to Mexican Independence* (New York: Oxford University Press, 2014) and Johan Höglund's *The American Imperial Gothic: Popular Culture, Empire, Violence* (Farnham: Ashgate, 2014). On the ways that the disciplinary organization and foci of mostly English department–based American studies, together with ethnic studies, have rarely produced comparative studies, see Dana D. Nelson, "From Manitoba to Patagonia," *American Literary History* 15, no. 2 (Summer 2003): 367–394. See also Susan Gillman and Kirsten Silva Gruesz, "Worlding America: The Hemispheric Text-Network," in *A Companion to American Literary Studies*, ed. Caroline F. Levander and Robert S. Levine (Malden, Mass.: Wiley-Blackwell, 2011), 228–231.

38. On this point, and for an overview of transnational American studies that takes stock of both the promise and pitfalls of this emergent mode of inquiry, see Donald Pease, "Introduction: Re-Mapping the Transnational Turn," in *Re-Framing the Transnational Turn in American Studies*, ed. Winfried Fluck, Donald Pease, and John Carlos Rowe (Hanover, N.H.: Dartmouth College Press, 2011), 1–46. Pease and Fluck have published many works on this topic. I cite only a few here: my concerns differ from theirs, and my interest in territories, spaces, sovereignty, and subjectivities is minimal. Some works that aim to avoid and redress that logic include Brian Lennon, *In Babel's Shadow: Multilingual Literatures, Monolingual States* (Minneapolis: University of Minnesota Press, 2010); and Yasemin Yildiz, *Beyond the Mother Tongue: The Postmonolingual Condition* (New York: Fordham University Press, 2012). Such provocations also inhere in Werner Sollors's and Marc Shell's works on multilingual American writing and in Caroline F. Levander's *Where Is American Literature?* (Malden, Mass.: Wiley-Blackwell, 2013).

39. See Kirsten Silva Gruesz, "Translation," in *Keywords for American Cultural Studies*, ed. Bruce Burgett and Glenn Hendler (New York: NYU Press, 2007), 85. Daniel Katz's *American Modernism's Expatriate Scene: The Labour of Translation* (Edinburgh: Edinburgh University Press, 2007), for instance, is admirable for its attempt to expand the sense of "translation" to include different types of cultural practices, but it barely engages the non-Anglophone texts that were central to

the translation practices of his subjects. The work of the New Americanists and of journals such as *Comparative American Studies* and the *Journal of Transnational American Studies* has had a salutary effect in revaluating the field of American studies, but their overwhelmingly dominant approaches have been along the expansionist lines mentioned above. The fuller bibliography on these topics, and on the remapping of American studies, is too extensive to list. Some key critics, in addition to those cited above, would include Rachel Adams, Colleen Glenney Boggs, Anna Brickhouse, Colin Dayan, Arif Dirlik, Robert S. Levine, Kirsten Silva Gruesz, Nicolás Kanellos, David Kazanjian, Laura Lomas, Joshua L. Miller, Carolyn Porter, Ramón Saldívar, and Elliot Young.

40. John Smith, *The Travels and Works of Captain John Smith*, part 1, ed. Edward Arber, intro. A. G. Bradley (New York: Burt Franklin, 1910), cxxvii.

41. Thomas Jefferson, Letter to Archibald Stuart, January 25, 1786; Letter to Peter Carr, August 10, 1787, in *Political Writings*, ed. and intro. Joyce Appleby and Terence Ball (Cambridge: Cambridge University Press, 1999), 9, 253. See also James E. Lewis Jr., *The American Union and the Problem of Neighborhood, 1783–1829* (Chapel Hill: University of North Carolina Press, 1998).

42. Henry Adams, *History of the United States*, 9 vols. (New York: Charles Scribner's Sons, 1889), 339, 341, 340.

43. Richard L. Kagan, "Prescott's Paradigm: American Historical Scholarship and the Decline of Spain," in *Spain in America*, ed. Richard L. Kagan (Urbana: University of Illinois Press, 2002), 247–276. American historians largely inherited this mode of thought from the English. James D. Fernández adds that "Longfellow's Law" was a corollary by which U.S. commercial interests in Latin America continually mediated American Hispanism. James D. Fernández, "'Longfellow's Law': The Place of Latin America and Spain in U.S. Hispanism, circa 1915," in ibid., 122–141.

44. James Turner, *Philology: The Forgotten Origins of the Modern Humanities* (Princeton, N.J.: Princeton University Press, 2014), 165; George Ticknor, *History of Spanish Literature*, 3 vols. (New York: Gordian, 1965), 3:438. Ticknor occupied the first prestigious Smith Chair at Harvard.

45. George Santayana, *Persons and Places*, 3 vols. (New York: Charles Scribner's Sons, 1945), 2:168.

46. George Santayana, "Spain in America: Written After the Destruction of the Spanish Fleet in the Battle of Santiago, in 1898," in *Poems of George Santayana*, ed. Robert Hutchinson (New York: Dover, 1970), 123. See also Paul Lawrence Dunbar's celebration of returning black troops, "The Conquerors"; Sutton Griggs's commentaries in *Imperium in Imperio* and *The Hindered Hand* (treated in James Robert Payne, "Afro-American Literature of the Spanish-American War," *MELUS* 10, no. 3 [Autumn 1983]: 19–32); and Bonnie M. Miller, *From Liberation to Conquest: The Visual and Popular Cultures of the Spanish-American War of 1898* (Amherst: University of Massachusetts Press, 2011).

47. Americans also read popular, often bestselling books on Spain full of stereotypes and Orientalisms, including H. C. Chatfield-Taylor's *Spain: Land of the Castanet* (1896), John Hay's *Castilian Days* (1899), Jeremiah Zimmerman's *Spain*

and Her People (1902), and Edward Gaylord Bourne's apologetic, pro-Iberian *Spain in America* (1904), and from England, George Borrow's works and Havelock Ellis's influential *Soul of Spain* (1908).

48. See Joshua L. Miller, *Accented America: The Cultural Politics of Multilingual Modernism* (New York: Oxford University Press, 2011).

49. William Graham Sumner, "The Conquest of the United States by Spain" (1899), in *War and Other Essays*, ed. and intro. Albert Galloway Keller (New Haven, Conn.: Yale University Press, 1911), 297, 313. See also Mark Twain's cynical "As Regards Patriotism," in *Collected Tales, Sketches, Speeches, & Essays, 1891–1910* (New York: Library of America, 1992), 476–78.

50. For a taxonomy of readings of the war in U.S. historiography, see Evan Thomas, *The War Lovers: Roosevelt, Lodge, Hearst, and the Rush to Empire, 1898* (New York: Little, Brown, 2010), 12–13. For a general account of the war, see Ivan Musicant, *Empire by Default: The Spanish-American War and the Dawn of the American Century* (New York: Henry Holt, 1998). For a Spanish perspective, see *España y Estados Unidos en el siglo XX*, ed. Lorenzo Delgado y María Dolores Elizalde (Madrid: CSIC, 2005).

51. For a classic historian's account that replicates the U.S. imperial logic, see Charles Gibson, *Spain in America* (New York: Harper & Row, 1966), which abruptly stops in the mid-nineteenth century. The exceptions to this logic have come from scholars not typically identified as Americanists: see *Spain in America*, ed. Kagan; Gustavo Pérez-Firmat, *Tongue Ties: Logo-Eroticism in Anglo-Hispanic Literature* (New York: Palgrave, 2003); and James D. Fernández, "The Discovery of Spain in New York, circa 1930," in *Nueva York: 1613–1945*, ed. Edward Sullivan (New York: SCALA, 2010).

52. Stanley T. Williams, *The Spanish Background of American Literature*, 2 vols. (New Haven, Conn.: Yale University Press, 1955): 1:xx. Eugenio Suárez-Galban's *The Last Good Land: Spain in American Literature* (Amsterdam: Rodopi, 2011) traces the use of Spain by U.S. writers in a manner that continues Williams's work; *Spain in Mind: An Anthology*, ed. and intro. Alice Leccese Powers (New York: Vintage, 2007), gathers such examples from beyond the United States, too.

53. Williams, *Spanish Background*, xxi.

54. See the collection of cartoons in *La gráfica política del 98* (Cáceres: Centro Extremeño de Estudios y Cooperación con Iberoamérica, 1998); and Joel C. Webb, "Drawing Defeat: Caricaturing War, Race, and Gender in Fin de Siglo Spain" (Master's thesis), http://scholarworks.umass.edu/cgi/viewcontent.cgi?article=136 5&context=theses.

55. See Christopher Britt-Arredondo, *Quixotism: The Imaginative Denial of Spain's Loss of Empire* (Albany: State University of New York Press, 2005), 1–3.

56. "Día nefasto," *El Liberal* (November 28, 1898): 1. The best narrative of the effects of the Disaster remains Sebastian Balfour's *The End of the Spanish Empire, 1898–1923* (Oxford: Oxford University Press, 1997). For a collection of primary documents, see *El desastre y sus textos*, ed. Julio Rodríguez-Puértolas (Madrid: Akal, 1999).

57. From *El Correo* (February 7, 1901), qtd. in Balfour, *End of the Spanish Empire*, 66.

58. Balfour, *End of the Spanish Empire*, 49. See also *Spain's 1898 Crisis: Regenerationism, Modernism, Postcolonialism*, ed. Joseph Harrison and Alan Hoyle (Manchester: Manchester University Press, 2000); Javier Krauel, *Imperial Emotions: Cultural Responses to Myths of Empire in Fin-de-Siècle Spain* (Liverpool: Liverpool University Press, 2013); and Henry Kamen, *Imagining Spain: Historical Myth and National Identity* (New Haven, Conn.: Yale University Press, 2008). The many works of historians such as John H. Elliott and literary scholars including Mary Lee Bretz, Sebastiaan Faber, Joshua Goode, Roberta Johnson, Susan Kirkpatrick, Jo Labanyi, William Luis, and Alejandro Mejías-López, in addition to those cited above, address elements of Spain's imperial mythology on either side of 1898.

59. Julián Juderías, *La leyenda negra: Estudios acerca del concepto de España en el extranjero* (Barcelona: Editorial Araluce, 1917), 24.

60. For a classic account, see Donald L. Shaw, *The Generation of 1898 in Spain* (New York: Barnes & Noble, 1975). An interesting historical document that I do not have the space to address here is Ricardo del Arco y Garay, *La idea de imperio en la política y la literatura española* (Madrid: Espasa-Calpe, 1944).

61. Most influential in naming this era for contemporary criticism was José-Carlos Mainer's *La edad de plata: Ensayo de interpretación de un proceso cultural* (Madrid: Cátedra, 1975). See also E. Inman Fox, *La invención de España: Nacionalismo liberal e identidad nacional* (Madrid: Cátedra, 1997).

62. Figures like Espronceda and Bécquer were key figures in Spanish romanticism but had nothing of the kind of international prestige that their English, German, or even American (if one includes Poe) peers found.

63. Francisco Silvela, "Without a Pulse," in *Modern Spain: A Documentary History*, ed. Jon Cowans (Philadelphia: University of Pennsylvania Press, 2003), 96.

64. See, for example, the Italian Hispanist Arturo Farinelli's Madrid lectures gathered in *España y su literatura en el extranjero á través dos siglos* (Madrid: M. Tello, 1902).

65. Qtd. in Sylvia L. Hilton, "The World in Black and White: Spanish Federalists on U.S. Democracy and Imperialism in 1898," *Comparative American Studies* 5, no. 1 (June 2007): 130. See also Hilton's "The United States Through Spanish Republican Eyes in the Colonial Crisis of 1895–1898," in *European Perceptions of the Spanish-American War of 1898*, ed. Sylvia L. Hilton and Steve J. S. Ickringill (Bern: Peter Lang, 1999), 53–70.

66. Charles Lummis, *The Spanish Pioneers* (Chicago: A. C. McClurg & Co., 1909), 12.

67. See Carlos Fernández-Shaw, *Presencia española en los Estados Unidos* (Madrid: Ediciones Cultura Hispánica, 1971); and David Arias, *Las raíces hispanas de los Estados Unidos* (Madrid: Editorial Mapfre, 1992).

68. See Frederick B. Pike, *Hispanismo: Spanish Conservatives and Liberals and Their Relations with Spanish America* (Notre Dame: University of Notre Dame Press, 1971). See also *El hispanismo en los Estados Unidos: Discursos críticos/prácticas*

textuales, ed. José M. Del Pino and Francisco La Rubia Prado (Madrid: Visor, 1999). Pike concentrates mostly on Spanish American/transatlantic versions, with rare attention to the United States.

69. Here I follow Elizabeth Amann's reading of Huntington's museum; see "Domesticating Spain: 1898 and the Hispanic Society of America," in *Institutions of Reading: The Social Life of Libraries in the United States*, ed. Thomas Augst and Kenneth Carpenter (Amherst: University of Massachusetts Press, 2007), 184–202.

70. Joaquín Sorolla, "A Spanish Painter's View," *Independent* (May 13, 1909): 1012. Sorolla would ride this wave of fame on to paint Taft's presidential portrait, and on the heels of his success, his compatriot Ignacio Zuloaga would put on another well-attended show at the HSA.

71. Lawrence Wilkins, "On the Threshold," *Hispania*, Organization Number (November 1917): 6.

72. Wilkins, "Spanish as a Substitute," 213; "Threshold," 10.

73. J. R. Spell, "Spanish Teaching in the United States," *Hispania* 10, no. 3 (May 1927): 141.

74. Mary Louise Pratt, "Language and the Afterlives of Empire," *PMLA* 130, no. 2 (March 2015): 355. For resources on the language politics of this moment, see *Language Loyalties: A Source Book on the Official English Controversy*, ed. James Crawford (Chicago: University of Chicago Press, 1992).

75. In 1920, Hispanic Americans were still only 1.2 percent of the population. See Brian Gratton and Myron Gutmann, "Hispanics in the United States, 1850–1990: Estimates of Population Size and National Origin," *Historical Methods* 33, no. 3 (Summer 2000): 137–153.

76. As Sebastiaan Faber writes, "between 1915 and 1922 German loses 95 per cent of its secondary-school enrollments (from 325,000 to less than 14,000) while Spanish enrollments increase sevenfold, from 36,000 to 252,000" ("Economies of Prestige," 14). Many histories of Hispanism exist; for overviews germane to the issues I discuss here, see Anne J. Cruz, "American Hispanism(s)," *South Atlantic Review* 73, no. 4 (Fall 2008): 86–106; Sebastiaan Faber, *Anglo-American Hispanists and the Spanish Civil War: Hispanophilia, Commitment, and Discipline* (New York: Palgrave Macmillan, 2008); *Ideologies of Hispanism*, ed. Mabel Moraña (Nashville, Tenn.: Vanderbilt University Press, 2005); *Spain Beyond Spain: Modernity, Literary History, and National Identity*, ed. Brad Epps and Luis Fernández Cifuentes (Lewisburg, Penn.: Bucknell University Press, 2005); and Iván Jaksić, *The Hispanic World and American Intellectual Life, 1820–1880* (New York: Palgrave Macmillan, 2007).

77. "Americans Visit Spain," *New York Times* (November 5, 1925): 25. This trend prompted, in part, Mario Praz's wonderfully critical *Unromantic Spain* (New York: Knopf, 1929).

78. See *Collecting Spanish Art: Spain's Golden Age and America's Gilded Age*, ed. Inge Reist and José Luis Colomer (New York: The Frick Collection, 2012).

79. Qtd. in Mitchell Codding, "Archer Milton Huntington, Champion of Spain in the United States," in *Spain in America*, ed. Richard L. Kagan (Urbana: University of Illinois Press, 2002), 161.

80. See James Fernández and Luis Argeo, *Invisible Immigrants: Spaniards in the U.S. (1868–1945)* (New York: White Stone Ridge, 2014).

81. Between July and December of 1918, *Four Horsemen* went through thirty-seven printings; twenty-four of Blasco Ibáñez's works were translated into English between 1911 and 1929. His novel *Sangre y arena* (1909) was adapted into another blockbuster Valentino film, *Blood and Sand* (1922), and four more of his novels would be made into films by 1926. See also James D. Fernández, "Poets, Peasants, Painters, Professors, and Performers in New York," in Stanley G. Payne et al., *When Spain Fascinated America* (Madrid: Fundación Zuloaga, 2010), 47–59; and Regina Galasso, "The Mission of *La Prensa*: Informing a Layout of the Literature of Hispanic New York," *Hispania* 95, no. 2 (June 2012): 189–200. See also César Domínguez, "Damaged in Transit? Valle-Inclán's *Tirano Banderas* Between Two World-Literatures," *Forum for World Literature Studies* 5, no. 1 (April 2013): 122–140; and Juan Herrero-Senés's forthcoming article on Putnam in *Hispanic Review*.

82. See, for example, Brian T. Edwards, "American Studies in Tehran," *Public Culture* 19, no. 3 (Fall 2007): 415–424.

83. See, for instance, Rafael María de Labra, "La literatura norte-americana en europa," *Revista de España* 67 (March 1879): 457–489.

84. John Delancey Ferguson, *American Literature in Spain*, Ph.D. diss., Columbia University (1916), 4.

85. Ibid., 180.

86. See Julián Juderías, "La literatura norteamericana en España. A propósito de un libro," *La Lectura* 1 (1918): 350–355.

87. See Enrique Díez-Canedo, "El país donde florece la poesía: USA," which I have translated as "A Spanish View of Modernist Poetry in American Periodicals (1925): 'The Country Where Poetry Flourishes: USA,'" *Journal of Modern Periodical Studies* 3, no. 1 (2012): 14.

88. See Francisco Lafarga and Luis Pegenaute, *Diccionario histórico de la traducción en España* (Madrid: Gredos, 2009).

89. See Miguel Gallego Roca, *Poesía importada: Traducción poética y renovación literaria en España, 1909–1936* (Almería: Universidad de Almería, 1996), 25–27. Gallego Roca is quoting Cipriano Rivas Cherif's article "La invasión literaria" (1920). See also Marta Giné and Solange Hibbs, *Traducción y cultura: La literatura traducida en la prensa española (1868–98)* (Bern: Peter Lang, 2011), on the previous decades.

90. See Pedro Guirao, "Los estudios de inglés en España," *Bulletin of Spanish Studies* (March 1924): 72–74. See also Sofía Martín-Gamero, *La enseñanza del inglés en España: Desde la Edad Media hasta el siglo XIX* (Madrid: Editorial Gredos, 1961).

91. Luis Araquistaín, *El peligro yanqui* (Madrid: Publicaciones España, 1921), 1.

92. See *Great Spanish Short Stories Representing the Work of the Leading Spanish Writers of the Day*, trans. Warre B. Wells, notes by J. G. Gorkin, intro. Henri Barbusse (Boston: Houghton Mifflin, 1932). "Gorkin" was a pseudonym chosen to honor Maxim Gorki; his given name was García. The leftist press Zeus issued

this volume, which features translations of short stories or sections of novels by Dos Passos, Hemingway, McKay, Jack London, Theodore Dreiser, Sinclair Lewis, Upton Sinclair, Sherwood Anderson, Ludwig Lewisohn, and Louis Bromfield.

93. See Vicente Uribe, *Yankee Imperialism in Spain* (New York: New Century, 1949).

94. Tomás Monterey, "Los estudios ingleses en España (1900–1950): legislación curricular," *Atlantis* 25, no. 1 (June 2003): 64–65; Tomás Monterrey, "Notes for a History of English Studies in Spain," in *European English Studies: Contributions Towards the History of a Discipline*, ed. Balz Engler and Renate Haas (Leicester: European Society for the Study of English, 2000), 33–52; and *Fifty Years of English Studies in Spain (1952–2002): A Commemorative Volume*, ed. Ignacio M. Palacios Martínez (Santiago de Compostela: Universidad de Santiago de Compostela, 2003).

95. Scholars including Esteban Pujals, Patricia Shaw, and Julio César Santoyo have both participated in and documented this work. See also *Treinta años de filología inglesa en la universidad española (1952–1981)*, ed. Pedro Guardia Massó and Julio-César Santoyo (Madrid: Alhambra, 1982).

96. John A. Macy, *The Spirit of American Literature* (New York: Doubleday, Page & Co., 1913), 17. The early issues of *American Literature* are germane documents here; the second issue surveys formations of "American literature" in Germany. Brooks considers the same topic with regard to England, too. Publications and courses on Old English still exponentially outnumbered those on American literature at the time.

97. See Eduardo Gómez de Baquero, *Letras é ideas* (Barcelona: Henrich, 1905); see chapter 3.

98. Glazener, *Literature in the Making*, 11.

99. Matthew Arnold, "On the Modern Element in Literature," in *Complete Prose Works*, ed. R. H. Super, 11 vols. (Ann Arbor: University of Michigan Press, 1960), 1:21–22; italics in original. Arnold's sense of "adequacy" was transtemporal itself— he saw classical Greece as "modern"—and thus, in one reading, should actually militate against the chronological alignments of political and cultural teleologies.

1. "Splintered Staves": Pound, Comparative Literature, and the Translation of Spanish Literary History

1. Kenner refers to a scene in which "Le Cid, tricky as Odysseus, has realized that a box of sand will pass at the moneylender's for a box of gold"; in fact, this scene occurs in the *Poema del Cid* but not in Corneille's *Le Cid*. Hugh Kenner, *The Pound Era* (Berkeley: University of California Press, 1971), 425.

2. Ezra Pound, "I Gather the Limbs of Osiris," in *Selected Prose, 1909–1965*, ed. William Cookson (New York: New Directions, 1973), 21.

3. Ezra Pound, Letter to Harriet Monroe, August 18, 1912, in *The Selected Letters of Ezra Pound, 1907–1941*, ed. D. D. Paige (London: Faber and Faber, 1982), 10.

250   1. "Splintered Staves"

The letter to Williams in the epigraph is from Pound to Williams, October 21, 1908, in ibid., 4.

4. The poem, whose original title is unknown, is variously referred to as the *Cantar de myo* [or *mío*] *Cid* or *Poema de myo Cid* ("Song of My Cid"). For simplicity and convenience, I will refer, as Pound does, to the *Poema del Cid*.

5. Ezra Pound, Letter to Isabel Weston Pound, February 23, 1910, in *Ezra Pound to His Parents: Letters 1895–1929*, ed. Mary de Rachewiltz, A. David Moody, and Joanna Moody (New York: Oxford University Press, 2010), 220.

6. The two best sources on what Pound understood as his failures in "Three Cantos" and his subsequent revisions across several publications prior to *A Draft of XVI. Cantos* (which the name "Ur-Cantos" means to gather) are *The Genesis of Ezra Pound's "Cantos"* (Princeton, N.J.: Princeton University Press, 1976); and Christine Froula, *To Write Paradise: Style and Error in Pound's "Cantos"* (New Haven, Conn.: Yale University Press, 1984). For simplicity, I will refer to the poems in "Three Cantos" as "Ur-Cantos," since I will address their variations and revisions.

7. Ezra Pound, Ur-Cantos autograph ms. and typescript, Box 69, folder 3101, Yale Collection of American Literature, Beinecke Rare Book and Manuscript Library. I thank Rebecca Beasley for pointing me to the allusions in these drafts.

8. Ezra Pound, *Gaudier-Brzeska: A Memoir* (London: John Lane, 1916), 136. Originally from an article in the *New Age* in 1915.

9. Ezra Pound to Louis Untermeyer, in *EP to LU: Nine Letters Written to Louis Untermeyer by Ezra Pound*, ed. J. A. Robbins (Bloomington: Indiana University Press, 1963), 15.

10. A. David Moody, *Ezra Pound, Poet: A Portrait of the Man and His Work*, 3 vols. (New York: Oxford University Press, 2007), 1:15.

11. Qtd. in Humphrey Carpenter, *A Serious Character: The Life of Ezra Pound* (Boston: Houghton Mifflin, 1988), 55.

12. See Ezra Pound, *Guide to Kulchur* (New York: New Directions, 1952), 158.

13. See Noel Stock, *The Life of Ezra Pound* (New York: Pantheon, 1970), 29.

14. Ezra Pound to Isabel Weston Pound, June 13, 1906, in *Ezra Pound to His Parents*, 80.

15. See Ezra Pound, "Mr. James Joyce and the Modern Stage," *The Drama* 6, no. 21 (February 1916): 122–132. Pound very likely influenced William Carlos Williams's decision to attempt a translation of Lope de Vega's *El nuevo mundo descubierto por Colón*.

16. In *Exultations*, Pound reprints, in the original Spanish, the final six lines that he translates. For a critique of this translation, see José María Rodríguez García, "How 'Modernist' Were Hispanic Literary and Artistic Modernities?" *Modernist Cultures* 7, no. 1 (2012): 6–7.

17. Gabriele Hayden discovered this manuscript in the Pound archives at the Beinecke Library at Yale University; I thank her for sharing her research.

18. The Cid's home is in Vivar (or Bivar, or Vivar del Cid), a small village about seven kilometers north of present-day Burgos.

19. Ezra Pound, "Burgos: A Dream City of Old Castile," *Book News Monthly* 25, no. 2 (October 1906): 91. Hereafter cited in the text as B. The other texts Pound

published in this series were "Interesting French Publications" and "Raphaelite Latin" (see below).

20. I quote from *Poema de mío Cid* (Burgos: Excmo. Ayuntamiento de Burgos, 1982), 46; this edition follows Menéndez Pidal's established orthography. Orthography in contemporary versions of the *Poema* varies wildly. See also the side-by-side edition in Old and modern Castilian produced by Pedro Salinas, *Poema de mío Cid: Puesto en romance vulgar y lenguaje moderno* (Madrid: Revista de Occidente, 1926).

21. Corneille's text, furthermore, was also a partial adaptation of Guillén de Castro's *Las mocedades del Cid* (ca. 1605–1615). Lope de Vega dedicated *Las almenas de Toro* (see below) to Guillén de Castro.

22. Ezra Pound, "Raphaelite Latin," *Book News Monthly* 25, no. 1 (September 1906): 31.

23. Ezra Pound, *The Spirit of Romance: An Attempt to Define Somewhat the Charm of the Pre-Renaissance Literature of Latin Europe*, ed. Richard Sieburth (New York: New Directions, 2005), 5. Hereafter cited in the text as *SR*.

24. Pound confessed in 1929 that the book was "a very raw summary of things in Rennert's seminar." Ezra Pound, "Post-Postscript" [1968], in *The Spirit of Romance*, 9.

25. Pound offered the book to Penn in 1920 in hopes of earning his Ph.D., but the university declined. He tried again with a paleographic edition of *Guido Cavalcanti: Rime* (1932) but was denied again. See K. K. Ruthven, *Ezra Pound as Literary Critic* (New York: Routledge, 1990), 15.

26. Richard Sieburth, introduction to Pound, *The Spirit of Romance*, viii.

27. Ezra Pound, "Provincialism the Enemy," in *Selected Prose*, 191. See Peter Liebregts, "The Classics," in *Ezra Pound in Context*, ed. Ira B. Nadel (Cambridge: Cambridge University Press, 2010), 173. See also Gail Macdonald, *Learning to Be Modern: Pound, Eliot, and the American University* (Oxford: Oxford University Press, 1993), 11–21; and see also Carlos Riobó, "The Spirit of Ezra Pound's Romance Philology: Dante's Ironic Legacy of the Contingencies of Value," *Comparative Literary Studies* 39, no. 3 (2002): 201–222. Pound's portrait of philology, of course, is reductive. For a more sympathetic and updated view, see Sheldon Pollock, "Future Philology? The Fate of a Soft Science in a Hard World," *Critical Inquiry* 35, no. 4 (Summer 2009): 931–961. On Pound's (and Kenner's) inconsistencies regarding philology, see Mark Smith, "The Energy of Language(s): What Pound Made of Philology," *ELH* 78, no. 4 (Winter 2011): 769–800. On Pound's inconsistencies in translation theory more generally, see Roland Végső, "The Mother Tongues of Modernity: Modernism, Transnationalism, Translation," *Journal of Modern Literature* 33, no. 2 (Winter 2010): 24–46.

28. See James Turner, *Philology: The Forgotten Origins of the Modern Humanities* (Princeton, N.J.: Princeton University Press, 2014); and Michael Holquist, "World Literature and Philology," in *The Routledge Companion to World Literature*, ed. Theo D'haen, David Damrosch, and Djelal Kadir (New York: Routledge, 2012), 150–152.

29. Ezra Pound, "The Renaissance," in *Literary Essays of Ezra Pound*, ed. T. S. Eliot (New York: New Directions, 1968), 223. Pound saw studies of Provençal and Occitan gaining prestige: they were offered regularly at most elite U.S. universities by 1904, the year that the poet and philologist Frédéric Mistral shared the Nobel Prize for Literature with Echegaray. Gaston Paris, by contrast, was nominated in 1901, 1902, and 1903 but never won.

30. See Rebecca Beasley, "Pound's New Criticism," *Textual Practice* 24, no. 4 (2010): 654–655. Beasley offers the best account of Pound's transitional years in the early 1910s from scholarship and criticism to a new art-critical fusion; see her *Ezra Pound and the Visual Culture of Modernism* (Cambridge: Cambridge University Press, 2007). On the separation of comparative literature from philology in this moment, see Natalie Melas, *All the Difference in the World: Postcoloniality and the Ends of Comparison* (Stanford, Calif.: Stanford University Press, 2007), 10–18.

31. In "L'Homme Moyen Sensual," Pound would like to "bury" Woodberry (*Little Review* 4, no. 5 [September 1917]: 9). Sharon Hamilton adds that, at Penn, Pound studied with (and butted heads with) Josiah Penniman; see her "The *PMLA* and the Background to Making Poetry New," *Journal of Modern Periodical Studies* 2, no. 1 (2011): 54–85.

32. Ezra Pound, "How to Read," in *Literary Essays*, 15n2. This essay from 1929 provides one of Pound's most trenchant critiques of the academies that shaped his early career.

33. Ezra Pound, "The Renaissance," in *Literary Essays*, 218.

34. Pound, "How to Read," in *Literary Essays*, 35.

35. Pound, "The Renaissance," in *Literary Essays*, 214. Pound would add the chapter "Psychology and Troubadours," written in 1912, to the 1932 edition of *The Spirit of Romance*.

36. This occurred despite Pound's appreciation of Paris's work of public education, which was an early model for his own plans in the *Cantos*, as he mentions in a 1915 draft of the "Ur-Cantos"; later, he also saw Paris's textbooks for general audiences as a model for his own *ABC of Reading*.

37. On the *Cantos* and Pound's antitelic and anti-imperialist arguments more generally, see Paul Stasi, *Modernism, Imperialism, and the Historical Sense* (Cambridge: Cambridge University Press, 2012), 60–81.

38. See George Ticknor, *History of Spanish Literature*, 3 vols. (New York: Gordian, 1965), 1:21. James Fitzmaurice-Kelly, too, quotes Ormsby's translation of this same passage in his *History of Spanish Literature* (New York: D. Appleton & Co., 1912).

39. *Poema de mio Cid*, 74; see Salinas, *Poema*, 60, 62.

40. John Ormsby, trans., *The Poem of the Cid* (London: Longmans, Green and Co., 1879), 76. The same lines can be found in Huntington's translation in *Poem of the Cid, reprinted from the unique manuscript at Madrid* (New York: Hispanic Society of America, 1942), n.p. (lines 722–729).

41. Ezra Pound, "The Renaissance," in *Literary Essays*, 217.

42. Ezra Pound, "Through Alien Eyes," *New Age* 12, no. 11 (January 16, 1913): 252.

43. See Ezra Pound, "Epilogue," in *Collected Early Poems*, ed. Michael King (New York: New Directions, 1982), 209.

44. A famous example is Ángel Ganivet's *La conquista del reino de Maya, por el último conquistador español, Pío Cid* (1897).

45. Menéndez Pidal, *The Cid and His Spain*, trans. Harold Sunderland (London: J. Murray, 1934), 15.

46. John Ormsby, introduction to *The Poem of the Cid*, 1.

47. Fitzmaurice-Kelly, *A History of Spanish Literature*, 51; James Fitzmaurice-Kelly, *Chapters on Spanish Literature* (London: Archibald Castle and Co., 1908), 10.

48. Archer M. Huntington, "The Most Famous of Spanish Manuscripts," *Bookman* (September 1896): 32.

49. Pound's portrait of the Cid thus lies close to the Chilean avant-garde poet Vicente Huidobro's *Mío Cid campeador: Hazaña* (1929) (translated by Warre B. Wells as *Portrait of a Paladin* [1932]); I thank Ignacio Infante, who is working on this text, for pointing me to it. Pound does not, on the other hand, go so far as to celebrate the mixture of Jewish, Islamic, and Christian cultures, as Spanish nationalists and Arabists had in the late 1800s and as María Menocal would in the early 2000s (see chapter 5).

50. Ezra Pound, *Patria Mia, and The Treatise on Harmony* (London: P. Owen, 1962), 9; all misspellings in the original. Hereafter cited in the text as *PM*.

51. Ibid., 12.

52. Pound, *Gaudier-Brzeska*, 134.

53. See Vincent Sherry, "Prose Criticism," in *Ezra Pound in Context*, ed. Ira B. Nadel (Cambridge: Cambridge University Press, 2010), 14–16.

54. Pound, "How to Read," in *Literary Essays*, 21.

55. Ezra Pound, "James Joyce: At Last the Novel Appears," *Egoist* 4, no. 2 (February 1917): 22.

56. Pound, *Gaudier-Brzeska*, 136.

57. Letter to Harriet Monroe, August 18, 1912, in *Selected Letters*, 10.

58. Ezra Pound, "What I Feel About Walt Whitman," in *Selected Prose*, 146, 145.

59. Pound, "The Renaissance," in *Literary Essays*, 221.

60. Ibid., 226.

61. Pound, "L'Homme Moyen Sensual," 10.

62. Ibid., 11.

63. Ezra Pound, Letter to Nancy Cox-McCormack, August 15, 1923, qtd. in Lawrence S. Rainey, "'All I Want You to Do Is to Follow the Orders': History, Faith, and Fascism in the Early Cantos," in *A Poem Containing History: Textual Studies in "The Cantos,"* ed. Lawrence S. Rainey (Ann Arbor: University of Michigan Press, 1997), 99.

64. Pound, "The Renaissance," in *Literary Essays*, 214.

65. Ezra Pound, "Appunti XIX: Traduzione," in *Ezra Pound's Poetry and Prose: Contributions to Periodicals*, ed. Lea Baechler, A. Walton Litz, and James Longenbach (New York: Garland, 1991), 5:310; original in Italian.

66. Ezra Pound, "Appunti II: Il mal francese," in *Ezra Pound's Poetry and Prose*, 5:251; original in Italian; "*forastiero*" [sic].

67. Ezra Pound to Barry, July 27, 1916, in *Selected Letters*, 91.

68. Ezra Pound, "I Gather," in *Selected Prose*, 22; Ezra Pound, *ABC of Reading*, intro. Michael Dirda (New York: New Directions, 2010), 29.

69. Ezra Pound, "Notes on Elizabethan Classicists," in *Literary Essays*, 232.

70. Pound, "How to Read," in *Literary Essays*, 34.

71. Ezra Pound, Letter to [?], January 20, 1911, qtd. in N. Christoph de Nagy, *The Poetry of Ezra Pound: The Pre-Imagist Stage* (Bern: Francke, 1968), 176, note g.

72. Kenner, *The Pound Era*, 150; Pound, Letter to A. R. Orage, April 1919, in *Selected Letters*, 149.

73. Ezra Pound, "I Gather the Limbs of Osiris," in *Selected Prose*, 24.

74. Qtd. in William McNaughton, "Ezra Pound's Meters and Rhythms," *PMLA* 78, no. 1 (March 1963): 136; Letter to Williams, October 21, 1908, in *Selected Letters*, 8. This letter appears with variant orthography in *Pound/Williams: Selected Letters of Ezra Pound and William Carlos Williams*, ed. Hugh Witemeyer (New York: New Directions, 1986), 8.

75. See Lawrence Venuti, *The Translator's Invisibility: A History of Translation* (New York: Routledge, 1995); and Daniel Tiffany, *Radio Corpse: Imagism and the Cryptaesthetic of Ezra Pound* (Cambridge, Mass.: Harvard University Press, 1995), 175–220. Scholars have recently acknowledged more fully the role of translation at the center of Pound's work and have untangled "modernist translation" from its close identification with Pound alone; see, for example, Steven G. Yao, *Translation and the Languages of Modernism: Gender, Politics, Language* (New York: Palgrave, 2002); Yao, "Translation," in *Ezra Pound in Context*, ed. Nadel, 33–42; and Ming Xie, "Pound as Translator," in *The Cambridge Companion to Ezra Pound*, ed. Ira Nadel (Cambridge: Cambridge University Press, 1999), 204–223.

76. Pound, *Gaudier-Brzeska*, 98.

77. Pound, "How to Read," in *Literary Essays*, 36.

78. Ezra Pound to William P. Shepard, April 1938, in *Selected Letters*, 311.

79. Ezra Pound, "Debabelization and Ogden," in *Ezra Pound's Poetry and Prose*, 6:251.

80. Ezra Pound to John Quinn, January 24, 1917, in *Selected Letters*, 104. Ronald Bush (*Genesis*, 111) dates it to September 1915 specifically.

81. Ezra Pound, Ur-Cantos autograph and transcript, Box 69, folder 3101, Yale Collection of American Literature, Beinecke Rare Book and Manuscript Library.

82. The genetic and compositional history of these cantos is very complex. See Bush, *Genesis*; John L. Foster, "Pound's Revision of Cantos I–III," *Modern Philology* 63, no. 3 (February 1966): 236–245; and Myles Slatin, "A History of Pound's Cantos I–XVI, 1915–25," *American Literature* 35, no. 2 (1963): 183–195. See also, more generally, Mark Byron, "Ezra Pound's *Cantos*: A Compact History of Twentieth-Century Authorship, Publishing, and Editing," *Literature Compass* 4, no. 4 (2007): 1158–1168.

83. Ezra Pound, "Three Cantos: I," *Poetry* 10, no. 3 (June 1917): 114.

84. These allusions actually begin with Martial, a Roman poet in Hispania (the province of the Iberian peninsula), and to the presence of the Moors in Spain. Pound also notes, as he will later explain in a letter to his father, "the wall-image / the cause" and mentions the "last auto da fe Spain 1757." Ezra Pound, Ur-Cantos autograph and typescript, Box 69, folder 3099; Three Cantos autograph ms. and typescript, Box 70, folder 3105; Ur-Cantos autograph and transcript, Box 69, folder 3101, Yale Collection of American Literature, Beinecke Rare Book and Manuscript Library. Pound's early drafts also include more attacks on German *kultur*.

85. Ezra Pound, "Three Cantos: II," *Poetry* 10, no. 4 (July 1917): 186.

86. Bush, *Genesis*, 117.

87. Pound, "Three Cantos: I," 113.

88. I include here and after "rivers" several lines from Pound's drafts that were deleted before publication; Ezra Pound, Three Cantos autograph ms. and transcript, Box 70, folder 3105, Yale Collection of American Literature, Beinecke Rare Book and Manuscript Library.

89. Pound, "Three Cantos: II," 184–185.

90. Ezra Pound, *Lustra of Ezra Pound* (New York: Knopf, 1917), 192.

91. Pound, "Three Cantos: I," 113.

92. *A Lume Spento* (1908) contains the poem "In Tempore Senectutis (An Anti-Stave for Dowson)," referring to the English decadent poet Ernest Dowson. Furthermore, in *Spirit*, he translates a Latin poem by Andrea Navgeri that includes the phrase "stave off the sun"; a footnote that he adds for "stave off" gives the original Latin, *arceo* ("shut off, protect, block"). *Spirit of Romance*, 224.

93. Pound, "Three Cantos: I," 117. On Pound, Noh, and translation, see Carrie Preston, *Learning to Kneel: Noh, Modernism, and Journeys in Teaching* (New York: Columbia University Press, 2016), 22–63.

94. Pound misspells *nueva* as "*neuva*" (late in his revisions before printing the poem, whereas it was correct in earlier drafts), gives Niebla as "Nieblas," and closes a quotation mark at the end of the phrase where it had never been opened; some of these mistakes were corrected by the time of the revisions for *Lustra*.

95. Ezra Pound to Barry, July 20[?], 1916, in *Selected Letters* 86; July 27, 1916, in *Letters*, 91.

96. Ezra Pound, "Some Notes on Francisco de Quevedo Villegas," in *Ezra Pound's Poetry and Prose*, 11:12. Hereafter cited in the text as SN. I have not been able to ascertain who translated this article into Spanish for *Hermes*.

97. Ezra Pound, *The Cantos of Ezra Pound* (New York: New Directions, 1996), 32. Hereafter cited in the text as *C*.

98. Pound refers to *The Tragicomedy of Calisto and Melibea* (1499) by Fernando de Rojas.

99. On Italy and Pound's ideas of patronage, see Lawrence Rainey, *Institutions of Modernism: Literary Elites and Public Culture* (New Haven, Conn.: Yale University Press, 1998).

100. Pound cheered the U.S. victory in the Spanish-American War when he was young, even composing a brief patriotic poem on its occasion.

101. Pound, "Provincialism the Enemy," in *Selected Prose*, 200.

102. Pound, *Guide to Kulchur*, 158; qtd. in Carpenter, *A Serious Character*, 554.

103. As John Foster notes, only three extended passages survive the revisions: those concerning Odysseus, the gods, and the Cid; other parts are cast throughout later parts of the *Cantos* (Inês de Castro in Canto XXX, for instance); see "Pound's Revision of Cantos I–III," 240.

104. Pound, "Three Cantos: I," 114.

105. I am assuming here that this allusion is otherwise not familiar enough that many readers would already know that Raquel and Vidas are Jewish.

106. Ezra Pound, Letter to Homer L. Pound, April 11, 1927, in *Selected Letters*, 210. Elvira, conveniently, is a character in both Lope de Vega's *Las almenas de Toro* and the *Poema del Cid*.

107. The references to Spanish history and politics are another story, mostly one that recounts the country's decline through bad trade deals and corrupt monarchy, culminating in what Pound saw as the disingenuous mess of the Spanish Civil War.

2. Restaging the Disaster: Dos Passos, Empire, and Literature After the Spanish-American War

1. Dos Passos traveled to Spain via Bordeaux. The biographical details of his many trips to Spain can be found in the two primary biographies: Townsend Ludington, *John Dos Passos: A Twentieth-Century Odyssey* (New York: Dutton, 1980); Virginia Spencer Carr, *John Dos Passos: A Life* (Garden City, N.Y.: Doubleday, 1984).

2. See Joshua L. Miller, *Accented America: The Cultural Politics of Multilingual Modernism* (New York: Oxford University Press, 2011), 167. Dos Passos's father predicted the same but in more explicitly racialized terms ("Anglo-Saxon"); see below.

3. Qtd. in Michael Clark, *Dos Passos's Early Fiction, 1912–1938* (Selinsgrove, Penn.: Susquehanna University Press, 1987), 25; Clark cites an unpublished manuscript of Dos Passos's, "Art and Baseball" (1917).

4. John Dos Passos, foreword to *Border of a Dream: Selected Poems of Antonio Machado*, trans. and intro. Willis Barnstone (Port Townsend, Wash.: Copper Canyon, 2004), xiv.

5. John Dos Passos, *Rosinante to the Road Again*, in *Travel Books and Other Writings, 1916–1941* (New York: Library of America/Penguin, 2003), 25. Hereafter cited in the text as *R*. Dos Passos revised and reprinted sections of Rosinante in *Journeys Between Wars* (1938).

6. Alfred Kazin, "Dos Passos and the Lost Generation," in *John Dos Passos: The Critical Heritage*, ed. Barry Maine (New York: Routledge, 1988), 228.

7. Letter to Rumsey Marvin, August 27, 1917, in *The Fourteenth Chronicle: Letters and Diaries of John Dos Passos*, ed. Townsend Ludington (Boston: Gambit, 1973), 98.

8. See Joseph Fichtelberg, "The Picaros of John Dos Passos," *Twentieth-Century Literature* 34, no. 4 (Winter 1988): 434–452.

9. John Randolph Dos Passos, *The Anglo-Saxon Century and the Unification of the English-Speaking People* (New York: Putnam, 1903), vii. Hereafter cited in the text as AS. See also Melvin Landsberg, "John R. Dos Passos: His Influence on the Novelist's Early Political Development," *American Quarterly* 16, no. 3 (Autumn 1964): 473–485.

10. See Elsa Nettels, *Language, Race, and Social Class in Howells's America* (Lexington: University Press of Kentucky, 1988), 53–54.

11. John R. Dos Passos, "The Negro Question," *Yale Law Journal* 12 (1903): 472.

12. Van Wyck Brooks, "Harvard and American Life," *The Living Age* 3362 (December 12, 1908): 649. See also Casey Blake Nelson, *Beloved Community: The Cultural Criticism of Randolph Bourne, Van Wyck Brooks, Waldo Frank, and Lewis Mumford* (Chapel Hill: University of North Carolina Press, 1990).

13. John Dos Passos, "The Evangelist and the Volcano," in *The Major Nonfictional Prose*, ed. Donald Pizer (Detroit, Mich.: Wayne State University Press, 1988), 25.

14. John Dos Passos, "A Humble Protest," in *The Major Nonfictional Prose*, 34.

15. John Dos Passos, "Against American Literature," in *Travel Books and Other Writings, 1916–1941* (New York: Library of America/Penguin, 2003), 587. Hereafter cited in the text as A.

16. Of course, the French realist novel was in many ways dominated by Russian models itself, so Dos Passos is also enjoining a series of endless regressions, much like the successive empires he sees in the translation of historical power from Europe to the United States.

17. Susan Hegeman, *Patterns for America: Modernism and the Concept of Culture* (Princeton, N.J.: Princeton University Press, 1999), 93.

18. Ludington, *John Dos Passos*, 92. Riaño, for his part, would marry an American woman and settle permanently in the United States, where he befriended Huntington and helped him build up the Hispanic Division of the Library of Congress.

19. Letter to Marvin, November 12, 1916, in *The Fourteenth Chronicle*, 51.

20. John Dos Passos, *The Best Times: An Informal Memoir* (New York: New American Library, 1966), 31.

21. See Carr, *Dos Passos*, 106–107. In the background of Dos Passos's travel writings is John Reed's *Insurgent Mexico* (1914), which Dos Passos admired greatly and reviewed for the *Harvard Monthly*.

22. Letter to Marvin, December 25, 1916, in *The Fourteenth Chronicle*, 64.

23. Letter to Marvin, December 4, 1916, in *The Fourteenth Chronicle*, 56–57.

24. Letter to Thomas P. Cope, January [?], 1920, in *The Fourteenth Chronicle*, 274.

25. Letter to Marvin, December 4, 1916, in *The Fourteenth Chronicle*, 56–57.

26. Letter to Marvin, May 29, 1916, in *The Fourteenth Chronicle*, 39.

27. Letter to Marvin, November 15, 1916, in *The Fourteenth Chronicle*, 53.

28. See the brief memoir by Dudley Poore, "On the Plain in Spain," *Virginia Quarterly Review* 58, no. 1 (Winter 1982), http://www.vqronline.org/essay/plain-spain.

29. Letter to Marvin, June 5, 1917, in *The Fourteenth Chronicle*, 73. See also Seth Moglen, *Mourning Modernity: Literary Modernism and the Injuries of American Capitalism* (Stanford, Calif.: Stanford University Press, 2007), 102.

30. [Waldo Frank], unsigned editorial, *Seven Arts* 1, no. 1 (November 1916): 53, 52.

31. See David Shumway, *Creating American Civilization: A Genealogy of American Studies as an Academic Discipline* (Minneapolis: University of Minnesota Press, 1994), 19–20.

32. On this topic, see Thomas Bender, *New York Intellect: A History of Intellectual Life in New York City from 1750 to the Beginnings of Our Own Time* (New York: Knopf, 1997); Edward Abrahams, *The Lyrical Left: Randolph Bourne, Alfred Stieglitz, and the Origins of Cultural Radicalism in America* (Charlottesville: University Press of Virginia, 1986); and Nelson, *Beloved Community*.

33. See Christine Stansell, *American Moderns: Bohemian New York and the Creation of a New Century* (New York: Metropolitan, 2000), 94.

34. Frank would also write elsewhere on "Young France." See Bruce Clayton, *Forgotten Prophet: The Life of Randolph Bourne* (Columbia: University of Missouri Press, 1998), 210; Hegeman, *Patterns for America*, 70; see also Ann Douglas, *Terrible Honesty: Mongrel Manhattan in the 1920s* (New York: Farrar, Straus and Giroux, 1995).

35. Echoing Dos Passos's "Against American Literature," Brooks also saw the incorporation of indigenous elements in Rubén Darío's works as an antidote to the homogeneity of U.S. writing and stated that Spanish American literature "is certainly an older, a richer, and a hardier growth than ours." See Van Wyck Brooks, "Review of *The Literary History of Spanish America*, by Alfred Coester," *Seven Arts* 1, no. 6 (April 1917): 668.

36. Letter to Gíner, February–March 1918, in *The Fourteenth Chronicle*, 153.

37. John Dos Passos, "Young Spain," *Seven Arts* 2, no. 4 (August 1917): 481. hereafter cited in the text as YS.

38. Letter to Lawson, January–February 1920, in *The Fourteenth Chronicle*, 277.

39. Letter to Marvin, November 1920 [?], in *The Fourteenth Chronicle*, 306.

40. William Dean Howells, *Familiar Spanish Travels* (New York: Harper & Brothers, 1913), 327.

41. William Dean Howells, "Criticism and Fiction," in *My Literary Passions, Criticism and Fiction* (New York: Harper & Brothers, 1895), 229. See his reviews of Palacio Valdés and Galdós in William Dean Howells, *Criticism and Fiction and Other Essays*, ed. and intro. Clara Marburg Kirk and Rudolf Kirk (New York: New York University Press, 1965), 122–138. Howells reviewed at least six of Palacio Valdés's novels and commented on those of Juan Valera as well. One of his pieces on Galdós was used as the introduction to the English translation of *Doña Perfecta* in 1896.

42. Howells, "Criticism and Fiction," 258; on his attempted translations, see William Dean Howells, "Heine," in *My Literary Passions*, 125.

43. William Dean Howells, "Valdés, Galdós, Verga, Zola, Trollope," in *My Literary Passions*, 181. Howells almost always renders Hispanic surnames incorrectly ("Valdés" for Palacio Valdés, "Ibanez" for Blasco Ibáñez); Dos Passos makes some similar mistakes.

44. William Dean Howells, "The Future of the American Novel," in *Criticism and Fiction*, 347.

45. William Dean Howells, "Editor's Easy Chair," *Harper's New Monthly Magazine* 131 (November 1915): 957.

46. Ibid., 958. Several years later, Howells wrote the introduction to the translation of Blasco Ibáñez's *The Shadow of the Cathedral* (1919).

47. Henry James to William Dean Howells, May 4, 1898, in *Letters, Fictions, Lives: Henry James and William Dean Howells*, ed. Michael Anesko (New York: Oxford University Press, 1997), 308–309.

48. Howells to James, July 31, 1898, in *Letters, Fictions, Lives*, 311.

49. Howells to James, April 17, 1898, in *Letters, Fictions, Lives*, 308.

50. James to Howells, August 19, 1898, in *Letters, Fictions, Lives*, 313.

51. Qtd. in Susan Goodman and Carl Dawson, *William Dean Howells: A Writer's Life* (Berkeley: University of California Press, 2005), 407. Howells published several brief articles on the war, including "Spanish Prisoners of War" (1898), that mostly lamented the effect of the war on the moral standing of the United States.

52. See Jonathan Arac, "The Age of the Novel, the Age of Empire: Howells, Twain, James Around 1900," *Yearbook of English Studies* 41, no. 2 (2011): 94–105. Arac has also examined the discussions of language "purity" and U.S. identity in these contexts, in "Babel and Vernacular in an Empire of Immigrants: Howells and the Languages of American Fiction," *boundary 2* 34, no. 2 (Summer 2007): 1–20.

53. Arnold Bennett, "The Future of the American Novel," *North American Review* 195 (January 1912): 76. Bennett notes that he wrote the essay in 1903, though it was not printed until 1912.

54. William Dean Howells, "Lazarillo de Tormes," in *My Literary Passions*, 106. Howells would soon turn away from Spanish and toward German with his studies of Heine.

55. S. Verdad [J. M. Kennedy], "Foreign Affairs," *New Age* 7, no. 25 (October 20, 1910): 58.

56. Letter to Mitchell, October 8, 1919, in *The Fourteenth Chronicle*, 263–264.

57. John Dos Passos, "In Portugal," in *The Major Nonfictional Prose*, 51.

58. On these themes, see Donald Pizer, *Towards a Modernist Style: John Dos Passos* (London: Bloomsbury Academic, 2013), 9–25. Pizer stretches his reading of *Rosinante*, however, by deeming it a work of "high modernism" and noting the qualities it shares with other expatriate modernist texts. Michael Clark links *Three Soldiers* and *Rosinante* through their shared, complex sense of the "gesture"; see *Dos Passos's Early Fiction*, 90–91. See also Eugenio Suárez-Galbán, *The Last Good Land: Spain in American Literature* (Amsterdam: Rodopi, 2011), 147–174; María

DeGuzmán, *Spain's Long Shadow: The Black Legend, Off-Whiteness, and Anglo-American Empire* (Minneapolis: University of Minnesota Press, 2005), xvi, 190; and Catalina Montes, *La visión de España en la obra de John Dos Passos* (Salamanca: Almar, 1980).

59. Baroja's novels did not appear in English until 1917, just when Dos Passos published "Young Spain," and his most famous work, *La lucha por la vida*, did not come out until 1922–1924 with Knopf.

60. Waldo Frank, Letter to José Ortega y Gasset, July 22, 1923, Archives of the Fundación Ortega y Gasset, Madrid.

61. Waldo Frank, *Virgin Spain: Scenes from the Spiritual Drama of a Great People* (New York: Boni and Liveright, 1926), 260.

62. John Dos Passos, "Spain on a Monument," in *The Major Nonfictional Prose*, 83, 84.

63. See Nancy Bredendick, "Baroja's Madrid in the Poems of 'Winter in Castile' by John Dos Passos," *Arizona Journal of Hispanic Cultural Studies* 3 (1999): 151–162.

64. Dos Passos, foreword to *Border of a Dream*, xiii–xiv.

65. Antonio Machado, *Campos de Castilla/The Landscape of Castile*, trans. Mary G. Berg and Dennis Maloney (Buffalo, N.Y.: White Pine, 2005), 33.

66. Ibid., 49.

67. Ibid., 253.

68. John Dos Passos, *A Pushcart at the Curb* (New York: George H. Doran, 1922), 21, 13, 14. Hereafter cited in the text as *P*.

69. One character in the novel, John Andrews, does fantasize, amid the horrors and drudgery of war, about escaping "to Spain and freedom." John Dos Passos, *Three Soldiers* (Boston: Houghton Mifflin, 1949), 211.

70. John Dos Passos, *Manhattan Transfer: A Novel* (New York: Mariner Books, 2003), 193; ellipses in original.

71. See Rubén Gallo, "John Dos Passos in Mexico," *Modernism/modernity* 14, no. 2 (April 2007): 329–345.

72. See ibid., 338.

73. John Dos Passos, translator's foreword to *Panama* (1918) by Blaise Cendrars, in *The Major Nonfictional Prose*, 134.

74. John Dos Passos, responses to questionnaire, reprinted in *The Major Nonfictional Prose*, 149–150.

75. John Dos Passos, *Fortune Heights*, in *Three Plays* (New York: Harcourt, Brace and Co., 1934), 210.

76. See Jon Smith, "John Dos Passos, Anglo-Saxon," *Modern Fiction Studies* 44, no. 2 (1999): 282–305.

77. John Dos Passos, *The Big Money: Volume III of the USA Trilogy* (New York: Houghton Mifflin, 2000), 371.

78. Anonymous, "Libros Yankis," *La Gaceta Literaria* 1, no. 8 (April 15, 1927): 5.

79. See John Dos Passos, *Rocinante vuelve al camino*, trans. Márgara Villegas (Madrid: Editorial Cenit, 1930).
80. Julián Gorkin, *10 novelistas americanos*, xvii. See also the introduction to this volume, above.
81. See John Dos Passos, "The Republic of Honest Men," in *Travel Books*, 339–368.
82. See Stephen Koch, *The Breaking Point: Hemingway, Dos Passos, and the Murder of José Robles* (New York: Counterpoint, 2005).
83. John Dos Passos, "Farewell to Europe!," in *Travel Books*, 622.
84. Smith, "John Dos Passos," 283.

3. Jiménez, Modernism/o, and the Languages of Comparative Modernist Studies

1. Juan Ramón Jiménez, qtd. in Ricardo Gullón, *Conversaciones con Juan Ramón Jiménez* (Madrid: Taurus, 1958), 113.
2. For more on this history in Anglophone criticism, see chapters 1 and 2 of Sean Latham and Gayle Rogers, *Modernism: Evolution of an Idea* (London: Bloomsbury Academic, 2015).
3. Juan Ramón Jiménez, *El modernismo: Apuntes de curso* (1953), ed. Jorge Urrutia (Madrid: Visor, 1999), 4; the phrases in brackets are Jiménez's. These and other collections of Jiménez's writings cited below bring together unpublished and published materials; the former are often scattered lecture notes or manuscript sketches, difficult to date precisely.
4. Emily Apter invokes a consonant sense of "untranslatability" in *Against World Literature: On the Politics of Untranslatability* (London: Verso, 2013).
5. I am treating primarily one strand of *modernismo*—the one most associated with Darío—which is necessarily pragmatic in this case. The historiography of *modernismo* is a complex and thorny issue in which many competing voices have intervened. A complete account is not necessary here: along with the figures discussed in this essay, Azorín, Pedro and Max Henríquez Ureña, Dámaso Alonso, Amado Nervo, Guillermo Díaz-Plaja, Pedro Laín Entralgo, Ricardo Gullón, Pedro Salinas, Ned J. Davison, Ángel Rama, Noé Jitrik, Lily Litvak, Gwen Kirkpatrick, and Eugenio Florit are some of the more prominent players. My case here does not rest on arguments about one or multiple modernities. The best overviews of these topics with regard to *modernismo* are Cathy Jrade, *Modernismo, Modernity, and the Development of Spanish American Literature* (Austin: University of Texas Press, 1998); and Alejandro Mejías-López, *The Inverted Conquest: The Myth of Modernity and the Transatlantic Onset of Modernism* (Nashville, Tenn.: Vanderbilt University Press, 2009). On the term and its nonportability even within Iberian languages, see Brad Epps, "'Modern' and 'Moderno': Modernist Studies, 1898, and Spain," *Catalan Review* 14, nos. 1–2 (2000): 75–116.

6. See Octavio Paz, *Children of the Mire: Modern Poetry from Romanticism to the Avant-Garde*, trans. Rachel Phillips (Cambridge, Mass.: Harvard University Press, 1974), 92.

7. Gerard Aching, "The Temporalities of Modernity in Spanish American *Modernismo*: Darío's Bourgeois King," in *The Oxford Handbook of Global Modernisms*, ed. Mark Wollaeger (New York: Oxford University Press, 2012), 109–117. See also Gerard Aching, *The Politics of Spanish American Modernismo: By Exquisite Design* (New York: Cambridge University Press, 1997); and Jaime Hanneken, "*Mikilistes* and *Modernistas*: Taking Paris to the 'Second Degree,' " *Comparative Literature* 60, no. 4 (Fall 2008): 370–388. The key critic in the background here, on the issue of derivation in Latin American writing, is Roberto Schwarz; see his *Misplaced Ideas: Essays on Brazilian Culture*, ed. John Gledson (London: Verso, 1992). In a related vein, see Fernando J. Rosenberg, *The Avant-Garde and Geopolitics in Latin America* (Pittsburgh, Penn.: University of Pittsburgh Press, 2006).

8. See Mary Lee Bretz, *Encounters Across Borders: The Changing Visions of Spanish Modernism, 1890–1930* (Lewisburg, Penn.: Bucknell University Press, 2001), 21–30; Mejías-López, *Inverted Conquest*, 1–2.

9. Astradur Eysteinsson, *The Concept of Modernism* (Ithaca, N.Y.: Cornell University Press, 1990), 111.

10. See Cathy Jrade, "The Spanish-American Modernismo," in *Modernism*, ed. Astradur Eysteinsson and Vivian Liska, 2 vols. (Amsterdam: John Benjamins, 2007), 817–830.

11. See José María Rodríguez García, "Introduction: How 'Modernist' Were Hispanic Literary and Artistic Modernities?" *Modernist Cultures* 7, no. 1 (2012): 1–14.

12. Ricardo Gullón has published most extensively on this topic; an excellent overview is *Juan Ramón Jiménez y el modernismo* (Mexico City: Aguilar, 1962). See also Richard Cardwell, *Juan R. Jiménez: The Modernist Apprenticeship, 1895–1900* (Berlin: Colloquium Verlag, 1977).

13. Michael P. Predmore, "Introduction to the Life and Works of Juan Ramón Jiménez," in *Diary of a Newlywed Poet: A Bilingual Edition of Diario de un poeta reciencasado*, trans. Hugh A. Harter, ed. and intro. Michael P. Predmore (Selinsgrove, Penn.: Susquehanna University Press, 2004), 24. Hereafter cited parenthetically in the text as *D*. This edition uses "*reciencasado*" in the title; I have given it above as "*recién casado*," as the first edition named it. See also Predmore, *La poesía hermética de Juan Ramón Jiménez: El "Diario" como centro de su mundo poético* (Madrid: Gredos, 1973).

14. See Cardwell, *Juan R. Jiménez*, 184. The references to Darío as "maestro" occur across many of the letters gathered in Juan R. Jiménez, *Epistolario*, ed. Alfonso Alegre Heitzmann (Madrid: Residencia de Estudiantes, 2006).

15. Rubén Darío, "To Juan Ramón Jiménez," in *Selected Writings*, ed. Ilan Stavans, trans. Andrew Hurley, Greg Simon, and Stephen White (New York: Penguin, 2005), 146; translation modified.

16. Rubén Darío, "I Seek a Form . . . ", in *Selected Poems*, trans. Lysander Kemp (Austin: University of Texas Press, 1965), 60.

17. Rubén Darío, "Ricardo Palma," *La Ilustración* 11, no. 530 (December 28, 1890): 822. Darío had used the term "expresión moderna" in 1888 when writing in the Chilean media on the Mexican Ricardo Contreras.

18. See Latham and Rogers, *Modernism*, 19–24.

19. The term *modernismo* entered the Spanish lexicon in José Cadalso's *Cartas marruecas* (1789), a novel in which one character speaks of two friends who lose their minds by being forced to study and absorb the "quintessence of modernism." José Cadalso, *Cartas marruecas* (Paris: Bobée é Hingray, 1827), 268. For more detailed citations and philological resources focusing on 1886 through 1890, see Gayle Rogers, "The Spanish Morgue and the Emergence of International Modernism," https://www.academia.edu/18995499/The_Spanish_Morgue_and_the_Emergence_of_International_Modernism_.

20. For an overview of the Catholic crisis over "*modernismo*" in Spain and its effects on Jiménez and Unamuno, see Gilberto Azam, *El modernismo desde dentro* (Barcelona: Anthropos, 1989), 43–70.

21. Matei Călinescu, *Five Faces of Modernity: Modernism, Avant-Garde, Decadence, Kitsch, Postmodernism* (Durham, N.C.: Duke University Press, 1987), 69.

22. Jrade, *Modernismo*, 1, 14.

23. Darío was able to promote himself further as the head of the movement when several other key figures (Gutiérrez Nájera, Martí, Casal, and Asunción Silva) were all dead by 1896.

24. Mariano Siskind, *Cosmopolitan Desires: Global Modernity and World Literature in Latin America* (Evanston, Ill.: Northwestern University Press, 2014), 7.

25. Rubén Darío, "The Story of My Books," in *Selected Writings*, 376. Darío is referring to Rafael María Baralt's *Diccionario de galicismos* (1855).

26. Ibid., 376. Darío adopted what he saw as the intensity of the French *azur* over the plainness of *bleu*.

27. Juan Valera, *Cartas americanas I* (Madrid: Fuentes y Capdeville, 1889), 219, 215.

28. Joseba Gabilondo points to an irony here in that Spanish nationalism in the nineteenth century had been modeled in important ways on Latin American independence movements. Joseba Gabilondo, "Historical Memory, Neoliberal Spain, and the Latin American Postcolonial Ghost: On the Politics of Recognition, Apology, and Reparation in Contemporary Spanish Historiography," *Arizona Journal of Hispanic Cultural Studies* 7 (2003): 247–266.

29. "modernismo," *Diccionario de la Real Academia Española*, http://www.rae.es.

30. See Alberto Acereda, *El antimodernismo: Debates transatlánticos en el fin de siglo* (Palencia: Cálamo, 2011). See also the bibliography in Carlos Lozano, *Rubén Darío y el modernismo en España, 1888–1920: Ensayo de bibliografía comentada* (New York: Las Americas, 1967).

31. See Max Henríquez Ureña, *El retorno de los galeones* (Madrid: Renacimiento, 1930). See also Ignacio Zuleta, *La polémica modernista: El modernismo de mar a mar, 1898–1907* (Bogotá: Instituto Caro y Cuervo, 1988).

32. See Mejías-López, *Inverted Conquest*, 196n25, 197n26. Mejías-López's reading extends the insights of Ángel Rama and José Luis Martínez, who addressed this conquest in different formulations.

33. Rubén Darío, "Prefacio," in *Azul . . . y Cantos de vida y esperanza*, ed. José María Martínez (Madrid: Cátedra, 2002), 334.

34. Rubén Darío, *España contemporánea* (Madrid: Visor, 2005), 29.

35. Rubén Darío, "El modernismo," in *Selected Writings*, 369; translation modified.

36. Rubén Darío, "El crepúsculo de España," in *El modernismo y otros ensayos*, ed. Iris M. Zavala (Madrid: Alianza, 1989), 167.

37. Ibid., 168.

38. Darío, "El modernismo," in *Selected Writings*, 371–72; translation modified.

39. Ibid., 372; Rubén Darío, "Black Spain," in *Selected Writings*, 554. Siskind notes that both Martí and Gutiérrez Najera critiqued the Spanish literary scene as moribund, too; see *Cosmopolitan Desires*, 110, 136. See also Robin Fiddian, "Under Spanish Eyes: Late Nineteenth-Century Postcolonial Views of Spanish American Literature," *Modern Language Review* 97, no. 1 (January 2002): 83–93.

40. Rubén Darío, preface to *Prosas profanas y otros poemas*, in *Selected Poems of Rubén Darío: A Bilingual Anthology*, ed. and trans. Alberto Acereda and Will Derusha (Lewisburg, Penn.: Bucknell University Press, 2001), 111.

41. Juan Ramón Jiménez, *Política poética*, intro. Germán Bleiberg (Madrid: Alianza Editorial, 1982), 184.

42. Jiménez called himself a "universal Andalusian," a term he had already ascribed to Bécquer. I owe this point, and the broader point about the shift from Castile to Andalusia, to José Luis Venegas.

43. Qtd. in Howard Young, "Anglo-American Poetry in the Correspondence of Luisa Grimm and Juan Ramón Jiménez," *Hispanic Review* 44, no. 1 (Winter 1976): 1–26; qtd. in Howard Young, *The Line in the Margin: Juan Ramón Jiménez and His Readings in Blake, Shelley, and Yeats* (Madison: University of Wisconsin Press, 1980), 72.

44. See José María Rodríguez García, "Introduction," 8.

45. Juan Ramón Jiménez, *Crítica paralela*, ed. Arturo del Villar (Madrid: Nárcea de Ediciones, 1975), 167.

46. See ibid., 187.

47. Ibid., 167.

48. See Carmen Pérez Romero, *Juan Ramón Jiménez y la poesía anglosajona* (Cáceres: Universidad de Extremadura, 1981).

49. See Gayle Rogers, "Translation," in *Global Modernisms: Toward a New Lexicon*, ed. Eric Hayot and Rebecca L. Walkowitz (New York: Columbia University Press, forthcoming); and Robert Johnson, "Juan Ramón Jiménez, Rabindranath Tagore, and 'la poesía desnuda,'" *Modern Language Review* 60, no. 4 (October 1965): 534–546.

50. Jiménez's biographer Francisco Garfias and Michael Predmore are among those who have made this claim. For a detailed documentation and bibliography of

Tagore's translation and reception in Spain, see Shyama Prasad Ganguly, "Spain and Latin America," in *Rabindranath Tagore: One Hundred Years of Global Reception*, ed. Martin Kämpchen and Imre Bangha (New Delhi: Orient BlackSwan, 2014), 476–498.

51. See Salomón de la Selva, "Rubén Darío," *Poetry* 8, no. 4 (July 1916): 200–204; Theodore S. Beardsley Jr., "Rubén Darío and the Hispanic Society: The Holograph Manuscript of ¡Pax!," *Hispanic Review* 35, no. 1 (January 1967): 1–42.

52. Jiménez, *Crítica paralela*, 181.

53. Juan Ramón Jiménez, *Alerta*, ed. Francisco Javier Blasco Pascual (Salamanca: University of Salamanca Press, 1983), 70.

54. I borrow this characterization of a hallmark of *modernista* poetry from Donald Shaw, *A Companion to Modern Spanish American Fiction* (Rochester, N.Y.: Tamesis, 2002), 33.

55. Predmore, "Introduction to the Life and Works," 48.

56. Jiménez, *Alerta*, 53.

57. See Nemes de Palua, *Vida y obra de Juan Ramón Jiménez* (Madrid: Gredos, 1957).

58. Jiménez reissued it as *Diario de poeta y mar* in 1948, with a few additions and slight alterations.

59. Jiménez, *Alerta*, 61.

60. Qtd. in Predmore, "Introduction to the Life and Works," 48.

61. Jiménez, *Política*, 185.

62. See note 5, above. The Francoist line is represented by Guillermo Díaz-Plaja's *Modernismo frente a noventa y ocho* (1951); Ricardo Gullón was among the most vocal to contest the separation of *modernismo* and the Generation of '98. Jiménez, in synthesizing the work of his critical and poetic forebears, is often still aligned with what is called the "epochal view" of *modernismo*, though I argue here that such a conception is too narrow.

63. Federico de Onís, *Antología de la poesía española e hispanoamericana* (New York: Las Americas, 1961), xv.

64. Cardwell, *Juan R. Jiménez*, 227.

65. Juan Ramón Jiménez, transcript of recorded lecture no. 3, in *El modernismo: Notas de un curso* (1953), ed. Ricardo Gullón and Eugenio Fernández Méndez (Mexico City: Aguilar, 1962), 260. Jiménez's notes are collected, with some differences, in two different editions, which I will cite accordingly.

66. Jiménez, *Alerta*, 31.

67. Jiménez, transcript, *Modernismo: Notas*, 261.

68. Jiménez, *Modernismo: Notas*, 100.

69. Jiménez, *Crítica*, 24.

70. Jiménez, *Modernismo: Apuntes*, 18.

71. Jiménez, *Política*, 181–182.

72. Jiménez, *Modernismo: Apuntes*, 19.

73. Jiménez, *Alerta*, 55.

74. Jiménez, *Modernismo: Apuntes*, 102.

75. Jiménez, *Política*, 179.
76. Jiménez, *Modernismo: Apuntes*, 103.
77. Jiménez, *Alerta*, 86.
78. Jiménez, *Política*, 179.
79. Jiménez, *Modernismo: Apuntes*, 103.
80. Jiménez does not make the point as clearly as Roberto Ignacio Díaz does that Spanish American *modernismo* itself was a multilingual movement that included writing in English by Martí, for example; see *Unhomely Rooms: Foreign Tongues and Spanish American Literature* (Lewisburg, Penn.: Bucknell University Press, 2002).
81. Jiménez, *Modernismo: Apuntes*, 97.
82. See David James and Urmila Seshagiri's critique of this tendency in "Metamodernism: Narratives of Continuity and Revolution," *PMLA* 129, no. 1 (January 2014): 87–100.
83. See, for example, Allison Schachter, *Diasporic Modernisms: Hebrew and Yiddish Literature in the Twentieth Century* (New York: Oxford University Press, 2011); Irene Ramalho Santos, *Atlantic Poets: Fernando Pessoa's Turn in Anglo-American Modernism* (Hanover, N.H.: University of New England Press, 2003).
84. Kelly Washbourne, introduction to *An Anthology of Spanish American Modernismo*, ed. and trans. Kelly Washbourne and Sergio Waisman (New York: MLA, 2007), xxxviii.
85. See also the role of translation as mapped by Hoyt Long and Richard So at the Chicago Text Lab: http://lucian.uchicago.edu/blogs/literarynetworks/.

4. Unamuno, Nativism, and the Politics of the Vernacular; or, On the Authenticity of Translation

1. Antoine Berman, "Translation and the Trials of the Foreign," in *The Translation Studies Reader*, ed. and trans. Lawrence Venuti (New York: Routledge, 2012), 250; italics in original. On the work of poeticizing dialects and vernaculars more generally in this period, see Matthew Hart, *Nations of Nothing but Poetry: Modernism, Transnationalism, and Synthetic Vernacular Writing* (New York: Oxford University Press, 2010).
2. Lawrence Venuti, *Translation Changes Everything: Theory and Practice* (New York: Routledge, 2013), 117. Venuti is discussing Victor Hugo, whom André Lefevere has also cited for pointing to such contradictions in nationalist thought.
3. Miguel de Unamuno, "Patriotismo espiritualista," in *Del patriotismo espiritual: Artículos en "La Nación" de Buenos Aires, 1901–1914*, ed. Victor Ouimette (Salamanca: Ediciones Universidad Salamanca, 1997), 329. Unamuno's thousands of publications are scattered across a number of collections and several incomplete editions of *Obras completas* with varying contents. A few have been translated into English, and I will quote from existing translations whenever possible, with my modifications noted.

4. Qtd. in Julio César Chaves, *Unamuno y América*, intro. Joaquín Ruíz Jiménez (Madrid: Ediciones Cultura Hispánica, 1964), 508.

5. Qtd. in Julio-César Santoyo, "Unamuno, traductor: luces y sombras," in *Historia de la traducción: quince apuntes* (León: Universidad de León, 1999), 192.

6. C. A. Longhurst characterizes Unamuno's thought as "schizophrenic" at points like this; see "Unamuno, Schleiermacher, Humboldt: A Question of Language," *Hispanic Review* 79, no. 4 (Autumn 2011): 582.

7. On the debates over Unamuno's socialism after 1897, see Stephen G. H. Roberts, "Unamuno and the Restoration Political Project: A Reevaluation," in *Spain's 1898 Crisis: Regenerationism, Modernism, Postcolonialism*, ed. Joseph Harrison and Alan Hoyle (Manchester: Manchester University Press, 2000), 68–80.

8. See José-Carlos Mainer, *Historia de la literatura española: Modernidad y nacionalismo, 1900–1939*, 9 vols. (Barcelona: Crítica, 2010), 6:250.

9. Miguel de Unamuno, *En torno al casticismo*, ed. Jean-Claude Rabaté (Madrid: Cátedra, 2005), 268.

10. Or, "one must make of the unfamiliar, the familiar": "Hay que hacer de lo extraño, entraño." Miguel de Unamuno, *De la enseñanza superior en España* (Madrid: Revista Nueva, 1899), 55.

11. Miguel de Unamuno to Antonio Machado, August 1903, in *The Private World: Selections from the "Diario íntimo" and "Selected Letters 1890–1936,"* trans. Anthony Kerrigan, Allen Lacy, and Martin Nozick (Princeton, N.J.: Princeton University Press, 1984), 169.

12. Miguel de Unamuno, "Españolarse," Poem 1437, in *Cancionero*, intro. Andrés Trapiello (Madrid: Akal, 1984), 417.

13. Miguel de Unamuno, "El Gaucho Martín Fierro," in *Obras completas*, ed. Manuel García Blanco, 9 vols. (Madrid: Escelicer, 1966–), 4:710. See Jo Labanyi, "Nation, Narration, Naturalization: A Barthesian Critique of the 1898 Generation," in *New Hispanisms: Literature, Culture, Theory*, ed. Mark I. Millington and Paul Julian Smith (Ottawa: Dovehouse Editions, 1994), 127–149.

14. Miguel de Unamuno, "Vocabulario," in *Vida de Don Quijote y Sancho* (Buenos Aires: Espasa-Calpe Argentina, 1952), 249.

15. Miguel de Unamuno, "Sobre el cultivo de la demótica," in *Obras completas*, ed. Manuel García Blanco (Madrid: Aguado, 1958), 7:476. See also Luis Álvarez Castro, *La palabra y el ser en la teoría literaria de Unamuno* (Salamanca: Ediciones Universidad de Salamanca, 2005).

16. Ibid., 7:477.

17. At the same time, Unamuno has been discussed as a forerunner to poststructuralist thought on language and human agency, especially because of the ways in which he repositions and theorizes the writer and reader in his experimental novels, which I do not have the space to treat here. See, for example, Iris M. Zavala, *Colonialism and Culture: Hispanic Modernisms and the Social Imaginary* (Bloomington: Indiana University Press, 1992).

18. Miguel de Unamuno, "Por España," in *Del patriotismo espiritual*, 98. See Josse de Kock, "Miguel de Unamuno y la lengua española de fin de siglo," in *Tu*

mano es mi destino, ed. Cirilo Flórez Miguel (Salamanca: Ediciones Universidad de Salamanca, 2001), 101–124.

19. Menéndez Pidal, *Manual elemental de gramática histórica española* (Madrid: Libería general de Victoriano Suárez, 1904), 8.

20. Letter to Victoria Ocampo, January 24, 1929, in *Epistolario inédito*, ed. Laureano Robles, 2 vols. (Madrid: Espasa Calpe, 1991), 2:260.

21. José Luis Venegas, *Transatlantic Correspondence: Modernity, Epistolarity, and Literature in Spain and Spanish America, 1898–1992* (Columbus: Ohio State University Press, 2014), 57.

22. Miguel de Unamuno, Poem 912, in *Cancionero*, 317.

23. Miguel de Unamuno, Poem 1164, in *Cancionero*, 392.

24. Miguel de Unamuno, "Hispanidad," in *Obras completas*, Escelicer ed., 4:1081.

25. Unamuno, *En torno al casticismo*, 155. See Jonathan Mayhew, "The Genealogy of Late Modernism in Spain: Unamuno, Lorca, Zambrano, and Valente," *Modernist Cultures* 7, no. 1 (May 2012): 77–97.

26. Unamuno, *Cancionero*, 363; Miguel de Unamuno, "La reforma de castellano," in *Obras completas*, Escelicer ed., 1:1003.

27. For a brief overview, see Barry L. Velleman, "Linguistic Anti-academicism and Hispanic Community: Sarmiento and Unamuno," in *The Battle Over Spanish Between 1800 and 2000: Languages, Ideologies, and Hispanic Intellectuals*, ed. José del Valle and Luis Gabriel-Stheeman (New York: Routledge, 2002), 14–41; and Robin Fiddian, "Under Spanish Eyes: Late Nineteenth-Century Postcolonial Views of Spanish American Literature," *Modern Language Review* 97, no. 1 (January 2002): 83–93.

28. Joan Ramon Resina, "'For Their Own Good': The Spanish Identity and Its Great Inquisitor, Miguel de Unamuno," in *The Battle Over Spanish Between 1800 and 2000*, 121. Unamuno's socialism, too, became less political and more cultural after 1897–1898.

29. Fiddian, "Under Spanish Eyes," 84.

30. See Miguel de Unamuno, "Sobre la lengua española," in *Obras completas*, Escelicer ed., 3:282.

31. Miguel de Unamuno, "El Gaucho," in *Obras completas*, Escelicer ed., 4:711.

32. Ibid., 4:715.

33. Miguel de Unamuno, "Sobre la literatura hispanoamericana," in *Obras completas*, Escelicer ed., 4:732.

34. Unamuno, "El Gaucho," 4:711.

35. Ibid., 4:712.

36. Ibid., 4:715.

37. See the bibliography in Unamuno, *Del patriotismo espiritual*, 21–31.

38. Qtd. in Jean-Claude Rabaté and Colette Rabaté, *Miguel de Unamuno. Biografía* (Madrid: Taurus, 2009), 129. For an overview of Unamuno's translations, see Carlos Serrano, "Sobre Unamuno traductor," in *Actas del VIII Congreso de la Asociación Internacional de Hispanistas*, ed. A. David Kossoff (Madrid: Ediciones Istmo, 1986), 581–590.

39. Miguel de Unamuno, "Contra el purismo," in *Ensayos*, 7 vols. (Madrid: Residencia de Estudiantes, 1917), 4:21, 22.

40. Miguel de Unamuno to Joan Maragall, January 4, 1907, in *The Private World*, 183–184.

41. Miguel de Unamuno to Federico Urales [1901], in *The Private World*, 165.

42. Miguel Unamuno, Poem 616, in *Cancionero*, 226–227.

43. Miguel de Unamuno, *Poesías* (Bilbao: José Rojas, 1907), 353. The word, derived from a Portuguese or Catalan stem, means roughly "in-store."

44. See Unamuno's preface to the Spanish translation of Benedetto Croce's *Aesthetics* from 1926.

45. José Lázaro Galdiano, founder of *La España Moderna*, also directed a publishing house for which Unamuno translated full-length German and English works. See Manuel García Blanco, "Unamuno, traductor y amigo de José Lázaro," *Revista de Occidente* 19 (October–December 1964): 97–106.

46. Santoyo, "Unamuno, traductor," 193.

47. Qtd. in Laureano Robles, "Unamuno, traductor de Th. Carlyle," *Daimon: revista de filosofía* 10 (1995): 16. Robles is quoting from a letter to Clarín from 1900.

48. Qtd. in Peter G. Earle, *Unamuno and English Literature* (New York: Hispanic Institute in the United States, 1960), 19. See also the overview in Manuel García Blanco, "Poetas ingleses en la obra de Unamuno," *Bulletin of Hispanic Studies* 36, no. 2 (1959): 88–106; 36, no. 3 (1959): 146–165.

49. Miguel de Unamuno, "En torno de Labouchère," in *Obras completas*, Aguado ed., 8:738.

50. Miguel de Unamuno, "Borrow y la xenofobia española," in *Obras completas*, Aguado ed., 8:756.

51. Miguel de Unamuno, "The English-Speaking Folk," in *Obras completas*, Escelicer ed., 4:507.

52. Ibid., 4:508.

53. Ibid., 4:508–509.

54. Review of "Alades" by E. Guanyabens, in *De esto y de aquello*, 4 vols., ed. and intro. Manuel García Blanco (Buenos Aires: Editorial Sudamericana, 1950), 1:463; Earle, *Unamuno and English Literature*, 22.

55. Miguel de Unamuno, "The Last Hero," *La Época* (May 14, 1896): 1. The title of this essay is originally in English. See also Thomas R. Franz, "La traducción de *The French Revolution*, factor importante en el aprendizaje literario de Unamuno," *Cuadernos de la cátedra Miguel de Unamuno* 27–28 (1983): 103–133.

56. Miguel de Unamuno to Juan Arzadun, December 12, 1900, in *The Private World*, 157.

57. Qtd. in Robles, "Unamuno," 15.

58. Ibid.

59. Qtd. in ibid., 16; Miguel de Unamuno, "Maese Pedro," in *Obras completas*, Escelicer ed., 1:1024. Robles is quoting a letter to Warner Fite from 1927.

60. Qtd. in Robles, "Unamuno," 19. On Carlyle's influence on Unamuno's *Niebla*, see Gayana Jurkevich, "Maese Pedro Unamuno: Carlyle and Narrative

Experiment in *Niebla*," *Canadian Review of Comparative Literature* 19, no. 4 (1992): 569–583.

61. See M. Thomas Inge, "Unamuno's Correspondence with North Americans: A Checklist," *Hispania* 53, no. 2 (May 1970): 277.

62. Miguel de Unamuno, "Los Hispanistas norteamericanas," in *Del patriotismo espiritual*, 58.

63. Ibid., 59.

64. Ibid., 61.

65. Miguel de Unamuno to Everett Ward Olmstead, April 7, 1917, in *Epistolario inédito*, 2:57.

66. Ibid., 2:58.

67. Miguel de Unamuno to Pedro de Múgica, January 2, 1898, in *The Private World*, 125.

68. Miguel de Unamuno, "The Spanish Spirit," *Bulletin of Hispanic Studies* 68, no. 3 (1991): 386.

69. Miguel de Unamuno, "Yanqueses," in *Obras completas*, Escelicer ed., 4:314.

70. This is not the same *Hispania* published by the American Association of Teachers of Spanish and Portuguese.

71. See Demetrios Basdekis, *Unamuno and Spanish Literature* (Berkeley: University of California Press, 1967), 20.

72. Miguel de Unamuno, *The Tragic Sense of Life*, trans. J. E. Crawford Flitch (New York: Dover, 1954), 125.

73. Ibid., xxxiii.

74. Ibid., xxxiv–xxxv.

75. Rodolfo Cardona, "Correspondencia entre el Profesor don Federico de Onís-Harriet de Onís (Wishnieff) y don Ramón del Valle-Inclán-Josefina Blanco," *Anales de la literatura española contemporánea* 32, no. 3 (2007): 132.

76. "Literary Gossip," *Athenæum* (September 24, 1920): 412.

77. Qtd. in David Callahan, "The Early Reception of Miguel de Unamuno in England, 1907–1939," *Modern Language Review* 91, no. 2 (April 1996): 384.

78. See T. S. Eliot, "Commentary," *New Criterion* 4, no. 2 (April 1926): 222. Eliot's Spanish correspondent for the journal, Antonio Marichalar, also discussed Unamuno throughout the 1920s and early 1930s.

79. Ezra Pound to Scofield Thayer, July 4–5, 1920, in *Pound, Thayer, Watson, and the "Dial": A Story in Letters*, ed. Walter Sutton (Gainesville: University of Florida Press, 1994), 62, 63.

80. Qtd. in Manuel García Blanco, "Unamuno and the United States," in *Unamuno Centennial Studies*, ed. Ramón Martínez López (Austin: University of Texas Press, 1966), 83.

81. Advertisement in the *Nation* 111, no. 2878 (August 28, 1920): 252. See Miguel de Unamuno, "The Cavern of Silence," *Dial* 76 (January 1924): 42–48.

82. See John Gould Fletcher, "Walt Whitman: I," *North American Review* 219, no. 820 (March 1924): 355–366.

83. Waldo Frank, *Virgin Spain: Scenes from the Spiritual Drama of a Great People* (New York: Boni and Liveright, 1926), 285, 282. Hereafter cited in the text as *VS*.

84. See Kirsten Silva Gruesz, "The Mercurial Space of 'Central' America: New Orleans, Honduras, and the Writing of the Banana Republic," in *Hemispheric American Studies*, ed. Caroline Levander and Robert S. Levine (New Brunswick, N.J.: Rutgers University Press, 2007), 140–165.

85. See also the profile of Unamuno by Andrés González-Blanco, "Miguel de Unamuno y sus dos últimas libros," *El Mercurio* (January 1914): 4.

86. Miguel de Unamuno, "Lengua y patria," in *Obras completas*, Aguado ed., 6:867.

87. Ibid., 6:868; "English-speaking folk" in original.

88. Miguel de Unamuno, "Sobre el imperialismo catalán," in *Obras completas*, Escelicer ed., 4:1305.

89. See M. Thomas Inge, "Miguel de Unamuno's 'Canciones' on American Literature," *Arlington Quarterly* 2 (Autumn 1969): 83; and M. Thomas Inge, "Unamuno's Correspondence with North Americans: A Checklist," *Hispania* 53, no. 2 (May 1970): 277–285.

90. Miguel de Unamuno, "Adamic Song," trans. Fernando Alegría, in *Walt Whitman and the World*, ed. Gay Wilson Allen and Ed Folsom (Iowa City: University of Iowa Press, 1995), 113. Alegría, García Blanco, and other Hispanophone scholars have documented Unamuno's citations of Whitman. Unamuno writes "poeta secular," invoking the sense of "secular" as both nonreligious and centuries-old. I thank Leslie Harkema for pointing me to this detail.

91. Miguel de Unamuno, "Abraham Lincoln y Walt Whitman," in *Obras completas*, Escelicer ed., 4:1411, 1409.

92. Walt Whitman, "The Spanish Element in Our Nationality," in *Complete Poetry and Collected Prose* (New York: Literary Classics of the United States/Viking, 1982), 1146, 1147. See also Walt Whitman, "Spain" (later titled "Spain, 1873–74"), in ibid., 591.

93. See Fernando Alegría, "Whitman in Spain and Latin America," in *Walt Whitman and the World*, 71–96.

94. Miguel de Unamuno, Poem 682, in *Cancionero*, 250.

95. Whitman, "Salut au Monde!", in *Complete Poetry*, 294.

96. Whitman, "Salut au Monde!", trans. Miguel de Unamuno, in *Obras completas*, 10 vols., ed. Ricardo Senabre (Madrid: Turner, 1995–2009), 5:1105.

97. See José Domínguez Búrdalo, "Del ser (o no ser) hispano: Unamuno frente a la negritud," *Modern Language Notes* 121 (2006): 322–342.

98. Sidney Lanier, "Sunrise," in *Select Poems of Sidney Lanier*, ed. Morgan Callaway Jr. (New York: Charles Scribner's Sons, 1895), 48.

99. Miguel de Unamuno, Poem 1616, in *Cancionero*, 539.

100. See Inge, "Miguel de Unamuno's 'Canciones,'" 83–97.

101. Qtd. in Manuel García Blanco, *América y Unamuno* (Madrid: Gredos, 1964), 410.

102. William Vaughn Moody, "Road-Hymn for the Start," in *The Poems and Plays of William Vaughn Moody*, vol. 1, intro. John M. Manly (Boston: Houghton Mifflin, 1912), 13.

103. Miguel de Unamuno, Poem 1295, in *Cancionero*, 428–429.

104. Miguel de Unamuno, Poem 1329, in *Cancionero*, 439. See Inge, "Miguel de Unamuno's 'Canciones,'" 245.

105. Unamuno's presence on the borders of the dominant narratives of modernism in cultural history is indicated by the fact that he is one of very few Spanish figures cited in Malcolm Bradbury and James McFarlane's famous timeline in their *Modernism: 1890–1930* (New York: Penguin, 1976).

106. See *La Gaceta Literaria* 78 (March 15, 1930).

107. "Unamuno Sees Europe 'Playing a Sly Game,'" *New York Times* (January 18, 1932): 8.

108. Qtd. in Callahan, "The Early Reception," 391. See also José Luis Mora García, "La recepción de Unamuno en lengua inglesa: un ejemplo: la revista *Hispania*," *Cuaderno gris* 6 (2002): 47–70.

5. Negro and *Negro*: Translating American Blackness in the Shadows of the Spanish Empire

1. W. E. B. Du Bois, "Looking Glass," *Crisis* 15, no. 3 (January 1918): 138; Du Bois points here to the "negro blood" of Cézanne too. See also Joseph F. Gould, "In Moslem Spain," *Crisis* 7, no. 6 (April 1914): 298–300. Du Bois's passage in the epigraph comes from "The Negro Mind Reaches Out," in *The New Negro*, ed. Alain Locke, intro. Arnold Rampersad (New York: Atheneum, 1992), 412–413. This is a slightly revised version of an essay Du Bois had published in *Foreign Affairs* in 1925.

2. Du Bois, "Negro Mind," 413.

3. Langston Hughes, "Hughes Bombed in Spain," in *The Collected Works of Langston Hughes*, ed. Arnold Rampersad, intro. Christopher C. De Santis, 16 vols. (Columbia: University of Missouri Press, 2002), 9:161.

4. Langston Hughes, "Hughes Finds Moors Being Used as Pawns by Fascists in Spain," in *Collected Works*, 165.

5. See Brent Hayes Edwards, *The Practice of Diaspora: Literature, Translation, and the Rise of Black Internationalism* (Cambridge, Mass.: Harvard University Press, 2003); Michelle Ann Stephens, *Black Empire: The Masculine Global Imaginary of Caribbean Intellectuals in the United States, 1914–1962* (Durham, N.C.: Duke University Press, 2005); Michel Fabre, *From Harlem to Paris: Black Writers in France, 1840–1980* (Urbana: University of Illinois Press, 1991); and Carrie Noland, *Voices of Negritude in Modernist Print: Aesthetic Subjectivity, Diaspora, and the Lyric Regime* (New York: Columbia University Press, 2015). Tyler Stovall and Robert Stepto laid important critical foundations here. The ideas of diaspora (in Edwards's work) and nation (in Stephens's) are invaluable but remain mostly in the background of this chapter.

6. See the essays in the recent collection *Paris, Capital of the Black Atlantic: Literature, Modernity, and Diaspora*, ed. Jeremy Braddock and Jonathan P. Eburne (Baltimore, Md.: Johns Hopkins University Press, 2013); and Tyler Stovall, *Paris Noir: African Americans in the City of Light* (Boston: Houghton Mifflin, 1996). The diasporic thought that I trace in this chapter, by contrast, rarely takes the Atlantic world as a unit of historical experience or cartography; Paul Gilroy's *The Black Atlantic: Modernity and Double Consciousness* (Cambridge, Mass.: Harvard University Press, 1993) is an important forerunner of the studies cited above and many others.

7. Google's Ngram viewer shows that "negro/a" saw sharp rises in use in the 1500s and 1600s in Spanish, then only small, sporadic use until a gradual, steady rise beginning in 1900. As the transfer of the term "negro" into English indicates, Iberian conceptions of racialized slavery strongly influenced slave practices in the United States. See James H. Sweet, "The Iberian Roots of American Racist Thought," *William and Mary Quarterly* 54 (1997): 143–166; Robin Blackburn, *The Making of New World Slavery: From the Baroque to the Modern, 1492–1800* (London: Verso, 1997); and Christopher Schmidt-Nowara, "Spanish Origins of American Empire: Hispanism, History, and Commemoration, 1898–1915," *International History Review* 30 (March 2008): 32–51. On the translation problems associated with "*negro*" between English and Spanish in general, see Vera M. Kutzinski, *The Worlds of Langston Hughes: Modernism and Translation in the Americas* (Ithaca, N.Y.: Cornell University Press, 2012), 4–5, 57.

8. *Raza* (race) is one of the most complex, diffuse, and fraught concepts in the Spanish language and has been used variously across history to signify biology, ideology, political and servile status, spirit, bloodlines and caste, ancestral heritage, language, geographic origins, Catholicism, and much more. On the universality of the "fusion" theory, see Joshua Goode, *Impurity of Blood: Defining Race in Spain, 1870–1930* (Baton Rouge: Louisiana State University Press, 2009), 1–19.

9. See Margaret R. Greer, Walter D. Mignolo, and Maureen Quilligan, introduction to *Rereading the Black Legend: The Discourses of Religious and Racial Difference in the Renaissance Empires*, ed. Margaret R. Greer, Walter D. Mignolo, and Maureen Quilligan (Chicago: University of Chicago Press, 2007), 1–15. See also Ania Loomba, "Race and the Possibilities of Comparative Critique," *New Literary History* 40, no. 3 (Summer 2009): 501–522.

10. Goode, *Impurity of Blood*, 25. This day is most commonly known as the Día de la Raza in the Americas and is also called the Fiesta Nacional de España and the Día de la Hispanidad in Spain.

11. See, for instance, [Anon.], "Ku Klux Klan," *Alrededor del Mundo* (November 7, 1921): 9. Another topic that I do not have the space to treat here is the way in which a U.S. notion of "whiteness" was imported into a country where it hardly had any purchase previously.

12. Qtd. in Magdeleine Paz, *Hermano negro*, trans. Juan Rejano (Madrid: Ediciones Hoy, 1931), 198. See below on variant translations.

13. The term "negro/a" in aesthetics had a residual history from Goya's *pinturas negras*, and artists around the turn of the twentieth century such as José Gutiérrez

Solana and Ignacio Zuloaga were associated—famously by Unamuno—with paintings of *España negra*. *España negra* also became the title of a travelogue coauthored by the Spaniard Darío de Regoyos and the Belgian Émile Verhaeren in 1899, and the term was invoked by Darío (see chapter 3).

14. See Emilio Carrere, "El Negro, Rey del Amor," *Flirt* 38 (October 26, 1922): 4.

15. The vanguardist Ramón Gómez de la Serna's collection *Seis falsas novelas* (Six fake novels, 1927) was a rare instance of Spanish "black writing," but it had more in common with the white-led fads in Paris than with New World (U.S. and Latin American) black writing that was being identified as *literatura negra*.

16. Jacquez Descleuze, "El arte literario francés," *La Revista Blanca* 4, no. 79 (September 1, 1926): 203.

17. [Anon.], "La literatura negra en los Estados Unidos," *Caras y Caretas* (March 4, 1926): 77. *Caras y Caretas* (Faces and masks) had a circulation exceeding 12,000 in Latin America and Spain. The citations of René Maran here and in other articles point to the influence of his winning the Prix Goncourt in 1921 and of his own article, "Le mouvement nègre-littéraire aux États-Unis" (1925), in the Hispanophone world.

18. [Anon.], *La Voz* (December 24, 1920): 5; Antonio Guardiola, "El hombre de goma," *La Libertad* (August 9, 1930): 4.

19. Antonio Marichalar, "Nota negra," in *Ensayos literarios*, ed. Domingo Ródenas de Moya (Madrid: Fundación Santander Central Hispano, 2002), 256.

20. Rafael Suárez Solis, "Brasas de ébano," *Crónica* (December 8, 1935): 12; Salvador Valverde, "El teatro negro en europa y su intérprete más famoso," *Nuevo Mundo* 39 (May 6, 1932).

21. Esteban Pavletich, "Un mensaje y un anuncio," *La Pluma* (Montevideo) 14 (April 1930): 13–16. This Latin American periodical saw Spanish circulation, too. Pavletich uses *"hermano negro"* for "darker brother" also.

22. Vicente Carreras, "Teatro negro en la ciudad de los blancos," *Mi Revista* (January 1, 1938).

23. Claude McKay [as "Claudio Mackay"], *Cock-tail negro*, trans. A. Rodríguez de León and R. R. Fernández-Andés (Madrid: Editorial Zeus/Ediciones Ulises, 1931), 34; hereafter cited in the text as C. The original line is from Claude McKay, *Home to Harlem*, intro. Wayne F. Cooper (Boston: Northeastern University Press, 1987), 29.

24. McKay, *Home to Harlem*, 134.

25. A separate consideration here is the terminology for sexual orientation, which I do not have the space to treat. The line in a cabaret song in McKay's novel that reads "It is a bulldycking woman and a faggotty man" is muted to "La mujer de la mujer y el hombre afeminado" ("A woman's woman and an effeminate man"). *Cock-tail negro*, 40.

26. An ad for *Cock-tail negro* in the *Heraldo de Madrid* (October 29, 1931): 10, listed it as the "middle course" in a feast of political literature, between César Arconada and Victoria Ocampo.

27. F. B., "Review of *Cock-tail negro* by Claude McKay, trans. A. Rodríguez de León and R. R. Fernández-Andes," *El Sol* (November 25, 1931): 6.

28. Adolfo Salazar, "Una novela negra: Claude McKay y el sionismo de color," *El Sol* (September 3, 1931): 2.

29. See José Francés, "La línea de color," *Nuevo Mundo* (August 11, 1933). Several years later, McKay's short story "Near-White" appeared in translation in Catalan as "Quasi Blanca" (1938). In a prologue, the translator, linguist, and writer Josep Miracle calls McKay a true "*negre*" from Harlem. Josep Miracle, preface to Claude McKay, *Quasi blanca*, trans. Josep Miracle (Barcelona: Biblioteca de la Rosa dels Vents, 1938), 5. The translation of this story struggles, as do the anthologies discussed below, to convey the full sense of "nigger": when a white character shouts "Damned buck nigger!", the translation only gives "Arri allà, el negre" ("Get outta here, you black!"), using the same Catalan word (*negre*) that means "black" without negative connotations (43).

30. Guillermo de Torre, "Literatura de color," *El Sol* (July 12, 1936): 5. As do other critics, Torre points also to the *jitanjáfora* of the Mexican writer Alfonso Reyes as having black roots.

31. Edwards, *The Practice of Diaspora*, 44. See also George Hutchinson, *The Harlem Renaissance in Black and White* (Cambridge, Mass.: Harvard University Press, 1995); and Jeremy Braddock, *Collecting as Modernist Practice* (Baltimore, Md.: Johns Hopkins University Press, 2012), 154–208. Anthologies of foreign writing had acquired a new vogue in Spain at the time, thanks to translator-editors such as Fernando Maristany and to editions such as *Antología de poetas orientales* (Barcelona: Editorial Cervantes, 1921); see Miguel Gallego Roca, *Poesía importada: Traducción poética y renovación literaria en España, 1909–1936* (Almería: Universidad de Almería, 1996), 3–27.

32. Cendrars's collection, perhaps most importantly, was translated into Spanish by Manuel Azaña for a press in Buenos Aires in 1930, just on the eve of his becoming prime minister of the new Second Republic. Sénghor's anthologies of African Francophone writing, especially after the Second World War, are valuable intertexts that I do not have the space to treat fully here.

33. Frank Andre Guridy, *Forging Diaspora: Afro-Cubans and African Americans in a World of Empire and Jim Crow* (Chapel Hill: University of North Carolina Press, 2010), 106; see 107–150 on these connections. See also Antonio López, *Unbecoming Blackness: The Diaspora Cultures of Afro-Cuban America* (New York: NYU Press, 2012).

34. See Jerome C. Branche, *Colonialism and Race in Luso-Hispanic Literature* (Columbia: University of Missouri Press, 2006), 171–173; Vera Kutzinski, *Sugar's Secrets: Race and the Erotics of Cuban Nationalism* (Charlottesville: University of Virginia Press, 1993), 155–159.

35. Victor de la Serna, "Poesía Negra: Harlem-Jesús María," *El Sol* (March 16, 1932): 6.

36. Ibid.

37. Federico García Lorca, "Play and Theory of the Duende," in *Deep Song and Other Prose*, ed. and trans. Christopher Maurer (New York: New Directions, 1980), 43.

38. Federico García Lorca, "A Poet in New York," in *Deep Song and Other Prose*, 93.

39. Federico García Lorca, "Dance of Death," in *Poet in New York*, trans. Pablo Medina and Mark Statman (New York: Grove, 2008), 41; italics in original.

40. Lorca, "A Poet in New York," in *Deep Song and Other Prose*, 101.

41. Federico García Lorca, "The King of Harlem," in *Poet in New York*, 26, 27.

42. Enrique Díez-Canedo, "Folklore y poesía," *El Sol* (April 20, 1935): 1.

43. Manuel Machado, "Prólogo," in Méndez Herrera, *Ébano al sol* (Madrid: Talleres Tipográficos Canarias, 1941), 8.

44. See José Luis Venegas, *The Sublime South: Andalusia, Orientalism, and the Making of Modern Spain* (forthcoming).

45. Guillermo Díaz-Plaja, "Review of Ballagas, *Antología de la poesía negra hispano-americana*," *El Sol* (January 31, 1936): 2.

46. Emilio Ballagas, *Antología de poesía negra hispano-americana* (Madrid: M. Aguilar, 1935), 180. Hereafter cited in the text as *A*.

47. Ballagas's glossary builds directly Fernando Ortiz's *Glosario de afronegrismos* (1924). On this and other anthologies, see Viviana Gelado, "Primitivismo y vanguardia: las antologías de 'poesía negra' hispanoamericana en las décadas del 30 y del 40," *Tinkuy* 13 (June 2010): 89–104. José Juan Arrom's important essay "La poesía afrocubana," *Revista Iberoamericana* 4, no. 8 (February 1942): 379–411, confirmed the Spanish origins of black writing that Ballagas posited.

48. Emilio Ballagas, *Mapa de la poesía negra americana* (Buenos Aires: Editorial Pleamar, 1946), 8, 9. Hereafter cited in the text as *M*.

49. Emilio Ballagas, "Situación de la poesía afroamericana," *Revista Cubana* 21 (January–December 1936): 51, 30.

50. In the anthology's glossary, local terms and idioms from across the Americas and references to Africa are all explained: *batey, baobab, bembón, congo, rag-time*. The glossary also asserts that northern Africa is white, sub-Saharan Africa is black. Pedroso's poem had already appeared identically in English, likely translated by Lloyd Mallan, in *New Directions No. 8* (Norfolk, Conn.: New Directions, 1944), 278–279.

51. José Sanz y Díaz, "Prólogo," *Lira negra: Selecciones afroamericanas y españolas* (Madrid: Aguilar, 1962), 11. Hereafter cited in the text as *L*.

52. V. F. Calverton, "The Growth of Negro Literature," in *Anthology of American Negro Literature*, ed. V. F. Calverton (New York: Modern Library, 1929), 4.

53. Ibid., 3.

54. Julio Gómez de la Serna, "Pórtico," in *Constelación negra: antología de la literatura negroamericana* (Barcelona: Aymá, 1942), 9. Hereafter cited in the text as P.

55. Kutzinski shows that several of Hughes's Spanish American translators used "hermano oscuro" for "darker brother" and that none used "más oscuro" until the 1950s; see *The Worlds of Langston Hughes*, 56–85, 276n90.

56. See ibid., 69. For a brief overview of Pereda Valdés's importance to Afro-Uruguayan culture and politics, see George Reid Andrews, *Blackness in the White*

Nation: A History of Afro-Uruguay (Chapel Hill: University of North Carolina Press, 2010), 99–102.

57. Ildefonso Pereda Valdés, introduction to *Antología de la poesía negra americana* (Santiago de Chile: Ediciones Ercilla, 1936), 9. Hereafter cited in the text as *AP*.

58. For example, Juan Felipe Toruño's *Poesía negra: ensayo y antología* (1953) reinforced the genealogy of black writing that the anthologies above had promulgated.

59. Vera M. Kutzinski's *The Worlds of Langston Hughes* is the most comprehensive of many treatments of this topic. See also *Langston Hughes in the Hispanic World and Haiti*, ed. Edward J. Mullen (Hamden, Conn.: Archon, 1977); Monica Kaup, "'Our America' That Is Not One: Transnational Black Atlantic Disclosures in Nicolás Guillén and Langston Hughes," *Discourse* 22, no. 3 (Fall 2000): 87–113; William D. Scott, "*Motivos* of Translation: Nicolás Guillén and Langston Hughes," *CR: The New Centennial Review* 5, no. 2 (Fall 2005): 35–71; and John Patrick Leary, "Havana Reads the Harlem Renaissance: Mistranslation and the Dialectics of Transnational American Literature," *Comparative Literature Studies* 47, no. 2 (2010): 133–158. Two essays that remain overlooked in this scholarship are Alain Locke, "The Negro in the Three Americas," *Journal of Negro Education* 13, no. 1 (Winter 1944): 7–18; and Dorothy Schons, "Negro Poetry in the Americas," *Hispania* 25, no. 3 (October 1942): 309–319. See also Edward J. Mullen, "The Emergence of Afro-Hispanic Poetry: Some Notes on Canon Formation," *Hispanic Review* 56, no. 4 (Fall 1988): 435–453.

60. Sebastian Balfour sees these wars and the Spanish Civil War as one continuous "epic" story in Spanish political history: see his *Deadly Embrace: Morocco and the Road to the Spanish Civil War* (Oxford: Oxford University Press, 2002), x.

61. Susan Martin Márquez, *Disorientations: Spanish Colonialism in Africa and the Performance of Identity* (New Haven, Conn.: Yale University Press, 2008), 252, 220. See also Balfour, *Deadly Embrace*; and Paul Preston, *The Spanish Holocaust: Inquisition and Extermination in Twentieth-Century Spain* (New York: Norton, 2012). Precise numbers are hard to find; estimates range from 30,000 to 78,000.

62. Qtd. in Hugh Thomas, *The Spanish Civil War* (New York: Modern Library, 2001), 403.

63. Preston, *The Spanish Holocaust*, 308.

64. Qtd. in ibid., 46.

65. Langston Hughes, "Negroes in Spain," in *Collected Works*, 156. For a broader view of the internationalist black left of this era, see the many works of Ernest Allen Jr., Robin D. G. Kelley, Winston James, William Maxwell, Barbara Foley, and Cary Nelson, along with those cited above.

66. Langston Hughes, "Soldiers from Many Lands United in Spanish Fight," in *Collected Works*, 181.

67. Hughes, "Negroes in Spain," in *Collected Works*, 156.

68. Ibid., 157.

69. Langston Hughes, *I Wonder as I Wander: An Autobiographical Journey* (New York: Rinehart, 1956), 349; hereafter cited in the text as *W*.

70. Hughes, "Hughes Finds Moors," in *Collected Works*, 161. See also Isabel Soto "'I Knew That Spain Once Belonged to the Moors': Langston Hughes, Race, and the Spanish Civil War," *Research in African Literatures* 45, no. 3 (Fall 2014): 130–146. V. B. Spratlin, the chair of Romance languages at Howard University for several decades, published extensively on the black Spanish professor of the 1500s Juan Latino; see his *Juan Latino: Slave and Humanist* (New York: Spinner, 1938).

71. Langston Hughes, "St. Louis Man's Spanish Helped Him Cheat Death," in *Collected Works*, 190.

72. See Langston Hughes, "'Organ Grinder's Swing' Heard Above Gunfire in Spain," in *Collected Works*, 167.

73. Ibid., 166, 168. Hughes called Guillén a "colored poet from Havana," praises Ballagas's anthologies, and notes that Canary Island Spaniards are partially African too (158).

74. Langston Hughes, "Around the Clock in Madrid: Daily Life in a Besieged City," in *Collected Works*, 200.

75. Langston Hughes, "Letter from Spain," in *The Collected Poems of Langston Hughes*, ed. Arnold Rampersad (New York: Random House, 1995), 201. The Moor here, many critics have noted, faintly echoes the tropes of the Moor's last sigh. Around eighty black Americans fought for the Loyalists; see Robin D. G. Kelley, *Race Rebels: Culture, Politics, and the Black Working Class* (New York: Free Press/Simon & Schuster, 1996), 123–158. See also *African Americans in the Spanish Civil War: "This Ain't Ethiopia but It'll Do,"* ed. Collum Danny Duncan (New York: G. K. Hall, 1992). Many on the black left in the United States saw the Spanish Civil War as an extension of the overtly racist Abyssinian War.

76. Hughes, "Letter from Spain," 201–202.

77. Carmen T. Sotomayor Blázquez, "El moro traidor, el moro engañado: variantes del estereotipo en el Romancero republicano," *Anaquel de Estudios Árabes* 16 (2005): 233–249; see also María Rosa de Madariaga, *Los moros que trajo Franco . . .* (Barcelona: Martínez Roca, 2002); and Caroline Brothers, *War and Photography: A Cultural History* (New York: Routledge, 1997), 58–75.

78. Qtd. in Sotomayor Blázquez, "El moro traidor," 240.

79. See Evelyn Scaramella, "Translating the Spanish Civil War: Langston Hughes's Transnational Poetics," *Massachusetts Review* 55, no. 2 (Summer 2014): 177–188.

80. Alberti [Antonio García Luque], "El moro fugado," in *Romancero de la guerra civil* (Madrid: Ministerio de Instrucción Pública y Bellas Artes, 1936), 51. The Republicans tried in vain to establish a Hispano-Moroccan Anti-Fascist Association.

81. See *El Mono Azul* 2, no. 29 (August 19, 1938): 1.

82. See Jonathan Mayhew, *Apocryphal Lorca: Translation, Parody, Kitsch* (Chicago: University of Chicago Press, 2009), 55–59. See also Michelle Woods and Sarah Wyman, "Aesthetic Radicalism: Langston Hughes's Lost Translation of Federico García Lorca's *Bodas de sangre / Blood Wedding*," *Modern Drama* 57, no. 4 (2014): 469–492.

83. Richard Wright, *Pagan Spain* (New York: Harper, 1957), 1. Hereafter cited in text as *PS*.

84. Wright also bought a group of letters from Spanish prostitutes that they had received from American sailors, several of them black. These letters were included in the French edition of *Pagan Spain* but not the American edition. See M. Lynn Weiss, "*Para Usted*: Richard Wright's *Pagan Spain*," in *The Black Columbiad: Defining Moments in African American Literature and Culture*, ed. Werner Sollors and Maria Diedrich (Cambridge, Mass.: Harvard University Press, 1994), 215n14.

85. Specifically, the *Formación política: lecciones para las flechas*, produced by the Falangists.

86. María DeGuzmán, *Spain's Long Shadow: The Black Legend, Off-Whiteness, and Anglo-American Empire* (Minneapolis: University of Minnesota Press, 2005), 232.

87. On the connections to Myrdal, see Guy Reynolds, "'Sketches of Spain': Richard Wright's *Pagan Spain* and African-American Representations of the Hispanic," *Journal of American Studies* 34, no. 3 (2000): 487–502. Claude McKay and Nella Larsen both spent time in Spain, too, but both trips were rather inconsequential.

88. Wright appears to have composed this passage, and thus used this term, before Norman Mailer made it famous with his essay "The White Negro" (1957).

89. See María Menocal, *The Ornament of the World: How Muslims, Jews, and Christians Created a Culture of Tolerance in Medieval Spain* (Boston: Little, Brown, 2002).

6. "Spanish Is a Language Tu": Hemingway's Cubist Spanglish and Its Legacies

1. Ernest Hemingway to Bernard Berenson, February 2, 1954, in *Selected Letters*, ed. Carlos Baker (New York: Scribner, 1981), 828.

2. Edmund Wilson, "Review of *For Whom the Bell Tolls*," in *Hemingway: The Critical Heritage*, ed. Jeffrey Meyers (Boston: Routledge and Kegan Paul, 1982), 322.

3. Ernest Hemingway, *By-Line Ernest Hemingway: Selected Articles and Dispatches of Four Decades*, ed. William White (New York: Scribner, 1967), 216.

4. See Christine Froula, "The Beauties of Mistranslation: On Pound's English After Cathay," in *Ezra Pound and China*, ed. Zhaoming Qian (Ann Arbor: University of Michigan Press, 2003), 49–71. In keeping with the idea that he saw this mode of writing as *more* faithful, Hemingway commented that *War and Peace* was "the most wonderful damn book and clearly and simply written that I've ever read." Ernest Hemingway to Morley Callaghan, October 22, 1925, in *The Letters of Ernest Hemingway, Volume 2: 1923–1925*, ed. Sandra Whipple Spanier et al. (Cambridge: Cambridge University Press, 2013), 405. One of the few critics

to address Hemingway and translation, though in very different terms, is Mimi Reisel Gladstein, "Bilingual Wordplay: Variations on a Theme in Hemingway and Steinbeck," *Hemingway Review* 26, no. 1 (2006): 81–95. See also Wolfgang E. H. Rudat, "Hemingway's Rabbit: Slips of the Tongue and Other Linguistic Games in *For Whom the Bell Tolls*," *Hemingway Review* 10, no. 1 (Fall 1990): 34–51. Apter and Spivak in particular have emphasized the importance of untranslatability and heterogeneity, thus taking a line of thought that one could follow from Walter Benjamin through Jacques Derrida, George Steiner, and Homi Bhabha and bringing it to bear on a historical negligence of translation in comparative literature that is most often associated with René Wellek. Lawrence Venuti recently has voiced his skepticism toward theories of untranslatability; see "Hijacking Translation," forthcoming in *boundary 2*. I am skeptical too, but I am using terms like "mistranslation" descriptively, not evaluatively, to note deviations from what were established norms and, in many cases, from preexisting translations of the same texts. To my mind, this obviates the danger of infinite regression in studies of translation when one refuses to accept at least a working sense of "translation" before revising or deconstructing it.

5. Ernest Hemingway, *For Whom the Bell Tolls* (New York: Scribner, 1995), 149, 171; hereafter cited in the text as *FW*. See also Alex Vernon, *Hemingway's Second War: Bearing Witness to the Spanish Civil War* (Iowa City: University of Iowa Press, 2011), 213.

6. Ernest Hemingway to Konstantin Simonov, June 20, 1946, in *Selected Letters*, 609. Kashkin was the central figure in the creation of what Alexander Burak calls the "cult of Hemingway": see his *"The Other" in Translation: A Case for Comparative Translation Studies* (Bloomington, Ind.: Slavica, 2013), 15. He published a biography of Hemingway in 1966 and translated many Anglophone authors. See Elizabetha Levin, "In Their Time: The Riddle Behind the Epistolary Friendship Between Ernest Hemingway and Ivan Kashkin," *Hemingway Review* 32, no. 2 (Spring 2013): 95–108.

7. Scott St. Pierre, "Bent Hemingway: Straightness, Sexuality, Style," *GLQ: A Journal of Lesbian and Gay Studies* 16, no. 3 (2010): 373, italics in original. See also Walter Benn Michaels, *Our America: Nativism, Modernism, and Pluralism* (Chapel Hill, N.C.: Duke University Press, 1995), 26–29, 73–74; and Daniel Worden, *Masculine Style: The American West and Literary Modernism* (New York: Palgrave Macmillan, 2011), 107–125.

8. Hemingway creates a version of what contemporary linguists call "interference," or the use of one language's elements when speaking another. We could theoretically posit a transhistorical speaking subject behind the dialogue in the novel, but the text does not support such a reading.

9. Qtd. in Allen Josephs, *For Whom the Bell Tolls: Ernest Hemingway's Undiscovered Country* (New York: Twayne, 1994), 22.

10. Qtd. in ibid., 155. Interested readers may hear his strained Spanish in this interview with Cuban television: http://www.youtube.com/watch?v=WZmjoE6y168.

11. Ernest Hemingway to Clarence Hemingway, November 6, 1923, in *Letters*, 2:72; Ernest Hemingway to William B. Smith Jr., February 17, 1925, in *Letters*, 2:252; Ernest Hemingway to Pound, November 10, 1924, in *Letters*, 2:179.

12. See Jeffrey Herlihy-Mera, "'He Was a Sort of Joke, In Fact': Ernest Hemingway in Spain," *Hemingway Review* 31, no. 2 (Spring 2012): 90.

13. Ernest Hemingway to Edmund Wilson, November 8, 1952, in *Selected Letters*, 794.

14. Ernest Hemingway to Charles Scribner, July 9–10, 1950, in *Selected Letters*, 704.

15. Ernest Hemingway, *Death in the Afternoon* (New York: Scribner, 1960), 81. Bullfighting terms make up the majority of the long "Explanatory Glossary." Hemingway's work as a translator in compiling the glossary is largely self-romanticizing.

16. See Michael North, *The Dialect of Modernism: Race, Language, and Twentieth-Century Literature* (New York: Oxford University Press, 1994).

17. Ernest Hemingway to Waldo Peirce, November 1–12, 1931, in *Selected Letters*, 343.

18. Ernest Hemingway to Arnold Gingrich, April 3, 1933, in *Selected Letters*, 385.

19. Ernest Hemingway, *The Sun Also Rises* (New York: Scribner, 2006), 158–159. Hereafter cited in the text as *S*.

20. See Mark Cirino, "'You Don't Know the Italian Language Well Enough': The Bilingual Dialogue of *A Farewell to Arms*," *Hemingway Review* 25, no. 1 (2005): 43–62.

21. Ernest Hemingway, "A Clean, Well-Lighted Place," in *The Short Stories of Ernest Hemingway* (New York: Scribner's Sons, 1953), 17.

22. Linguists debate the precise timing because it varied across contexts, and, in fact, "thou" has been retained in certain parts of northern England and southern Scotland and in some religious language.

23. Bruce Fleming is an exception; he correctly notes that Hemingway's "thou" is "a deformation (and a willful one at that) of the normal Spanish 'eres' and 'estás.'" Bruce Fleming, "Writing in Pidgin: Language in *For Whom The Bell Tolls*," *Dutch Quarterly Review of Anglo American Letters* 15, no. 2 (1985): 268.

24. Edmundo Desnoes, "Lo español en Hemingway," *Lunes de Revolución* 118 (August 14, 1961): 15. I thank Harris Feinsod for pointing me to this fascinating special issue.

25. The difference here depends on whether he is speaking with what is known in Spanish as *leísmo*, a dialectal mode of Iberian grammar that substitutes *le* for *lo / la*.

26. See Robert Van Gelder, "Ernest Hemingway Talks of Work and War," *New York Times* (August 11, 1940).

27. One passage reads, "'*Ya lo veo*,' he said in Spanish. 'I have seen him'" (*For Whom the Bell Tolls*, 36). Here, it is already clear that the original is in Spanish—all of the dialogue is presumed to be anyway—and Robert's repetition is unnecessary for a Hispanophone interlocutor and shifts the tense in the translation. Elsewhere, the translation of "mucho caballo" early in the novel is "much horse," while later, we find, "'*Eras mucho caballo*,' he said, meaning, 'Thou wert plenty of horse'"; later still, it is "much horse" again (313).

28. *A Farewell to Arms* sold over one hundred thousand copies, but none of Hemingway's works from the 1930s reached over 41,000 in sales.

29. See Thomas E. Gould, "'A Tiny Operation with Great Effect': Authorial Revision and Editorial Emasculation in the Manuscript of Hemingway's *For Whom the Bell Tolls*," in *Blowing the Bridge: Essays on Hemingway and "For Whom the Bell Tolls,"* ed. Rena Sanderson (New York: Greenwood, 1992), 67–81.

30. It is tempting to search for what might be a recovered Spanish "original" of the dialogue in *For Whom the Bell Tolls* as it was translated "back" into Spanish, as least as I am conceiving it. Despite various censorial bans and restrictions during the Franco regime, *For Whom the Bell Tolls* has appeared in six different Spanish editions (five Castilian, one Catalan) in just seventy years. The first five editions, however, simply render the dialogue in everyday, idiomatic Spanish, and instances of "obscenity" or "unprintable" are usually omitted. The popular 1968 version translated by Lola de Aguado employs a little-used Spanish verb—*tutear*, "to address as *tú*"—to denote switches to the familiar form of address. The most recent translation, by Miguel Temprano García in 2011, prints the word "[impublicable]" in brackets to indicate "[unpublishable]," as if it has been excised by a force beyond the narrator. Similarly, he brackets "[obscenidad]" for "obscenity," thus drawing attention to the substitution. See Ernest Hemingway, *Por quién doblan las campanas*, trans. Aguado (Barcelona: Planeta, 1968); and Ernest Hemingway, *Por quién doblan las campanas*, trans. Temprano García (Barcelona: Lumen, 2011).

31. In the opening pages of the novel, the character Golz is called, in phoneticized speech by a native Spanish speaker, "Hotze" and then "Comrade Heneral Khotze" (*For Whom the Bell Tolls*, 7). The echo of "Kurtz" is not far away, which in turn points to the sonic proximity of "Comrade" to "Conrad."

32. Qtd. in Dwight Macdonald, "Review of *For Whom the Bell Tolls*," in *Hemingway: The Critical Heritage*, 326.

33. V. S. Pritchett, "Review of *For Whom the Bell Tolls*," in *Hemingway: The Critical Heritage*, 348.

34. Carlos Baker, *Hemingway: The Writer as Artist* (Princeton, N.J.: Princeton University Press, 1972), 249n39.

35. Howard Mumford Jones, "Review of *For Whom the Bells Tolls*," in *Hemingway: The Critical Heritage*, 318.

36. Gilbert Highet, "Thou Tellest Me, Comrade," *Nation* 152 (March 1, 1941): 242.

37. See Arturo Barea, "Not Spain But Hemingway," in *The Literary Reputation of Ernest Hemingway in Europe*, ed. Roger Asselineau (Paris: Lettres Modernes, 1965), 208–214.

38. See Fleming, "Writing in Pidgin"; Milton M. Azevedo, "Shadows of a Literary Dialect: *For Whom the Bell Tolls* in Five Romance Languages," *Hemingway Review* 20, no. 1 (2000): 30–48; and Edward Fenimore, "English and Spanish in *For Whom the Bell Tolls*," *ELH* 10, no. 1 (March 1943): 73–86.

39. Ernest Hemingway to Ivan Kashkin, March 23, 1939, in *Selected Letters*, 480.

40. Ernest Hemingway to Harry Sylvester, February 5, 1937, in *Selected Letters*, 456; Ernest Hemingway to Maxwell Perkins, August 26, 1940, in *Selected Letters*, 515. See also Michael S. Reynolds, *Hemingway: The 1930s* (New York: Norton, 1997), 300.

41. One of the few studies to address this topic, regarding prose, is Wylie Sypher, "Gide's Cubist Novel," *Kenyon Review* 11, no. 2 (Spring 1949): 291–309.

42. Ernest Hemingway, *A Moveable Feast* (New York: Charles Scribner's Sons, 1964), 13.

43. For a representative selection of treatments and topics, see the essays in *Hemingway Repossessed*, ed. Kenneth Rosen (Westport, Conn.: Praeger, 1994); and Emily Stipes Watts, *Ernest Hemingway and the Arts* (Urbana: University of Illinois Press, 1971). For these critics, however, Hemingway's interest in art, especially by the time of *For Whom the Bell Tolls*, is almost purely formal—landscapes, colors, abstraction.

44. Worden, *Masculine Style*, 116–118.

45. Joseph Frank, "Spatial Form in Modern Literature," *Sewanee Review* 53, no. 2 (Spring 1945): 227.

46. Ernest Hemingway to Harvey Breit, November 14, 1955, in *Selected Letters*, 850.

47. See Joshua L. Miller, *Accented America: The Cultural Politics of Multilingual Modernism* (New York: Oxford University Press, 2011); and Christopher GoGwilt, *The Passage of Literature: Genealogies of Modernism in Conrad, Rhys, and Pramoedya* (New York: Oxford University Press, 2011).

48. Emily Apter, *The Translation Zone: A New Comparative Literature* (Princeton, N.J.: Princeton University Press, 2006), 210.

49. See Roman Jakobson, "On the Linguistic Aspects of Translation," in *Word and Language* (Paris: Mouton, 1971), 261–266.

50. Gilles Deleuze and Claire Parnet, *Dialogues*, trans. Hugh Tomlinson and Barbara Habberjam (New York: Columbia University Press, 1987), 4–5.

51. See also Evelyn Nien-Ming Ch'ien, *Weird English* (Cambridge, Mass.: Harvard University Press, 2004).

52. In order to focus on the United States and Spain, I am skipping over the bilingual writing of El Movimiento and of the Boom writers, whose fusions of English and Spanish have been explored amply by other critics; the best overview of this topic remains James Irby's "The Structure of the Stories of Jorge Luis Borges" (Ph.D. Dissertation, U of Michigan, 1962).

53. See Regina Galasso, "The Mission of *La Prensa*: Informing a Layout of the Literature of Hispanic New York," *Hispania* 95, no. 2 (June 2012): 189–200; María DeGuzmán, *Spain's Long Shadow: The Black Legend, Off-Whiteness, and Anglo-American Empire* (Minneapolis: University of Minnesota Press, 2005), 243–291.

54. Felipe Alfau, *Chromos* (Elmwood Park, Ill.: Dalkey Archive, 1990), 13. Hereafter cited in the text as *C*.

55. Ilan Stavans, "A Conversation with Felipe Alfau," http://www.dalkeyarchive.com/a-conversation-with-felipe-alfau-by-ilan-stavans/.

56. Jill Adams, "Felipe Alfau: A Retrospective," *Barcelona Review* 12 (1999), http://www.barcelonareview.com/12/e_fa_ret1.htm.

57. Malcolm Lowry, *Under the Volcano* (New York: Harper, 2007), 95; ellipsis in original. Hereafter cited in the text as *U*.

58. Stephen Spender argued that Hugh is a "caricature" of figures like John Cornford, the communist poet who was killed early in the war in Spain; introduction to Lowry, *Under the Volcano*, xxii.

59. In addition to Frederick Asals's guide, *The Making of Malcolm Lowry's* Under the Volcano (Athens: University of Georgia Press, 1997), the website "*Under the Volcano*: A Hypertextual Companion" provides excellent resources on this and other points of revision in the novel: http://www.otago.ac.nz/englishlinguistics/english/lowry/index.html. See also Patrick A. McCarthy, "Modernism's Swansong: Malcolm Lowry's *Under the Volcano*," in *A Companion to the British and Irish Novel, 1945–2000*, ed. Brian A. Shaffer (Malden, Mass.: Blackwell, 2005), 266–277.

60. Malcolm Lowry to Albert Erskine, June 22, 1946, in *Sursum corda!: The Collected Letters of Malcolm Lowry*, ed. Sherrill E. Grace (Toronto: University of Toronto Press, 1995), 1:586.

61. The sign then became the source of a pun for Lowry as he reread *Ulysses*: "Le gusta este Dujardin? Why is it Joyce?" Lowry to Erskine, May 4, 1952, in *Sursum corda!*, 1:581.

62. Ben Lerner, *Leaving the Atocha Station* (Minneapolis, Minn.: Coffee House, 2011), 19. Hereafter cited in the text as *L*. See Rebecca L. Walkowitz's reading of this text in *Born Translated: The Contemporary Novel in an Age of World Literature* (New York: Columbia University Press, 2015), 40–43.

Conclusion: Worlds Between Languages—The Spanglish *Quixote*

1. The bibliography of commentaries on Spanglish has become extensive. Paz and Roberto González Echeverría are two of the more prominent opponents; in differing ways, Gloria Anzaldúa and Tino Villanueva are proponents. For an overview and a taxonomy of varieties of Spanglish, see Roberto Maduro, "Spanglish and Its Influence on American English," http://198.178.194.52:8080/literature/Spanglish.htm.

2. Ilan Stavans, introduction to *Sentimental Songs/La poesía cursi*, trans. Ilan Stavans (Elmwood Park, Ill.: Dalkey Archive, 1992), xi.

3. Jorge Luis Borges, "Pierre Menard: Author of the *Quixote*," in *Labyrinths: Selected Stories and Other Writings*, ed. Donald A. Yates and James E. Irby (New York: New Directions, 1964), 40.

4. Ibid., 41.

5. See also Ilan Stavans's historical account of translations of *Don Quixote* into English, in "One Master, Many Cervantes: *Don Quixote* in Translation," *Humanities: The Magazine of the National Endowment for the Humanities* 29, no. 5

(September/October 2008), http://www.neh.gov/news/humanities/2008-09/OneMaster.html.

6. The common English word order of *adjective-noun* works in Spanish too, for instance, whereas the common Spanish word order of *noun-adjective* is ungrammatical in English.

7. These and all subsequent quotations are from Ilan Stavans, "'Spanglish: El heart en la palabra': *Don Quixote de La Mancha*, Miguel de Cervantes, First Parte, Chapter Uno, Transladado al *Spanglish* por Ilán Stavans," *Cuadernos Cervantes* 7, no. 36 (2001), http://www.cuadernoscervantes.com/art_40_quixote.html.

8. See Lourdes Torres, "*Don Quixote* in Spanglish: *Traducttore, traditore?*" *Romance Quarterly* 52, no. 4 (2005): 333. Torres has intentionally misspelled "*traducttore*" in his essay's title.

9. The entry for *ladino* in the dictionary of the Real Academia Española articulates this multiplicity: http://buscon.rae.es/drae/srv/search?val=ladino.

10. Ilan Stavans, *On Borrowed Words: A Memoir of Language* (New York: Penguin, 2002), 73.

11. See ibid., 191.

12. Miguel de Cervantes, *Don Quixote*, trans. Edith Grossman (New York: Harper, 2005), 873.

INDEX

Adams, Henry, 16
"Against American Literature" (Dos Passos), 8, 76, 83–85, 98
Alberti, Rafael, 110, 183–184, 194–195
Alfau, Felipe, 2, 12, 219–220; *Chromos*, 220–223
Altamira, Rafael, 23–24. See also *hispanismo*
American Association of Teachers of Spanish, 25–26
American Literature in Spain (Ferguson), 29–30
American studies, 2–4, 14; exceptionalism of, 4–6, 14–21; and the Franco regime, 31–32; institutionalization of, 6; and *literatura negra*, 10, 12, 169–170; masculinism of, 13; as a monocultural project, 18–19, 28; reciprocity with Hispanism, 23–25, 29–31; rise in Spain, 28–29; and translation, 7–9, 30; and Unamuno, 139–140; and U.S. empire, 15–16; and Williams, 19. See also comparative literature; Hispanism; modernist studies; *modernismo*; postcolonial studies; translation studies; transnational literary studies
anarchism, in Spain: and Darío, 117–118; and Dos Passos, 87–89, 95–98, 104; and Unamuno, 145
Anderson, Sherwood, 105, 133, 205
Anglophone modernism: and Jiménez, 110–111, 119, 122, 130, 134–136; and Marichalar, 31, 173–174; and *modernismo*, 112–114; and nativist literary historiography, 13, 19; and Pound, 38. See also American studies; comparative literature; Hispanism; *modernismo*
Anglo-Saxon Century, The (John Randolph Dos Passos), 80–83
Anthologie nègre (Cendrars), 177

288   Index

Antología de la poesía negra americana (Pereda Valdés), 189–190
Antología de poesía negra hispano-americana (Ballagas), 180–182
Apter, Emily, 218, 261n3
Arac, Jonathan, 93, 242n34, 259n52
Araquistaín, Luis, on American literature, 31
Arnold, Matthew, and literary historiography, 2, 33
Azorín, and the Generation of '98, 22
Azul... (Darío), 116, 124

Ballagas, Emilio, 2; *Antología de poesía negra hispano-americana*, 180–182; *Cuaderno de poesía negra*, 180; *Mapa de la poesía negra americana*, 182–183; and *negrismo*, 178. See also *literatura negra*; New Negro, the
Baroja, Pío, 1, 132; attitude toward Spanish letters, 33; Dos Passos's profile of, 89–90, 97–98; English translation of, 27; and the Generation of '98, 22; influence on Hemingway, 203
Baudelaire, Charles: and Darío, 116; and José de Espronceda, 135; and modernism/o, 131; and *modernismo*, 112, 114
Beasley, Rebecca, 46, 242n35
Bécquer, Gustavo Adolfo, 119, 131–132
Benavente, Jacinto, Dos Passos's profile of, 99–100
Benjamin, Walter, on translation, 2–3, 280n4
Bennett, Gwendolyn, 186, 188, 189
Berman, Antoine, 137
Bivar, Rodrigo Díaz de. *See* El Cid (Rodrigo Díaz de Bivar)
Black Legend, the: and Alfau, 222; and Hay, 17–18; and Juderías, 22, 172; and nativist literary historiography,

14; and Wright, 196–197. *See also* Spanish-American War
Blasco, Eusebio, on *modernismo*, 115
Blasco Ibáñez, Vicente, 5; Dos Passos's profile of, 90, 98–99; English translations of, 27
Borges, Jorge Luis, 228–229
Brooks, Van Wyck, 5, 83
Bush, Ronald, 63

Călinescu, Matei, 115
Calverton, V. F., 187
Campos de Castilla (Machado), 101–103
Camprubí Aymar, Zenobia, 13, 120–121
Cantos (Pound), 71–75
Carpentier, Alejo, 181, 183, 186
Castilianism, 239n17; and *casticismo*, 100, 142; and French symbolism, 111; and the Generation of '98, 23; and Hemingway, 215; and Juan de Mena, 67; and Machado, 99; and Menéndez Pidal, 144; and *modernismo*, 118; and the *Poema del Cid*, 54–56; and Stavans, 228, 230, 232–234; and Unamuno, 139, 141–142, 144–146, 148, 150, 152, 158; in U.S. language education, 26. See also Disaster, the; Hispanism; *modernismo*; Reconquista
Castro, Américo, 27
Cendrars, Blaise, 104, 177
Cervantes, Miguel de, 22; and Alfau, 220, 222; and Ballagas, 183; and Dos Passos, 79, 86–87, 94–96; and Frank, 157; and Hughes, 195; and Jiménez, 123; and Lowry, 223; and Pound, 54, 69–70; and Unamuno, 143, 153. See also *Don Quixote* (Cervantes)
Chromos (Alfau), 220–223
City Block (Frank), 103–104

Cómo se hace una novela (Unamuno), 148–49
comparative literature: and exceptionalism, 4, 59; and Franco's 1939 victory, 31; and *hispanismo*, 24–25; and literary historiography of the early twentieth century, 1; and *modernismo*, 113; and philology, 38, 46; and Pound, 3, 38, 40, 46, 48, 61; and translation, 7, 138; and U.S. empire, 15. *See also* American studies; Hispanism; philology; translation studies; transnational literary studies
Concept of Modernism, The (Eysteinsson), 113
"The Conquest of the United States by Spain" (Sumner), 18
Constelación negra (Gómez de la Serna), 187
"Coplas por la muerte de su padre Don Rodrigo" (Manrique), 95
Counter-Reformation, 22, 70
cosmopolitanism: and exceptionalism, 4, 19–20; and modernism/o, 131–132; and *modernismo*, 112–113, 130; and Spanish traditionalism, 117
Cuaderno de poesía negra (Ballagas), 180
Cullen, Countee, 173, 181, 186, 188; and Ballagas, 183–184; and Pereda Valdés, 190
Cuban War of Independence, 17–18
cubism, 14, 202, 214, 216. *See also* Hemingway, Ernest; Picasso, Pablo; Stein, Gertrude

Darío, Rubén, 5, 90, 110; *Azul . . .*, 116, 124; and *modernismo*, 112, 114–119, 121, 130, 261n5
DeGuzmán, María, 13, 196–197
Deleuze, Gilles, on literary bilingualism, 218

Der Schwarze Dekameron (Frobenius), 177
Díaz-Plaja, Guillermo, 180, 265n62
Dickinson, Emily: and modernism/o, 133; and Sor Juana Inés de la Cruz, 132; translation of by Jiménez and Camprubí, 120, 125, 128
Díez-Canedo, Enrique, on American poetry, 30
Diary of a Newlywed Poet (Jiménez), 3–4, 109–111, 121–130, 133
Disaster, the (1898), 11; and the Disaster at Annual, 191; and the Generation of '98, 22, 78, 85, 97; and Spanish thinking about blackness, 171–72. *See also* Castilianism; Hispanism; *hispanismo*; Spanish-American War
Don Quixote (Cervantes): and "Pierre Menard, Author of the Quixote" (Borges), 228–229; against *Robinson Crusoe*, 21; Spanglish translation of, 227–235. *See also* Borges, Jorge Luis; Castilianism; Cervantes, Miguel de; *Don Quixote* (Welles); Generation of '98; Stavans, Ilan
Don Quixote (Welles), 229
Dos Passos, John, 1–2, 9, 15, 75; "Against American Literature," 8, 76, 83–85, 98; critique of Galdós and Blasco Ibáñez, 93; and *Don Quixote*, 86; early travels to Spain, 85–87; *Fortune Heights*, 105; on Germany, 13; as a Hispanist, 11–12, 76–79, 87–89; *Manhattan Transfer*, 79–80, 103–104; 1919 trip to Spain, 94; 1933 trip to Spain, 105–106; *A Pushcart at the Curb*, 79, 101–104; repudiation of leftism, 80, 106; *Rosinante to the Road Again*, 1, 79, 94–98, 99–101; *Three Soldiers*, 94, 103; translation of Blaise Cendrars, 104–105;

Dos Passos, John (*continued*)
  translation of Manuel Maples Arce, 104; *U.S.A.* trilogy, 76, 105
Dos Passos, John Randolph, 80–83
Doyle, Laura, on inter-imperiality, 11
Du Bois, W. E. B.: on the blackness of Spain, 167–168; and Paz, 172. See also *literatura negra*; New Negro, the
Dunbar, Paul Lawrence, 173–174, 185. See also *literatura negra*; New Negro, the

Edwards, Brent Hayes, 10, 168
"El Camino de Harlem" (Guillén), 178, 189, 191
El Cantar de mio Cid. See *Poema del Cid*
El Cid (Rodrigo Díaz de Bivar), 38–39, 42. See also *Poema del Cid*
El desastre. See Disaster, the
Eliot, T. S., 69, 129; and Jiménez, 135; Spanish translation of, 30; and Unamuno, 155; *The Waste Land*, 237n2
"El moro fugado" (Alberti), 194–195
En torno al casticismo (Unamuno), 141–146
"The English-Speaking Folk" (Unamuno), 150
exceptionalism, 4–6, 14–21. See also American studies; Dos Passos, John; Dos Passos, John Randolph; Hispanism; *hispanismo*; Jiménez, Juan Ramón; Pound, Ezra; Unamuno, Miguel de
Eysteinsson, Astradur, 113

Familiar Spanish Travels (Howells), 91–92
Ferguson, John Delancey, 29–30
Fiddian, Robin, on post-1898 Spain, 146
Fitzmaurice-Kelly, James, 4, 54, 124
For Whom the Bell Tolls (Hemingway): and cubism, 216–217; initial reception of, 214–215; Lowry's *Under the Volcano* as rewriting of, 223–226; as a translation, 12–13, 200–203, 206–214, 279n4, 280n4, 282n30
Fortune Heights (Dos Passos), 105
Franco, Francisco: and American studies in Spain, 31; and Castilianism, 23, 54; and Hughes, 191; and *modernismo*, 130; and "Moorish" soldiers, 22, 169, 191; and political exiles, 32; and Spanish literature, 6; U.S. parallels to, 9; U.S. views of race relations under, 171, 191–198. See also Spanish Civil War
Frank, Waldo, 8, 77–78, 85; *City Block*, 103–104; on Unamuno, 156–157; *Virgin Spain*, 100–101, 156–157
French symbolism: *Diary of a Newlywed Poet* as Spanish variant of, 121–122, 129; Jiménez's genealogy of, 111, 131–132, 135; and translation, 238n6
Frère noir (Paz), 172
Frobenius, Leo, 177
Frost, Robert: and modernism/o, 128–129, 134; translation of by Jiménez and Camprubí, 120

Galdós, Benito Pérez, 33, 213; and Howells, 91, 93, 100, 258n41; and Pound, 40, 70
Generation of '27, 110
Generation of '98, 22–24, 78, 100, 130, 265n62. See also Spanish-American War
Gómez de la Serna, Julio, 187
Góngora, Luis de, 22, 183–185, 228
Gorkin, Julián, 31, 105, 176
"The Growth of Negro Literature" (Calverton), 187
Gruesz, Kirsten Silva, on American studies, 16

Guillén, Nicolás, 178, 189, 191
Gullón, Ricardo, 110, 262n12, 265n62

Hay, John, 17, 240n24, 244n47
Hegel, G. W. F.: and literary historiography, 2; translation of by Unamuno, 149
Hegeman, Susan, on Waldo Frank, 85
Hemingway, Ernest, 2, 27; *Death in the Afternoon*, 204; as a late modernist, 218–219; self-conception as a Spanish author, 3, 203; Spanglish correspondence of, 204–205; wartime pidgin in, 205–206. See also *For Whom the Bell Tolls* (Hemingway); *Sun Also Rises, The* (Hemingway)
high modernism, 79, 113, 199, 218, 259n58. See also American studies; Anglophone modernism; Hispanism; Jiménez, Juan Ramón; *modernismo*; modernist studies
Hispanic Society of America, 5, 13, 25, 41, 121, 247n69
Hispanism, 2–4, 14; and Arnold, 33–34; and *hispanismo*, 21–25; institutionalization of, 5–6, 25–27; and *literatura negra*, 169–170; masculinism of, 13; nativism of 21–22; and the *Poema del Cid*, 54–55; and Prescott's paradigm, 17, 25; and translation, 7–9. See also American studies; Castilianism; comparative literature; *literature negra*; *modernismo*; postcolonial studies; translation studies; transnational literary studies
hispanismo, 20–25, 29, 54–55, 78, 110
History of Spanish Literature (Ticknor), 17, 50
Home to Harlem (McKay), Spanish translation of, 174–176
Horne, Frank, 188–189. See also *literatura negra*; New Negro, the

Howells, William Dean, 8; as apologist for U.S. empire, 92–93; Dos Passos's critique of, 77, 90–91, 100; *Familiar Spanish Travels*, 91–92
Hughes, Langston, 2, 11, 173, 196, 217; on color lines in Spain, 167–169, 190–192; and Germany, 13; *I Wonder as I Wander*, 192; "Letter from Spain," 193–194; and *literatura negra*, 10, 170–171, 174, 176–177, 183, 185–190; as a panAmerican author, 177; in Spanish translation, 6, 8–9, 172, 181, 184; unpublished translations of Spanish Civil War poems, 194–195. See also *literatura negra*; New Negro, the
Humboldt, Wilhelm von, 139, 141, 144
Hume, Martin, 25, 151
Huntington, Archer Milton, 5, 13, 25–26, 28, 54–55, 126. See also Hispanic Society of America

imagism, 38, 63, 69, 104–105, 129, 134
Inquisition, the, 22, 40, 70
Irving, Washington, as Hispanist, 19–20, 77
I Wonder as I Wander (Hughes), 192

Jakobson, Roman, on translation, 218
James, Henry, 30, 33; and Pound, 58; and the Spanish-American War, 92–93
James, William, and Unamuno, 155, 158
Jameson, Fredric, on imperialism and literature, 10–11
Jefferson, Thomas, on Spain, 16
Jiménez, Juan Ramón, 1–2, 8–9, 12, 90; Anglophone reception of, 135–36; *Diary of a Newlywed Poet*, 3–4, 109–111, 121–130, 133; *Helios*, 119; influence on the Generation

Jiménez, Juan Ramón (*continued*)
of '98, 129; and *modernismo*, 10, 109–112, 114, 119–120, 125, 129–130, 132; *Ninfeas*, 114; theory of modernism/o, 129–136; translational poetics of, 119–121, 128; and Zenobia Camprubí Aymar, 13, 120–121
Johnson, James Weldon, 176–177, 183, 189, 190, 193. See also *literatura negra*; New Negro, the
Joyce, James, 62, 69, 134; *Finnegans Wake*, 199; influence on Hemingway, 204–205
Jrade, Cathy, 115
Juderías, Julián, 22–23; praise of Ferguson, 30; on the Spanish *raza* and African blackness, 172. See also Black Legend, the

Kenner, Hugh, 37, 46, 61

la leyenda negra. See Black Legend, the
Lanier, Sidney, and Unamuno, 140, 161–163
late modernism, 202: genealogies of, 12, 219
Lea, Henry Charles, 17, 80–81
Leaving the Atocha Station (Lerner), 225–226
Lerner, Ben, 225–226
"Letter from Spain" (Hughes), 193–194
Lindsay, Vachel, 109, 128, 134
Lira negra (Sanz y Díaz), 184–185
literatura negra (black literature): Ballagas's anthologies of, 180–184; and the black Caribbean, 177; emergence of, 169–171, 173–174; Gómez de la Serna's anthology of, 187–188; Guillermo de Torre on, 176–177; and *negrismo*, 178; Pereda Valdés's anthology of, 189–191; and political readings of Hispanophone literary culture, 190–195; and reconceptions of race under Franco, 195–198; Sanz y Díaz's genealogy of, 184–187; and the translation of "Negro," 168–169. See also American studies; Hispanism; *modernismo*; New Negro, the
Longfellow, Henry Wadsworth, 17, 19, 29, 77, 91, 183, 244n43
Lope de Vega, Félix, 22, 185–186, 213, 215, 228; dismissed in Pound's *Cantos*, 70, 74; and *modernismo*, 170, 184; Pound's early work on, 37, 40–42, 47, 52–53, 60, 66, 68–69; and Unamuno, 153
Lorca, Federico García, 5, 110, 170, 219, 225–226; assassination of, 6; and the Generation of '27, 110; and *literatura negra*, 170–171, 179–186, 188, 191, 195; *Poet in New York*, 126, 179
Lowell, Amy, 99, 109, 120, 125, 128, 132, 134
Lowry, Malcolm, 12; *Under the Volcano*, 223–225
Lummis, Charles, 24

Machado, Antonio: *Campos de Castilla*, 101–103; Dos Passos's profile and translation of, 90, 99; and the Generation of '98, 22; meeting with Dos Passos, 78; and *modernismo*, 112
Machado, Manuel, 102; and the Generation of '98, 22
Macy, John A., 32–33
Manhattan Transfer (Dos Passos), 79–80, 103–104
Manrique, Jorge, 95
Mapa de la poesía negra americana (Ballagas), 182–183
Maragall, Joan, Dos Passos's profile of, 99–100
Marichalar, Antonio, 31; and *literatura negra*, 173–174

Martí, José, 33, 133
Martín Fierro (Hernández), Unamuno on, 147
Masters, Edgar Lee, 84, 109, 127
McKay, Claude: "The Harlem Dancer," 184; and *literatura negra*, 10, 171–177, 183, 186, 189–190; Spanish translation of *Home to Harlem*, 174–176. See also New Negro, the
Mencken, H. L., 94, 98, 143
Méndez Herrera, José, and negrism, 180
Menéndez Pidal, Ramón, 23–24, 85, 144–145; *Cantar del mío Cid*, 54. See also Castilianism; El Cid; Unamuno, Miguel de
Mexican-American War, and American historiography, 16–17
modernismo: legitimation of, 117–119; and Marichalar, 31; nativist critiques of, 116, origins of, 112–15, 261n5, 263n19. See also Darío, Rubén; Jiménez, Juan Ramón; modernist studies
modernist studies, 109, 214, 240n22, 241n28; critique of, 134; transformations of, 10; and translation, 217; and U.S. empire, 15. See also American studies; Anglophone modernism; comparative literature; high modernism; Hispanism; Jiménez, Juan Ramón; *modernismo*; postcolonial studies; translation studies; transnational literary studies
Moody, William Vaughn: and Jiménez, 133; and Unamuno, 140, 161–163

negrism (European), 178
negrismo, 168, 178. See also *literatura negra*
négritude, 168, 178. See also *literatura negra*

New Negro, the: censorship under Franco, 197; and *literatura negra*, 10, 167–170, 178, 182–183. See also Bennett, Gwendolyn; Cullen, Countee; Du Bois, W. E. B.; Dunbar, Paul Lawrence; Horne, Frank; Hughes, Langston; Johnson, James Weldon; *literatura negra*; McKay, Claude; *negrismo*; *négritude*; pan-Africanism; *vogue nègre*; Wright, Richard

Onís, Federico de, 26–27, 110, 130, 156, 220. See also Hispanism; *hispanismo*
Orientalism: and Dos Passos, 95–96; and Hemingway, 203; and Hispanism, 5, 20, 244n47; and *literatura negra*, 178; and Pound, 42. See also Hispanism; *literatura negra*; *modernismo*
Ormsby, John, 50–52, 54–55, 64, 67. See also *Poema del Cid*; Pound, Ezra
Ortega y Gasset, José, 126

Pagan Spain (Wright), 195–98
pan-Africanism, 168, 173
Paris, Gaston: and the origins of comparative literature, 47; and Pound, 252n29, 252n36
Parnassianism, 109, 115, 125, 131, 135, 143. See also Baudelaire, Charles; Darío, Rubén; French symbolism; Jiménez, Juan Ramón; *modernismo*
Patria Mia (Pound), 56–57
Paz, Magdeleine, 172
Paz, Octavio, 134, 227; on *modernismo*, 112–113
Pease, Donald, 16, 243n37, 243n38
Pedroso, Regino: anthologization and translation of "Hermano negro," 182, 184; designation as "raza negroamarilla (sin otra mezcla)," 180–181

Pereda Valdés, Ildefonso, 189–190
philology, 170; and comparative literature, 138; and Franco, 31; and Pound, 3, 13, 38, 44, 45–48, 54, 60, 73; and statist Spanish literary history, 23; and Unamuno, 145. *See also* comparative literature; Pound, Ezra
Picasso, Pablo, 1, 14, 167–168, 176, 216
Pi y Margall, Francisco, on the United States, 23
"Pierre Menard, Author of the Quixote" (Borges), 228–229
Poe, Edgar Allen: and *Diary of a Newlywed Poet* (Jiménez), 127–128, 131–133; Dos Passos on, 77; and symbolism, 111; translation of by Jiménez and Camprubí, 120; and Unamuno, 158–159
Poema del Cid: history of translations of, 28, 54–55; Pound's work on, 38, 42, 48–52
Poesías (Unamuno), 149
Poet in New York (Lorca), 126, 179
postcolonial studies, and effects on modernist studies, 10, 240n22. *See also* American studies; comparative literature; Hispanism; modernist studies; translation studies; transnational literary studies
postmodernism, genealogies of, 12, 130, 202, 218–219
poststructuralism, 229–230
Pound, Ezra, 2, 4, 8; and "American Risorgimento," 57–60; *Cantos*, 71–75; *Cathay*, 61; correspondence with Unamuno, 155–156; early travels in Spain, 42–43; as a Hispanist, 12, 37–41; *Homage to Sextus Propertius*, 61; later attacks on Spanish literature, 69–75; on Lope de Vega, 40–42, 52–53, 66, 68, 73–74; *Patria Mia*, 56–57; and the *Poema del Cid*, 28, 43–44, 48–55, 62–68, 71–73, 253n49; rejection of philology, 13, 45–48; *The Spirit of Romance*, 45–47, 52–53, 56, 60, 66–67, 69, 71; "Three Cantos," 3; translational poetics of, 60–62, 149; translations of Li Po and Ghose, 136; on the university system, 58; the "Ur-Cantos," 39, 56, 62–68; on Whitman, 57–58
Pound Era, The (Kenner), 37, 46, 61
Pushcart at the Curb, A (Dos Passos), 79, 101–104
Pratt, Mary Louise, 11, 26
"Prescott's paradigm," 17, 25, 77, 244n43
primitivism: and *literatura negra*, 176, 178–179, 182; and white European writers, 170

Reconquista, 70, 145; and Castile, 239n17; and "El moro fugado," 194–195; and *Martín Fierro*, 147; and the *Poema del Cid*, 38, 54–55; racial theories of, 169; and the Spanish Civil War, 191. *See also* Castilianism; *Poema del Cid*; Spanish-American War; Spanish Civil War
regeneracionismo. *See* Generation of '98
Rennert, Hugo: in the *Cantos*, 73–74; and Pound, 25, 41–42, 45, 51
Resina, Joan Ramon, critique of Unamuno by, 146
Robles, José: friendship with Dos Passos, 87; murder of, 106; translation of Dos Passos, 105
Rolland, Romain, 120, 131
romanticism: and Darío, 114; and the Generation of '98, 22; and Jiménez, 119, 122–124, 131–122, 135; and philology, 138; and Unamuno, 161. *See also* Jiménez, Juan Ramón;

modernismo; Parnassianism;
    Unamuno, Miguel de
Romera-Navarro, Miguel, on
    Hispanism, 25
Roosevelt, Theodore, and white
    nativism, 18, 80–81
Rosinante to the Road Again (Dos
    Passos), 1, 79, 94–98, 99–101

Sandburg, Carl, 3, 105, 134, 140,
    161–162
Santayana, George: and Hemingway,
    199; on the Spanish-American War,
    17
Sanz y Díaz, José, 184–185
Silver Age, the, 13, 22. *See also* the
    Generation of '98
Smith, John (colonist), 16
socialism: and Hughes's reception, 174,
    190; and the realist novel, 9; in
    Spain, 31, 106
Song of Roland, The (*La Chanson de
    Roland*): and *Martín Fierro*, 147;
    Pound's work on, 47–48, 53, 55
Sorolla, Joaquín, and the Hispanic
    Society of America, 25, 247n70
Sotomayor, Carmen T., on Spanish
    Republican poetry, 194
Spanish-American War, 11, 17–18, 81,
    111, 245n50; and American studies
    and Hispanism, 2, 4, 6–8, 14, 20,
    29–31; and Darío, 117–118; and
    Frank, 100; and Jiménez, 133; and
    John Dos Passos, 77; and John
    Randolph Dos Passos, 80, 82;
    and Spanglish, 227; and Spanish
    attitudes toward the U.S., 20–21;
    and Unamuno, 139–140, 142,
    150, 153. *See also* American studies;
    Disaster, the; Generation of '98;
    Hispanism; Silver Age, the
Spanglish, 12, 16; controversy over,
    227; Unamuno and, 163. *See also*
    Stavans, Ilan

Spanish Civil War, 12–13, 21, 27, 80,
    164, 190–191, 202, 209, 277n60;
    and American studies in Spain, 31;
    ballads of, 3; Hughes and, 193–195;
    and Jiménez, 129, 135; and the
    Machado brothers, 102; "Moorish"
    soldiers in, 21–22, 167–69; and
    Pound, 256n107; and *Under the
    Volcano* (Lowry), 223–224. *See also*
    Franco, Francisco; Spanish-American
    War; World War II
*Spanish Background of American
    Literature, The* (Williams), 19–20
Spanish Pioneers, The (Lummis), 24
Spirit of American Literature, The
    (Macy), 32–33
Stavans, Ilan, 8, 12, 116; *Don Quixote*
    (Spanglish version), 228–235;
    theory of translation, 229–230.
    See also Cervantes, Miguel de;
    translation studies
Stein, Gertrude, 5, 134, 209; influence
    on Hemingway, 204–205, 216; and
    Picasso, 1, 14–15
Sumner, William Graham, 18
Sun Also Rises, The (Hemingway),
    translation in, 205

Tagore, Rabindranath, 187; Spanish
    translations of, 120, 136
Three Soldiers (Dos Passos), 94, 103
Ticknor, George, 9, 20, 244n44;
    History of Spanish Literature, 17, 50
Tragic Sense of Life, The (Unamuno),
    137, 154–155
translation studies, 230, 237n2, 238n6;
    and American studies, 7, 9–10, 16,
    27–28; and Hemingway, 214; and
    literary nativism, 138; and *literatura
    negra*, 170; and modernist studies,
    9–10, 111, 217; and Unamuno,
    141. *See also* American studies;
    comparative literature; Hispanism;
    transnational literary studies

transnational literary studies: effect on modernist studies, 10, 217, 241n28; and U.S. empire, 16

Unamuno, Miguel de, 2–3, 12, 132; Anglophone reception of, 152–156; *Cómo se hace una novela,* 148–149; correspondence with Pound, 155–156; "The English-Speaking Folk," 150; English translation of works by, 155; *En torno al casticismo,* 141–146; as founder of contemporary American studies in Spain, 139–141, 163–164; and the Generation of '98, 22; and *hispanismo,* 23, 25; legacy of, 164; on *Martín Fierro,* 147; and *modernismo,* 143; *Poesías,* 149; as poststructuralist forerunner, 267n17; and Spain's African past, 160–161; Spanish nativism of, 138–139, 141–147; *The Tragic Sense of Life,* 137, 154–155; translation of Carlyle's *The French Revolution,* 151–152; translational poetics of, 147–151; and U.S.–Spanish bonds, 157–158; on Whitman, 158–161; on Whitmanian U.S. poetry, 161–163
Under the Volcano (Lowry), 223–225. See also *For Whom the Bell Tolls* (Hemingway)
"Ur-Cantos" (Pound), 39, 56, 62–68
U.S.A. trilogy (Dos Passos), 76, 105

Valera, Juan, 24, 116, 118, 146
Valle-Inclán, Ramon del, 132; English translation of, 27; and the Generation of '98, 22
Venegas, José Luis, 145
Venuti, Lawrence, 138, 238n6, 280n4
Virgin Spain (Ferguson), 100–101, 156–157
vogue nègre, 168
vorticism, 38, 63

War of 1898. *See* Spanish-American War
Whitman, Walt: and Ballagas, 183; and Darío, 118; and *literatura yanqui* (Yankee literature), 6, 9, 29–31; and Lorca, 179–180; and modernism/o, 128, 132–133; and Pound, 57–58; and "proletarian literature," 105; translation of by Jiménez and Camprubí, 120; translation and interpretation by Unamuno, 140–141, 143, 149, 154, 156, 159–163
Wilkins, Lawrence, on Spanish-language instruction, 26
Williams, Stanley T., 19–20
Williams, William Carlos, 5, 61
World War I, 12
World War II, 12
Wright, Richard, 170–171; *Pagan Spain,* 195–198

GPSR Authorized Representative: Easy Access System Europe, Mustamäe tee
50, 10621 Tallinn, Estonia, gpsr.requests@easproject.com

www.ingramcontent.com/pod-product-compliance
Lightning Source LLC
Chambersburg PA
CBHW021937290426
44108CB00012B/865